HAUNTED GETTYSBURG

CAMPFIRE GHOST STORIES

Bonnie Wasel

BY

BOB WASEL
BONNIE WASEL

Distributed By:
Americana Souvenirs & Gifts
Gettysburg PA 17325

D1290179

Fascism's Return

Fascism's Return:
Scandal, Revision, and
Ideology since 1980

Edited by Richard J. Golsan

University of Nebraska Press
Lincoln and London

Portions of Robert Soucy, *French Fascism:
The Second Wave, 1933–1939*
(New Haven CT: Yale University Press, 1995), © 1995
Yale University Press, are reprinted, with
permission, in Robert Soucy's essay.
© 1998 by the University of Nebraska Press

Library of Congress Cataloging-
in-Publication Data
Fascism's return: scandal, revision,
and ideology since 1980 / edited by
Richard J. Golson.
p.   cm.—(Stages ; v. 10)
Includes bibliographical references
and index.
ISBN 0-8032-2159-2 (cloth: alk. paper).—
ISBN 0-8032-7071-2 (pbk.: alk. paper)
1. Fascism.   2. Right-wing extremists.
3. World politics—1945–
I. Golson, Richard Joseph, 1952–
II. Series: Stages (Series) ; v. 10.
JC481.F3373   1998
97-40783
320.53'3'09409045—DC21
CIP

For

Edward B. Hamer, Edouard Morot-Sir, and Walter A. Strauss

Contents

Acknowledgments

A project of this size involves the participation, support, and goodwill of a number of people whom I would like to thank here. First, the contributors to the volume have been enthusiastic about the project from the outset. I have learned a great deal from them and their essays here. Series editors Gerry Prince and Warren Motte have been most generous with their interest, support, and helpful advice. My own work on the book has been greatly facilitated by the continuing support of the Center for Leadership Studies at Texas A&M University and its director, Arnold Vedlitz. Special thanks are due to Charles Snodgrass, who prepared the bibliography and final manuscript.

First versions of many of the essays included here were originally presented at a conference entitled "Fascism's Return" held at Texas A&M University 10–11 November 1995, sponsored by the Interdisciplinary Group for Historical Literary Study. I would like to thank IGHLS and especially its director, Larry J. Reynolds, whose patience, support, and organizational skills (not to mention his tennis game) are nothing short of exemplary. I would also like to express my appreciation to conference participants Annette Lévy-Willard and Arnold Krammer.

Support for indexing costs for this volume have been generously provided by the Department of Modern and Classical Languages, the College of Liberal Arts, and the Interdisciplinary Group for Historical Literary Study.

Finally, I would like to thank my wife, Nancy, and my sons, James and Jody, who are, quite simply, the reasons why. This book is dedicated to Ed Hamer, Edouard Morot-Sir, and Walter Strauss—scholars, mentors, and friends, all.

Richard J. Golsan

Introduction

In 1994 the French historian and political commentator Jacques Julliard published a brief but highly polemical book in which he sought to
diagnose what he considered to be a dangerous malady afflicting contemporary Europe. The symptoms of the malady were numerous, he
argued, and could be detected in a variety of political, social, economic, and cultural developments. In Eastern Europe these included a
resurgence of nationalism and ethnic hatreds coupled with persistent
economic crises brought on by the collapse of communism. In Western
Europe, the indecisiveness and weakness of the democracies in dealing with events such as the crisis in the former Yugoslavia were accompanied by an inability to resolve economic problems, especially
chronic unemployment. Considered together, these symptoms formed
a pattern that, according to Julliard, was hauntingly familiar. The combination of the collapse of empire, the growth of virulent national-
isms, unrelenting economic miseries, and democratic impotence was
highly reminiscent of circumstances prevailing in Germany during
the decline of the Weimar Republic and the rise of Nazism. Indeed, all
the ingredients necessary for a new "fashogenesis" were present. Given
this assessment, it is not surprising that Julliard chose as the title of
his book *Ce Fascisme qui vient . . .* (This fascism that is coming . . .).[1]

The dire prediction implicit in the title *Ce Fascisme qui vient . . .* as
well as in Julliard's analysis of the European situation is not simply the
excessive or alarmist view of one commentator. In France especially,
other prominent intellectuals and public figures have recently compared the situation in the European democracies to the climate of the
Weimar period in its declining and crisis-ridden final years. After an
overview that embraces not only Europe but the recent genocide in
Rwanda and the ongoing crisis in Algeria, Bernard-Henri Lévy offers
the following apocalyptic assessment in *La Pureté dangereuse*: "When
I look through history for an analogue to this malaise, when I seek a
precedent for the disarray that is descending on the democracies, I can

think of only one example: the Weimarian moment which in Germany preceded the triumph of Nazism."[2]

Two years earlier Alain Finkielkraut assessed the narrower context of the war in Yugoslavia and the European democracies' inaction in the face of Serbian aggression, comparing the moment to another ominous episode in the decline of democracy and the rise of fascism leading up to World War II: the Munich accords of September 1938. In the form of a general European paralysis we were witnessing, according to Finkielkraut, a new form of appeasement, an appeasement that Finkielkraut, with his usual rhetorical verve, argued was implicitly revising history and reversing long held and indeed sacrosanct judgments concerning the past: "In other words, it was Chamberlain and Georges Bonnet who in 1938 were right to choose the path of appeasement and Pétain who, in 1940, was right to engage in a politics of collaboration with Germany."[3]

French intellectuals have, of course, long been known for their rhetorical flights, and if Tony Judt is to be believed, often as well for their resounding lack of political acumen and historical judgment.[4] But Julliard, Lévy, and Finkielkraut are certainly not thoroughly wrongheaded in noting parallels between the turmoil of the 1930s and events transpiring in contemporary Europe; nor are they, especially Julliard, alone in raising the possibility of a rebirth or return of fascism. The British historian Richard Bessel cites many of the same factors in a recent assessment of a generalized European disarray and finds Weimarian echos notably in the current situation in Russia. Under the circumstances, he continues, the study of fascism has assumed a new urgency because the "history of Europe during the first half of this century . . . of which the history of Fascism and Nazism forms a major part, no longer seems safely buried." What has sadly been buried under the weight of recent events is "the postwar, postfascist era in Europe."[5] By better understanding fascism's past, Bessel concludes, one might hope to head off its return in the future.[6]

Some might consider views such as these exceedingly pessimistic or based on faulty analyses. The fact remains, however, that a large number of European countries are experiencing political, economic, and social pressures that in many instances have reached crisis proportions reminiscent of dark moments in the recent past. Returning to the French context, the nation's economic difficulties, spurred on by high unemployment rates and other factors, erupted in strikes, protests, and a generalized national shutdown at the end of 1995.[7] The extent and duration of these events suggested not only a deepening structural crisis in the national economy but a crisis of confidence on the part of the French in their elected leaders. Following the ouster of the

Gaullists and the highly unpopular Alain Juppé as prime minister in the 1997 parliamentary elections, the Socialists under Lionel Jospin appear to be doing little better.

The situation in Italy is hardly better. The crisis of Italian democracy that began in the early 1990s continues largely unabated, with governments rising and falling, new parties and alliances being created, and old parties and political movements constantly transforming themselves into new ones.[8] Austria as well has seen its traditional postwar political alignments undergo significant political change recently under the pressure of a diminished economic prosperity and an influx of immigrants from Eastern Europe.[9] The situation in many former Communist Bloc European countries is of course as bad or worse, and the crisis in Russia as continuous as it is worrisome to the West, which is only too aware of the fragility of democracy and the instability of the Yeltsin government.

To add the final piece of the puzzle that justifies in general terms the comparison between the Europe of today and Europe, and especially Germany, in the 1930s, one need only note that in virtually all of the countries just cited, and in others as well, extreme right-wing nationalist movements and parties are on the rise. Many in France and elsewhere were shocked in the spring of 1995 when Jean-Marie Le Pen, leader of the Front National, obtained the highest percentage of votes (14.9 percent) he had ever received in the first round of the presidential elections. In summer 1995, the Front National made comparable inroads in regional and local elections, scoring over 30 percent in cities as large as Toulon and Perpignan and in the suburbs of major metropolitan areas like Marseille.[10] In February 1997, the Front National scored better than 50 percent in the mayoral elections in the town of Vitrolles. The losers, the Socialists, had all the other major parties lined up behind them.

In Italy, Silvio Berlusconi was elected prime minister in 1994 after building an alliance, Forza Italia, that included the neofascist Movimento Sociale Italiano (MSI) and the reactionary Lega Nord, or Northern League. At the same time, Mussolini's granddaughter was elected mayor of Naples on the MSI ticket. Although Berlusconi is no longer in power, the nation's political situation is far from certain, and major players still include the likes of Gianfranco Fini, head of the Alleanza Nazionale (AN), the heir to the recently dissolved neofascist MSI.

In Austria, parliamentary elections in December 1995 gave Jorg Haider, the youthful leader of the extreme right-wing and nationalist Freedom Party, 22.3 percent of the vote, down slightly from the previous parliamentary elections, held fourteen months before. For some, these results suggested that Haider's star was on the wane. But as Tony Judt warned shortly after the 1995 elections, the issues that helped make Haider popular in the first place had not disappeared; Judt concluded that "Haider and his like" may not simply harken back to fascisms past, but "stand for something far more serious: they are the ghosts of Europes yet to come."[11] The October 1996 European parliamentary elections seemed to bear out Judt's concerns. In these elections, Haider and the Freedom Party garnered almost 28 percent of the vote, just two percentage points less than the dominant and mainstream Socialist Party. As some commentators were quick to note, Haider now seems a legitimate threat to enter the government for the first time.[12]

Although no extreme right-wing nationalist movement or political party seems to be gaining momentum in a reunited Germany, as recently as the late 1980s Franz Schönhuber and his Republican Party were making electoral headway,[13] and neo-Nazi violence, as Ingo Hasselbach's recent memoir, *Fuhrer-Ex*, makes clear, continues to be a disturbing presence and legitimate threat to immigrant populations. In Russia, ultranationalist Vladimir Zhirinovsky may have lost ground recently, but he is still, as of this writing, a force to be reckoned with on the political landscape. Of all these extreme right-wing demagogues, Zhirinovsky's rhetoric is perhaps the most inflamed and bellicose, and his threat to deport bureaucrats to Siberia in cattle cars is all too reminiscent of the Final Solution in full swing.[14]

To return to the prediction/warning implicit in Julliard's title, could these extreme right-wing and ultranationalist movements considered together (or seperately) constitute a "fascism that is coming" or even the return of an older fascism dressed up in modern garb? As possible examples of the latter, one could cite the chic, "designer fascism" Richard Wolin identifies in contemporary Italian politics in his essay here. One could also mention the sleazy, media-age demagoguery that Tony Judt associates with Jorg Haider.[15] Whatever the case, the question of whether we are facing the advent of a new fascist paradigm or a return of earlier, "classic" fascisms raises a number of important theoretical and historical questions. If these are new fascisms, what distinguishes them from historical fascisms, while at the same time making them generically or typologically identifiable with these predecessors? This question, of course, raises another issue that has led political scientists, historians, and others to fill the pages of innumerable books, articles, and op-ed pieces: what is the definition of fascism? Finally, in what sense—beyond the question of general ideological compatibility between these "new" fascisms and the older "classic" forms—can one speak of a "return of fascism"? Did it, in fact, ever leave us in the first place?

In an essay on nationalism and the extreme Right in Eastern Europe,

Jill Irvine addresses the first of these questions, arguing that one important feature distinguishing these neofascisms (and she labels them as such) from historic fascisms is that neofascisms are not motivated by expansionist ambitions, while their predecessors were:

> Historical Fascism sometimes displayed a more universal, revolutionary perspective, or at least a dedication to expanding the Fascist state's dominion over the widest possible territory. Current neo-Fascism and the extreme right have eschewed this expansionist perspective in favor of what might be called the doctrine of "Fascism in one country," and their main preoccupation has been to achieve a "pure" nation-state based on national exclusivity.[16]

Other historians and political theorists have insisted on another important distinction between the new and the old: ultraright movements and parties such as Le Pen's Front National and Haider's Freedom Party are not antidemocratic or totalitarian in their aims, but in fact work within the confines of their countries' democratic systems. This ignores the fact that Hitler, for one, came to power within a democratic system. It also ignores the possibility that if the more recent ultraright or neofascist movements ever did come to power, they might not remain faithful to the democratic processes and practices that brought them there. Instead, they might well seek to impose a more authoritarian rule.[17] As Christopher Flood notes in his essay here, and as Jonathan Marcus has argued in his recent study of Le Pen and the Front National, the internal organization of the movement is hardly democratic and operates essentially on the *fuhrerprinzip* established by Hitler and the Nazis.[18] This does not of course make the Front National automatically totalitarian or fascist, but it certainly suggests that the movement's democratic impulses are only window dressing—skin deep at best.

In a recent book whose title alone, *A History of Fascism 1914–1945*, underscores the author's belief in a discontinuity between classic or historical fascism and postwar right-wing extremism, Stanley Payne insists on further distinctions between the interwar fascist dictatorships and postwar variants. For Payne, first of all, any possibility of a return of historic fascism in what he calls the "Western world" is very slight, not only because of the "enormous cultural, economic, and social changes" that have taken place since the heyday of the dictators, but also because of "the lengthy development of democratic systems."[19] Payne goes on to assert that "[all] the genuinely neofascist and neo-Nazi groups remain tiny circles of fringe activists" with no real political future.[20] Movements such as those led by Le Pen in France and Fini in Italy are for Payne not neofascist but "right radical parties" that will inevitably be forced to moderate their positions to increase their chances for political success. Other observers of these phenomena might well disagree with Payne on both counts.[21]

If Payne is correct in his assumption that there is very little likelihood of a reemergence of historical fascism in Europe or of a virulently neofascist movement coming to power, then, as he suggests in another context, continuing efforts to define fascism or provide a comprehensive taxonomy of the phenomenon may mercifully prove to be "strictly scholarly" exercises "faintly analagous to the classification of obscure Amazonian languages rapidly undergoing extinction."[22] No matter how colorful the analogy, however, and judging from past experience, efforts to define fascism in theoretical as well as historical terms have hardly proven to be dusty academic exercises where differences of opinion are unlikely to generate controversy. In fact, debates over the nature of fascism, ongoing now for more than half a century, have often been highly acrimonious and public and, in at least one well-known incident, landed the antagonists in court.[23]

This is not to say that all aspects of the debate have proven excessively contentious. Scholars have, for example, debated in relatively peaceful terms the degree to which Italian Fascism and Nazism can be considered homologous, given the two movements' divergence on the question of biological racism.[24] The issue of whether a regime must be totalitarian in order to qualify as fascist has also produced many arguments pro and con without, however, generating an extraordinary degree of vituperation.

But debates over the nature and identity of fascism almost of necessity become inflamed once they engage directly questions of memory, heritage, and national identity. The same potential for controversy is present when the debate over fascism and its heirs is caught up in current ideological confrontations or proves to be inextricably linked to disturbing political, social, or cultural developments in the present. Such linkages have, moreover, all too often proven inevitable. As a result, the debate over fascism becomes implicitly a debate over fascism's return, or perhaps its continuing and continuous presence in contemporary life.

For example, to return briefly to two of the ultraright movements and their leaders discussed earlier, any effort to determine dispassionately whether Jorg Haider and the Freedom Party in Austria or Jean-Marie Le Pen and the Front National in France are neofascist, fascist, or simply ultranationalist is inevitably complicated and indeed inflamed by real links between these leaders and movements and Europe's fascist past. Shortly before the 1995 Austrian parliamentary elections, Jörg Haider attended and spoke at a rally of former members of the Waffen ss, whom he lauded in his speech as "decent people." A videotape of the speech broadcast first in Germany created a public scandal, and later provoked controversy when broadcast in Austria.[25] Nor was this the first of Haider's pro-Nazi pronouncements. Speaking to another veterans' group in 1990 that also included former Waffen ss members, Haider assessed their contribution to the German war effort in terms reminiscent of the views of Hitler himself: "Your sacrifices will only be seen in the correct light in the years to come because the overall development of Europe will show clearly that the basis was laid by you for peace and freedom." On the subject of Kurt Waldheim's Nazi past, Haider stated that Waldheim "only did his duty,"[26] and he offered the same comment on the return to Austria in 1985 of Nazi war criminal Walter Reder. Statements such as these, combined with the fact that Haider was raised in a good Nazi family whose wealth reportedly came from the "aryanization" of Jewish property, have earned him the nickname "Hitler's grandson." Any assessment of Haider's politics and his party, no matter how objective, can hardly completely ignore the implied comparison.

Le Pen's personal connection to Europe's Nazi past is not as striking as Haider's, but it is certainly there. Le Pen is not the son of Nazi parents, nor does he speak at rallies of former members of the ss. But he has claimed among his friends the former head of the Belgium Rexist movement, Léon Degrelle.[27] He is also given to making thinly veiled anti-Semitic remarks and comments about the Holocaust that smack of historical revisionism of the most sinister kind. In an infamous comment to the press, Le Pen asserted that the Holocaust was in essence a "minor detail" in the history of World War II. Moreover, the presence of unrepentant supporters of Vichy and especially its fanatically profascist final years in important positions in the Front National is certainly telling. Among these individuals are former members of Vichy's pro-Nazi and paramilitary police force, the Milice, one of whom, Paul Malaguti, as Bertram Gordon notes in his essay here, is infamous for the slaughter of Resistance members near the end of the war. Another, Roland Gaucher, is a former member of Marcel Déat's wartime fascist movement, the Rassemblement National Populaire. In 1944, Gaucher attacked Pétain for being too soft on the Resistance and for failing to act quickly enough in drawing up lists of hostages to be executed to stymie the threat. Gaucher has also served as editor of the Front National's weekly magazine, the *National hebdo*.[28] Finally, those who have witnessed at close range the Front National's campaign tactics and the effect their coming to power creates among the populace find strong parallels with the rise of Nazism. In her study of the Front National's victory in the town of Dreux, *A Small Town in France*, Françoise Gaspard notes that she was inspired to write the book after rereading William Sheridan Allen's description in *The Nazi Seizure of Power* of a similar takeover by the Nazis of the small German town of Thalburg in the 1930s. In the epigraph to her book, Gaspard quotes from a newspaper article on an episode of neo-Nazi violence in Dreux inspired by the Front National's electoral victory on the preceding day.[29]

As noted earlier, the shadow of Nazism or Vichy hanging over far Right parties and movements is not the only factor that lends an emotional charge to discussions of fascism and neofascism. Efforts to write the history of fascism or define its manifestations in the context of specific national cultures inevitably entail an assessment of that national culture or identity, which all too often provokes controversy. As Tzvetan Todorov has recently asserted, "the memory of our past is a large part of our present identity, and one may not touch it without scandalous consequences."[30] One recent and fairly minor example occurred in summer 1995 when *Le Monde* published a favorable review of Robert Soucy's *French Fascism: The Second Wave 1933–1939*, in which Soucy labeled as fascist the 1930s paramilitary movement the Croix de Feu and its leader, Colonel de la Rocque. The review prompted a violently critical letter from La Rocque's son, who attacked Soucy's conclusions and facts. Neither La Rocque nor the Croix de Feu, the son insisted, were fascist. One could dismiss this episode as merely the case of a dutiful son protecting his father's name, were it not for the fact that French historians and political scientists in general have until recently been reluctant to acknowledge a fascism indigenous to France and have been generally prone to dismiss it as a foreign import. This explains in part the hostile reaction of many French historians and political scientists as well as public figures to the work of the Israeli historian Zeev Sternhell, who locates the birth of fascism in the Sorelian revolutionary syndicalism of late nineteenth- and early twentieth-century France. Moreover, Sternhell's insistence in his book *Ni droite ni gauche* that interwar French intellectual culture was "impregnated" with fascist ideology was also greeted by a storm of protest in France. One of those labeled as a fascist in the book, Bertrand de Jouvenel, sued Sternhell for defamation of character, and won. As Robert Wohl opined in the wake of the affair, those writing on the subject "should tread lightly and edit their manuscripts with a lawyer at their side."[31]

If efforts to write the history of French fascism from its disputed origins at the end of the nineteenth century to its manifestations in the interwar period lend themselves to controversy, the scope and magnitude of these debates are almost insignificant in comparison with the seemingly endless scandal surrounding efforts to come to terms with the history and memory of the Vichy period. For more than fifty years, as Henry Rousso demonstrates in his brilliant study *The Vichy Syndrome*, the disturbing memory of the Vichy past has erupted into the present in the form of political scandals and highly publicized judicial decisions and proceedings as well as in the screening of controversial films and the publication of innumerable histories and works of fiction dealing with the period. In the wake of the student uprisings of May 1968, the nation was shaken by films such as Marcel Ophuls's classic 1971 documentary, *The Sorrow and the Pity*, in which the Gaullist myth of a heroic and *résistante* France was shattered by personal testimonies of cowardice, indifference, and pro-Nazi sentiments. That same year, at the urging of high officials in the Catholic Church, President Georges Pompidou quietly pardoned Paul Touvier, a former intelligence officer in Vichy's Milice. Several months later, when the pardon became public knowledge, expressions of public outrage in the media and elsewhere were extraordinarily intense.

In 1974, the release of Louis Malle's *Lacombe Lucien* stirred another storm of protest after drawing early praise from numerous critics. Dealing with a young French peasant boy who joins the French Gestapo by chance after being turned down by the Resistance, the film painted a less than heroic picture of the nation during the Occupation. Such has been the impact of the movie that in 1992 Stanley Hoffmann labeled what he considered to be the overly pessimistic, collaborationist version of French history during the Occupation the "Lacombe Lucien myth."[32]

France's obsession with its Vichy past has only intensified since the late 1970s and early 1980s. The 1987 trial for crimes against humanity of Klaus Barbie, the former ss officer known as the "Butcher of Lyons" for his brutality there during the Occupation, stirred bitter memories, rekindled old debates, and prompted new ones as well. It also prompted renewed calls for Frenchmen guilty of similar crimes during the war to be tried. In 1989, the aforementioned Paul Touvier, charged with crimes against humanity in the early 1980s and in hiding in a series of right-wing Catholic monasteries since the 1970s, was arrested by French police; he would finally stand trial five years later. In 1991, René Bousquet, the former head of Vichy Police responsible for the roundup of some thirteen thousand Jews in Paris in July 1942 as well as other crimes, was also indicted on similar charges. Bousquet would have stood trial for crimes against humanity had he not been gunned down by a crazed publicity seeker in his own apartment in the summer of 1993.[33] More recently, in March 1996, hearings were held in a Bordeaux court to determine if Maurice Papon, a former Vichy functionary responsible for the roundup of Jews in Bordeaux during the war and later prefect of Paris police and minister of finance under Giscard d'Estaing, should stand trial on charges of crimes against humanity. In early 1997, the court decided in the affirmative, and Papon is scheduled to stand trial in late 1997 or 1998.

If the cases of Frenchmen charged with crimes against humanity have stirred controversy throughout the 1990s, these controversies are on a small scale compared to the scandal that erupted following revelations concerning then President François Mitterrand's extreme right-wing past during the interwar years and his lengthy service to Vichy, for which he eventually received the regime's highest honor, the Francisque. When Mitterrand discussed his Vichy past on French television in September 1994, he expressed no regrets, and discussed as well his postwar friendship with René Bousquet, whom he described as a "man of extraordinary stature." In a shocking misstatement of fact that smacked of a historical revisionism more typical of extreme right-wing ideologues than of a Socialist president, Mitterrand also asserted that the Vichy anti-Jewish statutes of 1940 and 1941 were directed only against "foreign Jews." For the French, as Henry Rousso and Eric Conan imply in the title of their recent book, Vichy has truly become "a past that will not pass."[34]

France is of course not alone in being haunted by its World War II past and the memory of fascism, nor is France the only European nation where these concerns are bound to burning questions concerning national identity in the present. In Austria as in France, the connection has also been complicated by the tenacity of the Austrian version of the Gaullist myth of resistance, which in essence exonerated the Austrians for their complicity with Nazism and transformed them into Hitler's victims rather than his cronies. As defined by Robert Knight, this "myth of Austria's foundation" affirms that

> Austrian nationhood and Austrian democracy were born (or reborn) of the war-time suffering of Austrian victims of Nazism and heroes of the Austrian resistance movement. After a short-lived euphoria following the Anschluss, it is claimed, disillusionment set in; Prussian carpetbaggers and Gestapo thugs descended on Austria and the Austrians turned away from National Socialism; eventually, Austria's national consciousness and her democratic commitment re-emerged united from under the Nazi jackboot.[35]

Regardless of the fact that, as Knight argues, the myth seriously underestimates Austrian loyalty to Nazi Germany once the war began, its traces can be found even in soothing Hollywood bromides purporting to represent Austrian attitudes during the war. In One, by One, by One Judith Miller describes a famous scene in The Sound of Music in which Baron von Trapp and his fellow Austrians in the audience at a songfest defiantly sing "Edelweiss" in the presence of angry Germans.

As Miller notes bitterly: "Had the film been historically accurate, the audience might have been singing with conviction, but they would have been singing a different song—something like 'Deutschland Über Alles.' For history, as opposed to Hollywood, tells us that the overwhelming majority of Austrians preferred the German national anthem to their own."[36]

The election of Kurt Waldheim as president in 1986, the continued and active presence since the war of former Nazis in Austrian politics, the relative failure of de-Nazification, and the continuing presence of anti-Semitism, not to mention the success of Jörg Haider, all point to the inaccuracy of Austria's postwar foundational myth in the past and in the present.[37] They also of necessity make any discussion of fascism past and present an emotionally charged issue. Trapped between a version of history that is difficult to renounce and a truth no one wishes to accept, Austria does not appear to be on the verge of constructing a viable national identity that would include a coherent and accurate account of the nation's Nazi past.

As opposed to France and Austria, the postwar Federal German Republic has not had its past whitewashed by a myth of resistance to fascism; nor, for that matter, has it been forced to come to grips with the painful consequences of the dismantling of such a myth, as has been the case recently in France. This is not to say, however, that Germany's efforts to come to terms with its Nazi past have not been painful or controversial, especially when they engage questions of national identity in the present. In fact, when the Historian's Debate erupted in the mid-1980s, the controversy centered as much on how the Nazi episode was to be accommodated in the nation's past as well as its present and future identity as it did on the nature and meaning of Nazism and the specificity of its crimes. Summing up these broader and more contemporary concerns, Herman Rudolph stated at the time:

the question that is now thrown open is: should the Third Reich be treated historiographically so that it no longer blocks the way to our past like some somber and monstrous monument, but rather itself becomes "history," past time, one epoch among other epochs? Or should it simultaneously remain as some admonitory memorial . . . because, in the speech of the biblical simile, this stone actually became the cornerstone of the new beginning after World War II? And should history provide orientation, awaken pride and self-consciousness, and thus become a starting point for "identity" and "national consensus"—or is its task much more one of unsettling what is customary, throwing into question what persists, and sharpening our vision for the future?[38]

Rudolph's comments, however, were not intended to suggest that the specificity of Nazism and its crimes were not also at the heart of the debate. It was in fact the efforts of right-wing intellectuals like Ernst Nolte to relativize the Holocaust by claiming that Hitler could conceivably have undertaken it as a preemptive strike to prevent a similar Holocaust from being visited on the Germans by Soviet Russia that generated the most heated response. Wasn't the Gulag, Nolte argued, more original than Auschwitz? Wasn't the "Bolshevik murder of an entire class . . . not the logical and factual prius of the 'racial murder' of National Socialism?"[39] Questions such as these, Nolte claimed, established comparisons that made possible a more objective assessment of the place of the Nazi episode in history.

Nolte's opponents were not convinced. In fact, as Charles Maier points out, Nolte's position had "given academic credentials to what hitherto was the underground discourse of the *Soldatenzeitung* or ss reunions."[40] In relativizing Nazism's crimes, Nolte and his supporters had muddied the historical waters and made real assessments of historical and moral responsibilty all the more difficult. In a provocative reference to the United States's, and specifically Ronald Reagan's, role in such dangerous revisionism, Maier refers to this form of history as "Bitburg history," which he defines as follows: "Bitburg history unites oppressors and victims, Nazi perpetrators of violence with those who were struck down by it, in a common dialectic. Bitburg history courts the danger that is reminiscent of Hegel's remarkable discussion of master and slave in *The Phenomenology of the Spirit*. It confuses the formal, logical dependence of victim and victimizer (there can by definition exist no perpetrator without a victim) with a shared responsibility for the wrong committed."[41]

If, as the preceding remarks suggest, fascism and its legacy have returned with a vengeance as the subject of heated public debate among historians and political scientists, the same can be said of other disciplines in what the French call "the human sciences" as well. With the publication of Victor Farias's *Heidegger et le nazisme* in France in 1987, the subject of the nature and duration of Martin Heidegger's commitment to National Socialism became the focus of an international controversy involving philosophers, literary critics, sociologists, and others. If the controversy had simply to do with Heidegger's political engagement, the debate in all likelihood would have died out fairly quickly. But equally at issue was the extent to which Heidegger's philosophy of Being was bound up with his pro-Nazi commitments. Given the degree to which that philosophy had influenced and in some instances defined poststructuralist thinking, Heidegger's Nazism could arguably be seen as "tainting" or "contaminating" these intellectual practices as well. Hotly contested in France, Germany, and the United States, the controversy continues to generate books, articles, and ancillary debates remakable for their acrimony. The broader philo-sophical and critical issues raised by the controversy, moreover, have hardly been settled to everyone's satisfaction.[42]

The controversy surrounding Martin Heidegger's Nazi past was fol-lowed in short order in this country by an equally vociferous and pub-lic debate over the past of another influential intellectual figure: Paul de Man, the Yale literary critic and proponent of deconstruction. Al-though certainly not of the stature of Martin Heidegger, de Man never-theless had a large following, especially among academic literary critics. News of his anti-Semitic and even pro-Nazi articles and book reviews in the pages of the Belgian collaborationist daily *Le Soir* during the war sent shock waves through literature departments. Many of de Man's friends, admirers, and disciples sought to minimize the damage either by claiming that his wartime journalism had nothing to do with his subsequent critical practice or by arguing, certainly more tenden-tiously, that his wartime writings were not in fact anti-Semitic or col-laborationist. Some even insisted that the articles in question were subtly resistant to Nazi hegemony.

The debate over Paul de Man's past has, of course, largely subsided. There is little doubt, however, that the scandal surrounding that past, coupled with Martin Heidegger's Nazism, has spurred considerable in-terest—and a fair amount of soul searching—concerning the degree to which the intellectual, cultural, and artistic practices of modernity and postmodernity are tied to the legacy of fascism. In this sense as well, the study of fascism's past inevitably engages questions of fas-cism's presence today, whether that presence is perceived as a return or as a painful, if oblique, continuity in Western culture.

The essays included in this collection take as their subject the return of fascism—or, stated less provocatively, its legacy in political, cul-tural, and historical terms since 1980. While the essays cover a wide variety of topics, their focus is restricted primarily to the Western Eu-ropean context and specifically the political movements and ide-ologies, historical and cultural debates, and trials of memory that have stirred controversy on the French, Italian, and German scenes for the last fifteen years. Thus Christopher Flood, Richard Wolin, and Jeffrey Schnapp examine extreme right-wing and neofascist ideologies and political movements, especially Jean-Marie Le Pen's Front National and the New Right in France, and Gianfranco Fini and the Alleanza Nazionale in Italy. Focusing on the debates over the nature and legacy of Europe's fascist past and the role that past plays in shaping national identity in the present, Wulf Kansteiner examines the German *Histo-rikerstreit* ten years later, while Robert Soucy and Bertram Gordon discuss, respectively, the debate over French fascism and its origins and role in French society and the ongoing history of the "Vichy Syndrome" in French public life. As part of the latter discussion, Richard Golsan examines the trial of Paul Touvier and the role played by these "trials of memory" in bringing closure to public and intellectual debates over *les années noires*. Along similar lines, Lynn Higgins discusses the Barbie trial and demonstrates the degree to which, in both legal and historical terms, French efforts to come to grips with Nazism in the person of Barbie were problematized by the irruption of troubling and explosive parallel memories of France's own role in the Algerian War.

In his essay on Ernst Junger and right-wing artists and intellectuals prominent in Germany today, Elliot Neaman explores disturbing continuities in Junger's cultural and political views and how these views, along with those of other troubling figures like Carl Schmitt, have informed the discourse of the new intellectual right in Germany today. Jeffrey Schnapp explores similar artistic and intellectual continuities from the Fascist era into the postwar republic—hence his title, "Fascism after Fascism." It is perhaps at the level of philosophical, artistic and intellectual discourse that the legacy of European fascism has made itself felt most in the United States since 1980; Reed Dasenbrock discusses this legacy in his essay here. Examining the Heidegger and de Man affairs and other more recent events, Dasenbrock finds "uncanny" resemblances between "post-structuralism, the post-modern in Lyotard's vocabulary, and the imaginative themes of fascism." For Tom Sheehan, fascism assumes a more concrete and wrenching form in the United States's policy of supporting Central American militarism and political murder. Such policies are for Sheehan the tragic outgrowth of a perverse commitment to a misguided American imperialism.

As these brief comments concerning the subjects of the essays suggest, no concise or all-inclusive definition of fascism as ideology or as political, social, or cultural practice emerges from a reading of the entire collection. Indeed, it should be noted that many of the contributors themselves entertain different notions of what is crucial to a definition of fascism in both historical and contemporary terms. Nevertheless, these essays do illustrate a multitude of ways in which fascism continues to make its presence felt in Western democratic societies, erupting with disturbing frequency as a "return of the repressed" in judicial and artistic scandals as well as in historical, critical, and political debates in Europe and the United States. It is in this sense that one may speak of a "return of fascism." One would perhaps be premature in speaking with Jacques Julliard of a "fascism that is coming," but abundant evidence in the essays here suggests that, at the very least, the ghosts of fascisms past are still very much with us today.

Notes

1. Jacques Julliard, *Ce Fascisme qui vient . . .* (Paris: Seuil, 1994).

2. Bernard-Henri Lévy, *La Pureté dangereuse* (Paris: Grasset, 1994), 10. For a refutation of the Weimar analogy deployed by Julliard, Lévy, and others, see Richard Wolin's essay here.

3. Alain Finkielkraut, *Comment peut-on être croate?* (Paris: Gallimard, 1992), 118–19. Unless otherwise noted, all translations are my own.

4. See Judt's now-classic study of French intellectuals in the immediate postwar years, *Past Imperfect: French Intellectuals 1944–1956* (Berkeley: University of California Press, 1992). He has been equally harsh in dealing with the political judgments of figures like Finkielkraut and Lévy and their engagements vis-à-vis Eastern Europe in "Paris and the Tribes of Europe," *French Politics and Society* 10, no. 2 (spring 1992): 34–47.

5. Bessel, *Fascist Italy and Nazi Germany*, 3.

6. Bessel's call for a renewed emphasis on the study of fascism as a generic concept is also linked to his concern, shared by a number of other historians, that studies of Italian Fascism and Nazism have become too "national specific." As a result, the concept of a generic fascism, discredited in the eighties as a holdover from earlier Marxist critiques, was losing its explanatory power. Therefore important links and parallels between fascist movements past and present were being obscured. Along these lines, see Tim Mason's classic essay "Whatever Happened to Fascism?" in Childers and Caplan, *Reevaluating the Third Reich*, 253–62.

7. Jacques Julliard has described the turbulent events of 1995 in France in a recent political memoir entitled *L'Année des dupes* (Paris: Seuil, 1996).

8. For an excellent and detailed account of the current Italian political crisis and its historical sources, see McCarthy, *Crisis of the Italian State*. The recent electoral victory in April 1996 of a center-Left coalition under Romano Prodi—and the defeat of Silvio Berlusconi—suggest that the crisis has generally abated in recent months, but it is perhaps too soon to tell if the new coalition's low-key approach will prove effective in the long run. For an account of the election and a discussion of Prodi and his allies, see Alexander Stille, "Italy: The Convulsions of Normalcy," *The New York Review of Books*, 6 June 1996, 42–46.

9. For a recent discussion of the situation in Austria, see Tony Judt, "Austria and the Ghost of the New Europe," *New York Review of Books*, 15 February 1996, 22–25.

10. I am grateful to my colleague Frank Baumgartner for this information.

11. See Judt, "Austria," 25.

12. For the Freedom Party's electoral success in the 1996 European parliamentary vote, see Alan Cowell, "Austria's Rightist Vote: No to Europe," *The New York Times*, 15 October 1996.

13. In 1989, the *Republicaner* garnered 7 percent in the West Berlin municipal

election of 1989, but the following year they garnered only 1 percent in national elections. See Payne, *History of Fascism*, 500.

14. In the June 1996 elections, Zhirinovsky's star appeared to be fading, but as the Communists gained momentum under Gennady Zyuganov, their support among extreme right-wing nationalists including the likes of Aleksandr Prokhanov was frequently noted. For a discussion of Zyuganov and the "red-brown coalition" he had formed, see David Remnick, "Hammer, Sickle, and Book," *New York Review of Books*, 23 May 1996, 45–51.

15. See Judt, "Austria," 23.

16. Jill A. Irvine, "Nationalism and the Extreme Right in the Former Yugoslavia," in Cheles, Ferguson, and Vaughan, eds., *The Far Right*, 147. Irvine's distinction between new and classic fascisms is not accurate in a number of instances. In *Fascism: An Informal Introduction to its Theory and Practice* (New Brunswick NJ: Transaction Books, 1976), Renzo de Felice notes that Italian Fascism originally concentrated on internal politics and presented itself as a government of peace in international affairs. It was only with the war in Ethiopia that aggression became the keynote of Italian foreign policy. See pp. 61–88.

17. In their *Dictionnaire historique des fascismes et du nazisme* (Brussells: Editions Complexe, 1992) Pierre Milza and Serge Berstein argue that totalitarianism is the most crucial defining feature of historical fascism. But in his recent *History of Fascism*, Stanley Payne argues that only Nazi Germany truly established itself successfully as a state along the lines of a totalitarian model. See Milza and Berstein's "Avant-propos" (*Dictionnaire*, 7–28), and Payne's "Generic Fascism?" (*History*, 462–70).

18. Marcus, *National Front*, 45–51.

19. Payne, *History of Fascism*, 518.

20. Payne, *History of Fascism*, 518.

21. There is no evidence to suggest that Le Pen moderated his views in his recent electoral successes, nor that his leadership style is not fundamentally fascistic, as suggested by the aesthetics of his rallies. The play of lights, the presence of monumental patriotic symbols, the cult of the leader, and the tone and message of Le Pen's harangues are all too familiar to those who have seen film footage of Nuremberg rallies. For the more complex case of Fini and the recently transformed MSI, see Jeffrey Schnapp's essay here.

22. Stanley Payne, "Historic Fascism and Neo-Fascism," *European History Quarterly* 23 (1993): 75.

23. Note reference to the Sternhell controversy below.

24. The role and importance of biological racism in Nazi ideology and culture has, on the other hand, been debated a great deal in recent years. In this context, see especially Charles S. Maier's "Foreword," in Childers and Kaplan, *Reevaluating the Third Reich*, xi–xvi.

25. See Alan Cowell, "Right's Rise Confronts Austria with its Nazi Past," *The New York Times*, 8 February 1996. The incident is also discussed in Judt, "Austria," 22–25.

26. Quoted in Robert Knight, "Haider, the Freedom Party and the Extreme Right in Austria," *Parliamentary Affairs*, 292.

27. Martin Conway, *Collaboration in Belgium: Léon Degrelle and the Rexist Movement* (New Haven: Yale University Press, 1993), 281.

28. For information on Gaucher, Malaguti, and other pro-Nazi collaborators in the Front National, see Eric Conan, "Enquête sur le retour d'une idéologie," *L'Express*, 17–23 July 1992, 20–27.

29. Gaspard, *Small City in France.*

30. Tzvetan Todorov and Annick Jacquet, *Guerre et paix sous l'occupation* (Paris: Arléa, 1996), 15.

31. Robert Wohl, "French Fascism, Both Right and Left: Reflections on the Sternhell Controversy," *Journal of Modern History* 63 (March 1991): 91. It is important to note that Sternhell's theses have been criticized by a large number of historians outside France, including Wohl in the essay just cited. For a detailed account of the broad parameters of the debate over French fascism, see Robert Soucy's essay here.

32. Stanley Hoffman, "Cinquante ans après, quelques conclusions essentielles," *Esprit* 181 (May 1992): 39. Malle has, of course, made a subsequent film about the Occupation, *Au Revoir les enfants*, which many, including Hoffman, consider a more balanced and authentic representation of the period.

33. For a detailed account of Bousquet's career and his murder, see Golsan, *Memory, the Holocaust, and French Justice.*

34. See Eric Conan and Henry Rousso, *Vichy, un passé qui ne passe pas* (Paris: Fayard, 1994). The book is forthcoming in English translation from the University Press of New England.

35. Robert Knight, "The Waldheim Context: Austria and Nazism," *tls*, 3 October 1986.

36. Miller, *One, by One, by One*, 61.

37. For a discussion of the Nazi presence in Austrian politics in the immediate postwar period, see Max E. Riedlsperger, *The Lingering Shadow of Nazism: The Austrian Independent Party Movement Since 1945* (New York: Columbia University Press, 1978). For the de-Nazification, the election of Waldheim, and anti-Semitism in postwar Austria, see the works by Miller, Knight, and Judt cited above.

38. Quoted in Charles S. Maier, *The Unmasterable Past: History, Holocaust, and National Identity* (Cambridge MA: Harvard University Press, 1988), 9.

39. Ernst Nolte, "The Past that Will Not Pass," in *Forever in the Shadow of Hitler?* trans. James Knowlton and Truett Gates (Atlantic Highlands NJ: Humanities Press, 1993), 22.

40. Maier, *Unmasterable Past*, 64.

41. Maier, *Unmasterable Past*, 14.

42. The number of publications generated by the Heidegger controversy is of course enormous, but a few suggestions as to basic texts are in order. Farias's book was published in English as *Heidegger and Nazism*. Initial responses by European intellectuals to Farias's book are included in the "Special Feature on Heidegger and Nazism" in *Critical Inquiry* 15, no. 2 (winter 1989): 407–88. A very detailed account of Heidegger's political activities in the 1930s is provided by Hugo Ott in *Martin Heidegger, A Political Life* (New York: Basic Books, 1993). Richard Wolin's *Politics of Being* explores the connection between Heidegger's philosophy and his politics, and Hans Sluga's *Heidegger's Crisis: Philosophy and Politics in Nazi Germany*

(Cambridge MA: Harvard University Press, 1993) provides a much needed contextualization in English of Heidegger's pro-Nazi commitment within the broader framework of the academic institution of philosophy in Germany at the time. For ancillary debates, see the exchange of letters and articles in the *New York Review of Books* in the spring of 1993 generally referred to as "L'affaire Derrida."

Christopher Flood

Organizing Fear and Indignation:
The Front National in France

The revival of the radical Right in Western Europe has been increasingly widely reported since the mid-1980s. Whether or not the parties representing this current can usefully be described as neofascist is debatable, since there is no consensus on what counts as fascism in the contemporary context.[1] Whatever the case, the more successful among the parties do not share the revolutionary stance, the socioeconomic corporatism, or the authoritarian rejection of democracy often associated with fascism. The commonly used label "national populist" seems to fit them well enough. Their message is certainly nationalistic, and they couch their appeal in distinctly populist terms. They have made the issue of immigration the centerpiece of their political platforms, and they have linked the presence of large immigrant populations to a wide range of social and economic problems. The prospect of huge waves of refugees, asylum-seekers, and economic migrants sweeping into Western Europe from the east or south is often the subject of apocalyptic warnings coupled with denunciation of the alleged weakness of mainstream political parties in facing the problem.

The emergence of radical right-wing parties is not related only to the immigration issue. It also reflects a more diffuse phenomenon some political theorists call societal insecurity.[2] That is to say, significant sections of European populations feel their collective identity and their material well-being are under serious threat. For the social scientist, the present period can be analyzed in the light of complex transnational and international factors of change such as economic modernization and globalization, the information-technology revolution, and the fluidity of international relations since the end of the cold war. For many ordinary citizens the issues seem less abstract. They see endemic unemployment and job insecurity. They see widening wealth gaps. They see the state losing its power to assure the welfare and safety of its citizens. They are frightened by media reports of rising crime, drug epidemics, and unrest among disaffected young people.

They distrust the political leaders on whom they are forced to depend. They want a civilized society that cares for its members, but they resent the taxes and the endless demands of those who claim to be deprived. They want peaceful relations with other countries, but they fear absorption by more powerful states or supranational groupings. Radical right-wing parties claim to have answers to these questions. While accepting elements of individualistic, market-oriented neoliberalism, they purport to reconstitute national community with a new, harder shell and with the restoration of internal stability.

In some countries the national populist Right is embodied in relatively new parties formed in the 1970s or later. Other parties have emerged from the revitalization of older groupings. Of course, the electoral importance of the phenomenon should not be exaggerated. In national contests the scores of these parties have tended to remain substantially below 10 percent.[3] However, there have been notable exceptions. For example, in Austria the *Freiheitliche Partei Österreichs* under Jorg Haider scored 16.4 percent in the 1992 presidential election, 22.5 percent in the parliamentary election of 1994, and 21.9 percent in that of 1995, making it the third largest party in the country (with even higher scores in the 1996 Vienna city election and in the 1996 national election to the European Parliament—more than 27 percent in both cases). In Italy Gianfranco Fini's Allianza Nazionale (the broader-based successor to the neofascist MSI) scored 13.5 percent in the parliamentary elections of 1994 and 15.7 percent in 1996.

The Front National (FN) in France is another important case. Politically and economically, France is a major regional power. It has played a historically important role in the integration of the European Union. It has residual influence in many of its former colonies and has considerable cultural prestige. Although the FN has not yet participated in government at the national level, and may never do so, the threat it poses as a significant pole of attraction for large numbers of right-wing voters—and even for some former left-wing voters—has already pulled the political agenda in a more nationalistic direction on a range of issues, especially concerning immigration. The FN has come a long way since its extremely modest beginnings in the early 1970s, and it has already marked one of the high points in the modern history of the French extreme Right.

Ideologically, the roots of the extreme Right in France can be traced back to the royalist counterrevolutionary theorists of the late eighteenth and early nineteenth centuries, with their rejection of the Enlightenment heritage of rationalism, universalistic humanism, economic liberalism, and constitutionalism, which fed into the French

Revolution. Since that time, the importance of reactionary monarchism has waned, and more modern forms of right-wing authoritarianism or even fascism have come to the fore.[4] The political fortunes of
the extreme Right have ebbed and flowed over time, according to historical circumstances. The high point in this century was during the
German occupation of 1940–44, when the reactionary, neotradition al-
ist wing of the Right was dominant in Marshal Pétain's government at
Vichy until the later stages of the wartime period, while the modernist, fascistic wing congregated in Paris. However, the price for that period of ascendancy, and for collaboration with the German authorities,
was the ignominy of the purges following the Liberation and the disgrace that drove the extreme Right to the edges of mainstream political life for many years afterward. Although Pierre Poujade's UDCA had
a brief flurry of electoral successes in 1956, the more consistent pattern under the Fourth Republic was one of impotence. That remained
the case until recently under the Fifth Republic, which succeeded the
Fourth during the crisis over Algeria in 1958. Despite all its extra-
parliamentary agitation, its conspiracies, and finally its acts of terrorism, the extreme Right was powerless to prevent General de Gaulle
from negotiating away France's most cherished colony, and it did not
have any significant impact on French politics until the mid-1980s.
The point is illustrated by Jean-Louis Tixier-Vignancour's 1965 presidential campaign, which achieved only 5.2 percent of the vote in the
first round—and even that can be seen as a relative success when compared with electoral scores for nearly twenty years afterwards.

The FN itself was founded in 1972 from a disparate group of neofascist organizations, in an attempt to unify the extreme Right and present a more acceptable face to the electorate.[5] During its first ten years
of existence the party followed the sterile tradition of the postwar extreme Right, spending much of its time on internal divisions, personal
animosities, expulsions, rivalry with breakaway groups, and occasional self-inflicted violence; it had no significant electoral impact,
never receiving even 1 percent of the national vote. The 1981 presidential election was particularly humiliating for the FN's leader, Jean-
Marie Le Pen. Having scored a mere 0.74 percent in the 1974 election,
he failed even to gain the five hundred signatures of public office-
holders needed to qualify as a candidate in 1981. Yet, within three years
of that disaster, the FN had begun its breakthrough into the national
arena. Since then, although the party has enjoyed only a brief period of
significant parliamentary representation, and has had setbacks, it has
established itself as a significant political force.

Like other parties of the radical Right in Western Europe, the FN has
placed opposition to immigration at the forefront of its political plat-

form, and this issue has been a major factor in its electoral appeal. It has been able to exploit the timidity of successive governments, and the sensitivity of public opinion, when faced with the problem of judging appropriate levels or types of immigration.[6] Equally, it has capitalized on the very real questions that arise in relation to the social and cultural integration of immigrants. During the great era of economic development from the early 1950s to the time of the first oil shock in 1973, France had willingly received huge numbers of immigrants. Since 1974, primary economic immigration by adult males has been very tightly restricted, but this has encouraged those who had already entered to stay permanently. In any case, the arrival and settlement of immigrants continues in the form of family regrouping, refugees and asylum-seekers, or illegal entrants. This raises complex issues of employment, geographical distribution and housing, welfare provision, and education, among others. Immigrants often appear to be competing with poorer sections of the native community, especially in areas of heavy geographical concentration. There are also problems of race and culture entwined with these other factors. In France, as in other countries with large immigrant populations, the targets for particular resentment have most often been the non-European, colored immigrants—especially those whose religious and other cultural traditions are markedly different from those of France and who are resistant to assimilation. Furthermore, people whose skin color or manner of dress identifies them as non-European will continue to be perceived as alien even after they become naturalized French citizens.

However, although the immigration issue has been of value to the FN, by itself it is not enough to account for the party's rise. A range of other conjunctural and structural factors have played their part in creating a space for the emergence of the FN by fostering a mood of anxiety and resentment in significant sections of the population. With the election of François Mitterrand to the presidency in 1981, followed by the election of a Socialist-dominated left-wing majority—including the Communists—in the National Assembly, France was offered the prospect of a radical transformation in the direction of democratic socialism, with a massive program of nationalizations, redistributive taxation, reductions in working hours, raising of the minimum wage, increased pension rights, extension of trade union power, and a range of other measures. The economic and financial crisis caused within the first eighteen months by the attempt to implement these policies confirmed the anxieties of conservatives and encouraged ideological polarization. The progressive abandonment of socialist objectives over the ensuing four years, while terribly disappointing to those who had voted for the Left, did not diminish the strident attacks from the mainstream Right. The climate of social and political tension began to offer the FN an audience for its explanation of France's ills. This was reflected initially in a handful of localities during the municipal elections of 1983, then in the European elections of 1984 (11 percent of votes cast, giving 10 MEPs), then in the cantonal elections of 1985 (averaging 10.4 percent in the seats it contested), then in the 1986 parliamentary elections (9.8 percent of votes cast, giving 35 *députés*) and regional elections (9.7 percent of votes cast, giving 137 councillors).

The swing of the political pendulum that produced a mainstream right-wing coalition government of the Gaullist Ralliement pour la République (RPR) and the Union pour la Démocratie Française (UDF) after the legislative elections of 1986 provided the opportunity for a trial of neoliberal ideas intended to galvanize the economy and society with a program of privatizations, deregulation, and supply-side economics inspired by Ronald Reagan's and Margaret Thatcher's governments. These were coupled with a tough stance on labor relations, law and order, and immigration. To some extent this stole the platform of the extreme Right, but it also helped to make the FN's concerns more respectable. In any case, the mainstream Right was damaged by the stock market crash of October 1987 and failed to regain sufficient momentum to win the 1988 elections.

Under the Socialist minority governments of 1988–93 and under the RPR/UDF governments up to the time of this writing, the period of grand ideas and ideological polarization gave way to a variable balance between moderate social-democratic and moderate conservative administrations, with particular emphasis on prudent economic management. Yet while the majority of people had a generally high standard of living, even during the economic downswing of 1992–94, the absence of grand but divisive projects did not produce consensus or reassurance in all sections of society. Rather, a sense of anxiety and cynicism spread among significant sections of the population. Public concern focused on persistently high unemployment levels and casualization of labor, especially among young people, amid the continuing effects of economic restructuring. Rising contempt for politicians was exacerbated by the pettiness of the power struggles within and between the major parties, and by the apparently endless series of corruption cases that came to light on both ends of the political spectrum. Sporadic riots in the run-down working-class suburbs served as a reminder of the two-speed society in which substantial minorities feel excluded from prosperity, while the majority themselves feel uncertain of the future. The wave of strikes and demonstrations by public-sector workers and university students in December 1995 showed the degree of resentment that could be aroused by government plans to impose budgetary freezes or cutbacks. Drugs, violent crime, burglary, and fear of a host of perceived social ills, including excessive influx of immigrants, loss of national identity because of the European Union, terrorism by Islamic fundamentalists, the costs of meeting the convergence criteria for European Monetary Union, and continuing decline in France's influence and autonomy as an international actor. These and other factors were deeply troubling.

None of this is to suggest that things have been all bad for France, or that everyone is discontented. If I have dwelt on the negative side, it is merely to explain why some sections of the French public feel that the country has been badly governed, and that its ruling elites have no clear sense of purpose beyond their own self-interest and the interests of their favored clienteles. The FN offers an outlet for public disaffection from the mainstream parties. Furthermore, in this climate of disillusionment the disadvantage of being unable to claim government expertise can be counterbalanced by the fact that the FN's personnel and policies have not yet been tarnished by the test of practice.

The FN is not merely a repository for the protest voters. The level and distribution of its support have become too solid for that to be an adequate explanation.[7] Of course, it has not all been smooth sailing for the FN since the first signs of electoral advance in the early to mid-1980s; there have been fluctuations in its progress. The FN's own predictions have repeatedly proven exaggerated. Toward the end of the 1980s, and again in 1994, public opinion polls and election results appeared to suggest that support for the party was stagnating or even dropping back. However, as of this writing, the more plausible assumption is that the FN has simply been implanting itself less rapidly than its supporters had hoped and its enemies had feared.

Le Pen's personal scores in the first rounds of the presidential elections of 1988 and 1995 were 14.4 percent and 15 percent respectively. These performances outstrip those of the FN in other elections. Nevertheless, in the regional elections of 1992 the FN scored 13.9 percent (239 councillors), compared with its 9.7 percent (137 councillors) in 1986. Equally, where it had received approximately 9.8 percent of the vote (but only 1 *député*) in the 1988 parliamentary elections, the FN made 12.4 percent in 1993 (though no *députés*). As I have said, 1994 was a bad year. In the European elections, where it had heavy competition from rival electoral lists for the anti-Maastricht vote, the FN's score slipped to 10.5 percent, as compared with 11.9 percent in 1989 and 11 percent in 1984 (though it maintained its level of representation in the European Parliament at 10 members). There was also slippage in the cantonal elections, to 9.8 percent from a high of 12.4 percent in 1992 (though it won 4 council seats in the 1994 race, as compared with 2 in 1992). Still, Le Pen's strong performance in the 1995 presidential election was followed by considerable success in the municipal elections in June of that year.[8] Although the party did not put up candidates in every municipality, it tallied 20–40 percent in a dozen towns of over thirty thousand inhabitants, and exceeded 40 percent in two others (compared with only seven towns over 20 percent in the 1989 municipal elections). It also scored well in many smaller towns. Its claimed tally of municipal councillors rose to 1,075 (992 according to the Ministry of the Interior), as compared with 360 in 1989 (489 according to the Ministry of the Interior). It gained overall control of the councils in Toulon, Marignane, and Orange, which it hoped to use as showcases for the party's policies. In the same election the city of Nice was won by the list headed by Jacques Peyrat, formerly a senior member of the FN, who had left the party for reasons of political opportunism rather than any fundamental change of heart on ideology or policy. In addition, the town of Vitrolles was subsequently won by the FN in February 1997, following annulment of the 1995 result due to electoral irregularities.

The momentum was maintained in the snap legislative elections called by President Jacques Chirac for 25 May–1 June 1997. The FN scored 15 percent in the first round, an advance of 2 percent on its 1993 result. Although it won only one seat in the second round, its candidates were sufficiently well placed to enter the runoffs in 133 constituencies. By refusing to stand down in all but 1 of those constituencies, it undoubtedly contributed to the overall defeat of the RPR/UDF by depriving the mainstream Right of vital votes.

Polling more strongly among men than among women, the FN gets its most substantial support from owners of small businesses, self-employed artisans and other traders, clerical workers, manual workers, and the unemployed.[9] Its support among managers and the liberal professions—after a brief flirtation in the 1984 European elections—is less substantial. As was illustrated by large-scale exit polls at the 1995 presidential election and the 1997 legislative elections, the occupational profile of the FN's electorate indicates that support was strongest among voters who considered themselves lower middle class, working class, or underprivileged.[10] It is noteworthy that no less than 76 percent of Le Pen's support came from voters who expressed anxiety concerning their personal and professional situation (a figure matched only by the Communist and Trotskyist candidates). From the FN's point of view it has to be encouraging that Le Pen attracted 21 percent of first-time voters in the 1995 presidential election, tying for second in this group with the Gaullist candidate, Jacques Chirac (eventual winner of the second round of voting), and only 2 percent behind the Socialist candidate, Lionel Jospin. Furthermore, a higher proportion (64 percent) of Le Pen's voters than those of any other candidate said they had made their decision several months earlier, which implies a firmer commitment than if the decision had been more recent.

Geographically, the FN's strongest support lies mainly east of a line running roughly from Le Havre to Valence then arching back to Toulouse, with particular concentrations in Paris and its region, the Lyon/ Saint-Etienne/Grenoble conurbation and its region, Alsace in the east-northeast, and a band across the south from Marseille and its region to Nice.[11] Obviously, many different local factors may contribute to this spread. In the Paris, Lyon, and Marseille areas at least, there is often a correlation with very high immigrant populations (especially North Africans), high crime rates, high unemployment, and problems of urban or suburban blight. However, the FN's popularity is not necessarily dictated by direct proximity to immigrant populations; there is also what has been called a halo effect of insecurity in areas neighboring those with high concentrations.[12]

In short, although the FN has failed to break the mold of French politics by gaining a stake in national government, it is solidly established as a competitor. Clearly it is the most successful repository for the protest vote. But the relative solidity of its support suggests that it has also succeeded in providing a genuine sense of affiliation and a message that is persuasive to many people, though they remain a minority.

One of the most striking features of the FN is the effort it devotes to matters of ideology, policy formation, and political communication. The aim has been to combine the organization of a mass party with the types of activity usually associated with the extreme Right's think tanks and clubs in the lineage of Charles Maurras's Action Française.[13] Although it is a broad, composite grouping that subsumes a number of different ideological traditions, the FN has devoted a great deal of effort to developing a central line intended to be reasonably acceptable to the main currents within the party and marketable to a wide electorate.[14] The structure of the FN reflects this.[15] In parallel with the Secrétariat Général, which runs the bureaucratic organization of the party, the Délégation Générale, formed in 1988 and directly answerable to the president of the party, is responsible for developing strategy and ensuring that the FN is potentially capable of governing the country according to a fully developed set of policies. Under the overall coordination of the Délégué Général and his staff, the Délégation includes a propaganda section responsible for the Atelier de Propagande, which produces posters, tracts, leaflets, stickers, cassettes, and so forth. There is a training section that runs the Institut de Formation Nationale to educate activists and organize conferences, evening lecture series, and other similar events. The study section runs a Centre d'Études et d'Argumentaires, which publishes reports and brochures to furnish arguments for the president and the movement. The communication section issues press releases and monitors the media; it is also responsible for producing the fortnightly magazine *Français d'abord, la lettre de Jean-Marie Le Pen*. There is a section devoted to spreading the FN's intellectual influence. This includes the Conseil Scientifique, which groups the party's leading intellectuals and produces the glossy theoretical journal *Identité* (relaunched in 1996 after ceasing publication in 1994). Finally, there is a section responsible for organizing major demonstrations, commemorations, festivals, and public meetings. In addition to the communication apparatus directly attached to the party, there are daily (*Présent, Le Français*) and weekly (*National hebdo, Minute, Rivarol*) newspapers, and other periodicals (*Le Choc du mois, Monde et vie, Itinéraires*, and *Militant*, for example), that support the FN and in some cases reflect the particular orientation of one of its internal currents.

Although it cannot boast any figures who possess the cultural stature achieved by Charles Maurras or Maurice Barrès earlier in this century, the FN has attracted a significant number of intellectuals. Among them are a number of theorists and publicists who were, or still are, associated with the New Right think tanks GRECE (Pierre Vial, Jean-Claude Bardet, Pierre de Meuse, Jean Haudry, and Jean Varenne, among others), or the Club de l'Horloge (notably Jean-Yves Le Gallou, Yvan Blot, and Bruno Mégret).[16] When the review *Identité* was launched in 1989, its editorial advisory board of twenty-five members included seventeen serving or former university teachers.[17] Le Pen himself is not merely a crude demagogue with a line in brutalistic charisma—though that is certainly an element of his behavior. He does, after all, have a degree in law and a postgraduate diploma (DES) in political science. He is no political philosopher—more a publicist and popularizer; but he is certainly capable of making a sophisticated argument. Besides the other books, newsletters, articles, and policy statements that appear under his name, he introduces, or otherwise contributes to, the annual lecture series organized by the Institut de Formation Nationale. Issues of *Identité* have normally been headed by one of his editorials.

The FN presents itself as the defender of the people against the Establishment. France is said to be dominated by a corrupt, inefficient, unaccountable oligarchy of politicians, bureaucrats, business elites, trade unionists, intellectuals, and media people who constitute a *no-menklatura* that pursues its own interests at the expense of the national good.[18] Thus, although the FN professes to differ from the old extreme Right in that it accepts democratic, republican principles, its contempt for all of the orthodox parties as equally indistinguishable, statist, incompetent, and self-serving provides a contemporary substitute for the extreme Right's traditional distrust of parliamentary democracy as such.

The FN's stance is one of injured innocence and courage in the face of persecution. Because it is the only force to defend the people, the FN claims, it is vilified by the Establishment. Because they are the only ones to tell the truth, Le Pen and his party assert, every effort is made to gag them by means of trumped-up legal cases and media campaigns, or sometimes physical violence.[19] The FN is branded as fascistic or extremist in order to conjure up frightening echoes of the past, and especially of the Vichy regime. But in reality, according to FN publicists, the party is not only not fascistic or extreme, but new and different, while the establishment remains lifelessly the same, unable to adapt to new times.[20] The parties of the establishment, besides being self-serving, soft-totalitarian oligarchies, are class parties catering to particular clienteles, whereas the FN has no specific class base, rather appealing to people throughout the social spectrum. People want change. The FN says it can provide it. In the political mythology of the party, the dynamism of the movement derives from the fact that it is a real community fused together in a common, redemptive cause for the benefit of the nation as a whole. Its history is presented as a process of refining its identity through struggle and sacrifice against the enemy.[21] Le Pen is portrayed in hagiographies as above all a man of the people, a natural leader, and the bearer of an unbreakable faith in the nation.[22]

Thus, the FN purports to have produced a new ideological synthesis. It is proud to acknowledge that it has its roots in the intellectual traditions of the extreme Right, but it denies that it is of the extreme Right today. The claim must be treated with caution, however. To declare loyalty to the extreme Right as it was in the past, while asserting that new times require new positions, leaves ample scope for ambiguity.[23] In any case, there can be a greater or lesser distinction between the party's official line on any given issue and the views expressed by particular factions or individual activists within the party. There are undoubtedly members of the party who hold racist, xenophobic, anti-Semitic, antidemocratic, and/or other opinions that would be classed as extremist in relation to the norms of the French political mainstream. What is said in private may differ from what is said in public, and what is said in public will be affected by the nature of the intended audience. When extremist opinions are aired publicly they can offer ammunition to the FN's enemies, but there is clearly a margin of tolerance in relation to writings and other public statements that do not appear directly under the auspices of the party. As Guy Birenbaum points out, newspapers and magazines that are notionally independent of the FN but nevertheless serve the party often have a more extremist tone than the official organs.[24] Furthermore, some of the books they promote for their readers are extremist.[25] The fact that the FN speaks with many voices allows a wide range of nuances of discourse, and the case of Le Pen himself illustrates how the register can vary from one site to another according to circumstances.[26]

But what of the claim to newness and modernity? The FN's argument is that whereas the old capitalism-versus-collectivism debate is outdated, the FN leads the new debate between those who uphold the values of national identity and those who advocate globalism and universalism.[27] The left and the soft Right coincide not only in their stifling attachment to social democratic values linking capitalism with the welfare state, but also in their woolly, antinational cosmopolitanism and the disastrous multiculturalism that has done so much to undermine the coherence of French society. The FN alone in France stands for cultural homogeneity and rootedness, national history, national community. There can be no compromise between the two. Furthermore, the FN represents itself as the harbinger of an international wave of renewed identitarian feelings. Its time is only just beginning; it is the the FN that has identified the need to confront the new North-South geopolitical conflicts now replacing the old East-West divide.

Here, then, the assertion is not so much that the concern with national identity is new in itself, but that it is entirely suited to the new historical situation. The ideology of rootedness, inherited from Barrès and others, is fused with the discourse of cultural identity and difference propagated by the New Right in place of the older, less publicly acceptable discourse of racial inequality.[28] Turning the discourse of the French left on its head, the FN views defenders of non-European immigration as anti-French racists, bent on undermining France's ethnocultural integrity. That is to say, according to FN writers, the political establishment claims France is in the grip of racism and calls for struggle against this alleged scourge, to which it gives higher priority than unemployment, insecurity, the declining birth rate, or immigration. The establishment preaches the cosmopolitan ideology of human rights, which reduces mankind to its lowest common denominator without taking account of racial or cultural particularities. In reality, therefore, "antiracism" is nothing more than anti-French racism, a disguised form of ethnocide.[29] French identity is obscured in the name of a purely abstract, juridical conception of nationality based on mere presence on French soil and possession of the right document, whereas the core of national identity is shared ethnicity and shared historical culture.

In more concrete terms, the FN constantly blames the influx of third-world immigrants for high unemployment and rising crime, urban decay, swamping and deterioration of schools, alien religious and cultural practices (such as polygamy or female circumcision), and the imposition of colossal burdens on the welfare system, hence on taxation.[30] In rhetoric that often verges on the apocalyptic, FN writers describe France as a dumping ground for the unemployed of North Africa, with the prospect of even more relentless pressure in the future. Meanwhile, positive discrimination in favor of immigrants means negative discrimination against French people. The types of solutions envisaged by the FN include a ban on new immigration; a ban on family regrouping; expulsion of unemployed immigrants; expulsion of immigrants convicted of criminal offenses; reform of the Nationality Code to make naturalization more difficult; restricted access to welfare, housing, and so on; quotas in schools; and an employment policy stipulating that immigrants be last in and first out. Le Pen's 1995 election program claimed that the compulsory repatriation of three million immigrants could be achieved over the course of seven years.[31] This would allegedly free up more jobs and secure better welfare benefits for French people. The principle of systematic privilege for French citizens over foreign residents would be enshrined in the constitution itself by the addition, to Title I, article 2, paragraph 1, of the words: "It [the French Republic] applies the principle of National Preference in relations between citizens and foreigners."[32]

In the social and moral spheres the message of the FN is largely traditional conservative. Not all FN publicists are religious devotees, but they agree on the need to restore a national sense of the sacred.[33] The argument is that Western society is the only one to have expelled the sacred from its social organization, considering it a superseded category of development, a vestige of religious obscurantism. This is represented by Western thinkers as historical progress, the triumph of scientific and technical reason over emotion and superstition. The religious societies of the Middle East, Africa, and Asia are treated with contempt. Yet Western societies have reached an impasse, where undeniable material progress has come at the expense of spiritual and cultural values. Fulfilling the heritage of materialistic values bequeathed by the Enlightenment, the economy takes precedence over everything else, imposing its own logic of profit and making money the normative judge of all social life, so that society itself becomes a market. Everything is evaluated at its price. Everyone is rated as a consumer from birth to the grave. Thus, capitalist countries have enjoyed high living standards, but at the price of rejecting values that gave meaning to life and provided a social framework. Western man thus lives in an existential void amidst a superabundance of goods and services. Exploitation of nature, exploitation of man, contempt for ancient traditions, substitution of man for God as origin and goal of everything—all of this has produced immense disillusionment.

This philosophical position underpins the FN's muscularly conservative social platform, which is based on the assumption that there is a need for strong codes of behavior, clear social duties, and strong social bonds supported by effective laws.[34] Restoration of traditional morality and the integrity of the patriarchal family should be encouraged by fiscal measures and an income for stay-at-home mothers of large families. Abortion should be banned, says the FN, and the relentless struggle against AIDS should express the war against moral depravity. Defense of the Church and support for private Catholic schooling also figure prominently in FN programs. Law and order should be restored, with ruthless suppression of violent crime, and restoration of the death penalty. For state education, the FN emphasizes restoration of discipline, competitive ranking of pupils, and return to grammar and basic skills, coupled with education in France's national history and national values. These very traditional concerns are given a neoliberal veneer by reference to the right to parental choice, increased autonomy of institutions, and competition between institutions as a spur toward higher standards.[35]

Its stands on environmental and human ecology give the FN a more modern-looking platform that links with the concerns of the New Right. It also generates appeal among the young and offers opportunities for extending influence through contact with Green groups (see below). At the same time the FN claims that ecologism, properly understood, is essentially conservative. This harks back to the Barresian emphasis on cultural and territorial rootedness and fits with the FN's stance on protection of French agriculture, especially the peasant smallholding and the rural way of life.[36] The FN holds that the political debate about conservation of nature has been falsely reduced to two extremes: the "good guys," the Greens, with their ideal of ending progress and returning to a state of nature; and the "bad guys," who want technological and economic progress at any price. This is a false dichotomy. The Greens have an ideology based on a retrograde utopian conception of nature, borrowed from Rousseau, that confuses science with fantasy. This must be opposed to a realist view of nature that takes account of man, its principal element, whose role is to impose his mark on nature precisely because he is a creator of culture. However, in the age of the rights of man, it must be remembered that man does not have a monopoly of rights, and that he needs to make sure of keeping his place in the wider order of nature. This requires a concerted effort to restore balances and get away from unbridled productivism. To face the technocratic planners, the statist socialists, the fanatical chasers of profits, and all those who indiscriminately disfigure the natural or the human environment, it is necessary to restore an ethics and aesthetics of life, and a sense of the long term, allowing the individual to rediscover his roots and his identity as a member of a community bonded to a particular site. In policy terms this means, for example, favoring alternative, renewable energy sources. It means promoting modern public transport systems to reduce dependence on motor vehicles in cities. It entails strict controls on chemical pollution. It requires close monitoring of biological research, especially in the field of genetics, which ought to have an international ethical commission. None of this is especially radical or controversial. But there have been hints that the old ethnobiologism of the extreme Right may still linger under the surface. Some FN leaders—including Le Pen himself—are professed admirers of Dr. Alexis Carrel, whose views on the ecology of the nation included the application of eugenics as a means of maintaining the quality of the stock.[37]

As regards the form and functions of the state, the FN claims to differ significantly from the old extreme Right on the grounds that it no longer advocates violent change and has not only espoused the principle of democracy, but even wishes to see its range of application, and its representativeness, extended in comparison with the existing situation. Furthermore, the party again echoes the neoliberals by advocating reduction of the role of the state, which it denounces as an omnipresent colossus crushing individual freedoms and leaving no scope for civil society.[38] Its illegitimate exercise of regulation and intervention in every sphere of national life has made it a universal, inefficient administrator, but it no longer governs in the sense of providing real political authority. As democracy declines, the state becomes more susceptible to lobbies and factions. Not only is it threatened from within by those whom it has reduced to dependence on it; it is undermined from outside by supranational institutions that see it as an obstacle to their own power or to extension of the global market. The present need, however, is not to get rid of the state, but to restore its proper role as guarantor of the higher interest and continuity of the nation, which should be limited as far as possible to providing internal and external security, making and enforcing law, defending French culture, and safeguarding national independence.

For this purpose the FN claims to represent the march toward a new Sixth Republic, which would embody important institutional reforms.[39] An appeal to democratic principle conveniently coincides with the FN's own self-interest when the party demands the reintroduction of proportional representation in parliamentary elections—which had brought so much benefit to the FN when it was used for the 1986 election, and corresponding disaster when it was replaced by the old system of single-member constituencies for the elections of 1988. On its populist platform the party also advocates Swiss-style national and local referenda by popular demand to initiate or veto legislation. It advertises this as a means of giving the people a real voice alongside the mainstream parties ("the Gang of Four"), the technocrats, the bureaucrats, the pressure groups, and the media, who have hijacked the nation's power to express their will. Reduction in the number of layers of local government and in the length of local electoral mandates likewise fits the demand for greater transparency and responsiveness in political processes. On the other hand, the principle and extensive powers of a directly elected presidency, as already established under the Fifth Republic, encounter no strong objection from the FN, although it has called in somewhat vague terms for a revitalization of parliament. At the same time, whatever the FN's democratic pretensions, the charismatic, authoritarian leadership of Jean-Marie Le Pen has encouraged a cult of personality within the party, and there is some evidence that many militants favor an authoritarian system of government over a republican system.[40] The demand for movement toward direct democracy no doubt involves an element of demagogy. But it is not entirely inconsistent with the nationalist Right's traditional assumption that although the people—the mass of decent, ordinary French people—are easily deluded by unscrupulous antinational forces, their cultural rootedness imbues them with an instinctive yearning for the national good. For the FN, which habitually assumes that the mainstream parties and their cronies all collude in the process of tricking the people into giving them a comfortable living with endless access to the appurtenances of power, more direct forms of democracy, coupled with a strong presidency, mean that the vast majority of French people, when addressed directly and able to express themselves directly in turn, will understand that the party is offering them exactly what they need. The examples of Switzerland and California show that such a system can serve a right-wing agenda.[41]

The aim of rolling back the state in the economic sphere extends the neoliberal component in the FN's agenda. Traditionally, the French extreme Right has not only been antisocialist and antisyndicalist, but has also shown at least a verbal hostility to unbridled liberal capitalism, especially when plutocracy could be linked to international finance, and above all when it was associated with Jews.[42] While private ownership of the means of production, distribution, and exchange has been sacrosanct, the extreme Right has tended in varying degrees to favor a corporatist and protectionist "third way" between socialism and free-market capitalism. Nowadays, although there are still currents in the party that favor the latter approach, the FN's official line is somewhat different. From the philosophical standpoint, the party argues that the economy needs to be restored to its proper function of serving society in subordination to higher political and social goals, not the other way around. Nevertheless, as the negative example of the Soviet bloc showed, the economic sphere has its own laws, which must be respected. No prosperous economy can exist without the right to property, free enterprise, free markets, and the profit incentive. Just as the political sphere must be freed from the economic, FN leadership argues that the economy must be freed from the stranglehold of the state in order to work effectively. Therefore, while the FN does not deny the need for political oversight of the economy, it also rejects the statist approach, which ends up destroying the economic vitality by means of a political straitjacket on businesses and returns. In policy terms the FN stands for giving maximal autonomy to enterprises within the public sector, reducing bureaucracy, denationalizing firms in the competitive sectors, deregulating the economy, and limiting the role of trade unions.[43] It is no coincidence that Le Pen had cordial contacts with some members of the right wing of the British Conservative Party during Margaret Thatcher's time as prime minister. Fewer and lower taxes will supposedly help to relieve unemployment. Popular capitalism will be promoted alongside protection of small businesses and extension of home ownership. The progressive reduction of the immigrant population and the restriction of immigrants' access to welfare benefits will help to reduce unemployment, finance improved access for French families to low-cost housing, and allow increases in welfare benefits and state pensions for French citizens while diminishing rather than increasing the tax burden. Reducing the weight of immigration and unemployment carried by the state will result in reduced charges levied on employers, and will thus allow the minimum wage to be raised for the benefit of lower-income workers.

The neoliberalism stops—and consciously distances itself from Thatcherism—when it comes to trade: just as the FN wants to protect

French workers from immigrant competition on classical nationalist lines, so it also wants to protect French products and services by means of trade barriers, though the existence of the Single European Market means that these barriers now have to be around the entire European Union.[44] In other words, the notion of community preference at the European level is intended to parallel the notion of national preference at the level of the French nation-state. FN publicists denounced the GATT agreement of 1993 on the grounds that no state, or group of states, should have international free trade imposed on it against its interests. Conversely, the FN views the principle of international free trade as the commercial expression of the destructive globalist ideology that allegedly envisions the world as a single, cosmopolitan space traversed by flows of products, services, and people under the omnipresent surveillance of a global superstate. Not surprisingly for a right-wing nationalist party, the FN has never been in favor of a fully federated European superstate. It looks to a Europe of nations, with each nation remaining firmly rooted in its own culture. Nevertheless, the FN 's vision of a loose confederacy allows for coordination in the fields of defense, economic protection, antiterrorism, and barriers to third-world immigrants. Statements made during the later 1980s, when the FN had ten members of the European Parliament, were by no means entirely negative on the subject of European integration in important areas, and were equivocal on the question of how much sovereignty should be pooled or in what form. For example, Le Pen himself did not appear to object to a common exchange currency alongside national currencies, or to an independent European Bank.[45] Equally, Le Pen argued the pressing need for a common European Community defense and security policy, including the development of multinational forces, in the face of the Soviet threat.[46] By the mid-1990s, however, under threat of being outflanked by anti-integrationist elements of the more orthodox Right and sections of the Left in the wake of the Maastricht and GATT debates, the emphasis had shifted significantly, so that it was placed primarily on denouncing the technocratic power of the European Commission and calling for its abolition, pointing to the dangers arising from the Schengen agreement (potentially allowing huge influxes of immigrants and criminals), calling for repeal of the Maastricht treaty and for Europe's withdrawal from the GATT agreements—all of this combined with warnings against the globalist ideology and the American expansionism underlying the prospective New World Order. The need for restoring France's national sovereignty by reasserting the primacy of French law over international law has become a theme in the party's discourse, coupled with demands for massive increases in defense spending to regain an independent geopolitical role in the face of new threats emerging in the aftermath of the cold war.[47]

In a more detailed study, it would be possible to dwell on the internal inconsistencies within the party's ideology and to question the practical (let alone the moral) validity of some of the policies proposed—most obviously, the massive reversal of immigration as a panacea for France's economic ills. For present purposes, however, it is sufficient to note that the effort put into the production and dissemination of ideology has undoubtedly been important in the development of the party. It has enabled the FN to present itself as a dynamic force of renewal, rather than a gang of superannuated fascist headbangers, at a time when other parties (Communists, Socialists, RPR/UDF neoliberals, even Greens) have appeared successively to lose ideological self-confidence and political direction.

Under Le Pen's leadership, the FN is a highly effective campaigning organization. In a country with a presidential political system there is a natural tendency to focus on the personalities and actions of the leaders of the parties contending for power. This tendency is reinforced by the way the media, especially television, seek to dramatize politics for popular consumption by concentrating on individual actors rather than on complex processes that have to be analyzed in abstract terms. The FN has been adept at taking advantage of the personalization of French politics. Le Pen, as president of the party, is a charismatic figure whose colorful past makes him all the more fascinating. His extremely humble origins in Brittany, the ups and downs of his career, his precocious experience as a parliamentarian in the 1950s, his military service in the colonies, his brawling and drinking excesses, his court appearances, and his eventual inheritance of a fortune under highly unusual circumstances, not to mention the scandals surrounding the breakup of his first marriage, all make him a larger-than-life figure.[48] He has been highly successful in attracting media attention. This has not always been to his advantage, and he has sometimes been trapped into costly mistakes, as with his dismissal of the gas chambers as a mere detail of the history of the Second World War.[49] In general, however, he appears to operate on the principle that any publicity is good publicity for a politician trying to break through from a marginal position. An early example of this technique came on the TV program "L'Heure de vérité," on 13 February 1984, when he remarked that France was not a brothel for the use of six million immigrants. To take another example, Le Pen was able to stir a massive wave of outrage from antiracist organizations, intellectuals, and politicians after he

announced at the FN summer school in 1996—and subsequently repeated—that he did not believe in the equality of races.

Of course, the FN does not consist of Le Pen alone. Although practice
can vary from one area of the country to another, the party is divided
into federations by *département*, subdivided into sectors grouping sets
of communes, and further subdivided into sections by commune. The
activity of secretaries of federations is coordinated by regional secretaries who are themselves responsible to the General Secretariat. Representatives from all levels meet in congress to elect the president and
the Central Committee every two to four years, and to debate matters
affecting the party. There is a National Council that meets two or three
times per year and includes members of the Central Committee as
well as the secretaries of regions and *départements*, local and national
politicians, and other invited notables. But Le Pen is more than a fig-
urehead and spokesman; he exercises very real authority and enormous power within the party. He is served directly by the staff of his
private office. He chairs the party's Executive Bureau (the general secretary, the general delegate, the three vice presidents, and the treasurer) and its forty-member Political Bureau, a policy-making body
made up of his own nominees. The Political Bureau, in turn, nominates
the secretaries of regions and *départements*. Le Pen is therefore in a position to exercise patronage or to purge dissidents. He also plays an important role in attracting financial backers. In practice, the party is run
on authoritarian lines from the top down.[50] Disloyalty and disobe-
dience are not tolerated.

The FN has a large network of affiliated organizations dedicated to
promoting its influence in different sections of society.[51] For example,
they include youth organizations—not only the Front National de la
Jeunesse, with its national network of cells in the *départements*, but
also school and university students' organizations. All of these are affiliated with Mouvement de la Jeunesse d'Europe. There is also the
paramilitary youth group attached to the Cercle National des Combattants, known as the Cadets, complete with uniform. There is the
Comité de Défense des Libertés Universitaires for university faculty.
In business there is the umbrella organization Fédération Nationale
Entreprise Moderne et Libertés, linking numerous small groups in the
private and public sectors, including farming, transport, industry,
medicine, law, commerce, banking, and so on. The FN also has campaigning organizations for restoration of the death penalty and ban-
ning of abortion. The list of affiliates continues with organizations for
the police (Front National pour la Police obtained 7.4 percent in the police trade union elections of December 1995, only a month after it had

been founded),[52] for prison staff, for military personnel and former servicemen, for tenants of public housing, for the unemployed and destitute, for women, for links with the integrist branch of the Catholic Church, for expatriates, for ex-colonialists, even for Jews.

The FN also seeks to extend its influence within nonaffiliated organizations. One such case was the Comité de Défense des Commerçants et Artisans (CDCA), which made news during the fall of 1995 with a violent attack on the city hall of Bordeaux, leading to 80 arrests.[53] At that time the CDCA was claiming 135,000 members, but was estimated to have about 80,000. It was originally of broadly Poujadist orientation in protest against high taxation, the spread of hypermarkets, and other factors that threatened small shopkeepers and artisans. In 1987 it became more militant and politicized under its new general secretary, Christian Doucet, an extreme right-winger who preached direct action against local tax and social security offices. In 1988 Jean-Gilles Malliarakis (formerly a leading figure in the neofascist groups L'Oeuvre Française, Mouvement Nationaliste Révolutionnaire, and Troisième Voie) joined and introduced a neofascist, neocorporatist ideology of anticapitalism, nationalization of trusts, elimination of welfare benefits for those who do not work, defense of the lower middle classes, etc., on lines reflecting his admiration for Mussolini. In 1991 Malliarakis, by then in charge of the Ile-de-France region of the CDCA, joined the FN, thus establishing a direct conduit for the latter's influence.

Attempts have likewise been made to use particular issues to establish links with special interest groups. Opposition to abortion is one case where FN groups or activists have sought to take over campaigns: thus the FN's Cercle National des Femmes d'Europe established close ties with the broader-based Laissez-les Vivre and SOS Tout-Petits. *Présent*, the main publication of the Catholic traditionalist current in the FN, sometimes carries reports on anti-abortion protests in which party activists have been involved alongside members of other groups.[54] Much the same thing has happened with environmental and animal-rights issues, where the FN's Cercle National pour la Défense de la Vie de la Nature et de l'Animal has sought to extend influence among the more reactionary elements of the environmental movement by campaigning alongside other pressure groups, without direct attempt at takeover, against the Loire dam, for instance, or the projected uranium mine at Pont-Callec in Finistère.[55]

Finally, it is worth mentioning the FN's patient work at building up local contacts. The FN is a highly activist party that advertises itself as the *parti-famille* in every sense. For example, in 1991, the FN leader at Meythet, a small town near Annecy, claimed to have activists in key positions in the local football club, the PTA, the bowling club, the folk

society, and other local associations.[56] He adopted the practice of invit-
ing people to use him as an intermediary for pressing the mayor on so
they would thank him if it produced results and blame the mayor if
nothing was done.

Any conclusion must, of course, be provisional and speculative, since
the history of the FN is still in the making. Thus far, the eidence of the
polls suggests that the FN has built up a genuine electoral constituency
since the mid-1980s. Some of the more pessimistic commentaries by
hostile French journalists and intellectuals give the impression that
there is an almost inexorable process at work as racism and xenophobia
spread among the population. But the party's support still comes from
a minority representing no more than 15 percent of the national electorate. The FN has not won the presidency and, barring unforeseen even-
tualities, it will have to wait until 2002 for its next opportunity. The
FN has not yet gained a place in a governing coalition. Although overt
or covert deals have been struck on occasion at the local level, the
party has not yet achieved an alliance or electoral pact with the orthodox Right at the national level. Short of a national alliance with the
mainstream Right and/or the reintroduction of proportional representation for future legislative elections, the party's prospects for rees-
tablishing itself as a significant presence at the parliamentary level
look rather dim. A potential danger for the FN is that the orthodox
Right could itself evolve in a more nationalistic and populist direction—as it has already shown the capacity to do—in matters such as
immigration, law and order, constitutional reform, perhaps even aspects of European integration, thereby encroaching further on the FN's
terrain. In the meantime, the party has the task of continuing to promote itself as a distinctive, potentially governmental, right-wing alternative to the RPR/UDF. This is not easy to do. Although the FN has
its showcase municipalities, as well as a significant core of committed
activists and supporters, distance from national power may in due
course heighten existing divisions between different tendencies
within the party as well as personal rivalries among its leadership.

On the other hand, if the PS-dominated left-wing majority elected in
June 1997 is unable to develop economic and social policies that mitigate national anxieties on such intractable issues as unemployment
and job insecurity, the maintenance of the welfare state, the funding of
public services or education, and European integration, the FN may
profit from the perceived failure. The advantage will be all the greater
if the RPR/UDF coalition lacks direction, and especially if it reverts to
its old habits of internal division and factionalism.

It would be futile to speculate further. Whatever happens, the FN has had an impact on French politics since the mid-1980s. Most obviously, it has changed the terms of debate over immigration and forced the major parties to fight on its own ground to a greater or lesser degree. The orthodox Right has adopted increasingly harsh positions. The PS has lost much of its credibility as defender of the weak. The FN has helped to crystallize doubts in certain quarters about European integration. It has attracted enormous attention from the media. It has undermined confidence in politicians of the major parties by demonstrating that they do not know how to face the FN down, even when its members say or do things that were once considered unacceptable. The FN has to be seen as a symptom as well as a contributory cause of a period of deepening uncertainty in the direction of French political life.

Notes

1. See for example Griffin, *The Nature of Fascism*, 161–79, for an attempt to classify postwar extreme right-wing movements in Europe; and for discussion of the equally problematic concept of the extreme Right in contemporary politics, Paul Hainsworth, "The Cutting Edge: The Extreme Right in Post-War Western Europe and the USA," in *The Extreme Right in Europe and the USA*, ed. P. Hainsworth (New York: St. Martin's, 1992), 1–28.

2. The concept is developed in Ole Waever et al., *Identity, Migration and the New Security Agenda in Europe* (London: Pinter, 1993).

3. See Hans-Georg Betz, *Radical Right-Wing Populism in Western Europe* (Basingstoke: Macmillan, 1994), 3, table 1.1, for electoral results of a range of West European parties from 1980 to 1994.

4. For overviews of the ideological and political history of the French extreme right, see for example Ariane Chebel d'Appollonia, *L'Extrême droite en France: De Maurras à Le Pen* (Brussels: Complexe, 1988); Michel Winock, ed., *Histoire de l'extrême droite en France*, 2d ed. (Paris: Seuil, 1994); and the monumental collection, Jean-François Sirinelli, ed., *Les Droites françaises: De la Révolution à nos jours*, 3 vols. (Paris: Gallimard, 1992).

5. On the early history of the FN, see Jean-Yves Camus, "Origine et formation du Front national (1972–1981)," in *Le Front national à découvert*, ed. Nonna Mayer and Pascal Perrineau (Paris: Presses de la Fondation Nationale des Sciences Politiques, 1989), 17–36; see also Gilles Bresson and Christian Lionet, *Le Pen: Biographie* (Paris: Seuil, 1994), 353–67.

6. On the immigration issue in France, see for example Marcin Frybès, "France: Un Équilibre pragmatique fragile," in *Immigrés en Europe. Politiques locales d'intégration*, ed. Didier Lapeyronnie (Paris: Documentation Française, 1992), 83–110; James F. Hollifield, "Immigration and Modernization," in *Searching for the New France*, ed. James F. Hollifield and George Ross (New York: Routledge, 1991), 113–50; Robert Miles and Jeanne Singer-Kérel, eds., *The Economic and Political Consequences of Post-1945 Immigration to France*, special issue of *Ethnic and Racial*

Studies 14, no. 3 (1991); and Patrick Weil, *La France et ses étrangers: L'Aventure d'une politique de l'immigration, 1938–1991* (Paris: Calmann-Lévy, 1991).

7. See for example Pierre Bréchon, *La France aux urnes: Cinquante ans d'histoire électorale* (Paris: Documentation Française, 1993), 35–56; Paul Hainsworth, "The Extreme Right in Post-War France: The Emergence and Success of the Front National," in Hainsworth, *Extreme Right*, 29–60; Jonathan Marcus, *The French National Front: The Resistible Rise of Jean-Marie Le Pen* (London: Macmillan, 1994); Mayer and Perrineau, *Front national*, chapters 2 and 12–16; and Pascal Perrineau, "Le Front national: 1972–1994," in Winock, *Histoire de l'extrême droite*, 243–99.

8. For statistics and analyses of the municipal election results in major towns, see *Le Monde*, 13 June 1995 (first round) and 20 June 1995 (second round); Florent Leclercq, "Front national: La Menace," *L'Express*, 22 June 1995, 8–10. The problem of estimating the numbers of FN councillors arises from the fact that some candidates run under labels of convenience rather than declaring their affiliation to the FN: see Christiane Chombeau, "Le Front national se prépare à appliquer son programme dans 'ses' villes," *Le Monde*, 18–19 June 1995, 6; but see also Institut de Formation Nationale (hereafter IFN), *Militer au Front*, 2d ed. (Paris: Editions Nationales, 1991), 31, where it is claimed that "more than 1,200 municipal councillors of the Front National were elected on 12 and 19 March 1989 in nearly 500 communes across France." The disparity in the FN's own claims may arise from a desire to maximize the apparent gain to the party by excluding councillors who stood under labels of convenience in 1989, but including them in 1995 (see Birenbaum, *Le Front national en politique* [Paris: Balland, 1992], 169, for 1989 figures that broadly coincide with those of the FN). On the implications of the FN victory in the February 1997 rerun at Vitrolles, see for example the dossier "Qui livre la France au Front national?" in *Le Nouvel Observateur*, 13–19 February 1997, 22–33.

For the FN's hopes of using Toulon, Marignane, and Orange as shop windows for its policies, see for example Bruno Mégret, "Dans le cadre légal, la préférence nationale ne peut s'exercer que de façon larvée," *Le Monde*, 18–19 June 1995, 6; Jean Roberto, "L'Expérience des villes laboratoires du FN peut-elle réussir?" *National hebdo*, 29 June–5 July 1995, 6–7; Cécile Chambraud, "Les Maires FN de Toulon, Marignane et Orange mettront en oeuvre la 'préférence Nationale,'" *Le Monde*, 1 November 1995, 8.

On Jacques Peyrat, see Alexis Liebaert and Bruno Aubry, "Les Contes de Peyrat font rêver les Niçois," *L'Evénement du jeudi*, 15–21 June 1995, 17; Alexis Liebaert, "La Vraie Nature de Jacques Peyrat," *L'Evénement du jeudi*, 22–28 June 1995, 16; Jean-Gabriel Fredet, "L'Homme qui a 'tombé' Nice," *Le Nouvel Observateur*, 22–28 June 1995, 32; and Jean-Pierre Laborde and Jean-Louis Saux, "Jacques Peyrat confirme son adhésion au RPR," *Le Monde*, 22 June 1996.

9. On the sociology of the FN electorate, see Christopher Husbands, "The Support for the Front National: Analyses and Findings," *Ethnic and Racial Studies* 14, no. 3 (1991): 382–416; Nonna Mayer and Pascal Perrineau, "Why Do They Vote for Le Pen?" *European Journal of Political Research* 22, no. 3 (1992): 123–41; Harvey Simmons, *The French National Front: The Extremist Challenge to Democracy* (Boulder CO: Westview, 1996), 169–85; for comparison with similar parties in other European countries, see Betz, *Radical Right-Wing Populism*, 141–68. The special is-

sues of the Dossiers et Documents series published by *Le Monde* after every national election are invaluable sources of data and analyses.

10. See *Le Monde*/Michel Noblecourt, ed., *L'Election présidentielle*, 23 April–7
May 1995, special issue of *Dossiers et Documents du Monde* (May 1995), 47–50;
Nonna Mayer, "Le Front national n'est plus le premier parti ouvrier de France," *Le
Monde*, 5 June 1997.

11. See Bréchon, "L'Extrême droite," esp. 51; *Le Monde*/Noblecourt, *L'Election
présidentielle*, 44; Christiane Chombeau, "Le Front national est en mesure de
maintenir ses candidats dans 133 circonscriptions," in *Le Monde*/Olivier Biffaud,
ed., *Elections législatives 25 mai–1ᵉʳ juin 1997: Le Président désavoué*, special issue
of *Dossiers et Documents du Monde* (June 1997), 47.

12. See Perrineau, "Le Front national: 1972–1994," 264–65.

13. Eugen Weber, *Action Française: Royalism and Reaction in Twentieth-Century France* (Stanford CA: Stanford University Press, 1962) remains a classic study of
Maurras's influential group.

14. On the composite nature of the FN and its internal currents, see Christophe
Bourseiller, *Extrême droite: L'Enquête* (Paris: François Bourin, 1991), 73–95. On the
synthetic nature of the party's ideology, see Alain Rollat, *Les Hommes de l'extrême
droite: Le Pen, Marie, Órtiz et les autres* (Paris: Calmann-Lévy, 1985); Pierre Milza,
"Le Front national: Droite extrême ou national-populisme?" in Sirinelli, *Droites
françaises*, vol. 1, 691–732; Marcus, *National Front*, 100–130; Christopher Flood,
"National Populism," in *Political Ideologies in Contemporary France*, ed. C. Flood
and Laurence Bell (London: Cassell/Pinter, 1997), 104–40.

15. An overview of the formal organization of the party is given in IFN, *Militer au
Front*, 24–37, and more up-to-date information is given by the FN's web site, http://
www.front-nat.fr. See also Birenbaum, *Le Front national en politique*, 213–19;
Marcus, *National Front*, 27–51.

16. On the New Right, see Anne-Marie Duranton-Crabol, *Visages de la Nouvelle
Droite: Le GRECE et son histoire* (Paris: Presses de la Fondation Nationale des Sciences Politiques, 1988); Pierre-André Taguieff, *Sur la Nouvelle Droite: Jalons d'une
analyse critique* (Paris: Descartes, 1994), drawing on his many excellent writings on
the subject; and Paul Piccone, ed., *The French New Right: New Right—New Left—
New Paradigm!* special double issue of *Telos* 98–99 (1993/1994).

17. See *Identité* 1 (May–June 1989): 3, for the list of members and their professional affiliations.

18. See, for example, the dossier of articles, "Les Nouveaux maîtres," collected in
Identité 5 (January–February 1990): 4–20. On this and most other aspects of the ideology IFN, *Militer au Front* provides a valuable condensation of the party's theoretical positions and strategic objectives.

19. See, for example, "SOS hystérie. Les Anti-Le Pen," special supplement hors série to *National hebdo* (n.d. [1990/91]), the message of which is signified visually by
the front cover, which shows a portrait of Le Pen with a gag over his mouth. In a similar vein, see "'Ils' l'attaquent parce qu'il vous défend," special issue of *La Lettre de
Jean-Marie Le Pen* 207 (November 1994).

20. This is the central theme running through the articles collected in the dossier
"La Modernité du Front national," in *Identité* 21 (January–February 1994): 4–20.

The arguments are anticipated by those produced in an earlier dossier, "Les Mutations idéologiques," in *Identité* 4 (November–December 1989): 4–21, and in books such as Bruno Mégret, *La Flamme: Les Voies de la renaissance* (Paris: Robert Laffont, 1990). See also Jean-Marie Le Pen, "Le Front national récuse la qualification d'extrême droite," *Le Monde*, 19–20 November 1995: 13. On the eternal question of whether or not the FN is extremist, see for example Milza, "Le Front national."

21. For a condensed version of the story to the end of the 1980s, see IFN, *Militer au Front*, 13–18. See also the official history, *Front National, 20 ans au Front: L'Histoire vraie du Front national* (Paris: Editions Nationales, 1993).

22. See for example Pierre Monnier, *Le Pen, le peuple et la petite fille espérance* (Saint-Cloud: Editions Nationales, 1994); also the strip-cartoon autobiography, Jean-Marie Le Pen, "Français passionnément! La Vie de Jean-Marie Le Pen en bande dessinée," special issue of *La Lettre de Jean-Marie Le Pen* 213 (March–April 1995); and IFN, *Militer au Front*, 19–22.

23. The program of evening lectures on the theme of "La Pensée nationale" given in 1989–1990 by FN intellectuals under the auspices of the IFN covers leading representatives of more or less all currents of the French extreme Right since the time of the Revolution, including the fascist collaborationist intellectuals Robert Brasillach, Pierre Drieu la Rochelle, and Louis-Ferdinand Céline, as well as the reactionary ultranationalists Charles Maurras and Xavier Vallat, whose thinking did much to influence the Vichy regime's attempted National Revolution. Although it includes few foreigners, and no Nazis, it does include Julius Evola, the Italian fascist intellectual whose writings have been influential in contemporary neofascist circles. The complete program of lectures is printed on the back cover of *Identité* 4 (November–December 1989).

24. Birenbaum, *Front national*, 253–54.

25. For example, the *National hebdo* list of recommended books has often included *Chants d'Europe*, edited under the name of François de Montfort (possibly a pseudonym for the neofascist Robert Allo, founder of Groupe Union Défense, a violent, ultraright student group), who was also the composer of some of the songs in it. The cover and many pages of the book are adorned with the Celtic cross and runic and other Nordic or Celtic symbols familiar from the iconography of neofascism and neo-Nazism. The book has a dedication to the executed fascist writer Robert Brasillach; to Roger Degueldre, leader of the Delta Commando of the OAS terrorist organization; and to others who, it says, "died for the New Europe." Many of the songs are associated with German Nazism, Italian and Spanish fascism, or their more recent imitators. Interestingly, the inside back cover invites the reader to obtain recordings of songs in the book from SERP, Le Pen's record company.

26. The left-of-center press has made a practice of monitoring the pronouncements of Le Pen and other party figures for evidence of extremism. See, for example, Robert Schneider, "Le Pen et les juifs," *Le Nouvel Observateur*, 17–23 May 1990, 32–33; and "La Vraie Nature de Jean-Marie," *Le Nouvel Observateur*, 18–24 September 1987, 28–29. For Le Pen's anti-Semitic comments in private company, see Bresson and Lionet, *Le Pen: Biographie*, 350–51. For other FN publicists' racist or anti-Semitic comments, see for example Maurice Moissonnier, "'Hommes veillez!'" in Jean-Pierre Cambier et al., *Lyon, capitale du négationnisme?* (Villeur-

banne: Golias, 1995), 29–41; Pierre-Jérome Biscarat, "Lyon III, L'Extrême droite en quête de légitimité universitaire," in Cambier et al., *Lyon*, 43–48; Florence Assouline and Richard Bellet, "Pas antisémites? Voici ce qu'ils écrivent," *L'Evénement du jeudi*, 17–23 May 1990, 18–19; Marie-France Etchegoin, "Ceux qui ne désarment pas," *Le Nouvel Observateur*, 25 September–1 October 1987, 38–39; Edwy Plenel and Alain Rollat, *L'Effet Le Pen* (Paris: La Découverte/*Le Monde*, 1984), 11–42. See Anne Tristan, *Au Front* (Paris: Gallimard, 1987) for the eyewitness account of a journalist who infiltrated the FN in Marseille. For a valuable analysis of contemporary anti-Semitism in France, see Pierre-André Taguieff, "La Nouvelle Judéophobie: Antisionisme, antiracisme, anti-impérialisme," *Les Temps modernes* 520 (1989): 7–80; and for an overview of the FN's anti-Semitism, etc., see Simmons, *French National Front*, esp. 123–41.

27. Again, this is a central theme running through the articles collected in the dossier "La Modernité du Front national," *Identité* 21 (January–February 1994): 4–20. The arguments are anticipated by those produced in an earlier dossier, "Les Mutations idéologiques," *Identité* 4 (November–December 1989): 4–21.

28. On the discourse of cultural identity and separate development in the writings of the New Right, see Franklin Hugh Adler, "Racism, *différence*, and the Right in France," *Modern and Contemporary France*, n.s. 3, no. 4 (1995): 439–51; Taguieff, *Sur la Nouvelle Droite*, 9–106. The definition of identity and the need for its preservation is the central focus of the articles collected in the dossier "Une Réalité: La France," *Identité* 13 (June–August 1991): 4–23. This theme, as well as the others discussed hereafter, is set out in relation to the party's policy proposals in FN, *300 mesures pour la renaissance de la France. Programme de gouvernement* (Paris: Editions Nationales, 1993).

29. On antiracism as anti-French racism, see the dossier "Le Montage antiraciste," *Identité* 9 (September–October 1990): 4–22; Jean-Yves Le Gallou, *Le Racisme antifrançais* (Paris: G. C. Conseils, 1988); Jean Madiran, Georges-Paul Wagner, and Jules Monnerot, *Le Soi-disant anti-racisme*, 4th ed., special number hors série of *Itinéraires* (1995).

30. The question of immigration figures in almost all FN writings on any political, social, economic, or cultural topic. See, for example, Jean-Yves Le Gallou and the Club de l'Horloge, *La Préférence nationale: Réponse à l'immigration* (Paris: Albin Michel, 1985), written before Le Gallou joined, but highly influential within the FN; Jean-Marie Le Chevallier, *Immigration en Europe: Attention danger* (Paris: Groupe des Droites Européennes, 1989); Pierre Milloz, "Le Coût de l'immigration étrangère," *Identité* 7 (May–June 1990): 23–26; Jean Mottin, "Immigration= chômage," *Identité* 12 (March–May 1991): 23–24, 34; François Vilmin, "Culture et immigration," *Identité* 17 (autumn 1992): 23–25, 34; IFN, *Militer au Front*, 104–109. Among the books regularly promoted in *National hebdo* has been Jean Raspail's novel, *Le Camp des saints*, 3d ed. (Paris: Robert Laffont, 1973), which imagines a nightmare scenario of a million immigrants in an armada of ramshackle ships making an unarmed invasion of southern France.

31. See Bruno Mégret, "Rapatrier trois millions d'immigrés en douceur," *National hebdo*, 16–22 February 1995, 8; Jean-Marie Le Pen, "Les Priorités de Jean-Marie Le Pen," supplement to *La Lettre de Jean-Marie Le Pen* 211 (February 1995): 9.

32. Le Pen, "Les Priorités de Jean-Marie Le Pen," 4.

33. See the dossier "L'Impératif du sacré," *Identité* 12 (March–April 1991): 4–22.

34. On the family, morality, abortion, etc., see for example Michel de Rostolan, *Lettre ouverte à mon peuple qui meurt* (Paris: Lanore/Sorlot, 1987); Marie-France Stirbois, "Rendre justice aux familles françaises," *National hebdo*, 30 March–5 April 1995: 12; Jean Cochet and Catherine Robinson, "Le Pen à Lyon: Pour la famille," *Présent*, 11 April 1995, 1–2. On law and order, see for example Jean-Marie Le Pen/Front National, *Pour la France: Programme du Front national* (Paris: Albatros, 1985), 97–109, and "Les Priorités de Jean-Marie Le Pen," 13–14.

35. On schooling, see the dossier "Reconstruire l'école," *Identite* 19 (summer 1993): 4–20; Le Pen, "Les Priorités de Jean-Marie Le Pen," 5.

36. On the FN's environmentalism, its links with cultural and geographical rootedness, revitalization of rural life and small farming, etc., see Jean-Marie Le Pen, *L'Espoir* (Paris: Albatros, 1989), 133–44; the dossier "Repenser l'écologie," *Identité* 7 (May–June 1990); Jean-Claude Martinez, "Un million de paysans en 2002," *National hebdo*, 9–15 March 1995, 12.

37. The admiration expressed by Le Pen and others has not included any specific endorsement of eugenics, as far as I am aware. It has been stated in more general terms, such as the following comments by Le Pen, in *L'Espoir*, 133–34: "For me, ecology is not [just] one more ideology, but a science, in this case the science of the harmony which exists, or ought to exist, between man and his natural environment. In this regard I consider the French Nobel prize-winner Alexis Carrel as the first environmentalist or if you prefer, the first modern ecologist, precisely because he committed himself to defining the relationships of natural harmony." For hostile discussion of Carrel in connection with the FN, see Lucien Bonnafé and Patrick Tort, *L'Homme, cet inconnu? Alexis Carrel, Jean-Marie Le Pen et les chambres à gaz* (Paris: Syllepse, 1992); Jean-Pierre Cambier, "Alexis Carrel: Un Médecin aux ordonnances tâchées de brun," in Cambier et al., *Lyon*, 7–16.

38. See Le Pen/FN, *Pour la France*, 47–60; and the dossier "Pour l'état souverain," *Identité* 16 (spring 1992): 4–20.

39. See for example Jean-Marie Le Pen/FN, *Pour la France*, 35–46; the dossier "Rétablir la démocratie," *Identité* 2 (July–August 1989); Yvan Blot, "Pourquoi la démocratie directe?" in Yvan Blot and the Club de l'Horloge, *La Démocratie confisquée* (Paris: Jean Picollec, 1989), 191–94. This was one of the central themes of Le Pen's 1995 presidential election campaign: see for example Le Pen, "Les Priorités de Jean-Marie Le Pen," 4, 10; Bernard Fontanges and Béatrice Absil, "'Mettre sur pied la VIe République,'" *Présent*, 21 March 1995, 1–2.

40. See Birenbaum, *Front national*, 324. A survey of delegates at the Nice congress of the FN in 1990 showed 96 percent of respondents in favor of social hierarchy. As regards the political system, 32 percent favored the existing Republic, 10 percent a popular democracy, 38 percent an authoritarian government, and 16 percent a monarchy.

41. See Pierre-André Taguieff, "Un programme 'révolutionnaire,'" in Mayer and Perrineau, *Le Front national à découvert*, 221–26 for discussion.

42. For analysis of this tradition, see Richard Griffiths, "Anti-Capitalism and the

French Extra-Parliamentary Right, 1870–1940," *Journal of Contemporary History* 13, no. 4 (1978): 721–40.

43. See the dossier "La Place de l'économie," *Identité* 17 (autumn 1992): 4–22; Le Pen, "Les Priorités de Jean-Marie Le Pen," 6–9, 11–12.

44. On the issues of European integration, trade, etc., see the dossier "Repenser l'Europe," *Identité* 1 (May–June 1989): 4–15; Jean-Claude Martinez, *Autant en emporte l'Europe* (Paris: Jean-Cyrille Godefroy, 1989); Hervé Morvan, "L'Eurocratie contre les peuples," *Identité* 5 (January–February 1990): 28–31; Carl Lang, "La Préférence nationale, c'est la préférence sociale," *National hebdo*, 1 February 1995, 13. On the distinction between the FN's conceptions and Thatcherism, see Pierre de Meuse, "Les Limites du thatchérisme," *Identité* 10 (November–December 1990): 24–26.

45. Le Pen, *L'Espoir*, 91.

46. This is a recurrent theme in the speeches collected in Le Pen, *Europe: Discours et interventions, 1984–1989* (Paris: Groupe des Droites Européennes, 1989): see for example "Défendre l'Europe," speech presented to the European Parliament, 17 October 1987, 71–73. See also Le Pen, *L'Espoir*, 53–84, for an overview of defense issues.

47. See Le Pen, "Les Priorités de Jean-Marie Le Pen," 8; and on defense, see also Le Pen, "Restaurer la France et son armée," *National hebdo*, 9–15 February 1995, 8–9; and "Le Pen: La Nation est l'avenir de l'homme," interview with Bruno Racouchot and Muriel Plat, *National hebdo*, 26 October 1995, 6–9.

48. For an interesting account of Le Pen's life to 1988, see Bresson and Lionet, *Le Pen: Biographie.*

49. For the circumstances under which Le Pen made the remarks, see Bresson and Lionet, *Le Pen: Biographie*, 451–59.

50. See IFN, *Militer au Front*, 24–31 for an idealized model; and Birenbaum, *Front national*, 53–73 and 195–219 for more detail as well as analysis of how it works in practice.

51. On the network of affiliated and allied organizations, see IFN, *Militer au Front*, 32–35; Birenbaum, *Front national*, 220–86. There have been substantial investigations in weekly magazines: see for example the dossier "Des Vérités qui font mal," *L'Evénement du jeudi*, 12–18 March 1992, 38–67; the dossier "Comment Le Pen tisse sa toile," *L'Express*, 4 October 1991: 24–35; the dossier "Les Réseaux secrets de Le Pen," *Le Nouvel Observateur*, 19–25 April 1990: 4–11; and the dossier "Enquête sur les réseaux Le Pen," *Le Nouvel Observateur*, 31 October–6 November 1996, 4–12. See also Christiane Chombeau, "Le FN veut s'appuyer sur des syndicats et des associations 'amies,'" *Le Monde*, 28 December 1995, 5.

52. See Erich Inciyan, "L'Impartialité de la police mise en cause par la poussée de l'extrême droite," *Le Monde*, 20 December 1995, 10; and various articles in *Libération*, 18 December 1995, 6–7. A further 5.8 percent voted for the FPIP, another extreme-right trade union with which the FN has had informal links in the past: see Hervé Gattegno, "Ces Flics qui virent au brun," *Le Nouvel Observateur*, 19–25 April 1990, 6–7.

53. On the links between the CDCA and the FN, see Jacques Rollan, "Le CDCA ou les petits boutiquiers du national-socialisme," *L'Evénement du jeudi*, 12–18 March

1992, 64–65; Armelle Thoraval, "Manip chez les artisans," *L'Express*, 4 October 1991, 29–30; and on the CDCA riot at Bordeaux, Paul Webster, "Juppé's City Hit by the Worst Rioting since 1968," *The Guardian*, 1 November 1995: 13.

54. See for example Olivier Mirande, "Contre l'avortement, les défenseurs de la vie," *Présent*, 11 April 1995, 8.

55. See Murielle Szac-Jacquelin, "Les Ecolos dans la marée brune," *L'Evénement du jeudi*, 11–17 January 1990, 34–35; and "Le FN chasse aussi sur les terres écolos," *L'Evénement du jeudi*, 12–18 March 1992, 66–67; Dominique de Montvalon, "Entrisme chez les écolos," *L'Express*, 4 October 1991, 26–28.

56. See Florent Leclercq, "Ceux qui rallient le Front," *L'Express*, 4 October 1991, 32–35, for the Meythet case and other examples of FN local activism.

Richard Wolin

Designer Fascism

The "positive nihilism" of Nietzsche has no other sense than this: one can build only where the ground has been razed. . . . If we want to give birth to a New Right, everything remains yet to be done. And given the delay to be made up, we have about a century in which to succeed. Which means there isn't a minute to lose.
Alain de Benoist, Les Idées à l'endroit

Many discussions of right-wing extremism in contemporary Europe have focused on comparisons with Weimar Germany. There is a natural tendency to perceive parallels between the neofascist movements that are making inroads across the European political landscape today and what I would like to call "historical fascism": the first wave of fascist movements that swept across Europe in the 1920s and 1930s. Such comparisons can be seductive, but they must be approached cautiously, for a number of reasons.

Although neofascism bears important ideological affinities with the fascisms of yesteryear, it is extremely unlikely to attain power or to exercise a destabilizing effect analogous to that of historical fascism. In this respect it is important to understand that historical fascism was a phenomenon highly specific to the interwar period. It was very much a response to a series of crises—extreme political instability, economic catastrophe, and the Bolshevik threat—that emerged on the European scene following World War I. Its spirit of militarism and imperialistic quest for living space led to unprecedented dislocations and cataclysms—according to some estimates, during World War II 50 million people (most of them, of course, civilians) lost their lives in the European theater alone. This is a phenomenon very few in Europe—including most of today's neofascist leaders—are anxious to repeat. One should also recall that the leading fascist parties of the interwar period had at their disposal mass paramilitary organizations (the SA in Hitler's case and the squadri in Mussolini's), whose function was to foment disorder as well as to terrorize the opposition. Thus, the orientation of the interwar fascist parties was avowedly extra- and anti-parliamentary. In all these respects, the programmatic differences between historical fascism and the parties of the new European Right are striking.[1] Finally, the economic programs of most of today's European far-right parties are resolutely laissez-faire or "liberal"—a fact that contrasts sharply with the corporatist orientation of historical fascism.

While contemporary neofascism has taken root in a very different and more stable historical context, this doesn't mean we should be unconcerned with it or that there is nothing to worry about. On the contrary, neofascism retains the capacity to exercise a distinctly destabilizing influence on the state of contemporary European democracy. In sum, just because the neofascists come outfitted in Italian suits rather than jackboots and brownshirts (hence my title) does not mean they shouldn't be taken seriously. What is especially disconcerting about the steadily growing influence of the parties of the New European Right is that their finely honed and "modernized" political programs have considerable contemporary appeal. Thus, unlike the neofascist parties of the immediate postwar period, they cannot easily be dismissed as historical anachronisms or throwbacks that need not be taken seriously. As a recent commentator has astutely noted, "Unlike the stodgy, splintered parties of the 1960s and 1970s, run by old Nazis and backward-looking nationalists, the streamlined New Right parties of western Europe (and those gradually emerging in eastern Europe) offer a far-right ideology with a modern, democratic veneer."[2] Though they lack the mass electoral appeal of historical fascism, and though they have tried concertedly to distance themselves from the bellicose claims of the fascism of old, a number of their fundamental aims are quite similar: they seek to roll back as far as possible the libertarian spirit of the contemporary democratic order and to replace it with an ethnically homogeneous authoritarian state. Although contemporary fascism may be only a shadow of its former self, "it is a shadow which is cast menacingly across society and politics in Western Europe, not least because it can reduce the overall level of tolerance and democratic pluralism in society as other parties try to contain the success of the extreme right by taking over some of its ideas, a development obvious both in France and Germany in the course of the 1980s."[3]

A brief survey of some recent political developments will help illustrate the nature and extent of the extreme-Right threat. In October 1994 Belgium's anti-immigrant Flemish Block Party (Vlaams Blok), led by Filip Dewinter, gained over 25 percent of the vote in Antwerp city elections. On the very same day, the Austrian Freedom Party (FPO), led by the youthful and charismatic Jörg Haider, increased its electoral share to nearly a quarter of the country's vote in general elections. Commenting on these results, France's newspaper of record, *Le Monde,* remarked: "It is as if in one day the mythic gateways of the Ancient Continent—its North Sea port and the capital of Central Europe—had been swept away by a wave of extremism moving across Europe."[4] These recent electoral results confirm the fact that in today's Western European democracies, up to 20 percent of the electorate frequently displays a distinct preference for parties of the far Right whose programs are often characterized by an ethnopopulist agenda.

Thus, the electoral results in Belgium and Austria, far from being exceptions, confirm a disturbing new trend. In the Scandinavian states of Denmark and Norway, the anti-immigrant Progress Parties have been successful in pushing a far-Right agenda, regularly attracting 6–12 percent of the electorate. Over the last ten years Europe's most successful extreme Right party, Jean-Marie Le Pen's National Front, has become a permanent fixture on the French political landscape. In the 1988 French presidential elections, Le Pen garnered an impressive 14.4 percent of the vote. In the 1995 presidential contest, he improved slightly to an even 15 percent. Despite the frequent political obituaries written about them by journalists and others, the National Front's share of the French electorate has remained remarkably stable. In the parliamentary elections of March 1993, they gained a respectable 12.5 percent of the vote; in the 1994 European elections, they won 10.5 percent.

In April 1994 Italy's National Alliance Party, formerly the neofascist MSI (Movimento Sociale Italiano), was incorporated into Prime Minister Silvio Berlusconi's government, after having gained an unprecedented 13.5 percent of the vote in parliamentary elections. Although Berlusconi's government collapsed ten months later under the weight of corruption scandals, such developments do not seem to have adversely affected the future of National Alliance leader Gianfranco Fini, whom many are touting as a leading player in Italy's political future.[5]

At the same time, there are other less discouraging developments in far-Right party politics that one must also take into account. For example, over the last six years German politics has been haunted by two extreme-Right parties: the Republicans, led by former ss leader Franz Schönhuber; and the neofascist German People's Union (Deutsche Volksunion). Both parties have been able to surmount the 5 percent threshold in city and regional elections in recent years. Yet, in the national elections of October 1994, both the Republicans and the German People's Union failed to break the 5 percent barrier and are now in disarray. Schönhuber has been ousted from Republican leadership, and despite a much-discussed merger, the two parties now seem to be of at best marginal importance on the German political scene.

An optimistic assessment of these developments in the German case would be premature, however. One of the key reasons for the electoral decline of the political Right is that the mainstream political parties have been steadily incorporating key aspects of their program: above all, aspects pertaining to xenophobia and restrictions on immigration. Thus, in June 1993, the Christian Democrats and Social Democrats joined together in a coalition of shame, transforming Germany's immigration law from the most liberal in Europe into one of the most restrictive. This legislation, coming in the aftermath of several deadly and highly publicized attacks on foreign immigrants, seemed like an ex post facto endorsement of such xenophobic outbursts, the equivalent of blaming the victim. For German politicians the perceived solution to neo-Nazi violence was in effect to limit the influx of asylum-seekers rather than to punish the perpetrators. However, the hollowness of such measures soon became apparent. The 1993 arson attack in Solingen, in which five Turkish immigrants were killed, occurred well *after* the parliamentary agreement limiting asylum rights.

The process whereby mainstream parties broaden their platforms rightward for the sake of returning errant voters on the extreme Right to the fold is one of the major consequences of the rise of a new European Right. It is, moreover, a far from innocent development. For in this way one sees the political spectrum gradually edging to the right on key questions concerning tolerance and civic openness.

In the observations that follow, I will concern myself with the rise of the far Right in France. This means addressing two separate (though interrelated) phenomena: the so-called New Right as it emerged in the late 1970s, and its filiations to Jean-Marie Le Pen's National Front.

When one speaks of the French New Right or Nouvelle Droite, one is referring to a group of intellectuals, many of whom had prominent ties to fascist groups during the 1960s. Their agenda has been relatively straightforward: in a postwar era in which the extreme Right had been delegitimated owing to the taint of collaboration, they have sought to bring right-wing ideas into the political mainstream once again. And while, as intellectuals, many of the leading figures of the Nouvelle Droite have remained marginal, in historical retrospect one would have to say they succeeded in their aim. In essence, they have been able to relegitimate a discourse of race and racism that has had an insidious influence on the French politics of the 1980s and 1990s.

Originally the French New Right consisted of two organizations: GRECE (Groupement de Recherches et d'Études pour une Civilisation Européene) and the Club de l'Horloge. Although the Club de l'Horloge, founded in 1974, shared many positions with GRECE, it maintained closer ties with the mainstream French conservative parties (the Union pour la Democratie Française [UDF] and the Rassemblement pour la République [RPR]). It also defended market capitalism in the tradition of "national liberalism" in a way that GRECE would never have countenanced. Moreover, it is worthy of note that in the early 1980s a number of the Club's leading officers (Jean-Yves Gallou, former secretary-general; Yvan Blot, the Club's president until 1985; and Bruno Mégret, who would later become the National Front chairman) abandoned their ties to the mainstream Right and joined Le Pen's National Front.

GRECE was co-founded in 1968 by Alain de Benoist, who in many ways remains the mastermind behind the program of the Nouvelle Droite in France as well as the New European Right in general. Thus in 1994 Benoist was warmly received by Alexander Dougine, the Russian nationalist leader and founder of a Russian New Right, who is also a leading advisor to Vladimir Zhirinovsky. A Russian edition of one of Benoist's journals has just begun publication. Benoist also maintains close ties to representatives of the New European Right in Italy, Spain, Germany, and Belgium.[6]

The 1960s and 1970s were the wilderness years for the extreme Right in France. During this period the mainstream Right, as represented by de Gaulle, Pompidou, and Giscard d'Estaing, enjoyed twenty-three continuous years of electoral success, keeping political extremists like Le Pen and others wholly on the margins. Paradoxically, however, France was dominated culturally and intellectually by the Left. It was specifically in order to put an end to left-wing cultural hegemony that Benoist and his disciples began to formulate a new program in the late 1970s. In fact, Benoist would explicitly dub his strategy at the time a "right-wing Gramscianism," his aim being to replace a left-wing cultural dominance with one of the Right. This struggle in the domain of cultural politics was intended to prepare the terrain for a future extreme Right political movement. Benoist would thus aptly characterize his efforts as a "metapolitical" struggle. In the words of Pierre-André Taguieff:

GRECE's great innovation was to take cultural questions seriously from the standpoint of the Right. The political Right had abandoned the intellectual-cultural field to the Marxist Left, while the radical nationalist movements (the "extreme Right") were engaged in an anti-intellectual activism, which bore resemblances to the anti-intellectualism of poujadisme and which was linked to a type of populist revolt. In this respect GRECE reestablished links with the tradition of historian-writers of the Action française.[7]

In his attempt to revitalize fascist ideology, Benoist strove for a type of intellectual saturation effect—as he once put it, "the intellectual education of everyone in whose hands the power of decision will come to rest in the coming years." To this end, he established an international network of publications, study groups, and front organizations designed to ensure that extreme Right ideas would be received by French and European political elites.

Originally, the GRECE program drew on the biological racism of figures such as the Italian fascist Julius Evola—whose racial thinking was so extreme that Mussolini had him arrested in the early 1940s.[8] However, over the last ten years GRECE has pursued a new line, minimizing the Nouvelle Droite's ties to a discredited historical fascism in order to facilitate more general acceptance. And while the Nouvelle Droite has certainly gained an ear among the parties of the traditional French Right, Le Pen's National Front has undoubtedly been the main beneficiary of its success in rehabilitating a politics of race that, following World War II, had for decades remained confined to the political fringe.[9]

The filiations between the Nouvelle Droite and the National Front are far from straightforward: Le Pen, a Poujadist deputy in the 1950s, espouses the values of an authoritarian national populism. Benoist, conversely, is a confirmed elitist. The National Front has sought to exploit the reactionary, antirepublican symbols of French Catholicism. Benoist, following Nietzsche and the tradition of German fascism, has long espoused a new European paganism that harks back to mythological, pre-Christian, Indo-European traditions—clearly not a program destined to win a large following in contemporary Europe.[10]

In general, Benoist's political sense and timing have left much to be desired. For example, during the 1984 European elections, Benoist, contemptuous of mainstream political parties on both the Left and the Right, and enamored of his new media visibility, announced he would vote for the Communists. Of course, this artless avowal was viewed as akin to heresy by a number of his fellow rightists, who proceeded to abandon GRECE in droves. Moreover, his hyperbolic anti-Americanism (Benoist's hypermythological understanding of the United States doesn't seem to get very far beyond Hollywood films and McDonald's hamburgers) and pseudorevolutionary third-worldism (in keeping with his claim that the peoples of Europe have more in common with the freedom fighters of Third World liberation movements than with the United States or the former Soviet Union) have not exactly endeared him to the influential cadres of the mainstream French Right.[11]

The Nouvelle Droite's breakthrough came in 1979 when the editor of *Le Figaro*, Louis Pauwels, began systematically publishing articles by Benoist and other figures of the French New Right. Suddenly a fixture in the Sunday supplement of one of France's leading conservative newspapers, Alain de Benoist became a household name in a matter of months. Within a short period of time nearly two thousand articles (according to some estimates) were published on Benoist, who until that point had been a virtual unknown.[12] A major debate raged in the press as to whether Benoist's views were fascist, reactionary, conservative, neofascist, or any of a number of other things. Gallons of scholarly and journalistic ink were devoted to analyzing and dissecting this Nouvelle Droite phenomenon—much of it supplied by the French Left. After all, were there to be a new threat on the horizon from the extreme Right, this would stand to increase the political currency of the stalwartly antifascist socialist and communist Left.

In the last analysis, it seems that had the Nouvelle Droite not existed, the French Left would have had to invent it. The Nouvelle Droite's very presence, as well as its suspect ties to the conservative establishment, represented a potential taint for the mainstream Right, just as it embodied a galvanizing force for a Left that had been excluded from political power for more than twenty years. One should also keep in mind that these were the years, following a long hiatus, of increased public awareness concerning the ignominies of Vichy. Hence, any suggestion of continuities between the far Right of the past and that of the present were predestined to become matters of intense national scrutiny.[13]

Let me now turn to the important question of what is "new" about the New Right. An answer to this question will help us to distinguish the "neofascism" of contemporary Europe from the outmoded interwar version of fascist ideology.

After flirting for many years with the more orthodox fascist concept of biological racism, in the early 1980s the Nouvelle Droite came up with a clever new strategy for distancing itself from an out-of-fashion historical fascism, permitting it to convey an analogous racist message in a more acceptable guise. It was at this point that the Nouvelle Droite shifted its emphasis from the concept of "race" to that of "culture": abandoning specious and outmoded arguments for biological racism, it moved in the direction of what might be called a "cultural racism." Under the banner of preserving the sanctity and integrity of cultures, the Nouvelle Droite argued against immigration, the mixing of cultures, and cosmopolitanism. For the sake of reaching a broader audience, it cynically appropriated the universalist values of tolerance and the right to difference for segregationist ends. Thus, it was the cosmopolitans who were the true racists, insofar as they forced immigrants to submit to the brutal rites of assimilation. Further, it was claimed that "anti-racism itself is a form of racism, a witch-hunt used against individuals and intended to extinguish 'French' France to the benefit of a 'cosmopolitan' non-society."[14] Benoist, sounding like a liberal's liberal, argued instead for what one might call a "differentialist racism" that was in principle nonhierarchical: no culture was intrinsically better than another, but they were all different, and these differences should be preserved.[15] Practically speaking, this meant that the place where Algerians should enjoy civil liberties was Algeria. "France for the French" (an old racist slogan from the 1930s), Europe for the Europeans, and so on. As Benoist remarked in the early 1980s: "The truth is that the people must preserve and cultivate their differences. . . . Immigration merits condemnation because it strikes a blow at the identity of the host culture as well as the immigrants' identity."[16]

Let us pause for a moment to compare Benoist's justification of ethnic particularism with a contemporaneous claim made by Jean-Marie Le Pen: "Peoples cannot be summarily qualified as superior or inferior, they are different, and one must keep in mind these physical or cultural differences."[17] "I love North Africans," continues Le Pen, "but their place is in the Maghreb. . . . I am not a racist, but a national. . . . For a nation to be harmonious, it must have a certain ethnic and spiritual homogeneity." It is therefore necessary "to resolve, to France's benefit, the immigration problem, by the peaceful, organized return of immigrants."

The upshot of the National Front political program has been what one might call a type of parliamentary ethnic cleansing. In 1991 the National Front went so far as to demand not only an end to French immigration, but a review of the citizenship status of all immigrants since 1974—the first time since Vichy that ex post facto legislation had been publicly recommended. They have proposed an ominous "dismantling" of ethnic ghettoes, an end to the construction of mosques, and restrictions on the number of Islamic cultural centers and schools. Under National Front proposals, children of immigrants would no longer receive free education, and quotas would be established for immigrant children in classrooms. Acquisition of French citizenship would no longer be automatic, but instead based on blood rights.[18]

The move from a discourse of race to one of culture and the embrace of a nonhierarchical, differentialist racism proved a crucial strategy in rehabilitating a right-wing discourse of ethnopolitics that had long been discredited. And though the rhetorical tactics are new, the argumentative strategy is quite old: in truth, it goes back to the anti-universalist sentiment one finds at the dawn of the European counterrevolution. As Joseph de Maistre famously remarked in his *Considerations on the French Revolution* (1797): "In my life I have seen Frenchmen, Italians,

Russians, and so on. I even know, thanks to Montesquieu, that one can be Persian. But as for *man*, I declare I've never encountered him; if he exists he is unknown to me."[19] Maistre's classical affirmation of the primacy of the ethnos is indeed only a hair's breadth removed from Le Pen's infamous "concentric circle" approach to politics: "I like my daughters better than my cousins, my cousins better than my neighbors, my neighbors better than strangers, and strangers better than foes."[20]

Emphasis on the degeneracy that threatens a nation that succumbs to racial or cultural mixing has been one of the linchpins of counterrevolutionary (in truth, protofascist) ideology, from Comte Arthur Gobineau's *Essay on the Inequality of the Races* (1854) and Edouard Drumont's *La France juive* (which sold hundreds of thousands of copies in the 1880s) to the anti-Semitic legislation of Nuremberg and Vichy. Nor has Le Pen's xenophobic discourse been free of the anti-Semitism that has historically marked French fascism. In a gesture of solidarity with Holocaust deniers, he once observed that the extermination of the Jews was no more than a mere "detail" in the overall course of World War II. He is fond of referring to those with AIDS as "sidaiques," recalling the derisory Vichy characterization of Jews as "judaiques." Of course, according to the classical doctrines of European racism, Jews, like those afflicted with AIDS, are also carriers of a "virus" or "bacillus." Finally, Le Pen never tires of identifying Jewish members of the Socialist party as "Frenchmen of recent origin" (*français de fraîche*).

By disingenuously situating themselves within the Republican tradition, by claiming to support the present constitutional order, Le Pen and the Nouvelle Droite can allege that the attempt to link them with the extreme Right is merely a cynical maneuver on the part of leftwing critics to discredit them. And although for now there is no question of the National Front gaining power (because of the majoritarian system of voting, they are currently unrepresented in the French Chamber of Deputies; but in 1986–88, under the system of proportional representation, they claimed as many as 34 delegates), they have been able to exercise an illiberal and debilitating influence on contemporary French political culture.

Since the National Front has steadily attracted from 10 to 15 percent of the vote in presidential, European, and regional elections, mainstream parties on both Left and Right have vied to steal its thunder on the immigration issue. The incentive for the center-Right parties to ingratiate themselves with Le Pen's constituency has become a mathematical imperative: Jacques Chirac's loss to Mitterrand in the 1988 presidential elections is directly attributable to the National Front's erosion of the traditional Right's electoral base. Having learned the lessons of their defeat, both Chirac and Giscard d'Estaing began pandering to Le Pen's supporters. In the summer of 1991 Chirac spoke of the plight of the French worker who sees a Muslim "family with a father, three or four wives, and about twenty kids, who without working, pull down $10,000 in social benefits"; the smells emanating from their kitchens, he continued, were surely offensive to the average Frenchman.[21] For his part, Giscard suggested the need to abandon France's longstanding tradition of openness to immigrants, openly flirting with the idea of the need to base citizenship on the principle of *jus sanguinis* rather than *jus solis*.

In June 1993, the newly elected conservative parliamentary majority, borrowing a page from Le Pen's playbook, passed a new series of strict immigration laws. It included stop and search legislation on the basis of race, revoking a longstanding republican tradition of tolerance. Moreover, citizenship for those born on French soil is no longer automatic; instead, one must now apply at age seventeen, with the outcome of the application process far from a foregone conclusion.

Nor have the Socialists been immune from pandering à la Le Pen to the electorate's baser instincts. In summer 1991, then–Prime Minister Edith Cresson, in an attempt to outdo both Le Pen and Chirac, expressed her interest in repatriating prospective immigrants via government-sponsored charter flights. Two years earlier, in 1989, when the controversy erupted concerning Arab women sporting Islamic headdress (the Foulard) in the arch-secular French public school system, a contingent of leading Socialists, including Mme. Mitterrand, signed a widely circulated petition supporting a ban. And a recent book by three journalists (*La Main droite de Dieu*) has unmasked Mitterrand's personal efforts to aid Le Pen in gaining political credibility, in full knowledge that National Front prominence would wreak havoc among the traditional Right.

In no uncertain terms, Le Pen's political competitors have de facto allowed him to set the tone and agenda for French political debate in the 1980s and 1990s. Thus a good part of the National Front's success is attributable to the political void that has resulted from the failure of the Socialist program in the 1980s, as well as the manifest lack of alternatives offered by the traditional conservative parties. In retrospect, the National Front has stepped into this political void with a vengeance. As the philosopher André Glucksmann has astutely remarked:

we have a rather extraordinary phenomenon in France today, which is that 80 percent of people who are neither communist nor supporters of Le Pen talk about nothing but Le Pen. I suggest that we in Europe are all in danger of talking about the fascist danger because we have nothing to say. . . . Words create things, and it is because of the absence of discussion about European integration, about the development of democracy in every country, that there is a fascist danger, not because of a few fascists.[22]

The fact is that until the mainstream parties on both Left and Right cease thinking in terms of immediate political self-interest or the next election and instead unite in a stance of principled opposition to the mentality of hatred and fear that Le Pen has been so successful in sowing, the National Front will remain a blot on the French political landscape.

In conclusion I wish to examine more closely some of the larger social and economic changes often considered to be responsible for the surprising emergence of a New European Right as a major force in contemporary European politics.

Here, too, the differences with the fascism of the interwar period are instructive. Historical fascism was able to draw upon a fairly large middle-class electoral base: farmers and residents of small towns, proprietors of small businesses, the lower middle classes, and white-collar workers. Often, this group has been collectively characterized as the "losers of the modernization process": that is, those most vulnerable and exposed to the social dislocations involved in industrialization. As the political sociologist Seymour M. Lipset once expressed this thesis, the fascist movements appealed to

segments of the middle class displaced or threatened by the emergence of centralized, large-scale industry and the growing power and status of organized labor. Oppressed by developments fundamental to modern society, small entrepreneurs, small farm owners, and other insecure members of the middle strata were particularly prone to mobilization by fascist movements opposing both big labor and big capital. These developments represented in part a revolt against modernity.[23]

The constituency of the New European Right is also heavily composed of potential "losers of the modernization process." Yet, the nature of the modernization process itself has changed dramatically between the interwar period and today, a fact that accounts, at least in part, for neofascism's more delimited mass base.

Since the early 1980s many of the countries of Western Europe have experienced a level of structural mass unemployment in excess of 10 percent. This fact has given the lie to the traditional welfare state goal of full employment. Instead, recent commentators have begun referring to the Western European democracies as a "civilisation du chomage"—a "civilization of unemployment." To be sure, the predominant electoral constituency of the far Right parties does not appear to derive in the main from the ranks of the unemployed. On the whole, however, it does bear a significant correlation with those social groups who feel in danger of being left behind by new developments in a postindustrial economy—an economy in which the values of education, cultural capital, and knowledge have become the primary determinants of salary, status, and social advancement. As one commentator has noted:

> The transition from industrial to postindustrial capitalism is in large part characterized by a process of dissolution, fragmentation, and differentiation [vis-à-vis the norms of class societies], which has its roots in a general acceleration of individualization process. These create new challenges to the individual's capability to adapt to rapidly changing circumstances. This, in turn, puts a premium on cultural capital, individual entrepreneurship, and flexibility.[24]

As such, postindustrial society assumes an increasingly technocratic cast, in which positions of power and influence are occupied by elites possessing specialized knowledge or training. Correspondingly, it appears that, in a majority of cases, those attracted to parties of the extreme Right are young men of lower- or lower-middle-class background whose prospects for upward social mobility appear bleak owing to lack of either education or suitable training. They are the potential losers of a postindustrial society. Since the 1980s there has been much discussion among European sociologists of the "two-thirds society": a society in which two-thirds of the population lives in relative affluence, while the other third leads a marginal existence, barely getting by. It is this latter group that makes up the reserve army of the chronically under- and unemployed: persons who are cut off from the glitz of consumption-oriented, postmodern lifestyles, and who instead perform menial, dead-end, low-paying "Mcjobs." It is predominantly from the forgotten lower echelons of the two-thirds society that the New European Right has been able to draw its support. Nor is it a coincidence that these parties have been able to cultivate a hard-core following among the young in a European Community where youth unemployment has in recent years hovered around the 15 percent level. The aforementioned trends in occupational structure are likely to be exacerbated in the near future. The "technological elimination of unskilled and semiskilled jobs means that a great many people will be caught in a world of despair, lacking marketable skills or hope for the future."[25] The pronounced ideological emphasis in the discourse of the New European Right on "values" and questions of "collective identity"—be it ethnic, regional, or national—is consciously cultivated. It is intended to compensate for the instability and disorientation sensed by those who have become supernumeraries in a profoundly threatening global economy or "world society"—a highly impersonal, brave new cybertechnological order. For world society has had the effect of eroding and destabilizing traditional networks of social solidarity on which individuals previously could rely as a source of normative integration: family and extended family, occupational groupings, neighborhoods, communities—even the hitherto sacrosanct autonomy of the traditional nation-state. Thus, analyses of the constituency of the New European Right abound with examples of how "feelings of anxiety and social isolation, political exasperation and powerlessness, loss of purpose in life, and insecurity and abandonment" provide social conditions propitious for the success of extreme-Right political views.[26] New Right politicians are skilled at playing on such feelings and fears. Unfortunately, there is no reason to suspect that their demagogic tactics will not continue to reap a good measure of success.

Notes

1. For more on this point, see Roger Eatwell, "Why are Fascism and Racism Reviving in Western Europe?" *The Political Quarterly* 65, no. 3 (July–September 1994): 323–25.

2. See Paul Hockenos, "Jörg Haider: Austria's Far Right Wunderkind," *World Policy Journal* (fall 1995): 75.

3. Geoffrey Harris, *Dark Side of Europe*, 15.

4. Cited in *The Economist*, 15 October 1994, 68.

5. I have examined the events surrounding Fini's rise to power in "Mussolini's Ghost," *Tikkun* (June–July 1994): 11–16.

6. For an analysis of the pan-European dimensions of the new European Right, see Mark Wegierski, "The New Right in Europe," *Telos* 98–99 (winter 1993–spring 1994): 55–70.

7. Pierre-André Taguieff, *Sur la Nouvelle Droite* (Paris: Descartes, 1994), 18.

8. For a good discussion of Evola's doctrines in relation to Benoist, see Thomas Sheehan, "Myth and Violence: The Fascism of Julius Evola and Alain de Benoist," *Social Research* (spring 1981): 45–73.

9. As one commentator has remarked: "It is clear that Le Pen . . . has been strengthened by the work of the intellectuals of the Nouvelle Droite, whose conscious aim has been to make the ideas of the extreme right dominant in French political life" (Harris, *Dark Side of Europe*, 89). Another observer has noted: "Heavily influenced by the ideas of various right-wing think tanks collectively known as the *Nouvelle Droite*, the National Front programme began to emerge as a curious mix of in-vogue monetarism and traditional authoritarian values. Bolstered by the intellectual kudos of the various recruits from the *Nouvelle Droite*, Le Pen was able to counter the accusations of fascism and extremism leveled at his party" (Jim Wolfreys, "An Iron Hand in a Velvet Glove: The Programme of the French National Front," *Parliamentary Affairs* 46, no. 3 [July 1993]: 415).

10. See Alain de Benoist, *Comment peut-on être païen?* (Paris: Albin, 1981).

11. For Benoist's third-worldism, see *Europe, Tiers Monde: Même combat* (Paris: R. Laffont, 1986).

12. This figure is given by Wolfreys, "Iron Hand," 417. One of the Nouvelle Droite's earliest supporters was ex-Vichyite and author of *Qu'est-ce que le fascisme?* (1961), Maurice Bardèche. See his article, "Les Silences de la Nouvelle droite," *Défense de l'Occident* (December 1979): 19. For a fascinating interview with Bardèche, see Alice Yeager Kaplan, *Reproductions of Banality*, 161–92. Bardèche was the brother-in-law of fascist scribe Robert Brasillach, who was executed after the war for "intellectual collaboration."

For a good discussion of the at times tense relationship between the Nouvelle Droite and the mainstream French Right, see Pierre Milza, *Fascisme français: Passé et présent* (Paris: Flammarion, 1987), 373–75.

13. On this point see the standard work by Henry Rousso, *Vichy Syndrome*.

14. D. S. Bell, "The French National Front," *History of European Ideas* 18, no. 2 (1988): 228.

15. For an excellent analysis of this phenomenon, see Pierre-André Taguieff, "De la race à la culture," in *Sur la Nouvelle Droite*, 7–106. See also Taguieff, "The New Cultural Racism in France," *Telos* 83 (spring 1990): 109–23. Taguieff is undoubtedly the leading political analyst of the French Nouvelle Droite. For the best introduction to the ideas of the French New Right in English, see the double issue of the journal *Telos* 98–99 (winter 1993–spring 1994), "The French New Right: New Right, New Left, New Paradigm?" One of the focal points of the issue is Benoist's alleged "left turn" during the 1980s, as well as the collaboration between prominent figures on the French Left (e.g., Jean Baudrillard) with the Nouvelle Droite in its new, academically respectable guise, as embodied by the journal *Krisis* (founded by Benoist in 1988).

16. Robert de Herte [Alain de Benoist], "Avec les immigrés contre le nouvel esclavage," *Eléments pour la Civilisation Européene* 45 (spring 1983): 2.

17. Jean-Marie Le Pen, "Le Pen et l'eglise" (interview), *National hebdo* 44, no. 19 (April 1985): 15.

18. Wolfreys, "Iron Hand," 424.

19. Joseph de Maistre, *Considerations on the French Revolution*, trans. R. Lebrun (Montreal: McGill–Queens University Press, 1974), 97.

20. Cited in M. Vaughan, "The Extreme Right in France: 'Lepénisme' or the Politics of Fear," in Cheles, Ferguson, and Vaughan, *Neo-Fascism in Europe*, 221.

21. See P. Merkl and L. Weinberg, eds., *Encounters with the Contemporary Radical Right* (Boulder CO: Westview, 1993), 226.

22. Evidence presented to the EP Committee of Inquiry, Annexe G. Cited in Harris, *Dark Side of Europe*, 68.

23. Lipset, *Political Man* (Baltimore: Johns Hopkins University Press, 1981), 489. Also see Thomas Childers's important study, *The Nazi Voter* (Chapel Hill: University of North Carolina Press, 1983).

24. Hans-Georg Betz, *Radical Right-Wing Populism in Western Europe* (New York: St. Martin's, 1994). For one of the best recent characterizations of the new postindustrial condition, see Ulrich Beck, *The Risk Society* (Newbury Park CA: Sage, 1992).

25. J. Hage and C. H. Powers, *Postindustrial Lives: Roles and Relationships in the 21st Century* (Newbury Park CA: Sage, 1992), 41.

26. Betz, *Radical Right-Wing Populism*, 177. For three recent surveys of fascism that devote considerable attention to the phenomenon of "neofascism" as well as the New European Right, see Roger Eatwell, *Fascism: A History*; Stanley Payne, *History of Fascism, 1914–1945*; and Walter Laqueur, *Fascism: Past, Present, Future*.

Jeffrey T. Schnapp

Fascism after Fascism

The paradoxical loop in my title refers to two January days on which the noun *fascism* crossed a fatal threshold and underwent modifications so substantial that the very survival of the political phenomenon to which the noun refers could be cast in doubt. The first of these was 1 January 1948: the day of Alcide De Gasperi's proclamation of the Italian Republic—a republic whose constitution relegated all openly fascist parties to outlaw status. The second came forty-seven years later, on 28 January 1995. This was the date on which Gianfranco Fini, leader of the Movimento Sociale Italiano (MSI), the principal party that had kept the torch of fascism burning at the murky periphery of the Republic's electoral system, officially proclaimed his party's dissolution, as well as the abandonment of the ideological stances, symbols, gestures, and salutes that had closely identified it with the Mussolinian past. In the MSI's place, Fini announced the foundation of an entity without any real precedents during the fascist and post-fascist eras: a neoliberal right-wing movement, called Alleanza Nazionale, committed to the democratic process, centrist in orientation, and opposed in its very constitution to anti-Semitism, xenophobia, and racism. A right-wing movement that now did not hesitate to recognize what only years before would have been a heresy: namely, that its roots were to be sought less in fascism than in the antifascist struggle. The Resistance, Fini averred, to the shock of the MSI old guard (who, with Giorgio Pisanò and Pino Rauti, promptly walked out), represents "the key historical precondition for the return to the democratic values that [historical] fascism had suppressed." "Let us leave fascism," he concluded, "to the historians."[1]

Such, at least, is the official story, the one intended by two political actors whose founding acts claimed to have effected a two-stage burial of the Mussolinian past: first, a burial of the fascist regime and of the totalitarian state apparatus it had created; and second, a burial of its neofascist offspring, with its antidemocratic ideology, its dream of a corporatist "third way," and its apology for historical fascism.

The dead, however, are not easily disposed of in Roman soil; Italian history has repeatedly demonstrated that their ghosts cannot be held down by even the heaviest tombstones. And any historical account that relies upon externalia such as dates, shifts in personnel, and founding gestures is bound to underestimate the ghostly afterlife of a phenomenon as significant for modern Italian history as fascism. For better or for worse, fascism cut a distinctly Italian path toward modernization in the spheres of economic, social, political, and cultural organization. The path in question did not, as the philosopher Benedetto Croce famously claimed, simply mark a parenthesis or accident in the nation's history.[2] It represented, rather, a significant and irreversible break with the prefascist order. This break so strongly conditioned the postfascist order that only recently, in the midst of the current collapse of Italy's party system, have many of fascism's legacies been overcome. But have they been overcome? Is the burial complete? Or have the ghosts simply changed shirt colors? Firm answers are hard to come by within the contemporary political phantasmagoria, but it is in the pursuit of an answer to such questions that I will recount one version of the story of fascism's return. First, in relation to the initial January day, I will say something about the complex of fascist traces that succeeded in crossing over the barrier that separates the Republic of Salò from the new Republic, ruled by a center-Left coalition of forces that included Christian Democrats, Liberals, Republicans, Socialists, and Communists. Second, in relation to the second January day and by way of a conclusion, I will reflect briefly upon the demise of both anticommunism and antifascism as the foundation stones of the postwar order. In their absence, new ideological and cultural spaces have opened up on the Right: spaces currently being fought over by Fini's Right neoliberal alliance, by Berlusconi's centrist Forza Italia (or "Let's Go Italy"), and by the federalist, regionally grounded leagues led by Umberto Bossi—spaces, in my view, with a mostly oblique relation to historical fascism or to French movements like Le Pen's Front National.

A final word of caution: I am a cultural and not a political historian, so my remarks' emphasis will fall on the cultural side of the divide. But even if I were better equipped to offer an analysis of the contemporary political scene, the circumstances of the Italian new Right remain so highly mutable in the era of *tangentopoli* and *affittopoli* that all observations, not to mention conclusions, are fated to remain little more than guesses.[3] This is particularly true in the domain of culture, where the sudden collapse of the center-Left and resurgence of the Right in the early 1990s has yielded only one unmistakable result: namely, a situation so thoroughly confused that it is virtually uninterpretable. I remember well when this volume's editor first asked me to contribute an essay on the culture of the Italian new Right. The invitation was irresistible, yet I doubted my ability to get a handle on such an elusive topic. On the one hand, I was worried by the relative paucity of policy pronouncements on cultural matters by the new Right itself. Bossi's Lega Lombarda, for instance, had largely jettisoned the regionalist linguistic and cultural polemics that had characterized its start-up phase in order to transform itself into the metaregional force known as the Lega Nord (Northern League), whose triumph in the 1994 elections led to its inclusion in the Berlusconi government. Aside from regular sallies against the state cultural bureaucracy, its main cultural-political contribution had been the new, brash political style crystallized by Bossi's slogan: "La Lega c'è l'ha duro!" (roughly, The League has balls of steel).[4] Fini's alliance had developed a far less colorful rhetoric of virility. But it too had been reticent on matters of culture, celebrating free market doctrines, endorsing a generic nationalism and Europeanism (with mild anti-American overtones), attacking the Left's stranglehold on cultural institutions, and criticizing the privileges enjoyed by the state television (RAI) in the name of a "raising of the ethical level of the nation."[5] This said, I felt certain that the topic of fascism's "return," at least in the sense of intellectual fashions, was pertinent. A decisive watershed has indeed been crossed within Italian intellectual life over the past decade; the signs seem beyond dispute. Previously taboo phrases like *la cultura di destra* (the "culture of the right") have become a publishing industry marketing tool. Philosophers like Massimo Cacciari, once one of Italy's key Marxist thinkers, are singing the praises of Carl Schmitt and Ernst Jünger. Mario Sironi, Massimo Bontempelli, Giovanni Gentile, and any number of other cultural protagonists of the fascist era have been rehabilitated, and heroes of the Resistance and Resistance myths are falling one after another. I have even experienced this shift in terms of the reception context of my work. When I began my researches into the cultural dimensions of fascism back in the late 1970s, I often found myself under attack on the grounds that fascism and culture were antithetical terms and that any challenge to this principle was inherently apologetic. Now I sometimes encounter the opposite peril: the tendency to suppose a facile equation between fascist politics and cultural modernism.

In short, somewhere in the interstices between the reticence of the new Right on matters of culture and the recent surge of interest in once-accursed cultural-political currents, a revolution is underway that may shed some light on fascism's return and/or non-return. In the following reflections, my focus will be historical, but my sights will be set on the latest and perhaps final chapter in fascism's ghostly afterlife: that marked by the metamorphosis of the MSI into Alleanza Nazionale. Firm conclusions being beyond my reach, my aim will instead be to contextualize, to wander among the ghosts so as to sort out the recently returned from the departed.

As already noted, the formula "fascism after fascism" refers in the first instance to that complex of doctrines, laws, institutions, mentalities, and cultural projects from the interwar period that carried over into the postwar context. Just how significant was the carryover? The answer will surprise some readers. At the end of World War II, the Mussolinian state was thoroughly discredited, having lost all but a fraction of the popular support it had once enjoyed. Its demise had brought even the fascist faithful face to face with the gap between its reformist pretenses and actual practice, between its bellic bluster and military blundering, between the rosy promises and the grim realities of its colonial empire; and with the failure of its efforts to achieve anything like economic autarchy (a principal policy goal of its later years). The constitution of the new model republic was thus deliberately shaped so as to contrast sharply with the fascist antimodel. Yet the overlap remains considerable, far greater than is sometimes assumed.[6]

On the highest level of generality, one might say that, while its external trappings were designed to extinguish any remaining trace of the totalitarian past, the new state's economic character and many of its vital organs were simply transplanted from its fascist predecessor. And not unintentionally so. In the name of antifascism, De Gasperi and the new Republic's founders had wished to endow their state with precisely the same sort of centralized powers and high degree of autonomy and agency that the dictatorship had arrogated to itself. Their aim was noble and twofold: to allow the Republic to defend itself against the enemies of democracy; and to allow it to undertake the task of national reconstruction with the same tools the fascist regime had used to pursue its ill-fated economic and military policies. The results were some uncanny doublings in the socioeconomic domain, where, despite the restoration of labor union freedoms, traces of fascist corporatism and the fascist social state abound.

In the wake of the Great Depression, the fascist regime embarked on a series of reforms analogous to those instituted by Franklin Roosevelt under the New Deal, but more aggressive. Designed to illustrate the fascist "third way" to industrial development combining the advantages of centralized planning with those of liberal decentralization, these reforms resulted in the creation of a mixed economy with a degree of state ownership of private industry second only to the Soviet Union. Its defining features were, first, "corporations" that coupled workers and capitalists within state-sponsored corporate units, each responsible for a given sector of the economy as well as for coordinating their policies at the national level; and second, entities such as the Istituto Mobiliare Italiano (IMI) for the control of credit and the Istituto per la Ricostruzione Industriale (IRI) for the coordination of industrial policy. If the IMI and IRI began modestly enough, by 1939 the former had a solid handle on the banking world and the latter had become the owner of fully 44 percent of the capital in the Italian stock market and of nearly 18 percent of the nation's total capital. This rendered the state the nation's key entrepreneur, venture capitalist, and insurer (its coinvestments just about guaranteed that it would provide bailout funds when anything went wrong). As much a political as an economic actor, the state enjoyed near-total control over the banking and credit system. All of these features, save the fascist corporations, were carried over into the Republic, with the IRI being explicitly written into the constitution. Soon the IRI would be joined by other government trusts such as the ENI, ENEL, and ENEA, in a system of government economic control so extensive and elephantine that only the recent wave of privatizations carried out by the so-called "government of professors" has begun its dismantling. During Italy's so-called "economic miracle" years the system was praised and admired by many on the Left and Right. Yet its costs—in both fiscal and institutional terms—were enormous, and particularly so the forms of collusion and confusion between private interests and the public trust it bred.[7]

An analogous centralism also characterized the postwar era in the domains of mass media and culture. The fascist state's authority over radio and television was retained (at least until the deregulation of broadcasting in 1975) to a considerable degree, with responsibilities and control simply being reallocated according to the new logic of *lottizzazione* (the parceling out of spoils according to party allegiances) and *partitocrazia* (the rule of parties). Likewise, in the area of filmmaking, fascism's key innovations—the Centro Sperimentale di Cinematografia, Cinecittà (the Italian Hollywood), and a generous system of government subsidies—were all preserved, as was the same cast of administrators, directors, and actors, from Alessandro Blasetti through Vittorio de Sica. The case of the theater is even more striking inasmuch as Royal Decree #773, passed in 1931 and revised in 1935, was adopted without modification as the postwar law governing censorship. Prohibiting the staging in public of works that were contrary to "the public order, morality, and healthy customs," it required that all scripts be submitted to and receive the approval of a central censor's office, just as had been the case under fascism.[8] In addition, legal decree #538 committed the Republic to adopting precisely the system of taxes and subventions devised by the now defunct Corporation of Spectacle. Gate receipts were taxed to create a capital fund to be redistributed to theater companies that "were engaged in the continuous professional activities," especially for "theatrical events deemed of special artistic and social importance."[9] The national commission devised for this purpose was under no greater pressure than the Corporation of Spectacle to make its deliberations public or to define or justify its conception of "special artistic and social importance," which is to say that its disciplinary function and ability to impose a given cultural-political line remained intact. Nor were its cultural horizons very different inasmuch as, on grounds of cultural nationalism, it too reserved special subsidies for "original works by Italian authors" and for "elaborations, translations, and reworkings of original works in ancient Greek and Latin."[10] (As a matter of fact these laws were strengthened during the 1950s, a period during which even Machiavelli's *Mandragola* and Pirandello's *Six Characters in Search of an Author* were subject to censorship in one notorious case.)

The latter commitment to cultural nationalism points to a further prewar/postwar carryover: that of a politics of spectacle and tourism founded upon the staging of open-air shows in the ancient ruins, theaters, and temples, before the Italian masses and foreign tourists. As I have demonstrated at length elsewhere, the history of theater performances in ancient Greek and Roman archeological sites is a long one on the Italian peninsula, antedating Mussolini's March on Rome and, in the case of Verona's coliseum, even extending back to early modern times.[11] But there is no disputing the fact that fascism, though it can hardly claim to have discovered these sorts of shows, was singlehandedly responsible for their diffusion within a setting it infused with political (not to mention imperial) symbolism. Only a small handful of Italy's ancient theaters had been in even occasional use before 1922. By the late 1930s the list of ancient theaters and performance sites in recurrent use for stagings of operas and works from either the Greco-Roman or the modern theater repertory had mushroomed to include Paestum, Siracusa, Taormina, and Verona, as well as numerous sites (like Rome's Baths of Caracalla and Milan's Castello Sforzesco) in irregular use. This network of theaters was the product of a cohesive regional and national politics that aimed to provide modern "hygienic" outdoor alternatives to the decadent interiors of fin-de-siècle theaters; that sought to popularize elite forms of culture; that strove to forge a new sense of national identity both by promoting interregional tourism and by placing the Italian masses face to face with their race's past, present, and future; and that aimed, last but not least, to place this ultramodern yet venerably ancient Italy on display before large numbers of foreign visitors. This fascist politics of spectacle and tourism, stripped of its theoretico-ideological framework and lictorial ornaments, was taken over by the new republican cultural bureaucracy with only slight adjustments.[12]

My purpose in citing these examples of continuity is not to cast doubt upon the revolutionary changes democracy wrought, nor to suggest that there is something inherently "fascist" about the viewing of *Aida* in Verona's Roman arena. Rather, it is to underscore the fact that antifascism dictated a strong central government cast in the image of its fascist nemesis to the degree that its sphere of action would encompass not only the classical public sphere, but also significant sectors of the economy, social welfare system, communications media, and the world of culture. Much as under fascism, the latter continued to be viewed from a strictly "top-down" perspective both on the center-Right and on the Left, at least until the countercultural revolts of the 1970s. Culture was imagined, that is, as the product and possession of an enlightened governing elite whose sense of social responsibility and/or commitment to democratic nation-building drove it to devise means of diffusion that could reach the masses—masses conceived of in a mostly passive, receptive role, not fundamentally unlike the feminized oceanic mobs envisaged by Il Duce. A legitimate and potent tool for the forging of a Right society, culture remained state business in the new Republic.

The story of these ghostly carryovers extends beyond the state's laws and its transplanted organs. It is the story of how a paternalistic "social" state developed protections for a wide array of social categories—mothers, state employees, artists, and so on—and fostered a politics of clientelism that fascism inherited from the past and merely modernized. But it is also, and most especially, the story of a large number of individuals: individuals who managed to reinvent themselves during the wartime era; individuals whose careers and intellectual projects were shaped by and within the fascist era but were barely interrupted by fascism's demise. Cases of sustained and intransigent antifascism are not uncommon among those who fought in World War I. But they are the exception among the leading figures of the fascist/antifascist bridge generation. What prevails instead are biographies that begin with an early conversion to fascist corporatism, often reinforced by participation in the elite youth groups and in the even more elitist Littoriali—the fascist Olympiads of art and culture intended to serve as the breeding ground for the new ruling class.[13] The regime's imperial conquests bring this faith to its peak intensity, suggesting the fundamental importance of nationalist drives (even nonfascists like the novelist Alberto Moravia would celebrate the foundation of Italian East Africa). Disaffection first sets in around the time of the proclamation of the 1938 racial laws, gradually increasing as a function of declining economic conditions, unfulfilled promises, or the political ascendancy of conservative elements within the Fascist National Party. The moment of an active switch to the antifascist resistance (and often of conversion to socialism or communism) usually awaits the war years. This pattern recurs in the lives of Elio Vittorini, Vitaliano Brancati, Pietro Ingrao, Vittorio Zincone, Delio Cantimori, Alessandro Blasetti, and countless others. With notable variations, it is also repeated by prominent members of the Italo-American scholarly community such as Columbia University professor Howard Rosario Marraro, who published a body of apologetic works celebrating Giovanni Gentile, the fascist reform of Italian educational institutions, Mussolini's imperial aspirations, and the fascist youth groups, and then reversed his conclusions in the early 1940s in a series of antifascist publications.[14] But how to explain the pattern's regular recurrence? Was the early fascist faith of these individuals a matter of fear, opportunism, and/or self-interest? Or, as many have claimed, were they simply deceived by a great communicator and a highly effective propaganda machine? Certainly opportunism and self-interest might be invoked to explain why only eleven university professors, out of a total of twelve hundred, refused to swear an oath of allegiance to the fascist faith in 1931. (During the immediate postwar period, only a very few university professors or high school teachers were removed from their positions because of pro-fascist political stances or activities.) All were cognizant of Mussolini's cynicism regarding intellectuals. Their Leftism, he averred in conversations with Emil Ludwig, Yvan de Begnac, and others, was the result of material insecurities: insecurities Il Duce set out to remedy through a system of sometimes generous inducements he proffered to academics, journalists, artists, and writers including Sibilla Aleramo, Filippo Tommaso Marinetti, Julius Evola, Curzio Malaparte, Sandro Penna, Vasco Pratolini, Salvatore Quasimodo, Giuseppe Ungaretti, and Pietro Mascagni.[15]

Not all of these individuals were genuine fascist converts. Some were apolitical; others were "fair weather" fellow travelers; others were simply blindly nationalistic. But many had embraced the fascist faith no less sincerely than they would disavow it during or after the war. The shift in political faith experienced by this last group requires further explanation, because it rarely corresponds to any deep disjunction between their pre- and postwar work. The continuity suggests that, far from a simple matter of opportunism, self-interest, deception, or fear, they embraced fascism because of its success in elaborating a complex of modern myths of individual and collective sovereignty just as compelling as the democratic myths of the Resistance and Republic. Fascism's chameleon-like ideology, of course, helped to smooth over the transition. Two examples will have to suffice: the first a broad one; the second narrow.

One of the key cultural-political myths codified in the course of the late 1940s (and still firmly in place in today's literary manuals) was the reputedly intimate connection between the experience of the Resistance and the documentarist aesthetic referred to as Neorealism and associated with now legendary names such as Visconti, De Sica, Vittorini, and Pavese. Tightly coupling the worlds of film and narrative to Italian social reality, Neorealism was, in the words of Alberto Asor Rosa's *Dizionario della letteratura italiana del Novecento*, "a movement that arose with the literature of anti-fascism and the Resistance."[16] The definition continues:

The experience of the war and of the partisan struggle engendered in writers hopes of a palingenesis, not to mention a new feeling of responsibility to speak for and about those realities that decadent aestheticism and the formalism of the *rondisti* and hermetics had entirely ignored: in particular, the South, and, more generally, the world of the underclass. Beyond the undeniable divergences—Vittorini spoke of "so many neorealisms"—one must recognize that the immediate post-war forced intellectuals to confront the moral (and, indeed, the historico-ideological) dilemma of giving expression to a new world and to do so via a literature informed by [social] contents and, therefore, endowed with documentary and critical value. (In this regard, Gramsci's historicist teaching and the recovery of De Sanctis's lesson would play determining roles.) The war, anti-fascism, the peasant revolts, the conditions of the working class were rendered with immediacy by means of a naked and essential language.[17]

There are multiple problems with such an account. The invocation of Gramsci's writings, while appropriate for the early 1950s, is misleading as regards the genesis of Neorealism, inasmuch the first *Quaderni del carcere* began to appear only in 1948. (Publication was completed only in 1965.) A graver problem still is that it elides the fact that Neorealism was a product not of "the experience of the war and of the partisan struggle," but of fascist cultural debates involving many of the same fascist/postfascist bridge generation writers.[18] Indeed, much of the fascist cultural field of the 1930s had shaped itself around the terms "realism" and "neorealism," which were slippery enough to accommodate a wide array of contradictory aesthetic endeavors, extending from factual novelizations of the world of the factory by Bilenchi and Bernari to Massimo Bontempelli's realism juiced up with myth to Futurist industrial magic realism. Within these debates "realism" was variously understood as denoting a rejection of naturalist description in the name of a return to certain universal, elemental forces shaping society and nature; a paratactic "choral" mode of narration favoring the collective over the individual; a grappling with human particularities and practicalities (as opposed to human ideals); a sober but heroic ethos that alternates between recognition of life's tragic nature and struggle to overcome the real; and a transformative, socially grounded concept of art. If the definitions seem confused, so they would remain when applied in the postwar Neorealist context.

A second example, and one I have written about at greater length in a recent essay, is that of the fascist/antifascist engineer Gaetano Ciocca.[19] Author of *Giudizio sul bolscevismo*, *Economia di massa*, and *La Strada guidata*; inventor of the "fast house" and of the "guided street," Ciocca dedicated himself to building a new society—first fascist, then democratic—through technical innovation. This enterprise took him from the battlefields of World War I through the fascist era through the period of postwar reconstruction and on into the antinuclear movement of the 1960s. But his activities during the 1930s and 1940s form the core of his biography; during those decades Ciocca emerged as a key mediator between Mussolini's Italy and the countries he considered the "two most genuine representatives of class capitalism": the Soviet Union and the United States. In his writings on these two countries, Ciocca contributed to defining the corporatist "third way" to industrialization the fascist regime claimed to have devised. In his influential mass theater projects, Ciocca responded to Il Duce's 1933 call for the creation of a theater "of masses for masses": a theater much like those Ciocca had encountered during a two-year residency in Moscow (under the employ of Fiat), but brought into line with the fascist ideals of discipline, hierarchy, and Romanity. In his architectural experiments he developed industrially produced peasant and worker housing units ("house machines"), rational in design and entirely prefabricated so that they could be built as if on an automobile assembly line. In his ventures into animal husbandry, he brought to the agrarian world the same enthusiasm for rationalization and standardization he had brought to the design of corporatist city plans, fast houses, and mass theaters. And he labored tirelessly (albeit in vain) to bring about his most enduring dream: the construction of a nationwide transportation system of self-steering vehicles on guided roadways—a system that would reconcile the need for mass transit with private circulation, the best interest of the collectivity with individual interests.

Ciocca spent the entire 1930s identifying this array of projects with fascism's corporatist ideal of "cooperation inside the orbit of the state between all the forces active within society, whether individual or collective, whether of the body or of the mind ... [forces] brought together in order to insure that the nation's productive energies achieve maximum results and that the resulting benefits are distributed in a manner that is both equitable and in keeping with a collective good; a collective good that is less material than it is moral and whose ultimate expression is the nation's spiritual grandeur and power."[20] But late in World War II, as would be the case with many other fascist intellectuals, Ciocca's allegiances shifted. The same engineer who had once celebrated Hitler as possessing the "genius and intuition of an exceptional leader" and had actively pursued potential clients both in the fascist ministries and among the Nazi top brass, now began spying for the Italo-British regional military command. Between 1943 and the early 1950s Ciocca became a planner in the reconstruction of the Lombard region under the Fanfani Plans of 1945 and 1949. That these activities predate even the end of the world conflict is far more typical than atypical, to judge by the issues reviews like *Stile* (directed by Giò Ponti) and *Graficus* (directed by Luigi Gianolio) were already devoting to postwar reconstruction as early as 1942.[21]

In any event, by the end of 1945, the year of fascism's collapse and Italy's liberation, Ciocca the (re)builder of the Italian Republic was every bit as active as had been Ciocca the builder of fascist corporatism. At the beginning of 1946, he was one of the presenters of the new city plan for Milan, the fourth article of which proposed "the preparation of the current athletic zone for mass spectacles."[22] Later in the same year he stood before the National Congress for Industrial Reconstruction pleading his case for the assembly-line production of prefabricated housing as a solution to Italy's postwar housing woes and filed a proposal for building "small serially produced houses of rapid construction" in Milan. Many projects later, he was erecting the Necchi corporation Garden-Village in Pavia: a worker housing complex directly inspired by his 1930s designs, intended to demonstrate the efficiencies that could be achieved via industrialized construction. By the mid-1950s he returned to designing cinemas, auditoriums, drainage canals, and sewage systems, and in 1959 saw the Milanese public transit authorities adopt a subway system very similar to his vision of the guided roadway (minus the prior symbolism of reconciling individual and collectivity as according to the fascist Third Way).

If Ciocca's story and the others I have recounted share a common moral, it is that the breach in the order of institutions marked by De Gasperi's January 1948 proclamation of the Italian Republic was far from absolute. Key ideas, bodies of law, and institutions overleapt the gap with little difficulty, as did a complex of attitudes sedimented over many centuries: attitudes blending political pragmatism with deep cynicism, founded on a vision of human interactions in clientelist terms. Much the same can be said for the careers of even the most politicized members of the fascist/antifascist bridge generation. Animated by a credo of intellectual activism, by strong nationalist feelings, by a vision of the state as a forceful agent of social coordination, modernization, and reform, and by populist convictions always teetering on the edge between authoritarianism and democracy, many found the transition from fascism to antifascism relatively smooth.

As stated in this essay's prefatory remarks, the phrase "fascism after fascism" points not only to certain ghosts from the early postwar era, but also to a contemporary question: namely, what sort of meanings can be assigned to the noun "fascism" after 28 January 1995, the date on which Fini abolished the MSI and refounded it as a neoliberal party called Alleanza Nazionale? Has the move from fascism to antifascism now been supplanted by a move from antifascism to postfascism? And does the current resurgence of interest in fascism's cultural-intellectual background and dimensions mark a continuing fascination or merely the demise of a taboo, which sets the stage in turn for its wholesale disappearance? In these brief closing reflections, I begin to address these questions from the perspective of the history of neofascist movements in Italy.

During the fifty years since Mussolini's fall, fascism has had only one true heir and representative on the Italian scene: the Movimento Sociale Italiano (Italian Social Movement—MSI). This is not to deny that an array of neofascist or fascistoid currents arose during the postwar decades to contest the MSI's exclusive claim to that legacy. The most visible surfaced after the 1950s and assumed the form of radical anti-institutional movements more in line with German, English, and French neo-Nazism, or, more recently, with the French Nouvelle Droite, than with the corporatist traditions of the MSI.[23] A few originated as MSI splinter groups: the Fasci di Azione Rivoluzionaria and Ordine Nuovo, for instance. More typical are those that appeared during the 1970s or "years of lead" (so named because of the rain of terrorist bullets): Stefano della Chiaie's Avanguardia Nazionale, Valerio Borghese's Fronte Nazionale di Junio, Carlo Fumagalli's Movimento di Azione Rivoluzionaria, and Amos Spiazzi's Rosa dei Venti, to name but a few.[24] Mostly immune to electoral ambitions and representing little more than the black flip side of red extraparliamentary movements like the

Red Brigades and the Proletarian Armed Nuclei, these groups usually amounted to small cells built around a charismatic founder-leader. Strategically speaking, they placed themselves somewhere in the twilight zone between armed struggle and university-based activism. From the standpoint of ideology, most stood at the convergence point between the far Right and the far Left. With the extraparliamentarian Left they shared a fierce hostility toward the Republic's institutions and party system, were sketchy in their accounts of the political alternative proposed, and adopted as the backbone of their program the pursuit of a "strategy of tension" aimed at polarizing the electorate and inciting the state to abrogate freedoms. Like their left-wing counterparts, they have left no real progeny on the current political scene.

An account of this category would be incomplete without some mention of the loosely structured array of skinhead groups referred to by Italians as "Naziskins." The label lends itself to misunderstandings inasmuch as the core group of neofascist skinheads is extremely small—according to Italian Ministry of the Interior statistics, it numbers around one thousand, with only two to three thousand sympathizers or fellow travelers.[25] Concentrated in the Lazio region and in the industrial peripheries of major northern and central industrial cities, it overlaps only slightly with a much larger netherland made up of skinhead "ultraist" soccer fans, whose ideology varies, but who have adopted much the same repertory of symbols, looks, and poses. The Naziskin core has developed very limited connections to the current political system, though some of its membership is made up of former activists from MSI youth groups who broke off in the wake of the MSI's transformation into Alleanza Nazionale. This said, I would argue that it constitutes less a neofascist "movement" than a regionally grounded avatar of an international counterculture of reaction and protest (as indicated by the centrality in their belief system of anti-Semitism and xenophobia [both interregional and international], neither of which was a defining feature of Italian fascism).[26] Not one of these groups has ever been more than trivially present on the Italian political scene; nor has any ever achieved significant popular support or a mass following. Their principal impact on public debates has been via sporadic hate crimes, symptomatic of broader social tensions and therefore indicative, but amplified by sensationalist media coverage.

All of which leaves the MSI as the key protagonist of fascism's postwar struggle for survival.[27] In the case of the MSI, the genealogical ties to the prewar era could hardly be more solid or sustained. Every single one of the MSI's historical leaders (first and foremost, Giorgio Almirante) was a public official during the fascist regime's final incarnation:

the Repubblica Sociale Italiana, better known as the Republic of Salò.[28] The direct heir of this final militant, socially progressive, but violent and authoritarian phase of fascism, the MSI was relegated to a state of paralegality because it refused to acknowledge the legitimacy of the new republic, and it was denied legitimacy by the latter's constitution. This said, there are good reasons why it was tolerated. The MSI's shadowy place at once inside and outside the postwar party system proved convenient for nearly all of the postwar Republic's key political actors. Highly convenient for the communist Left because the Italian Communist Party (PCI) was the principal proprietor and beneficiary of the myth of national Resistance. For it, as for the Socialists, the MSI provided ocular proof that, however faded or faint, the fascist threat was never dead, thereby validating the Left's democratic credentials and its claim that, just as during the war years, it was the sole reliable champion of popular sovereignty. The MSI's value to the Christian Democrats is equally obvious. The mere fact of the party's existence pointed to a disjunction between the antidemocratic and democratic Right, between fringe and mainstream forms of conservatism. Stigmatized by its borderline constitutionality and by its small and economically backward constituency, the MSI proved of special symbolic weight during the crucial years in which De Gasperi managed to push the Left out of his coalition government, thereby forging the highly effective yet inefficient democratic machine that would rule Italy for the next forty years. The MSI was crucial to the operation because, by covering the right-wing flank, it helped to situate the Christian Democrats squarely at the center of a centripetal force field sustained by two contradictory but complementary urges: antifascism and anticommunism. In between the authoritarian anticommunism of the Right and the (putatively) authoritarian antifascism of the Left, in between the red scares and the black scares, the Italian center-Right coalition managed to identify itself with a balanced approach merging the defense of democratic values, the call for law and order, an elaborate spoils system, and a Catholic-inspired credo of state protections and guarantees in the socioeconomic sphere. Antifascism had been the cornerstone of the new Republic; when supplemented by the anticommunism of the cold war, it gave rise to what, contrary to legend, became the industrial world's most stable political system: a system that, despite the constant rotation of governments, not only insured the continuous rule of a single party for forty years, but also fostered so intense a game of musical (ministerial) chairs that a single individual, Giulio Andreotti, was able to retain one ministerial position or another uninterruptedly from 1946 through the early 1990s (although at this writing he is standing trial for corruption, alleged Mafia contacts, and possible complic-

ity in the murders of Aldo Moro and a journalist who held damaging
information on Andreotti's activities).[29]

How exactly did the MSI interpret its role as keeper of the fascist
torch? Mostly in a nostalgic mode, loyal to the fascism of the Republic
of Salò, but out of touch even with the conservative motivations of its
small southern electorate. The array of themes remained nearly iden-
tical for forty years: advocacy of a third way in between liberal capitalism and social-communism; rejection of the party system; intransigent anticommunism; appeals for a strengthening of the executive
branch and a weakening of labor unions; support for aggressive government intervention in the social domain; opposition to the guiding role
of the superpowers in international politics. This militant mix, which
excluded anti-Semitism but not an occasional complacent nod cast in
the direction of right-wing terrorism, received only lukewarm support
from the party's voting base, which, concentrated in the rural backwa-
ters of Sicily, was motivated more by a desire to protest the disruptive
effects of industrialization and modernization and to seek special protections than by a firm belief in fascist corporatism. This gap made the
MSI the perfect target for Left and center antifascism. On the one hand,
it cast the party itself in the role of symbol of the past. Its core of militants appeared as an isolated and aging cadre of radical irredentists unable to confront the failure of their pseudo-revolutionary ideals. On
the other hand, the reactionary tendencies of the MSI electorate could
be used to confirm that the militants' progressive and modernizing
pretenses were in fact little more than a pseudorevolutionary smoke
screen.

This said, the MSI's electorate did undergo a gradual evolution, even
if its national election results show it stuck around or below the 5 percent range. In the immediate postwar period this electorate was made
up mostly of members of the southern underclass and of the rural
oligarchy. In the 1960s inroads began to be made into the urban lower-
middle classes. The 1970s saw a sudden (but momentary) surge in support thanks to protest votes cast by the urban underclass and to middle-class anxiety over the world petroleum crisis and the possibility of
a communist seizure of power.[30] These demographic shifts in turn encouraged a number of ideological adaptations. In the late 1970s the
movement's historical leader, Giorgio Almirante, introduced the concept of the Euroright (or Eurodestra) and established a formation joining the MSI to the Spanish Fuerza Nueva and to the French Parti des
Forces Nouvelles. He embraced new themes such as anticonsumer-
ism, the defense of the environment, and protection for the disabled,
and he propounded the reintroduction of the death penalty. But there
was little electoral effect. After Almirante's death in 1988, his protégé

Fini assumed the party's helm. The first party secretary belonging to the post–Republic of Salò generation, Fini followed a cautious line aimed at assuaging the MSI old guard, though he did add to the standard ideological mix new anti-immigrant themes worthy of the French Front National. In 1990–91, he was succeeded by Pino Rauti, who led the party along an opposite tack, pursuing what he called European "africanism": a policy that conceived of Western Europe as an anti-imperialist "proletarian nation" (a coinage of Enrico Corradini) opposed symmetrically to the state capitalism of Eastern Europe and to the liberal capitalism of North America, and therefore called upon to be the privileged interlocutor and defender of the Third World. Once again, the electoral results did nothing to alter the MSI's marginal status.

All of which brings us to the brink of the second historical moment with which this essay began. In October 1992, with Fini again at its helm, the MSI commemorated the seventieth anniversary of the March on Rome. The event was celebrated with solemnity and pomp, accompanied by fascist hymns, salutes, banners, slogans, uniforms, and oaths of loyalty: all of the trappings, in short, necessary to reaffirm the MSI's ties to the fascist decades and, in so doing, to enforce its relegation to the margins of the political system. The anniversary's principal highlight was a rally held in Rome's Piazza Venezia, where, beneath the balcony from which in 1936 Mussolini proclaimed the advent of Italian East Africa to an oceanic crowd, extraparliamentary elements like the Naziskins were seen rallying alongside the old men of the MSI and fascist veterans. An ideal device for solidifying Fini's support among aging party stalwarts, perhaps, but hardly a harbinger of the neoliberal revolution to come. Six months later the event would be revealed as the last hurrah of the wartime/postwar generation with direct ties to Salò. The MSI would have transmogrified into an almost unrecognizable neoliberal party with a new generation at the helm. And it would have been rewarded for doing so by being included in the Berlusconi government as an equal partner.

Facing anticipated elections due to the political crisis brought upon by a spreading corruption scandal known as *tangentopoli*, Fini (like many other political leaders of his generation) saw the writing on the wall. He concluded that the prior party system was now definitively on the rocks; confident that the October 1992 celebrations had consolidated his hold on the MSI leadership, he made a bold move. He began several months of backroom negotiations out of which emerged a loosely structured federation made up of parties of the Right, all untainted by *tangentopoli*. The federation ran its candidates on a single unified electoral list under the rubric of Alleanza Nazionale (or "National Alliance"), which title referred, in the first instance, to a plurality of forces and not just the refounded MSI. The same writing on the wall also dictated Fini's conversion to a new religious faith: Reagan republicanism. Gone were the Roman salutes, the black shirts, the banners, the corporatist slogans, the calls for stronger state authority, the strident anticommunism, the assertions of continuity between neo-fascism and historical fascism, the invocations of Italy as a proletarian nation. In their place appeared a new gospel: that of private initiative and free markets, seconded by a noninterventionist, stripped-down concept of the state, and by a denunciation of all forms of dictatorship, totalitarianism, *partitocrazia*, and racial intolerance.

Was the change sudden? By all means (though there were many hints of its coming). But it was no more sudden, in any event, than the fall of the Berlin wall or the mushrooming of *tangentopoli*. Was it absolute? Not at all. In a series of 1994 interviews, published as *La mia Destra* (or My right), Fini sounded his new faith in liberal democracy alongside some familiar neofascist themes: the conviction that "there is nothing more all-encompassing and clear than the concept of Nationhood"[31]; that the Right necessarily affirms a "hierarchy of values, without which a people can be reduced to an indistinct complex of individuals and loses its dignity and soul"[32]; that a campaign promoting increased birth rates must be undertaken in Italy (a favorite Mussolinian policy)[33]; that the Right must oppose "lawless capitalism"[34]; and that environmentalism is the "natural corollary to [AN's] non-materialist vision of life" even if it is necessary to reject the views of those who would "bring the Pontine marshes back into being where [thanks to the fascist reclamation projects] cities have now arisen."[35] Among his recent contributions to the political debate there have also been proposals—for instance, for the creation of a national council of technocrats, industrialists, and labor leaders—that smack of prewar corporatism. Nonetheless, Fini's overarching ideological stance has remained consistently neoliberal since January 1993. "The social and economic model advanced by the fascist regime was everything but a liberal democratic model," he has repeatedly insisted, "but if today the Right defines itself and is, as we define ourselves and are, post-fascist, and if it fights not only for civil but also economic freedoms, it is self-evident that the liberal-democratic model is perfectly compatible." All of which brings us to a final decisive question: was the change authentic? Is a liberal-democratic MSI believable? I would hazard an affirmative answer on the basis of two interrelated factors. First, there is the evidence provided by the altered profile of Fini's electorate. Polling data from 1994 and 1995 consistently indicate that nearly two thirds of MSI supporters now strongly approve of the capitalist system and that a vast majority hold favorable views regarding the privatization of state industries—a heretical view from the standpoint of (neo)fascist corporatism. Moreover, the polling data demonstrates beyond a doubt that, despite the resignations of several historical MSI leaders, the old electorate did not depart, but rather embraced the change of shirts, suits, ideologies, and faces with greater vigor than its had embraced the nostalgic policies of Almirante and Rauti. All of which begins to explain Alleanza Nazionale's sudden spurt of growth between 1994 and 1996. As early as its second outing, the national elections of March 1994, Fini's new alliance succeeded in nearly tripling its prior results, capturing fully 13.5 percent of the total ballots and electing 105 deputies and 43 senators, a number of these in center and center-north areas where the MSI had never polled more than 2 percent. The result was that a party that once stood for an illegitimate past enshrined by the nation's most backward regions now found itself in the government alongside other recent upstarts like Bossi's Lega Nord. Foremost among its policy goals was the dismantling of precisely those features of the Republican state that had proven to be fascism's most tenacious historical legacy.

So transformation there was—but within the confines of a systemic crisis that required nearly every actor on Italy's political stage to assume a new and unexpected role. Alleanza Nazionale's emergence out of the ashes of the moribund, regionally grounded old MSI was but a single instance of a more general, but far more spectacular collapse: the collapse of an entire party system built around the poles of antifascism and anticommunism. On the Left, trouble had been brewing for some time. The fall of the Iron Curtain and the Soviet Union's demise had thrown Italy's principal opposition force, the Communist party, into a disarray from which it has only gradually emerged (rebaptized as the Democratic Party of the Left and, as of the May 1996 national elections, at power's doorstep). At the center and center-Right, a seemingly endless sequence of corruption and bribery scandals had decimated the ranks of every single party that had held power since 1948: particularly, the Socialists, Social Democrats, and Christian Democrats. Exposed to the world for the first time was a system of secret and not-so-secret complicities between the private sector and the state, administered by political parties for their common benefit but at the expense of the citizenry. The large-scale social state, whether Left or Right, whether socialist, Catholic, social democratic, or fascist, had fallen into disgrace and traditional electorates were wavering and wandering. Within such a setting, there could be no fascism after fascism that went by any other name than postfascism. Legitimacy was reserved for political outsiders alone—but for outsiders wearing unfamiliar uniforms.

Notes

1. Cited from Roberto Chiarini, *Destra italiana dall'Unità d'Italia a Alleanza Nazionale* (Venice: Marsilio, 1995), 158, 160.

2. On Croce and Italian analyses of fascism, see Renzo De Felice, *Interpretations of Fascism*, trans. B. H. Everett (Cambridge: Harvard University Press, 1977), 14–27.

3. *Tangentopoli* (or "bribe city") is the word devised by the Italian press to describe the corruption scandals that erupted in the wake of the *Mani pulite* ("Clean Hands") investigation undertaken by the Italian magistrates over the past half decade. *Affittopoli* (or "rent city") refers instead to a more recent scandal involving several prominent figures in the Democratic Party of the Left (ex-Communist Party) who were found to be renting luxury apartments at nominal rates thanks to political connections.

4. On the history and sociology of the Leagues the best source is Ilvo Diamanti, *La Lega. Geografia, storia e sociologia di un soggetto politico*, 2d ed. (Rome: Donzelli, 1993).

5. "Alleanza Nazionale directly connects [the question of the quality of television programming] to the need to raise the Nation's ethical level [il livello etico del Paese]." Cited from Paolo Francia, *Fini — La mia destra* (Rome: Viviani, 1994), 65.

6. The most lucid examinations of the institutional and generational overlap between the pre- and postwar eras are Claudio Pavone's *Le origini della Repubblica. Fascismo, antifascismo e continuità dello Stato* (Bologna: Il Mulino, 1995) and his groundbreaking prior work *Una guerra civile. Saggio storico sulla moralità nella Resistenza* (Turin: Bollati Boringhieri, 1991). Both have stirred up enormous controversy within Left historical circles because Pavone, a one-time Resistance fighter, undertakes a meticulous dismantling of the prevailing postwar mythologies. Although there are specific points on which I would diverge from his analysis, I find Pavone's overall account of the period at once stimulating and persuasive.

7. Perhaps the most infamous case of costly collusion was that which saw the public takeover of the Ferruzzi group and its subsequent collapse.

8. Cited from Bruno Sanguanini, "La politica culturale e il finanziamento dello stato al teatro in Italia," reprint (Trento: Dipartimento di Teoria, Storia e Ricerca Sociale, Università degli Studi di Trento, 1983), 15. Along with this study see also Sanguanini's "L'attivazione culturale delle masse," in *Potere e consenso—Tre ipotesi di studio*, ed. P. G. Rauzi, B. Sanguanini, and V. Romitelli (Trento: Libera Università degli Studi, 1981), 27–65; and "L'attivazione culturale delle masse. Le culture dell'associazionismo social-comunista ed i periodici di cultura (1947–1957)," in *Il mutamento culturale in Italia (1945–1985)*, ed. Giovanni Bechelloni (Naples: Liguori, 1987), 239–49.

9. Cited in Sanguanini, "La politica culturale," 10–11.

10. Cited in Sanguanini, "La politica culturale," 11.

11. Schnapp, *Staging Fascism*.

12. The changes involved the abolition of some of the national institutes that had overseen the festivals held at individual sites and their replacement with regionally based boards, often connected directly to the regional tourist authorities. The same system of national subventions and supports (often consisting in hotel and airfare/train packages) was employed, however, to facilitate the work of regional orga-

nizers. For a more complete account of the fascist open-air theater movement, see chapter 2 ("Staging the Miracle of the Corporative Age") of my *Staging Fascism*.

13. On the lictorial games and their impact on the bridge generation see Marina Addis and Ugoberto Alfassio, *Cultura a passo romano. Storia e strategie dei Littoriali della cultura e dell'arte* (Milan: Feltrinelli, 1983); Tracy H. Koon, *Believe, Obey, Fight: Political Socialization of Youth in Fascist Italy, 1922–1943* (Chapel Hill: University of North Carolina Press, 1985); and Giovanni Lazzari, *I Littoriali della cultura e dell'arte* (Naples: Liguori, 1979).

14. My research remains incomplete at this point, but among Marraro's pro-fascist publications the most notable are: "Education in Italy under Mussolini," *Current History* (February 1926): 705–9; "Italy's Program of Empire," *Current History* (July 1926): 545–50; *Nationalism in Italian Education* (New York: Italian Digest and News Service, 1927); "The New Education in Italy," *Current History* (February 1933): 571–76; "The Fascist Record in Italy," *Current History* (May 1935): 158–62; *The New Education in Italy* (New York: Vanni, 1936); and "The Child in Italy Today," *Il Progresso Italo-Americano*, 5 July 1936. During this early phase of his career, Marraro corresponded with several prominent figures in the regime and with Giovanni Gentile in particular, whom he greatly admired. (Numerous letters composed between 1929 and 1940 are preserved in the Gentile Archive in Rome.) His July 1926 article, for instance, prompted Giuseppe Bottai to reply that "I received the issue of *Current History* with your piece: a magnificent essay on Italian imperialism, in my opinion. I will call it to the attention of His Excellency, the Chief of State. I should be extremely grateful if you would consider contributing to our review [*Critica Fascista*—one of the regime's leading intellectual forums], especially by submitting studies concerned with American political life. You might also become our conduit to American writers, conveying to them our interest in publishing their work." Cited from a letter, dated 8 July 1926, from Bottai to Marraro, in box 4, "Miscellaneous Correspondence" folder, Marraro Archive, Columbia University. Perhaps because Marraro's pro-fascist convictions seem to have been inspired at least as much by ultranationalism as by an active embrace of fascist doctrine, he did not accept Bottai's invitation to become *Critica Fascista*'s American correspondent. By December 1942 he appears to have completed his reversal, to judge by an (unpublished) letter to the editor of the *New York Times* written on 3 December 1942, denouncing Mussolini's speech of the previous day on the "deep and abiding antagonism" between England and Italy. The letter was followed by additional antifascist publications like "The Secondary School in Liberated Italy," *The Educational Forum* 10, no. 1.1 (November 1945): 75–91. Marraro went on to pursue a successful career as a Risorgimento historian and was the founder of the "Marraro Prize in Italian Studies," administered to this day by the Modern Language Association.

15. Among the documents seized by the Allied Joint Command at the end of World War II is a report (#42) listing subventions accorded by the Ministry of Popular Culture between 1933 and 1943 (reel 26, frames 12622–12642, Mussolini, Personal Papers, microfilm 815; University of Chicago Library). It documents at least 235,000 Lire given to Aleramo; 424,000 Lire distributed to Futurist writers and artists (Bragaglia, Cangiullo, Conti, Dottori, Govoni, Marinetti, Prampolini, Vasari);

48,000 to the philosopher Julius Evola; 75,000 to the poetess Ada Negri; 41,000 to the journalist/writer Corrado Sofia and 11,000 to his collaborators in 18 BL, Alessandro Blasetti and Giorgio Venturini; 144,000 to the poet Giuseppe Ungaretti; a whopping 1,290,000 to maestro Pietro Mascagni; 210,500 and 157,300 respectively to the playwrights Sem Benelli and Rosso di San Secondo; and even 35,000 to the troublesome Curzio Malaparte. Other names on the list are Bruno Corra, Enrico Falqui, Massimo Bontempelli, Achille Campanile, Pino Masnata, Sandro Penna, Salvatore Quasimodo, Stefano Pirandello, Ottone Rosai, and Emilio Settimelli. It is worth emphasizing that these gifts were usually presented in Mussolini's name and were often the outcome of an audience and/or of a plea made in person or through intermediaries. Styling himself a man of culture, Mussolini took an active role in these sorts of matters.

16. "Neorealismo," entry by Graziella Pulce, in *Dizionario della letteratura italiana del Novecento*, ed. Alberto Asor Rosa (Turin: G. Einaudi, 1992), 368.

17. Pulce, "Neorealismo," 368.

18. Pulce does briefly note that "already in the preceding decades there had been a substantial literary tendency to pursue realist dictates with openings towards symbolic and psychological language, all of which constitutes a happy anticipation of true neorealism" ("Neorealismo," 368). She then lists some of the characteristic works from this prehistoric phase without ever noting the political inspiration of its main authors. For a more accurate view, see Ruth Ben-Ghiat, "The Politics of Realism: Corrente di Vita Giovanile," *Stanford Italian Review* 8, nos. 1–2 (1988): 139–64.

19. See "Between Fascism and Democracy: Gaetano Ciocca—Builder, Inventor, Farmer, Engineer," *Modernism/modernity* 2, no. 3 (September 1995): 117–57.

20. Cited from *Giudizio sul bolscevismo* (Milan: V. Bompiani, 1933), 33–34.

21. *Graphicus*'s May 1942 issue was, for example, dedicated to "F. T. Marinetti: The Art of Typography at War and After the War" ("L'Arte Tipografica di Guerra e Dopoguerra"). Marinetti had used the war/postwar formula as early as 1940, the year of Italy's entry into World War II on the side of Nazi Germany.

22. Cited from Gaetano Ciocca, Amos Edallo, Augusto Magnaghi, Luigi Mattioni, and Mario Terzaghi, *Linee di massima per il nuovo piano regolatore di Milano* (Milan: Edizioni Framar, 1946), 21.

23. Information regarding these movements can be found in the collective volumes *Al di là della destra e della sinistra* (Rome: Lede, 1982); *Le forme del politico. Idee della Nuova Destra*, ed. Marco Tarchi (Florence: La Roccia di Erec, 1984); *C'eravamo tanto a(r)mati* (Vibo Valentia: Settecolori, 1984); Enzo Raisi, *Storia ed idee della nuova destra italiana* (Rome: Settimo Sigillo, 1990), and M. Zucchinali, *A destra oggi in Italia* (Milan: Sugarco, 1986).

24. On the extra- or anti-MSI radical right in Italy, see Franco Ferrarresi, "La destra eversiva," in his *La destra radicale* (Milan: Feltrinelli, 1984), 54–119; Marco Revelli, "La nuova destra," 119–213 in the same volume, as well as his *La cultura della destra radicale* (Milan: Franco Angeli, 1985); E. Pisetta, "Per una storia del terrorismo nero," *Il Mulino* 32 (1983): 738–70; and G. Galli, *La destra in Italia* (Milan: Gammalibri, 1983). Also useful is the "Destre" special issue of *Democrazia e diritto* 1 (1994).

25. Cited in The Anti-Defamation League, *The Skinhead International. A Worldwide Survey of Neo-Nazi Skinheads* (New York: ADL, 1995), 49.

26. On Italian skinheads in general see *The Skinhead International*, 48–52. The lone exception is perhaps the minuscule Movimento Politico Occidentale, run out of Rome by Maurizio Boccacci, now redubbed (to evade closure under the Mancino edict, which restricts hate speech and other forms of racial, ethnic, and religious discrimination) I Camerati (The Comrades).

27. On the MSI's history, see in particular Chiarini's *Destra italiana* and Piero Ignazi's *Il polo escluso. Profilo del Movimento Sociale Italiano* (Bologna: Il Mulino, 1989) and *Postfascisti? Dal Movimento Sociale Italiano ad Alleanza Nazionale* (Bologna: Il Mulino, 1994).

28. Almirante is a typical case in point. Close to Telesio Interlandi, he served as editor of *Il Tevere* and *La Difesa della Razza* in the prewar period. During the Republic of Salò he was appointed to the position of cabinet chief in the Ministry of Popular Culture, where his principal charge included propaganda sector work. In the postwar period he was one of the founders of the MSI and edited and wrote for the MSI newspaper *Il Secolo d'Italia*. The postwar period saw no substantial shift in Almirante's RSI-based views, though he was willing to acknowledge that "mistakes had been made."

29. The current turmoil has placed the four decades of relative stability in an unfavorable light, but less than a decade ago there were those who, like Joseph LaPalombara, were ready to proclaim the system an overall success. See his *Democracy, Italian Style* (New Haven: Yale University Press, 1987).

30. On this subject see Ignazi, *Il polo escluso*, 359–408.

31. "It is true that there is nothing more all-encompassing and clear than the concept of Nationhood, which contains within itself no hidden allusion to 'paternalism' or, worse, a desire for 'aggression' or 'imperialism.' I would say, rather, that in the present moment Nation signifies more than ever before the ancient and, therefore, eternal concept of Fatherland [l'antico e, proprio perchè antico, eterno concetto di Patria]." *La mia Destra*, 33.

32. "Our cultural, economic, and social stance contains within itself the seed of true civil progress and true social justice. It affirms a stance that is considered 'right-wing' in antithesis to that of the Left, whose positions it clearly and substantially improves upon. It has much in common with many of the political forces on the European scene. The Right's superiority consists entirely in the maintenance and respect for a hierarchy of values, without which a people can be reduced to an indistinct complex of individuals and loses its dignity and soul." *La mia Destra*, 43.

33. "It has nothing to do with fascism. There is nothing embarrassing in asserting that policies to promote demographic growth need to be put into action. Italy has by now reached zero growth. The immediate result is that every working Italian carries the weight of the retired sector of the population. Sooner or later we won't be able to cover all retirees." *La mia Destra*, 51.

34. "[We are] anti-capitalists in the sense that we are unfavorably disposed towards a lawless capitalism [un capitalismo selvaggio]." *La mia Destra*, 56–57.

35. "It is no exaggeration to speak of nature's agony. To address environmental problems will be among the main concerns of Alleanza Nazionale. . . . It's little

more than a natural corollary to a non-materialist vision of life." *La mia Destra*, 71.
"Though the environment must be well protected from destruction, this must be
done in accordance with man's tendency to make progress. If such a conception is
violated one ends up with the paradox of environmentalists who would bring the
Pontine marshes back into being where cities have now arisen or who oppose the
construction of roadways because a tree would have to be felled." *La mia Destra*, 73.

Wulf Kansteiner

Between Politics and Memory: The *Historikerstreit* and West German Historical Culture of the 1980s

GUNTER GRASS: My age group is too young to have become Nazis or to have become guilty. . . . After some years, however, I recognized that belonging to this age group is no achievement.

GUNTER GAUS: A grace?

GUNTER GRASS: In this case a grace but also a responsibility. This generation carries the burden to mediate between the abused fifty and sixty year olds and the twenty-five year olds. *ZDF interview, aired 28 September 1965*

A Political Scandal and Its Resolution

On 10 November 1988 a political scandal with unprecedented conse-quences erupted at the center of the West German political establish-ment. Literally overnight, the second highest official of the Federal Republic, Philip Jenninger, the president of the Federal German parlia-ment, was removed from office because the members of that body al-most unanimously disapproved of the speech he delivered on the occa-sion of the fiftieth anniversary of the "Night of the Broken Glass." The fact that a high-ranking representative of the governing conservative party was forced to resign due to "improper" remarks about National Socialism, and also the speed of his removal from office, suggest that the speech violated some basic rules of West Germany's historical culture.[1]

Jenninger had tried to deliver a very ambitious speech, one to put him on par with President Richard Weizsäcker, whose remarks on the occasion of the fortieth anniversary of the end of World War II had brought him international acclaim.[2] Jenninger eschewed the conven-tional empty formulas about the need for remembrance and engaged in an exercise of self-critical memory-work by focusing on Hitler's popu-larity with the German people. In the process he managed to commit three major political mistakes.

In practical political terms Jenninger's excursion into the history of everyday life during Nazism contradicted the political objectives of his own party, the Bavarian Christian Socialist Union, which was struggling to retain the loyalty of West Germany's right-wing electorate after the death of Franz-Josef Straua, who had secured these votes for the Christian Democratic/Christian Socialist Union for more than two decades. In this situation, the last thing the party needed was a self-critical analysis of Hitler's popularity.[3] In addition, the speech violated the collective identity of the German parliament. In 1988, some of the most prominent members of parliament still identified themselves as victims and opponents of Hitler's regime, and the younger members, especially on the Left, are best described as ex post facto resistance fighters—that is, politicians who had spent a considerable portion of their political life fighting fascisms of all kinds to make up for their parents' generation's lack of resistance to Nazism. Both of these groups had been instrumental in bestowing democratic legitimacy upon the West German political establishment. Naturally, both the original and the ex post antifascists resented Jenninger's urge to identify, albeit momentarily, with the perspective of the bystanders of the Holocaust.[4] Last, and most important, Jenninger's remarks violated a tacit agreement about the nature of the Holocaust that represents one of the cornerstones of West Germany's historical culture. Especially since the 1970s, the "insistence on the Holocaust's uniqueness and inexplicability allowed the West Germans to see the Holocaust as something that could not be explained even in the context of the Third Reich. The Holocaust thus lost all the characteristics of a historical event and was transferred to the realm of the ahistorical that defies explanation and renders the question of responsibility obsolete."[5] Jenninger's remarks reclaimed the Holocaust as a historical, maybe even explicable event and thus, at least implicitly, raised the question of concrete historical responsibility.

All these "shortcomings" of the speech were exacerbated by Jenninger's poor performance. Not a gifted speaker in the first place, Jenninger lost all control over his subject matter once he noticed his colleagues' staunch opposition. In particular, he could not separate his attempt to elucidate the German population's fascination with Hitler in the 1930s from his own fascination with this topic. Past—including quotes from original documents—and present became hopelessly intermingled.[6] Thus, Jenninger not only transformed the Holocaust from an ahistorical into a historical event; he subsequently also transformed the past into a present event, provoking an outcry among his offended colleagues, who rightly felt that Jenninger's performance called into question their complacent antifascism or antitotalitarianism. Ultimately, Jenninger singlehandedly, if inadvertently, managed to undercut the elaborate defense strategies the West German political establishment had erected to safeguard their democratic identity from the contamination emanating from the Nazi era. This rhetorical fiasco cost him his job.

This explains Jenninger's speedy removal from office, but it does not explain his ambitious objective of describing the National Socialist anti-Semitic policies from the perspective of the bystanders and of identifying with the bystanders' passivity in the face of the persecution of Europe's Jews. Although more research on this topic is needed I would suggest that Jenninger's remarks and intentions reflect the dilemma of a specific political generation, the Hitler-Youth Generation. This generation grew up during Nazism and was coopted into the state youth organization, the "Hitler-Youth"; the majority of its members identified with the National Socialist cause during adolescence. After 1945 they faced the task of completely reworking their political and moral identity—a task they accomplished successfully because, unlike their older compatriots, they were not held responsible for the Nazi crimes. Subsequently, the Hitler-Youth Generation played an important part in shaping West German democracy, especially in the 1970s and 1980s, when its members dominated the political and professional elites of the Federal Republic.[7] In the late 1980s, however, before leaving the public arena, some of these politicians and intellectuals readdressed the issue of their double-layered identity by probing into the emotional and political proclivities of their lives during Nazism. Although these initiatives sparked an interesting research proposal,[8] they primarily reflected an uncritical identification with the viewpoint of the German population during Nazism. As the Jenninger affair and the Historians' Debate indicate, the attempts to recover and revalue memories from the Third Reich in a public setting produced a problematic emotional stance that for good reasons had been omitted from West Germany's official historical culture; they resulted in a misplaced empathy with the bystanders of the Holocaust.

The Parameters of the *Historikerstreit*

In November 1988, when Jenninger was forced to retire as president of parliament, the Historians' Debate about the singularity of the Holocaust had subsided. In a nutshell the Jenninger affair featured all the elements that had figured in the volatile discussions among German historians and the interested public for two years. The following analysis and contextualization of the German Historians' Debate of 1986 through 1988 reveals a conglomeration of political, professional, and generational factors similar to that which surfaced in the Jenninger affair, albeit on a larger scale.

It is not my objective to recall and comment in detail on the arguments advanced during the Historians' Debate; such introductions and comments have been provided elsewhere.[9] Rather, I want to probe into the short- and long-term causes of the debate by offering an analysis and critique of its origins in West German party politics, by relating it to the paradigm of the history of everyday life advanced by West Germany's subculture and its mass media, by studying the political-philosophical underpinnings of the discussions, and by integrating the *Historikerstreit* within its wider historiographical context. Finally, I will concentrate on the generational dynamics played out in the debate that illustrate the extent to which the issues discussed in the Historians' Debate reflect the specific experiences and attitudes of the Hitler-Youth Generation. Analysis of these multiple factors locates the Historians' Debate within the wider context of West Germany's historical culture, that is, within the diverse representations and interpretations of the past that provided West German society with models of historical orientation and historical change in the 1980s. Understood in these terms the concept of historical culture cuts across various institutional settings and various fields of social practice and professional expertise, including academic research and writing, the arts, the political sphere, the mass media, the educational system, and leisure activities.[10] As a public debate of exceptional proportions, the Historians' Debate affords the opportunity to study the interplay of some of these fields of historical knowledge and collective memories. Thus, the Historians' Debate gives us a chance to study historical culture "in action" and to draw some conclusions on the compatibility, interdependence, and relative autonomy of different visions and concepts of the Nazi past that were in use in the Federal Republic's historical culture at the time.

Between 1986 and 1988 the Historians' Debate produced some twelve hundred texts, ranging from single newspaper columns to extended monographs, at one point appearing at the rate of one hundred articles per month.[11] The debate began in the feuilleton pages of the major German dailies and weeklies, especially *Die Zeit* and the *Frankfurter Allgemeine Zeitung*, and was carried over into numerous historical, political, and cultural journals, eventually becoming the focus of more than ten edited volumes and ten monographs.[12] Particularly in its early stages, the *Historikerstreit* continued an important cultural tradition in Germany reflected in the close cooperation between highbrow print media and academics, especially historians. While historians, with the exception of the philosopher/sociologist Jürgen Habermas, were the most visible and outspoken among the discussants, cultural journalists outnumbered them and played an important role in keeping the debate going.

The high profile of the Historians' Debate should not, however, deflect from the fact that at every stage the *Historikerstreit* remained a strictly intellectual affair. The great majority of the West German population was unaware of the course and the intellectual stakes of the debate because it "was conducted well above the heads of the wider public."[13] The local papers covered the debate only very sporadically, and the electronic media paid little attention to it. With the exception of some radio debates and some television features in the political magazines of the German public television stations, the Historians' Debate did not fill the airwaves to the same extent that it clogged the national papers. Apparently, the TV and radio journalists felt the discussions had little entertainment value. Thus the Historians' Debate marks "one of the last triumphs of the print media" in Germany.[14]

After the fact, almost all participants agreed that the *Historikerstreit* had been intellectually unproductive. The debate did not settle any methodological disputes, nor did it help find new material or interpretive avenues for the study of the history of National Socialism and the "Final Solution." With the possible exception of Ernst Nolte's *Der Europäische Bürgerkrieg*, the historians and journalists never took note of the academic publications and achievements of any of the participants.[15] Instead, they focused on a few arguments and quotations from the marginal works of the historians involved, taken from textbook essays, newspaper articles, essay collections, or utterances made during the debate. The impressive bibliography of the debate stands in stark contrast to the very slim textual base from which the conflict originated and from which it never departed. This characteristic of the dispute can also be attributed to the fact that the *Historikerstreit* was never much of a debate. It produced an amazing fallout, but never surpassed two rounds of exchanges between the original participants. By mid-1987 both camps were merely repeating their initial positions, and declined to engage in further discussion, especially after the liberal/Social Democratic side declared victory.[16] A decade later, it is also safe to say that the Historians' Debate has not inspired any new research.[17] More recent research about Nazism and the "Final Solution" conducted in Germany addresses issues like the interdependence of National Socialism and modernity and thus, at least implicitly, rejects arguments about Nazism's singularity that were still hotly discussed during the Historians' Debate.[18] In addition, despite the current interest in the politics of memory and commemoration, especially with regard to the Nazi past, few scholars have discussed the *Historikerstreit* within the context of the history of (West) German efforts to come to terms with Nazism. The few texts that have recently reconsidered the Historians' Debate were written by participants who felt that their voice was not heard in the heat of the battle.[19]

On the surface, the Historians' Debate dealt with three major issues and accusations. First, the participants discussed the concept of the singularity of the Holocaust and its comparability with other genocides, especially with the Stalinist crimes in the Soviet Union. This topic was raised in response to a number of essays by Ernst Nolte, who had argued that in implementing the "Final Solution" Hitler and the Nazi leadership acted upon their fear of Bolshevik class warfare and that, above and beyond this causal connection, the extermination of the Jews represented a radicalized version of the mass exterminations in the Soviet Union. Nolte's critics, Jürgen Habermas and a number of liberal historians, denied both the causal and the phenomenological linkage and insisted on the Holocaust's status as an exceptional historical event.[20] Second, the discussants argued about the need for today's historians to take sides and identify with the historical actors of the Nazi period. This issue was brought about by a slim volume in which Andreas Hillgruber suggested that German historians should identify with the perspective of the German troops on the Eastern Front in their defensive battle against the Red Army in 1944–45. Hillgruber's critics principally questioned the need to identify with past actors and asserted that, if they were to do so at all, historians had to empathize with the victims of the regime, especially with the inmates of the camps, with the many civilians and soldiers who would have survived if the Eastern Front had collapsed earlier.[21] Third, the critics assumed that Nolte and Hillgruber were part of an overall conservative effort to normalize the representation of the Nazi past and to remove the major conceptual and emotional obstacles to revival of a traditional German national historical identity. In their eyes this conservative agenda had already been pursued at Bitburg in 1985, where Helmut Kohl and Ronald Reagan had staged a symbolic reconciliation between the former enemies—the United States and Germany—over the graves of German soldiers who had died in World War II, including some members of the ss.[22] Also, the critics thought this agenda was clearly laid out in the recent political writings of the historian and former advisor to Chancellor Kohl, Michael Stürmer, who had argued that the Federal Republic's future depended on its citizens' identification with a national cause and a national history and who was, therefore, included in the critique. Habermas and the liberal historians denied West Germany's need for conventional forms of historical identity and claimed that the allegiance to the constitution West Germans had developed after the war represented the most appropriate type of collective identity in the present postnational environment, and assured West Germany's membership in the community of Western nations.[23]

In the context of these three main concerns the participants in the Historians' Debate raised a number of related questions: they discussed the validity of traditional geopolitical models, reintroduced by the conservative historians, for the interpretation of modern and contemporary German history;[24] they questioned the allegedly defensive nature of Hitler's attack on the Soviet Union in light of Nolte's remarks;[25] and most important, the Historians' Debate overlapped with heated discussions about two national historical museum projects championed by the federal government. Shortly after taking over the chancellorship in 1982, Helmut Kohl had announced that the new conservative government would sponsor a museum for German history to be opened in 1987 in Berlin on the occasion of the city's 750th anniversary, and a museum in Bonn dedicated to the history of the Federal Republic. After concepts had been circulated in 1984 and 1985, both projects were challenged by liberal critics, who charged that the conservative government intended to found two institutions that would promote the conservative national political agenda.[26]

The Political Dimension of the Historians' Debate

The *Historikerstreit* was first and foremost a political battle. In a country where academics in the humanities, especially in history, are firmly aligned with one or the other of the established political forces—that is, the conservatives of the CDU/CSU or the Social Democrats of the SPD—and where politicians and academics keep track of how many research chairs belong to the power base of each camp, it should not come as a surprise that the intellectual seasons tend to follow the political calendar.[27] Therefore, as many commentators pointed out, Habermas's initiative in July 1986 must also be interpreted within the context of the elections for the eleventh Bundestag in January 1987, in which the Social Democrats hoped to regain control of the federal government, which they had lost in 1982–83 under particularly humiliating circumstances. However, while the timing of the debate can only be understood in relation to the election, there was more at stake for the participants of the *Historikerstreit* than the electoral results. It is important, therefore, to recall briefly West Germany's political developments since the 1960s and the impact these developments had on academic politics in order to understand the political motivations with which the historians entered into the debate.

A massive expansion of the civil service system on the state and federal levels from the mid-1960s to the mid-1970s had created a large number of well-paid jobs, especially for graduates in the humanities. These jobs were filled by members of the first postwar generation, the generation that staffed the student movement, the great majority of whom firmly supported Willy Brandt's reform politics. As a result, the middle ranks, and ultimately also large sections of the higher ranks, of local, state, and federal administrations, of research institutions, of the state school system from kindergarten through secondary education, and of the media, absorbed a considerable number of liberal-minded academics who shaped these institutions for several decades. Although this transformation varied widely from region to region and although it never tipped the balance in the sense that conservatives suddenly found themselves outnumbered throughout the country, it had a lasting impact on West Germany's social and political climate.[28]

Thus, the intensity and virulence of the Historians' Debate has to be partly attributed to the fact that by the mid-1980s many conservative intellectuals were deeply frustrated by having to deal with a well-positioned, firmly entrenched liberal/Social Democratic establishment in the civil service and the media (and for conservative historians that also included thriving new scholarly journals like *Geschichte und Gesellschaft*) despite the fact that the conservative parties they belonged to had regained the political majority on the federal level five years earlier and had held the majorities in most states throughout the reform era. The liberal intellectuals, on the other hand, were highly motivated to defend their power base in light of the conservative offensive, and to put their weight behind the Social Democratic campaign. Their strong allegiance to the liberal cause might also be attributed to the fact that almost all of them had gained entry to the professorial elite during the aforementioned expansion of the university system in the 1960s and 1970s.[29]

These political constellations and allegiances in the Federal Republic of the mid-1980s, in conjunction with the imminent federal elections, help explain three political misperceptions liberal and conservative historians held in common. According to their habit of thinking in terms of clear-cut political borders and close-knit political networks, both sides perceived the debate primarily as a political campaign or even a political conspiracy, especially with regard to their respective foes' motivation and strategy. Liberals and conservatives alike assumed that they faced deliberate campaigns designed to attain or defend cultural/political hegemony; thus both failed to take note of the more complex and more interesting aspects of the debate.[30] In addition, both sides overestimated their influence with the electorate and their general public appeal. The intellectual skirmishes of the Historians' Debate had no impact at all on the outcome of the elections. Finally, conservative and liberal intellectuals shared a political objective that negatively influenced the course and the outcome of the Historians' Debate. The 1987 elections marked a departure from the stable three-party system that had dominated West German politics since the mid-1960s; with the Green party, a political force representing the substantial but highly divided political movements to the left of the Social Democrats entered the federal arena. The defensive attitude of the political establishment toward these movements was mirrored in the behavior of the arguing professoriate, which throughout the debate ignored comments originating from the radical Left of West Germany's political spectrum.[31]

Although it was strongly influenced by party politics, politicians never interfered in the Historians' Debate. To some extent, this surprising restraint might be attributed to the politicians' respect for the autonomy of the cultural/academic sphere; they did not feel comfortable addressing questions of historical uniqueness and comparability when even the sociologist Habermas was chided for his alleged lack of historical expertise.[32] In addition, unlike the historians, the politicians probably recognized that there was nothing to be gained politically by entering a debate that was for the most part inaccessible or uninteresting to the electorate. They engaged in discussions about the appropriate interpretation and representation of the Nazi past when they saw an opportunity to score politically, as for instance during the Bitburg and Jenninger affairs immediately before and after the Historians' Debate. Finally, unlike other areas of West Germany's historical culture, the political establishment of the Federal Republic remained for decades closely attached to the interpretations of Nazism that had served it very well nationally and internationally in the 1950s. Thus, conservative politicians in particular held on to the interpretive framework of antitotalitarianism that had eased West Germany's entry into the Western alliance, and declined to engage in debates that might render that useful tool ineffective.[33]

In light of its limited political impact, the most tangible political effect of the Historians' Debate is particularly deplorable: it marks one of the few moments in the history of the Federal Republic when elements of right-wing, apologetic renditions of the history of the Third Reich found their way into the mainstream media. Nolte's philosophical meanderings about Hitler's right to intern the Jews and his vivid descriptions of the Soviet threat perceived by Hitler and his followers can be distinguished from right-wing propaganda only after close scrutiny, if at all.[34] Not surprisingly, Nolte subsequently received unsolicited (but apparently not unwelcome) support from German neo-Nazis.[35] Even more importantly, however, Nolte's idiosyncratic revisionism seems to have inspired a number of younger scholars, who have followed his lead.[36]

The Subcultural and the Popular Dimension

Elie Wiesel coined the term "gang of four" with respect to the four conservative historians (Stürmer, Nolte, Hillgruber, and Klaus Hildebrand, who published a favorable review of one of Nolte's essays) Habermas singled out for his attack. Wiesel thus nicely captured the conspiratorial air of Habermas's critique, but not the essence of the debate. The conservative historians' publications were never coordinated, nor did they follow the same agenda. Stürmer's contribution was the least complex, lacking any political or historiographical depth. However, its one-dimensionality exposed the political and philosophical naiveté behind all the talk of national and postconventional identity during the *Historikerstreit*. Stürmer's call for a consistent conservative national history that would focus on the success story of the Federal Republic and provide the population with a sense of historical self was designed to render West Germans immune to right-wing ideological temptations and turn them into a reliable, predictable political entity, nationally as well as internationally.[37] As mentioned above, Stürmer's project can be interpreted as a historiographical extension of the government's 1985 Bitburg initiative and the two museum projects. Stürmer's vision must have had considerable appeal, especially for politicians facing an unpredictable electorate, but it did not even come to terms with the blatant conceptual problem of Germany's division after 1945. Stürmer failed to explain how it was possible simultaneously to construct a consistent national identity for West Germans and still insist on the national unity of the two Germanys, a theme regularly invoked by conservative politicians in their dealings with the East German state and population. Moreover, Stürmer and his colleagues in the conservative think tanks close to the government, as well as their critics on the Left, never addressed the question of how to popularize their respective designs for a West German collective identity. The conservative side apparently assumed that West Germany's political culture suffered from a debilitating identity crisis and that the existing "vacuum" would be filled instantaneously once the intellectuals decided to release their historical visions. The liberal side went even further, by maintaining that West Germans had drawn the only appropriate conclusion from the Nazi experience by internalizing Western democratic values, which superseded outdated conventional sentiments of national and historical identity. Consequently, in principle, the liberals should not even have expected the population to accept the conservative offer of normalization, although Habermas's massive intervention seems to indicate that he himself did not trust the postnational equilibrium.

There are good reasons to assume that both sides were wrong, that at the time of the *Historikerstreit* the majority of Germans neither suffered from an identity crisis nor had given up on traditional forms of collective identity. In the late 1970s, but especially the early 1980s, a part of West Germany's historical culture underwent a massive transformation only insufficiently captured by the term *Alltagsgeschichte* (everyday history). This phenomenon was by no means limited to West Germany; in one way or another it encompassed most of Western Europe, the United States, and Japan. As Georg Iggers argues: "Not since the Enlightenment has there been a similarly parallel, international discursive event."[38] *Alltagsgeschichte* developed in West Germany in two distinct forms: as an intellectual phenomenon based in the Left subculture with few links to the academic establishment, and as a popular phenomenon that encompassed all mass media, print and electronic. In either variety, *Alltagsgeschichte* lacked a clear conceptual focus but featured a primary interest in relating to past events on a tangible, emotional, and subjective level in a way that afforded the opportunity of identifying with past actors—preferably hitherto unknown or marginalized—and concrete local traditions and practices. In keeping with its emotional emphasis, and unlike more conventional ways of studying the past, *Alltagsgeschichte* put particular emphasis on visual records and forms of representation, such as paintings, photographs, and especially moving images. Also, for the same reasons, the producers and consumers of *Alltagsgeschichte* preferred conventional narrative frameworks and tried to capture past phenomena that in one way or another—often enough only in an imaginary way—could be considered close to home: for example, phenomena that evoked the multifaceted sounding board "Heimat."[39] The movement dealt with diverse topics, including the early modern period and Prussian history, but in Germany it focused primarily on the history of National Socialism.

As an intellectual movement *Alltagsgeschichte* represented a critical appropriation of a number of different traditions: the neo-Marxism of the Frankfurt School, in particular Habermas's writings and those of independent Marxist philosophers like Ernst Bloch; the phenomenological and ethnological traditions of German sociology, reaching as far back as Husserl; the debates on fascism that occupied West Germany's Left intellectuals in the 1960s; and various imports like Anglo-

American anthropology (for instance Clifford Geertz), Foucault's theory of power, and Bourdieu's theory of practical action, as well as microhistorical and neo-Marxist role models like the works of Carlo Ginzburg, Natalie Davis, and E. P. Thompson.[40] With few exceptions, however, the practitioners of *Alltagsgeschichte* took a decidedly antitheoretical stance.[41] Consequently, these traditions have often only been acknowledged in passing, and core concepts of the new movement, like *Alltag* (everyday life) and *Erfahrung* (experience), have never been accurately defined. Institutionally the movement had four focal points: the Max Planck Institute in Göttingen, the Open University in Hagen, the Institute for Contemporary History in Munich, and, most important, a large number of local, grassroots initiatives loosely organized in an association of history workshops. The latter in particular were firmly rooted in the new social movements of the 1970s, such as the ecological, peace, and women's movements.[42] *Alltagsgeschichte* was launched by the first postwar generation, scholars born after 1938, many of them veterans of the student movement who, unlike their predecessors, could no longer find jobs in the shrinking university system.[43] Participation in the history workshops afforded them the opportunity to continue their involvement with Left politics after the end of the Social Democratic/liberal reform era, to partake in a continued antifascist intellectual endeavor after theorizing about fascisms had exausted itself and proven politically ineffectual, and to engage with history on a semiprofessional level after they had been denied access to academia proper.

As a popular phenomenon *Alltagsgeschichte* went far beyond the pet projects of a group of highly motivated, unemployed, left-wing historians. It produced "a flood of literature aimed at the general audience"[44] and resulted in an unprecedented wave of exhibitions and new museums. *Alltagsgeschichte* even sparked new ways of doing history, like the history workshops, and boosted hitherto marginal historical projects like student competitions into the national limelight. Most important, however, it changed West German television, especially its image of Nazism. German public television, until 1986 without any private competition, had always very diligently and responsibly addressed the topic of Nazism, albeit often in a detached, "objective," and heavy-handed manner. Since the late 1970s, however, a new generation of television producers and executives have bought and produced programs in large numbers that present the history of the Third Reich from the perspective of the "average" citizen. These shows were visually very attractive and cast in successful television formats, such as TV films featuring standard, popular plot types. Consequently, they were also very successful with audiences. The wave of new media images included critical probings into the population's passivity during the Third Reich, but most of the time presented a vision of everyday life during Nazism devoid of the historically most important groups of victims (i.e., Jews, gypsies, political dissidents, and Soviet POWs). By 1984, television had already achieved what historians only started to consider after the Historians' Debate: it had historicized Nazism by integrating it within the continuity of modern German history by means of pleasurable historical narratives, taking the viewpoint of the bystanders as the ultimate reference point. Nevertheless, *Alltagsgeschichte*, understood in these broad terms, was probably the only moment in West German history when the population as a whole, and not just intellectuals or other subgroups, confronted the Nazi past.[45]

Both varieties of *Alltagsgeschichte* developed in distinct cultural and political settings, the popular rendition lacking the clear critical, political focus of its subcultural counterpart. However, both together unravelled the traditional center of West Germany's historical culture by exposing crucial blind spots of the West German historical profession, which had neither researched the intricacies of everyday life during Nazism nor been able to produce histories with popular appeal. Moreover, unlike the historical profession, both the public broadcasting systems and the left-wing intellectuals were attuned to parallel international trends they incorporated in their new vision of the history of the Third Reich. Not surprisingly, both varieties of everyday history received sharp criticism from professional historians.[46] *Alltagsgeschichte* thoroughly transformed West Germany's historical culture, but even in hindsight it remains difficult to assess its impact; it produced self-congratulatory celebrations of local resistance groups as well as self-critical probings into the half-forgotten histories of local concentration camps; stated otherwise, it encompassed *Heimat* as well as *Holocaust*.[47]

In almost all respects *Alltagsgeschichte* as a social phenomenon amounted to the exact opposite of the writings of the participants of the Historians' Debate: visually instead of discursively oriented, popular instead of intellectual and academic, designed for subjective experience instead of objectification. This said, however, it is clear that the *Historikerstreit*, unlike the academic routine of its participants, shared some of the characteristics of *Alltagsgeschichte*. During the Historians' Debate the participants sought the greatest publicity they could achieve while staying within their traditional realm, the print media. Also, in contrast to their usual academic publications they included subjective assessments of National Socialism and conducted the debate on a very personal level. In this respect the *Historikerstreit* was also a belated reaction to the eruption of *Alltagsgeschichte*, which had caught the intellectuals very much by surprise. The various conservative initiatives as well as Habermas's preventive critique tried, unsuccessfully, to reclaim lost ground and reestablish historians and intellectuals in what they considered their traditional role as the primary arbiters of the agenda of West Germany's historical culture. However, throughout the *Historikerstreit*, the intellectuals of both camps misjudged the population's need for historical guidance and overestimated their own ability to provide and shape the popular historical imagination. Possibly due to their ignorance of the historical culture of a media society, the intellectuals misconceived the process of historical identity formation in West Germany's post-Nazi society. The competition and incompatibilities between the academic sector on the one hand and the mass media and subcultural sectors of West Germany's historical culture on the other stand out more clearly when considered from inside the academic discourse of historians and philosophers. In particular the philosophical writings on the question of West Germany's postwar collective identity, which provided the guidelines for the intellectuals during the Historians' Debate, reveal to what extent the academic perspective was out of touch with the areas of West Germany's historical culture more closely attuned to the actual development of those collective identities.

The Political-Philosophical Dimension

The philosophical underpinnings of the conservative agenda for the construction of a conventional national historical identity were provided by Hermann Lübbe, who was also very instrumental in justifying the relative unwillingness of West German society to address the problem of the Nazi past in the 1950s. In his philosophical considerations Lübbe strictly differentiates between historical identity and moral self-definition. According to his reasoning, the individual comes to terms with the historical forces, which shape his or her life but which are clearly located outside the person's own sphere of influence, through the process of historical self-identification. Recognizing and adapting to these essential forces represents an important element of human self-identity, precisely because they define the parameters and processes to which the individual is exposed without having any power to alter them. The realm of moral self-identity, on the other hand, is limited to the individual's personal sphere, where his or her actions can make a decisive difference and where self-identity is indistinguishable from moral responsibility.[48] Lübbe's stance systematically unburdens the individual's historical memory vis-à-vis such a phenomenon as Nazism. Since he transposes this model onto the level of collective processes of historical and moral identity formation, Lübbe interprets the German population's postwar silence in the face of the Nazi crimes as a realistic and in this sense "responsible" tacit agreement between former victims and former perpetrators, who decided to further the cause of rebuilding the shattered society and state by ignoring past struggles.[49] Lübbe's ideas are helpful in understanding the silence of the 1950s; he is its foremost apologist and—with the Mitscherlichs[50]—also its foremost theoretician. But his writings have little to say about the much more active phases of *Vergangenheitsbewältigung* in West Germany from the 1960s through the 1980s, which constantly interweave moral and historical issues on both the personal and the collective level, as the example of *Alltagsgeschichte* aptly illustrates. Nevertheless, Lübbe's ideas are relevant today because they render explicit the radical dissociation of moral and historical questions that informs conservative initiatives like Stürmer's.

The Left counterpart to Lübbe's position, developed by Jürgen Habermas, is also questionable, if for other reasons. As already mentioned, Habermas argues that the philosophical problems highlighted by Nazism call for a reflexive, postnational identity that avoids the pitfalls of traditional ideologies by generating guidelines for social action on the basis of intersubjective principles of communicative reason. For Habermas, these principles provide a healthy and necessary corrective in our dealings with the past because they put us in a position to choose which traditions we will continue and which we will dissociate ourselves from. More concretely, after Auschwitz, these principles help us distance ourselves and our society from the traditions that led to Auschwitz—with nationalism, racism, and authoritarianism among the most prominent. Habermas has identified two resources in contemporary German society that embody these rational principles and facilitate their future adaptation and implementation. While Western constitutions like the German Grundgesetz provide an adequate modern rendition of Enlightenment traditions, the radical democratic practice of grassroots initiatives, like the new social movements of the 1970s, provides the necessary impetus to revise the constitutions in light of social, political, and economic change. For Habermas, the formal procedures of the Rechtsstaat and the democratic grassroots movements afford us the opportunity to deal with the past in a self-critical, postnational fashion.[51] In the same way, Habermas most recently elaborated upon his earlier writings on discourse ethics in an attempt to outline a philosophy of law and ethics that avoids the shortcomings of more traditional approaches, especially abstract universalist ethics and moral pragmatism. His results are similar to those of his less ambitious and extensive probings into the groundings of postnational identity, and he lays the foundation for a postconventional moral consciousness rooted in rational discursive practices as well as universal procedural principles of justice.[52] Obviously for Habermas, unlike Lübbe, the very essence of moral problems is the fact that our realm of moral responsibility extends beyond our sphere of influence, so that in his eyes not only bystanders but also subsequent generations share the moral responsibility for the Holocaust.

The problem with Habermas's theoretical position on the issue of postwar West German collective identity derives from the peculiar juxtaposition of social analysis and philosophical ideals that is characteristic of most of his writings, including those of his texts that pertain to the issues of the Historians' Debate.[53] With regard to the moral and historical aspects of West Germany's collective identity, Habermas maintains that above and beyond providing the philosophical groundwork and practical outline for future politics and discursive practices, his writings reflect the essential aspects of the postwar development. Thus, he claims repeatedly that 1945 induced a change of mentality that led to a postnational consensus in West Germany.[54] But many elements of postwar West German history, including the events recalled above with regard to *Alltagsgeschichte,* suggest that the population never underwent a mentality change of significant proportions, let alone reached a consensus about such important matters as what lessons to draw from the Nazi period. Detlev Claussen has expressed this critique of Habermas most bluntly: "Habermas' position is weakened by the fact that he stipulates a post-1945-consensus about the National Socialist past which is completely fictitious. . . . Unfortunately, such a postwar consensus never existed."[55] In an ironic turn of events, it seems that in particular the social movements Habermas entrusts with the further development of postconventional identities and practices combine a radical democratic agenda with thoroughly conventional ways of imagining the past and passing moral judgment, as the example of *Alltagsgeschichte* indicates.

In sum, Lübbe and Habermas offer three choices: either historical identity without ethics, moral identity without history, or formal principles of communicative action as far removed as possible from both history and ethics, at least in the traditional sense. Thus, both systematically exclude from consideration the *mixtum compositum* of historical and moral identity that in practice has thus far provided the best results in the history of *Vergangenheitsbewältigung* in West Germany. Whenever larger numbers of West Germans have been motivated to confront the Nazi legacy, the reference point or catalyst has provided them with a strong moral appeal in combination with an image of the National Socialism they accepted, for one reason or another, as an authentic rendition of "their" history. Media events like *The Diary of Anne Frank, Heimat, Holocaust,* and to a lesser extent *Schindler's List,* as well as grassroots movements like the history workshops of the 1970s, offered the audience or participants a tangible sense of historical and moral identity on their own terms. Thus, in hindsight it has become obvious that the philosophers either underestimated the population's willingness to contemplate historical responsibility with regard to actions for which they bear no responsibility (Lübbe), or overestimated the population's capacity and willingness to break radically with traditional forms of moral and historical orientation (Habermas). In either case, they underestimated the particular emotional appeal, entertainment value, didactic-philosophical pleasure, and moral historical education perpetrators and bystanders and the descendants of perpetrators and bystanders could derive from standardized historical narratives that interlace historical and ethical elements in very conventional ways.[56] The TV series *Holocaust,* for instance, provided such moral education through the unihibited use of the genre of the soap opera for the representation of the destruction of the Jews of Europe. *Heimat,* more pleasurable than disturbing to the German audience, gave "images, history, stories, and symbolic contour to a word and concept that only exists in German."[57] Both television shows successfully appealed to viewers' sense of justice, veracity, and historical identity.

In contradistinction to the philosophers' viewpoint, the perspective of *Alltagsgeschichte* developed above suggests that the development of West Germans' historical identities might be sketched as follows: Due to the overwhelming difficulties with traditional forms of national identity after Nazism, its crimes and collapse, after the permanent loss of formerly German territories in Eastern Europe, the division of Germany, and the Americanization of West German culture, many West Germans neither surrendered to a historical vacuum nor found emotional refuge in a form of constitutional patriotism; rather, over the course of three decades, they rekindled traditionally stable and satisfying local and regional historical identities. From this "safe" ground, artificially removed from the turmoil of high politics, they even addressed the problem of the Nazi past. However, while the philosophers' discourse did not reflect the actual postwar development, it was a very important reference point for West German historians. In particular, the work of the social historians who joined in the critique of Nolte et al. during the Historians' Debate represents the historiographical pendant to Habermas's philosophical perspective on modern German history.

The Historiographical Dimension

Although the participants in the *Historikerstreit* were to a great extent politically motivated, the issues under discussion reflect the themes and topics that had been at the center of the West German historiographical efforts to understand and explain the Nazi past throughout the postwar period. This applies in particular to the historiographical issues raised since the 1960s when the methods, concepts, and interpretive frameworks for the study of Nazism multiplied. In this respect, the historians involved in the *Historikerstreit* focused on the historiographical past and did not aspire to shape the historiographical future. On the basis of the discussion of the Holocaust in German history, its comparability with other genocides, and its implications for West Germany's collective identity, the participants reconsidered the theoretical, conceptual, and methodological differences that had occupied them throughout their professional careers. Since all the participants were very familiar with the applicable background, they never spelled out all the implications of their arguments. Therefore, it is necessary to consider the historiographical context and prehistory of the Historians' Debate in order to recognize in which specific way the debate represents the unproductive closure to a very productive phase in the history of the German historical profession.

Six historiographical issues were touched upon in the Historians' Debate, and also concerned West German historians in the decades before the debate: the discussions about the concepts of totalitarianism versus fascism; the methodological disputes between social historians and neohistoricists, and more precisely the clashes between intentionalists and functionalists; the debate about the notion of Germany's special path to modernity; the historiographical debates about *Alltagsgeschichte*; the issue of the exceptionality of the Holocaust; and the so-called Fischer Debate. For our purposes, the Fischer Debate, which occupied the West German historical establishment from 1960 through 1965, was the most important precursor to the Historians' Debate. The topics of the two debates are unrelated, but in both cases we are dealing with historiographical discussions that spilled over into the print media, involved the entire West German intellectual elite, and had important political ramifications. In addition, the intensity and tone of the debates, especially the ad hominem attacks, as well as the age groups of the scholars and intellectuals involved, indicate that they marked a generational shift in West German historiography and intellectual life. Unlike any other historiographical disputes in the history of the Federal Republic, the Fischer Debate and the *Historiker-*

streit destabilized a hitherto unproblematic consensus, thus opening the field to new methods and interpretive frameworks crafted according to the interests and intellectual needs of new generations of scholars.

In the early 1960s the Hamburg historian Fritz Fischer and some of his students challenged the widespread opinion that all European powers were equally responsible for the outbreak of World War I. Prior to Fischer's intervention, the historians agreed that an exhaustive study of the archival record had proven that none of the European governments was particularly interested in starting an all-out military campaign in 1914. The specific circumstances immediately before the outbreak of the war—diplomatic mishaps, treaty obligations, the intricacies of mobilizing large modern armies and the like—constituted the only salient reason the governments suddenly found themselves entangled in warfare almost against their will. Applying standard historiographical methods to new as well as already known archival material, Fischer revealed the particularly excessive war aims of the German government and argued that the German side was primarily responsible for the outbreak of World War I. More specifically, Fischer exposed the parallels between the German war aims in World War I and World War II, thus proposing a continuity in German politics that was particularly disturbing to a generation of scholars who still identified with (and had grown up during) the Kaiserreich and who had mostly dealt with Nazism by bracketing it away from its specifically German historical context.[58]

The Fischer Debate certainly changed the perception of German involvement in World War I, although Fischer could not establish a new orthodoxy as some of his students have claimed.[59] More importantly, however, the debate prepared the ground for the historiographical innovations of the 1960s because some of the older scholars, most notably Gerhard Ritter, thoroughly undermined their own authority through their overly emotional and aggressive criticism. Also, while Fischer used conventional methods, he introduced a different, less literary, more "objective" style of writing, which had more in common with the "scientific" style of the emerging social historians than with the style of Fischer's contemporaries and predecessors. Finally, by introducing the question of continuity within twentieth-century German history, at least up to 1945, Fischer captured the underlying motif of the younger historians, especially the social historians, who were then writing their dissertations and *Habilitationen* and who were studying the nineteenth and twentieth centuries in order to understand the origins of Nazism and Germany's special path to modernity.

The comparison between the Fischer Debate and the Historians' Debate clarifies the specificity of the *Historikerstreit* and highlights the generational dynamics at the core of the evolution of the representation of National Socialism in West German historiography. This evolution proceeded in three steps. From the immediate postwar period through the 1950s German historians and intellectuals tended to "export" Nazism by projecting its origins onto forces and historical events external to German history, such as fate, diabolic elements, or the French Revolution.[60] Even the first systematic studies of the Nazi regime—presented by political scientists and not historians—applied a theoretical framework that linked Nazism to the contemporary Soviet system rather than the German past.[61] Thus, most of German history, with the possible exception of the last years of the Weimar Republic, remained available for positive identification and, as the Fischer Debate revealed, was also used for these purposes. This construction was destabilized by Fischer and his disciples and irreversibly overturned by the next generation of scholars, especially the social historians, who constructed a negative continuity embracing Nazism and most of modern German history. Building upon explanatory strategies developed during the war and in the immediate postwar period outside of Germany, social historians and social scientists argued in the 1960s that the rise of Nazism was linked to a basic discrepancy between rapid technological and industrial modernization on the one hand and delayed social, political, and cultural modernization on the other. The social historians considered this a detrimental combination that made Germany a special case within the context of the modernization of the Western countries since the nineteenth century. In addition, in contrast to the historians of the 1950s, the second generation perused other national pasts, especially the Anglo-American tradition, for methodological and political traditions worth identifying with. In short, if the first postwar generation of German historians spent some effort on bracketing Nazism, the next generation turned this implicit notion of an almost mythic historical exceptionality into an explicit research agenda trying to grasp the concrete specificity of Germany's path to modernity as well as the particular aspects of Hitler's government and the Nazi society.[62]

Unlike their predecessors, the second generation also advanced research on the Holocaust, although only a few members of this generation made it their primary research focus. Nevertheless, the notion of the Holocaust as a singular historical event served an important purpose in the community of historians, which had rapidly turned into an intellectually and methodologically diverse and competitive field since the 1960s; the exceptionality of the Holocaust became a concept that tied together West German scholars of various political and methodological creeds. As Otto Dov Kulka put it: "One of the most remarkable developments in German historiography during the 1960s and '70s appears to have been the gradually reached, overwhelming consensus on the central role of anti-Semitism in National Socialist ideology and politics. It was identified as the only constant element and as such, a key to the understanding of the inner contradictions of the Third Reich, Hitler's unconventional war aims, and the singularity of the Holocaust."[63]

The next turning point occurred in the 1980s and took several years to reach its conclusion in the Historians' Debate. There might have been widespread agreement among German scholars during the 1970s about the historical exceptionality of Nazism and its prehistory, especially with regard to the Holocaust, but starting in the early 1980s the second generation of West German historians, with help from historians from abroad, undermined step by step the various notions of exceptionality that had informed their work on modern German history. Thus, the *Historikerstreit* was merely the last in a line of similar debates that relativized and ultimately discarded the interpretive framework of historical singularity. This dismantling process took place against the backdrop of the above-described historiographical and popular interest in *Alltagsgeschichte*, which, due to its emphasis on the "normal," everyday aspects of life during the Third Reich, presented a massive challenge to all historiographical notions of exceptionality, and which was for this reason harshly criticized by many professional historians. In the scholarly realm, the process included the fundamental critique of the theory of Germany's special path to modernity. The critique was advanced by young, Left-oriented scholars from Britain and conservative historians in West Germany, who pointed out that the theory was based on problematic assumptions about a "normal" path to modernity that did not fit the actual development in any Western country, including Britain.[64] At the same time, in the early 1980s, West German historians discussed the structuralist interpretation of the origins of the "Final Solution," which challenged the assumption that the Nazi leadership had followed a long-term plan in their anti-Jewish policies. In their writings on the origins of the Holocaust the structural historians challenged the idea that Hitler's exceptional ideological commitments and his exceptional position within the power structure of the Third Reich were the decisive causes of the "Final Solution." Instead, they argued that many "normal" bureaucrats, party functionaries, and even members of the German army and the police force played a decisive role in the design and implementation of the "Final Solution."[65] Thus, at least implicitly, the social historians had already challenged the limits of the concept of the Holocaust's singularity before it was contested during the Historians' Debate. This development indicates that during the 1980s notions like the singularity of the Holocaust or assumptions concerning Germany's special path to modernity lost their function as shared interpretive guidelines and common political signposts after they had been explicitly defined and subsequently challenged.[66]

Unlike prior debates in the early 1980s that addressed similar conceptual issues, the Historians' Debate, due to the relative age of participants and audience and to its historiographical and political context, represents a generational and intellectual divide just as the Fischer Debate did almost three decades earlier. In the historical profession, the Fischer Debate marked the end of the Adenauer era and the onset of the Social Democratic reform process, while the Historians' Debate, somewhat belatedly, attested to the end of that reform era and the onset of the neoconservative offensive in West Germany's intellectual and political life. In both cases, the future generations of scholars were themselves only marginally involved in the discussions. In addition, both debates paved the way to new lines of continuity in modern German history. The Fischer Debate broke the continuity barrier of "1933"— that is, after the Fischer debate Nazism could be conceived as a decidedly German historical event with a long prehistory within the German past. The *Historikerstreit* discarded the continuity barrier of "1945," which had been respected by the first and second generations of West German historians who in one way or another believed that German history had been radically altered after the war. Today, for the first time since 1945, the third generation of scholars within the German historiographical establishment are probing into the elements that link the Kaiserreich, the Weimar Republic, the Third Reich, and the Federal Republic. And, also for the first time, in some cases this probing is undertaken with the explicit aim of uncovering positive elements of continuity that encompass Nazism and are worth identifying with.[67]

This short survey of the debates and developments in the West German historical profession since the 1960s attests to the impressive innovative zeal and methodological diversity of the discipline. However, at the same time the historians developed and debated the new concept of social history, West Germany's historical culture as a whole also underwent a massive transformation. The student movement in the mid-1960s added a critical and very distinct voice to the discussions about the meaning of the Nazi past, a voice that by way of different metamorphoses and dead ends gave rise to the intellectual side of *Alltagsgeschichte*. In addition, the mass medium of television, which in West Germany only reached a mass audience beginning in the early

1960s, added a completely new dimension to the business of representing history. As a result, the historians' contribution to West Germany's historical culture took on a more marginal role despite the exceptional productivity of the discipline. This became particularly apparent during the Historians' Debate, when the historians tried to reach out to a larger public but had little resonance outside their established audience in academia and the highbrow national print media.

The Generational Dimension

Some of the participants in and commentators on the Historians' Debate have already pointed out that the great majority of the players in the debate belong to the age cohort born between 1920 and 1931 (for example: Ernst Nolte, 1923; Andreas Hillgruber, 1925; Joachim Fest, 1926; Jürgen Habermas, 1929; Eberhard Jäckel, 1929; Hans and Wolfgang Mommsen, 1930; Imanuel Geiss, 1931; and Hans-Ulrich Wehler, 1931).[68] These intellectuals are part of the Hitler-Youth Generation, which has been defined as encompassing "the age groups which were born during the Weimar Republic (1918–33) and raised and educated during the twelve years of the Nazi regime."[69] As mentioned earlier, members of this generation rose to power in the Federal Republic in the late 1960s and represented the West German political, economic, and cultural-intellectual elite through the late 1980s. This age cohort has been closely studied by West German sociologists and historians because its members have developed distinct characteristics, which were already manifest in the first postwar surveys. Many factors indicate that we are dealing with a picture-perfect case study of what the sociologist Karl Mannheim termed in 1926 a political generation: an age group whose members shared a number of historical experiences in their youth that shaped their emotional and political horizon of expectation for the rest of their lives.[70] In the case at hand these experiences include living through Nazism, World War II, and the subsequent years of deprivation—experiences shared with other age groups—but also two experiences unique to this political generation: having grown up and been educated during National Socialism within institutions either appropriated or founded by the Nazis, and having willingly or unwillingly served a criminal regime at a young age without, therefore, being primarily responsible for the rise of Nazism and the crimes committed under the auspices of the German state. With reference to its common educational background, this generation has been called the Hitler-Youth Generation. Its peculiar relationship to the complex of guilt and responsibility for the Nazi crimes, especially among its younger members, has been captured in the infamous phrase of the

"Gnade der späten Geburt"—that is, the mercy or privilege of late birth.[71]

The age limits set for this political generation vary slightly from study to study, with a maximum spread of birthdates ranging from 1918 to 1933. Sociologists have pointed out that the Hitler-Youth Generation comprises various subgroups whose experiences differ markedly from each other: for instance, the experiences of a young soldier versus those of a Hitler-Youth member. Also, and more importantly, the model focuses on the experiences of the male members of the generation and would have to be substantially revised in order to account for the experiences of women as well. Nevertheless, it provides an excellent point of departure, especially when dealing with a still almost exclusively male profession like the German academic elite. For our purposes, it is not important to linger on the general characteristics ascribed to this generation, which, based on Helmut Schelsky's 1957 study, has been repeatedly described as disillusioned with politics, focused on family and career, motivated by an extraordinary need for financial and emotional security, and equipped with an astute sense of realism.[72] The historians under consideration, representing only a tiny fraction of their generation and working within a small profession, do not necessarily fit this image. As a prod to further inquiry, I want to focus on the peculiar situation of the historians of this generation perched uneasily, as the *Historikerstreit* revealed, between history and memory.

In 1926 Mannheim described in theoretical terms the case of a political generation whose "natural worldview"—acquired during youth, and the yardstick against which all subsequent experiences are measured—is radically challenged by a sudden and substantial reversal of the political and social environment. He concluded that "the first impressions remain alive and predominant even if the subsequent life is spent negating and working through the 'natural worldview' acquired during youth."[73] Therefore, it is not surprising that members of the Hitler-Youth Generation, and especially historians, return to the memories of their youth and even reidentify, albeit momentarily, with the moral and political perspectives taken on during adolescence. Unlike the case of Stürmer, who was born in 1938 and does not belong to the Hitler-Youth Generation, Hillgruber's and Nolte's disturbing utterances in the prelude to the *Historikerstreit* are not so much part of a political program as markers of the surfacing of bits and pieces of troubled memory. While after the war most Germans came to recognize the unprecedented criminality and gigantic self-destruction they had taken part in, from the perspective of many participants at the time, and especially the committed youth, the attempts to defend German territory and the German population in the face of overwhelming odds in 1944–45 amounted to the ultimate test of their patriotism, if not their commitment to the Führer. A reflection of that devotion appears in Hillgruber's need to identify with the Eastern troops and Nolte's anticommunism and anti-Semitism.

For the historians of the Hitler-Youth Generation, the task of objectifying the Nazi past within the parameters of the discipline on the one hand, and the interest of keeping in touch with personal memories of the period that often did not mesh with the objectified image on the other, created a conflict that was acted out during the Historians' Debate. The historians gave public testimony to their generation's troublesome position between history and memory, a position exacerbated for the intellectuals among them, who for professional reasons had spent decades producing objectifications of the past that systematically delegitimized some of their own memories. While only a few of the intellectuals acted out their memories and put them into print, the harshness of the critics' response and the overall aggressive tone and ad hominem attacks launched during the *Historikerstreit* attest to the violence involved in a lifelong struggle with one's "natural worldview." From this perspective, in addition to the political, philosophical, and historiographical issues described above, the *Historikerstreit* also addressed the question of the legitimacy and illegitimacy of the pleasure of subjective reidentification after a total reversal of the official, collective system of values. This issue, which I would identify as a central motive of the debate, is meaningless for subsequent generations and explains why the issues of the *Historikerstreit* quickly became outdated. The texts of the Historians' Debate became "sites of memory" only for a well-defined subgroup, the West German historians and similarly oriented intellectuals of the Hitler-Youth Generation.[74]

While the very fact that some members of the Hitler-Youth Generation felt compelled to return to their origins, even in a public setting, should not come as a surprise, the timing of this return creates somewhat of a riddle: why in the late 1980s? First, the late 1980s offered the Hitler-Youth Generation its last chance to influence what Jan Assmann has called the transition from communicative to cultural memory. For Assmann, communicative memory represents the part of a society's historical culture "based exclusively on everyday communications"; it is highly group specific, and operates within a temporal horizon of not more than one hundred years. The term cultural memory, on the other hand, designates the areas within a given historical culture that provide objectified representations of the past: texts, images, buildings, monuments, rituals, and so on that represent "the culturally institutionalized heritage of a society."[75] By the time of this writing, at the end of 1995, almost all of the historians of the Hitler-Youth Generation have retired, and have thus lost the opportunity to shape the cultural memory of Nazism *ex cathedra*, with the authoritative voice of a full professor, and from the very particular communicative memory of their generation.

In addition, the timing of the debate, especially the late surfacing of the historians' more personal recollections, was determined by a factor Lutz Niethammer has expressed very succinctly with regard to the victims of genocidal policies, but which I would argue also holds true (if in a less traumatic sense) for the members of the Hitler-Youth Generation. Only after West Germany's historical culture had provided an interpretive structure for the understanding of Nazism—a structure composed primarily of mass media representations but also including historical research that provided both a protective layer between the individual and his/her troublesome memories and a challenge to the authenticity of these memories—did the individuals feel compelled to express their memories in order to amend or contradict the media images they found themselves confronted with.[76] In the German case, the renewed interest in history, the wave of everyday history, the programs on West German television on the topic of Nazism, and the historians' own prior work created such a framework beginning in the late 1970s. Against this backdrop the historians of the Hitler-Youth Generation expressed memories they had held in check for decades. Now they felt challenged to tell the younger generations, who had researched everyday life in the Third Reich and who put such emphasis on the subjective angle in their pursuit of *Alltagsgeschichte*, what it had really felt like growing up during Nazism.

Without obliterating them, the generational factor cuts across the institutional and discursive boundaries of a given historical culture, as shown by the parallels between the Jenninger affair and the Historians' Debate. The Hitler-Youth Generation as a whole, and not just the historians among its members, sought explanations for the historical riddle of the rise and nature of Nazism. Through this shared focal point the generation differs markedly from the political generation preceding it. The generation of Germans who had been adults during the Third Reich showed little inclination after the war to come to terms with the specificity of the Nazi era. But the Hitler-Youth Generation also differs from its successors, the first postwar generation, whose members are much more concerned with the question how Nazism fits within the overall history of modern Germany and how Nazi society is related to their own social context. To this end they have pursued everyday history, and the historians among them are currently investigating in which ways Nazism represents a typically modern phenomenon. In this process, the parameters the intellectuals of the Hitler-Youth Generation introduced for the study of Nazism have been quickly displaced. Nevertheless, the Hitler-Youth Generation, and especially its historians, will most likely remain the age cohort—situated between the generation of the Nazi perpetrators and by-standers and the postwar generations—that has provided the most substantial and committed, if idiosyncratic, contribution to the task of *Vergangenheitsbewältigung.*

Historians and Historical Culture

The contribution of the academics of the Hitler-Youth Generation to the historical culture of the Federal Republic was informed by the motive of defining a solid ground for the postwar democracy as far as possible removed from the Nazi past; politically, by excluding extremists of any kind from their own ranks and conducting their discussions within the parameters of the political mainstream; philosophically, by delineating concepts of collective identity removed from conventional types of identity thought to be involved in the catastrophe of National Socialism; and historiographically, by corroborating the decisive turning point of 1945 and by quarantining the events of the "Final Solution" through the double-edged concept of historical singularity. The consensus fell apart when some members of the profession became more actively involved in the conservative cultural offensive of the 1980s, when important developments in other sectors of the historical culture undermined key notions of this consensus, and when the historians, at the end of their careers, found themselves caught between the conflicting interests of providing objective accounts of Nazism and of relating their more personal memories of the era to the public. These factors combined brought about the Historians' Debate in 1986.

During that debate the historians very successfully mobilized their traditional constituency, the "educated public" represented by other academics and the producers and consumers of the national print media. This audience was attuned to the specificities of the historiographical perspective on Nazism and to the conflict between memories and historiography played out in the debate. But the historians could not make significant inroads into other areas of West Germany's historical culture that were not compatible with the parameters of the historians' discourse, as for instance television. The abstract concepts and the elaborate historiographical models, especially those developed by the social historians, are unsuitable for visual representation and could not be brought to the screen in an interesting fashion. In addition, the hierarchical and paternalistic structure of West Germany's academic establishment, which normally works to the advantage of the professoriate, in this case contributed to its relative isolation. In the late 1980s the universities were the only significant sector of West Germany's historical culture still clearly dominated by representatives of the Hitler-Youth Generation. In all other sectors, with the possible exception of the political sphere, the image of Nazism was already shaped by the first postwar generation. These younger intellectuals had brought *Alltagsgeschichte* to the screen and into the museums and had little inclination to return to the issues addressed during the Historians' Debate. The importance of the generational divide next to the institutional/mediatic divides is exemplified by the fact that even the younger professional historians who had initiated the study of the history of everyday life contributed very little to the Historians' Debate.[77]

The limited impact of the Historians' Debate within West Germany's historical culture reveals another factor that might have contributed to the viciousness of the debate. Having spent their careers designing representations of Nazism geared toward what they perceived as the political needs of the postwar democracy, the historians of the Hitler-Youth Generation might have realized in the 1980s that they had been beaten to the task by a medium that hardly existed when they received their professional training in the 1950s and early 1960s. As the above excursion into *Alltagsgeschichte* exemplifies, at least since the late 1970s television and other visually based media had become culturally and politically the most relevant sectors of West Germany's historical culture: "[T]he mass media have become the most effective (and least acknowledged) institutional vehicles for shaping historical consciousness."[78]

After the *Historikerstreit* the historians had little time to contemplate the limited influence of their trade within the larger historical culture. Like the development of the electronic media, albeit more swiftly, German unification once again radically changed the social and political context of their profession. This time around the conservative historians found themselves in a better position. Once again considerably overestimating the potentials of their profession, they quickly attacked the social historians for having been unable to foresee the historic events of 1989–90. In response to the events and/or the critique, the social historians have indeed considerably revised their position. They have taken their distance from the *Sonderweg* paradigm and the notion of a postnational identity, and have tried "to recapture nationalism for the political left."[79] Thus, some of the central ideas that were still vigorously and successfully defended during the

Historians' Debate have now, only a few years later, become obsolete. The latest reshuffling of Germany's historical culture within the rediscovered parameters of national history will certainly influence future interpretations of Nazism. Perhaps, in a few years, the only aspects vaguely reminiscent of some of the key interpretive tools of West Germany's historiography, like the Sonderweg theory and the exceptionality of the Holocaust, might be an astute awareness of the specificity of Germany's postwar history between 1945 and 1989.

The different fields of knowledge and modes of representation we have brought to bear upon each other to contextualize and explain the event of the Historians' Debate have in recent years often been explored through the concept of memory. Terms like social memory, collective memory, vernacular memory, countermemory, public memory, and so forth have been applied in different ways to explore socially constructed and socially transmitted representations of the past. Besides their dizzying multiplicity and at times contradictory implications, these terms also suffer somewhat diminished use-value in that they, at least implicitly, stay within the conceptual framework of the classic studies in the field that define history and memory as mutually exclusive ways of learning about and representing the past. From Nietzsche and Maurice Halbwachs to, more recently, Pierre Nora, Yosef Yerushalmi, and Jacques LeGoff, all the classical theorists of memory have differentiated between objective, timeless, academic representations of the past and "living," collective memories sustained by social groups for the purpose of historical identity formation.[80] Even if scholars have more recently emphasized the intertextuality between different kinds of social memory, they have rarely studied historians and their work in the same terms.[81] Thus the traditional dichotomy between history and memory has been reconfirmed, often inadvertently. This interpretive bias inherent in the term collective memory is clearly at odds with the preceding case study on the Historians' Debate, which illustrates that the historical profession represents a very context-specific, timebound, and socially determined approach to the study and representation of the past. In addition, there exists another reason to prefer a more technical term, like historical culture, over the term memory. Even the more sophisticated revisions of the classical dichotomy between history and memory, like Assmann's model, are not very helpful when analyzing the interdependencies among different representations of the past in today's media societies. The differentiation between communicative and cultural memory, for example, does not apply to the often neglected medium of television, which is produced centrally by cultural elites closely attuned to the parameter of the "official" cultural memory but at the same time consumed locally and thus closely linked to numerous communicative memories. This example indicates that it is more important to pay close attention to the social, institutional, and discursive base of a given "way of doing history," and to study its internal proceedings and external linkages, its modes of storage and distribution, than to try to figure out where to locate it within the continuum between history and memory.

Rhetorical Recycling

In December 1995 Ignaz Bubis, the executive director of the Association of German Jews, revealed that he himself had used large parts of Jenninger's speech on two occasions in 1989. Bubis said that after twenty years in the public arena, and after having delivered numerous memorial speeches, he had been pressed for new ideas and found many of Jenninger's remarks to the point and thought-provoking.[82] This recycling of Jenninger's speech by the highest political representative of Germany's Jews is neither scandalous nor inconsistent. In 1988 many West German Jews had come out in favor of Jenninger, arguing that finally a German politician had emphasized the real problem with Nazism: Hitler's popularity with the German people. In addition, as mentioned, many critics pointed out that Jenninger's failure was more a question of performance than content. Nevertheless, Bubis's revelations are remarkable for other reasons. Although Bubis's public appearances are regularly and carefully followed by journalists and politicians' aides, nobody noticed in 1989 what must have been obvious parallels between Bubis's and Jenninger's discourse. This fact completely disappeared in the context of the historic event of the fall of the Berlin Wall. Thus, only a year after Jenninger's resignation and the end of the Historians' Debate, Bubis's—or better, Jenninger's—speech no longer represented a noticeable transgression of the rules of West Germany's rapidly changing historical culture. It is only consistent, therefore, that six years later, in 1995, Bubis's revelations were hardly noticed by the media.

In the course of a decade, the parameters for any acceptable representation of Nazism and the "Final Solution" in Germany's historical culture have changed to the point that Jenninger's performance, if repeated today, would probably no longer result in his resignation. However, having sketched out West Germany's historical culture at the time of the Historians' Debate, we see more clearly how Jenninger failed in 1988. He combined state-of-the-art conceptual models of *Alltagsgeschichte* with a personal interest in rectifying the negative image of the German population's performance during Nazism. Once introduced into the political realm of high politics this combination formed a volatile mixture because it undermined the founding myth of the West German democracy, which had been preserved in parliament for over three decades. Inadvertently, Jenninger called into question the belief that the Federal Republic originated from an anti-Nazi consensus.

Notes

I gratefully acknowledge the support of the Monkarsh Fellowship Fund at UCLA as well as the Institut für Europäische Geschichte in Mainz, Germany; both have facilitated research and writing of this essay. Also, for their helpful comments on earlier drafts of this essay I would like to thank Peter Baldwin, Sande Cohen, Elisabeth Domansky, Beatrice Dumin-Kansteiner, Saul Friedlander, Claudio Fogu, Joe Golsan, Friedrich Jäger, Kerwin Klein, David Myers, Hans Rogger, Martin Vogt, and Richard Wolin.

1. On the Jenninger affair see Armin Laschet and Heinz Malangré, eds., *Phillip Jenninger: Rede und Reaktion* (Aachen: Einhard, 1989) and most recently Peter Reichel, *Politik mit der Erinnerung: Gedächnisorte im Streit um die nationalsozialistische Vergangenheit* (Munich: Hanser, 1995), 313–20. The best interpretation of the Jenninger affair has been provided by Elisabeth Domansky, "'Kristallnacht,' the Holocaust and German Unity: The Meaning of November 9 as an Anniversary in Germany," *History and Memory* 4 (1992): 60–94; see also Domansky, "Die gespaltene Erinnerung," in *Kunst und Literatur nach Auschwitz*, ed. Manuel Köppen (Berlin: Erich Schmidt, 1993).

2. Weizsäcker's speech and the favorable reactions have been documented in Ulrich Gill and Winfried Steffani, eds., *Eine Rede und ihre Wirkung: Die Rede des Bundespräsidenten Richard von Weizsäcker vom 8. Mai 1985* (Berlin: Rainer Röll, 1986); a more critical interpretation of the speech has been most recently developed by Peter Reichel, in *Politik*, 295–96.

3. See Lutz Niethammer, "Jenninger: Vorzeitiges Exposé zur Erforschung eines ungewöhnlich schnellen Rücktritts," *Babylon* 5 (1989): 40–46.

4. Niethammer, "Jenninger," 44.

5. Domansky, "Kristallnacht," 79.

6. On Jenninger's poor performance see the entertaining critique by Klaus Theweleit, "Kann es denn Zeitungen geben 'nach Auschwitz'?," *Taz hoch* 10: Zehn Jahre Pressefreiheit (special tenth anniversary edition of the Left daily *Die Tageszeitung,* 1989), 16–23, 17; and Katherina Oehler, "Glanz und Elend der öffentlichen Erinnerung: Die Rhetorik des Historischen in Richard von Weizsäcker's Rede zum 8. Mai und Philipp Jenningers Rede zum 9. November," *Jahrbuch für Geschichtsdidaktik* 3 (1991–92): 121–35.

7. On the definition of the Hitler-Youth Generation see the section of this chapter on "The Generational Dimension." For an interpretation of Jenninger's speech as symptomatic of the return of the repressed in West Germany's political culture see Hans-Jürgen Wirth, "Der Fall Jenninger und unsere Schwierigkeiten mit der deutschen Vergangenheit," *Psychosozial* 11 (1988–89): 55–61.

8. Martin Broszat, "A Plea for the Historicization of National Socialism," in Bald-

win, *Reworking the Past*, 77–87; see also Saul Friedlander, "Some Reflections on the Historicization of National Socialism," in Baldwin, *Reworking the Past*, 88–101; and Broszat and Friedlander, "A Controversy about the Historicization of National Socialism," in Baldwin, *Reworking the Past*, 102–34.

9. The best introductions and analyses of the Historians' Debate in English have been supplied by Charles Maier, *The Unmasterable Past: History, Holocaust, and German National Identity* (Cambridge: Harvard University Press, 1988); Richard Evans, *In Hitler's Shadow: West German Historians and the Attempt to Escape from the Nazi Past* (New York: Pantheon, 1989); Geoff Eley, "Nazism, Politics, and the Image of the Past: Thoughts on the West German *Historikerstreit* 1986–1987," *Past and Present* 121 (1988): 171–208; Peter Baldwin, "The *Historikerstreit* in Context," in *Reworking the Past*, 3–37; Ian Kershaw, "Living with the Nazi Past: The 'Historikerstreit' and After," in *The Nazi Dictatorship: Problems and Perspectives of Interpretation*, 2d ed. (London: Edward Arnold, 1989), 168–91; and Saul Friedlander, "'A past that refuses to go away': On Recent Historiographical Debates in the Federal Republic of Germany about National Socialism and the Final Solution," *Zeitschrift für Religions-und Geistesgeschichte* 39, no. 2 (1987): 97–110. See also Konrad Jarausch, "Removing the Nazi Stain? The Quarrel of the German Historians," *German Studies Review* 11 (1988): 285–301; John Torpey, "Habermas and the Historians," *New German Critique* 44 (1988): 5–24; Stephen Brockmann, "The Politics of German History," *History and Theory* 29 (1990): 179–89; Beatrice Heuser, "Museums, Identity and Warring Historians: Observations on History in Germany," *The Historical Journal* 33 (1990): 417–40; and Martin Travers, "History Writing and the Politics of Historiography: The German *Historikerstreit*," *The Australian Journal of Politics and History* 37 (1991), 246–61. Unfortunately, the most recent English-language publication on the Historians' Debate provides an unsystematic, highly impressionistic, and at times even altogether inaccurate analysis of the debate and its historiographical context (Alfred Low, *The Third Reich and the Holocaust in German Historiography: Toward the* Historikerstreit *of the Mid-1980s* [Boulder CO: East European Monographs, 1994]).

10. The concept of historical culture, Geschichtskultur, has been developed by Jörn Rüsen. It avoids some of the interpretive bias of the term collective memory, which is conventionally used in the study of socially constructed representations of the past. See Rüsen, "Geschichtskultur als Forschungsproblem," *Jahrbuch für Geschichtsdidaktik* 3 (1991–92): 39–50; and especially Rüsen, "Was ist Geschichtskultur? Überlegungen zu einer neuen Art, über Geschichte nachzudenken," in *Historische Faszination: Geschichtskultur heute*, ed. Klaus Füamann, Heinrich Theodor Grütter, and Jörn Rüsen (Cologne: Böhlau, 1994), 3–26; see also Sand Cohen, *Historical Culture: On the Recoding of an Academic Discipline* (Berkeley: University of California Press, 1986). The choice of terminology is discussed further in a later section of this paper.

11. The most complete bibliography of the Historians' Debate has been compiled by Helmut Donat, Diether Koch, and Martin Rohkrämer, "Bibliographie zum Historikerstreit," in *"Auschwitz erst möglich gemacht?": Überlegungen zur jüngsten konservativen Geschichtsbewältigung*, ed. Helmut Donat and Lothar Wieland (Bremen: Donat, 1991), 150–214.

12. The core texts by the main protagonists have been assembled in *Historikerstreit: Die Dokumentation der Kontroverse um die Einzigartigkeit der nationalsozialistischen Judenvernichtung* (Munich: Piper, 1987), which was translated by James Knowlton and Truett Cates as *Forever in the Shadow of Hitler?* See also the following monographs and essay collections, organized according to the authors' political orientation. For the liberal camp see, for example, Dan Diner, ed., *Ist der Nationalsozialismus Geschichte? Zu Historikerstreit und Historisierung* (Frankfurt am Main: Fischer, 1987); Donat and Wieland, *"Auschwitz"*; Gernot Erler et al., *Geschichtswende? Entsorgungsversuche zur deutschen Geschichte* (Freiburg: Dreisam, 1987); Wieland Eschenhagen, ed., *Die neue deutsche Ideologie* (Darmstadt: Luchterhand, 1988); Hilmar Hoffmann, ed., *Gegen den Versuch, Vergangenheit zu verbiegen* (Frankfurt am Main: Athenäum, 1987); Hans Mommsen, *Auf der Suche nach historischer Normalität: Beiträge zum Geschichtsbildstreit in der Bundesrepublik* (Berlin: Argon, 1987); and Hans-Ulrich Wehler, *Entsorgung der deutschen Vergangenheit: Ein polemischer Essay zum Historikerstreit* (Munich: Beck, 1988). For comments from independent left critics, see Heide Gerstenberger and Dorothea Schmidt, eds., *Normalität oder Normalisierung: Geschichtswerkstätten und Faschismusanalyse* (Münster: Westfälisches Dampfboot, 1987); Wolfgang Fritz Haug, *Vom hilflosen Antifaschismus zur Gnade der späten Geburt*, 2d ed. (Hamburg: Argument, 1987); Eike Hennig, *Zum Historikerstreit: Was heißt und zu welchem Ende studiert man Faschismus?* (Frankfurt am Main: Athenäum, 1988); Heinrich Senfft, *Kein Abschied von Hitler: Ein Blick hinter die Fassaden des "Historikerstreits"* (Cologne: Volksblatt, 1990). For reactions from the conservative side see Klaus Hildebrand, ed., *Wem gehört die deutsche Geschichte? Deutschlands Weg vom alten Europa in die Europäische Moderne* (Cologne: Bachem, 1987); and Ernst Nolte, *Das Vergehen der Vergangenheit: Antwort an meine Kritiker im sogenannten Historikerstreit* (Berlin: Ullstein, 1987). In addition, there have been two unsuccessful reconciliation attempts, by Christian Meier, *Vierzig Jahre nach Auschwitz: Deutsche Geschichtserinnerung heute*, 2d ed. (Munich: Beck, 1990); and Imanuel Geiss, *Die Habermas-Kontroverse: Ein deutscher Streit* (Berlin: Siedler, 1988). See also Geiss, *Der Hysterikerstreit: Ein unpolemischer Essay* (Bonn: Bouvier, 1992).

13. Walter H. Pehle, "Vorbemerkungen des Herausgebers," in *Der historische Ort des Nationalsozialismus: Annäherungen*, ed. Pehle (Frankfurt am Main: Fischer, 1990), 7.

14. Hennig, *Zum Historikerstreit*, 35.

15. Not surprisingly, Nolte's *Der Europäische Bürgerkrieg 1917–1945: Nationalsozialismus und Bolschewismus* (Berlin: Propyläen, 1987) drew heavy fire when it came out at the end of 1987, but it did not introduce any new aspects into the debate; see for example the reviews by Hans Mommsen, "Das Ressentiment als Wissenschaft," *Geschichte und Gesellschaft* 14 (1988): 495–512; and Wolfgang Schieder, "Der Nationalsozialismus im Fehlurteil philosophischer Geschichtsschreibung," *Geschichte und Gesellschaft* 15 (1989): 88–114.

16. See for the most overt declaration of victory Wehler, *Entsorgung*, 197–98.

17. A volume on teaching German history represents one of the few productive

initiatives triggered by the dispute: Klaus Oesterle and Siegfried Schiele, eds., *Historikerstreit und politische Bildung* (Stuttgart: Metzler, 1989).

18. On the various recent interpretations of National Socialism as a specifically modern event see Norbert Frei, "Wie modern war der Nationalsozialismus?" *Geschichte und Gesellschaft* 19 (1993): 367–87; Axel Schildt, "NS-Regime, Modernisierung und Moderne: Anmerkungen zur Hochkonjunktur einer andauernden Diskussion," *Tel Aviver Jahrbuch für deutsche Geschichte* 13 (1994): 3–22; and Wulf Kansteiner, "Emplotment and Historicization: Recent German Histories about National Socialism and Modernity," *Storia della Storiografia* 25 (1994): 65–87.

19. That applies in particular to Immanuel Geiss, who was ridiculed by the Left for his assumption of the role of arbiter (most vehemently by Volker Ulrich, "Der Schlichter als Provokateur—Immanuel Geiss und der 'Historikerstreit,'" in Donat and Wieland, *"Auschwitz,"* 140–49) and who was the last to revisit the site of the Historians' Debate in print, in 1993—see Geiss, *Hysterikerstreit* and *Habermas-Kontroverse.*

20. The best critique of Nolte's comparisons and the best exploration of the methodological problems of comparative history raised by the Historians' Debate has been provided by Charles Maier, "A Holocaust Like the Others? Problems of Comparative History," in *Unmasterable Past,* 66–99; see also Herbert Jäger, "Über die Vergleichbarkeit staatlicher Groaverbrechen: Der Historikerstreit aus kriminologischer Sicht," *Merkur* 43, no. 6 (1989): 499–513; Hans-Heinrich Nolte, "Inwieweit sind russisch-sowjetische und deutsche Massenmorde vergleichbar?" in *Von der Verdrängung zur Bagatellisierung: Aspekte des sogenannten Historikerstreits,* ed. Niedersächsische Landeszentrale für politische Bildung (Hannover: Saade, 1988), 49–58; Wehler, *Entsorgung,* 167–74; Hans-Walter Schmuhl, "Der Holocaust—Ein transzendentaler Vernichtungsprozea?," in Donat and Wieland, *"Auschwitz,"* 119–29; Manfred Funke, "Braune und rote Diktaturen—Zwei Seiten einer Medaille? Historikerstreit und Totalitarismustheorie," in *Streitfall deutsche Geschichte: Geschichts- und Gegenwartsbewuatsein in den 80er Jahren,* ed. Landeszentrale für politische Bildung Nordrhein-Westfalen, (Eessen: Hobbing, 1988), 161–70; and compare to Eckhard Jesse, "Der sogenannte 'Historikerstreit': Ein deutscher Streit," in *Die Last der Deutschen: Kontroversen zur deutschen Identität,* ed. Thomas Gauly (Cologne: Wissenschaft und Politik, 1988), 24–31.

21. For a critique and contextualization of Andreas Hillgruber's *Zweierlei Untergang: Die Zerschlagung des Deutschen Reiches und das Ende des europäischen Judentums* (Berlin: Siedler, 1986), see Wehler, *Entsorgung,* 47–68; Haug, *Antifaschismus,* 239–44; Adelheid von Saldern, "Hillgrubers 'Zweierlei Untergang'—der Untergang historischer Erfahrungsanalyse," in Gerstenberger and Schmidt, *Normalität,* 160–69; and Perry Anderson, "On Emplotment: Two Kinds of Ruin," in *Probing the Limits of Representation: Nazism and the "Final Solution,"* ed. Saul Friedlander (Cambridge: Harvard University Press, 1992).

22. On the Bitburg affair see especially Geoffrey Hartman, ed., *Bitburg in Moral and Political Perspective* (Bloomington: Indiana University Press), 1986; and Hajo Funke, "Bergen-Belsen, Bitburg, Hambach: Bericht über eine negative Katharsis," in Funke, ed., *Von der Gnade der geschenkten Nation* (Berlin: Rotbuch, 1988), 20–34.

23. The interdependence between historical writing and the question of national identity in the Federal Republic has been covered by Bernd Faulenbach: "Der Streit um die Gegenwartsbedeutung der NS-Vergangenheit: Ein Literaturbericht," *Archiv für Sozialgeschichte* 28 (1988): 627–33; and "Identität durch Geschichte? Zur aktuellen Diskussion über die Bedeutung der deutschen Vergangenheit," in Landeszentrale, *Streitfall*, 237–49; see also Meier, *Vierzig Jahre*, 50–76; Hennig, *Zum Historikerstreit*, 108–15; and Wehler, *Entsorgung*, 171–74. Stürmer's position is most clearly developed in two collections of his essays: *Dissonanzen des Fortschritts: Essays über Geschichte und Politik in Deutschland* (Munich: Piper, 1986); and *Deutsche Fragen oder die Suche nach der Staatsräson: Historisch-politische Kolumnen* (Munich: Piper, 1988).

24. On the rennaissance of geopolitical explanatory models see especially Wehler, *Entsorgung*, 174–89.

25. For a summary and evaluation of this aspect of the debate see for instance Wolfram Wette, "Über die Wiederbelebung des Antibolschewismus mit historischen Mitteln Oder: Was steckt hinter der Präventivkriegsthese," in Erler, *Geschichtswende*, 86–115; and Bianka Pietrow, "Deutschland im Juni 1941—ein Opfer sowjetischer Aggression?" *Geschichte und Gesellschaft* 14 (1988): 116–35.

26. A bibliography of the debate about the two museum projects is integrated in the general bibliography of the Historians' Debate: see Donat, Koch, and Rohkrämer, "Bibliographie." The debate is documented in Christoph Stölzl, ed., *Deutsches Historisches Museum: Ideen, Kontroversen, Perspektiven* (Berlin: Propyläen, 1988); and Geschichtswerkstatt Berlin, ed., *Die Nation als Austellungsstück: Planungen, Kritik und Utopien zu den Museumsgründungen in Bonn und Berlin* (Hamburg: VSA, 1987); see now also Reichel, *Politik*, 249–57.

27. For an excellent example of this mentality see Wehler, *Entsorgung*, 189–96.

28. On the transformation of the cultural and political spheres of the Federal Republic, initiated by the student movement of 1968 but institutionalized by the subsequent expansion of the civil service sector, the educational reforms of the 1970s, and extensive state subsidies for freelance cultural and educational projects, see Hermann Glaser, *Die Kulturgeschichte der Bundesrepublik Deutschland III: Zwischen Protest und Anpassung 1968–1989* (Frankfurt am Main: Fischer, 1990), 289–98; Thomas Ellwein, *Krisen und Reform: Die Bundesrepublik seit den sechziger Jahren*, 2d ed. (Munich: dtv, 1993), 109–15, 118–21; Ulf Preuss-Lausitz et al., "Was wir unter Sozialgeschichte verstehen," in *Kriegskinder, Konsumkinder, Krisenkinder: Zur Sozialisationsgeschichte seit dem Zweiten Weltkrieg*, 3d ed. (Weinheim: Belt, 1991), 11–25.

29. To name just four examples: Eberhard Jäckel, Stuttgart, 1967; Hans Mommsen, Bochum, 1968; Wolfgang Mommsen, Düsseldorf, 1968; Hans-Ulrich Wehler, Bielefeld, 1971. See also the statistics provided by Wolfgang Weber, *Priester der Klio: Historisch-sozialwissenschaftliche Studien zur Herkunft und Karriere deutscher Historiker und zur Geschichte der Geschichtswissenschaft 1800–1970* (Frankfurt am Main: Lang, 1984), 536–77.

30. Allegations of political conspiracy abound in the texts of the Historians' Debate; Hillgruber's statement that Habermas's critique "amounts to nothing but the unleashing of a campaign of character assassination" that was quickly imple-

mented by Habermas's "fellow-travelers and disciples" represents one of the most blunt accusations of this kind. Hillgruber, "Jürgen Habermas, Karl-Heinz Janaen, and the Enlightenment in the Year 1986," in Knowlton and Cates, *Forever*, 222–36, 223.

31. For comments from the "independent" Left see for instance Senfft, *Kein Abschied*; Haug, *Antifaschismus*; and Hennig, *Zum Historikerstreit*.

32. Hillgruber, "Habermas," 235.

33. This continuity in the interpretation of Nazism by conservative politicians is very well illustrated in Reichel, *Politik*. For a case study on the persistence of anti-totalitarianism in Germany see most recently Susanne Thoma, *"Vergangenheitsbewältigung" am Beispiel der Auseinandersetzungen um die Neue Wache* (Berlin: Scheibel, 1995).

34. See Nolte, "Between Historical Legend and Revisionism," 8–9; and "The Past that Will Not Pass," 21–22, both in Knowlton and Cates, *Forever*.

35. See for instance Rolf Kosiek, *Historikerstreit und Geschichtsrevision*, 2d ed. (Tübingen: Grabert, 1988), 49–53; and for Nolte's ambivalent relationship to positions espoused by neo-Nazis and revisionists, see Nolte, *Streitpunkte: Heutige und künftige Kontroversen um den Nationalsozialismus* (Berlin: Propyläen, 1993), 304–19.

36. See in particular Uwe Backes, Eckhard Jesse, and Rainer Zitelmann, eds., *Die Schatten der Vergangenheit: Impulse zur Historisierung des Nationalsozialismus* (Berlin: Propyläen, 1990).

37. On Stürmer's motives and background see in particular Volker Berghahn, "Geschichtswissenschaft und Groae Politik," *Aus Politik und Zeitgeschichte* 11 (1987): 25–37; and Hans-Jürgen Puhle, "Die neue Ruhelosigkeit: Michael Stürmers nationalpolitischer Revisionismus," *Geschichte und Gesellschaft* 8 (1987): 382–99.

38. Georg G. Iggers, *Geschichtswissenschaft im 20. Jahrhundert* (Göttingen: Vandenhoek & Ruprecht, 1993), 75.

39. While *Alltagsgeschichte* has been widely discussed as a historiographical paradigm, its history as a social and historical phenomenon remains to be written. For the astonishing impact of *Alltagsgeschichte* see for instance Volker Ullrich, "Entdeckungsreise in den historischen Alltag: Versuch einer Annäherung an die 'neue Geschichtsbewegung,'" *Geschichte in Wissenschaft und Unterricht* 36 (1985): 403–15; Gerhard Paul and Bernhard Schoaig, "Geschichte und Heimat," in *Die andere Geschichte: Geschichte von unten, Spurensicherung, ökologische Geschichte, Geschichtswerkstätten*, ed. Paul and Schoaig (Cologne: Bund, 1986), 15–30; Detlev Peukert, "Das 'Dritte Reich' aus der Alltagsperspektive," *Archiv für Sozialgeschichte* 26 (1986); and especially *Der Spiegel* 23 (1983): 36–42.

40. On the intellectual origins and the development of *Alltagsgeschichte* see especially Gi-Bong Kim, *Der Historismus und die neue Kulturgeschichte: Eine neue Konfiguration des Historismus in der Postmoderne* (Ph.D. diss., University of Bielefeld, 1995); also Geoff Eley, "Labor History, Social History, *Alltagsgeschichte*: Experience, Culture, and the Politics of the Everyday—a New Direction for German Social History?" *Journal of Modern History* 61 (1989): 297–343; and Eley, "Wie denken über Politik? Alltagsgeschichte und die Kategorie des Politischen," in *Alltagskul-*

tur, Subjektivität und Geschichte: Zur Theorie und Praxis von Alltagskultur, ed. Berliner Geschichtswerkstatt (Münster: Westfälisches Dampfboot, 1994), 17–36; Iggers, *Geschichtswissenschaft,* 73–87; Alf Lüdtke, "Einleitung: Was ist und wer treibt Alltagsgeschichte?" in *Alltagsgeschichte: Zur Rekonstruktion historischer Erfahrungen und Lebensweisen,* ed. Lüdtke (Frankfurt am Main: Campus, 1989), 9–47; Hans Medick, "'Missionare im Ruderboot'? Ethnologische Erkenntnisweisen als Herausforderung an die Sozialgeschichte," in Lüdtke, *Alltagsgeschichte,* 48–84; Lutz Niethammer, "Einführung," in *Lebenserfahrung und kollektives Gedächnis: Die Praxis der "Oral History,"* ed. Niethammer (Frankfurt: Suhrkamp, 1985), 7–33; Niethammer, "Fragen—Antworten—Fragen: Methodische Erfahrungen und Erwägungen zur Oral History," in *"Wir kriegen jetzt andere Zeiten": Auf der Suche nach der Erfahrung des Volkes in nachfaschistischen Landern,* ed. Niethammer and Alexander von Plato (Bonn: Dietz, 1985), 392–445; and Winfried Schulze, ed., *Sozialgeschichte, Alltagsgeschichte, Mikro-Historie* (Göttingen: Vandenhoek & Ruprecht, 1994).

41. The most theoretically precise historian of *Alltagsgeschichte* is Alf Lüdtke, whose important contributions have been assembled in Lüdtke, *Eigensinn: Fabrikalltag, Arbeitererfahrungen und Politik vom Kaiserreich bis in den Faschismus* (Hamburg: Ergebnisse, 1993).

42. On the origins, further development, and recent demise of the history workshops in Germany see Alfred Georg Frei, "Geschichtswerkstätten als Zukunftswerkstätten," in Paul and Schoaig, *Die andere Geschichte,* 258–80; and Frei, "Die Geschichtswerkstätten in der Krise," in Berliner Geschichtswerkstatt, *Alltagskultur,* 315–27. For a succinct characterization of the new social movements in West Germany see most recently Andrei Markovits and Philip Gorski, *The German Left: Red, Green and Beyond* (New York: Oxford University Press, 1993), 79–112.

43. Due to the exceedingly long training period for academic personnel in Germany the expansion of the university sytem in the 1960s had provided secure employment for the historians of the Hitler-Youth Generation and not, as in other professions, for the first postwar generation. For the figures illustrating the expansion in the 1960s see Udo Wengst, "Geschichtswissenschaft und 'Vergangenheitsbewältigung' in Deutschland," *Geschichte und Gesellschaft* 46 (1995): 189–205, 198.

44. Eley, "Labor History," 298.

45. Like the history of *Alltagsgeschichte* as a social phenomenon, the role of television in the history of coming to terms with Nazism in the Federal Republic has not yet been written. The topic is, for instance, not covered in recent surveys like Reichel, *Politik;* Peter Dudek, *Der Rückblick auf die Vergangenheit wird sich nicht vermeiden lassen: Zur pädagogischen Verarbeitung des Nationalsozialismus in Deutschland (1945–1990)* (Opladen: Westdeutscher Verlag, 1995); or Rolf Steininger, ed., *Der Umgang mit dem Holocaust: Europa-USA-Israel* (Vienna: Böhlau, 1994). For notable exceptions see Michael Geissler, "The Disposal of Memory: Fascism and the Holocaust on West German Television," in *Framing the Past: The Historiography of German Cinema and Television,* ed. Bruce Murray and Christopher Wickham (Carbondale: Southern Illininois University Press, 1992), 220–60; Georg Feil, *Zeitgeschichte im Deutschen Fernsehen: Analyse von Fernsehsendungen mit historischen Themen, 1957–1967* (Osnabrück:

Fromm, 1974); and Knut Hickethier, *Das Fernsehspiel der Bundesrepublik: Themen, Form, Struktur 1951–1977* (Stuttgart: Metzler, 1980). The interpretation of *Alltagsgeschichte* on West German television is also based on research conducted in the archives of the ZDF, the second West German public television station, which provided approximately 50 percent of the national television programming between the early 1970s and the mid-1980s. In the history of the ZDF four phases of *Alltagsgeschichte* stand out: an early "trial" phase in 1971–72, two ambitious and successful phases in 1978–79 and 1982–84, and another series of successful shows in 1987–88.

46. For an assessment of the contribution of the history workshops to the study of fascism see Gerstenberger and Schmidt, *Normalität*. Among the numerous discussions about the problems and virtues of *Alltagsgeschichte* see in particular Franz Brüggemeier and Jürgen Kocka, eds., *"Geschichte von unten—Geschichte von innen": Kontroversen um die Alltagsgeschichte* (Hagen: Fernuniversität, 1985); and Institut für Zeitgeschichte, ed., *Alltagsgeschichte der NS-Zeit: Neue Perspektiven oder Trivialisierung* (Munich: Oldenbourg, 1984). For the critique of *Alltagsgeschichte* from the perspective of West Germany's social historians see in addition Hans-Ulrich Wehler, "Neoromantik und Pseudorealismus in der neuen 'Alltagsgeschichte,'" in *Preussen ist wieder chic . . . : Politik und Polemik* (Frankfurt am Main: Suhrkamp, 1983), 99–106; the more substantial but less entertaining Jürgen Kocka, *Sozialgeschichte: Begriff, Entwicklung, Probleme*, 2d ed. (Göttingen: Vandenhoek & Ruprecht, 1986), 132–76; and Klaus Tenfelde, "Schwierigkeiten mit dem Alltag," *Geschichte und Gesellschaft* 10 (1984): 376–94.

47. For the media events "Holocaust" and "Heimat," which have been studied closely, see especially Peter Märtesheimer and Ivo Frenzel, eds., *Im Kreuzfeuer: Der Fernsehfilm Holocaust; Eine Nation ist betroffen* (Frankfurt: Fischer, 1979); Yizhak Ahren et al., eds., *Das Lehrstück "Holocaust": Wirkungen und Nachwirkungen eines Medienereignisses* (Opladen: Westdeutscher Verlag, 1982); Friedrich Knilli and Siegfried Zielinski, eds., *Holocaust zur Unterhaltung: Anatomie eines internationalen Bestsellers* (Berlin: Elefanten, 1982); the special issue on *Heimat* of *New German Critique* 36 (1985); and Anton Kaes, *From Hitler to Heimat: The Return of History as Film* (Cambridge: Harvard University Press, 1989), 161–92.

48. For Lübbe's concepts of historical and moral identity see chapters 12 and 14–17 in Lübbe, *Geschichtsbegriff und Geschichtsinteresse* (Basel: Schwabe, 1977); Lübbe, "Handlungssinn und Lebenssinn: Über die Reichweite von Rationalitätspostulaten," in *Handlungssinn und Lebenssinn: Zum Problem der Ranalität im Kontext des Handelns*, ed. Lübbe et al. (Freiburg: Karl Alber, 1987), 11–35; Lübbe, "Wer kann sich historische Aufklärung leisten? Der Streit um die politische Funktion der Geisteswissenschaften," in *Logik, Ethik, Theorie der Geisteswissenschaften*, ed. Günther Patzig et al. (Hamburg: Felix Meiner, 1977), 35–45; Lübbe, "Die Politik, die Wahrheit und die Moral," *Geschichte und Gegenwart* 3 (1984): 288–304; and Lübbe "Aneignung und Rückaneignung," in Georg Kohler and Heinz Kleger, *Diskurs und Dezision: Politische Vernunft in der wissenschaftlich-technischen Zivilisation* (Vienna: Passagen, 1990), 335–71. For a critique of Lübbe's position see Emil Angehrn, *Geschichte und Identität* (Berlin: de Gruyter, 1985), 297–

303; and especially Jörn Rüsen, "Zur Kritik des Neohistorismus," *Zeitschrift für philosophische Forschung* 33 (1979): 243–63.

49. Hermann Lübbe, "Der Nationalsozialismus im deutschen Nachkriegsbewuatsein," *Historische Zeitschrift* 236 (1983): 579–99; Lübbe, "Verdrängung? Über eine Kategorie zur Kritik des deutschen Vergangenheitsverhältnisses," in *Die Gegenwart der Vergangenheit: Historikerstreit und Erinnerungsarbeit*, ed. Hans-Hermann Wiese (Bad Segeberg: Wäser, 1989), 94–106; and Lübbe, "Der Nationalsozialismus im politischen Bewuatsein der Gegenwart," in *Deutschlands Weg in die Diktatur: Internationale Konferenz zur nationalsozialistischen Machtübernahme*, ed. Martin Broszat et al. (Berlin: Siedler, 1983), 329–49. The conference volume also documents a long discussion of Lübbe's paper by journalists, politicians, and historians: "Podiumsdiskussion zum Thema des Abschluavortrages," in Broszat et al., *Deutschlands Weg*, 350–78.

50. Alexander and Margarete Mitscherlich, *Die Unfähigkeit zu trauern*, 21st ed. (Munich: Piper, 1990); Margarete Mitscherlich, *Erinnerungsarbeit: Zur Psychoanalyse der Unfähigkeit zu trauern* (Frankfurt am Main: Fischer, 1987).

51. For Habermas's concept of postnational identity see his contributions to the Historians' Debate in Knowlton and Cates, *Forever*, 43–44, 165–66; and especially Habermas, "Historical Consciousness and Post-Traditional Identity: The Federal Republic's Orientation to the West," in *The New Conservatism: Cultural Criticism and the Historians' Debate* (Cambridge: MIT Press, 1989), 249–67; as well as Habermas, "Grenzen des Neohistorismus," in *Die nachholende Revolution* (Frankfurt am Main: Suhrkamp, 1990), 149–56. For the philosophical underpinnings of the concept see Richard Wolin, "Introduction," in Habermas, *Conservatism*, vii–xxxi; and Martin Matustik, *Postnational Identity: Critical Theory and Existential Philosophy in Habermas, Kierkegaard, and Havel* (New York: Guilford, 1993), esp. 3–28.

52. Habermas's philosophical works on discourse ethics comprise three major contributions: *Moral Consciousness and Communicative Action* (Cambridge: MIT Press, 1990); *Justification and Application: Remarks on Discourse Ethics* (Cambridge: MIT Press, 1993); and especially *Between Facts and Norms: Contributions to a Discourse Theory of Law and Democracy* (Cambridge: MIT Press, 1996). For an introduction to Habermas's discourse ethics see Ciaran Cronin, "Translator's Introduction," in Habermas, *Justification*, xi–xxxi; and in particular William Rehg, *Insight and Solidarity: A Study in the Discourse Ethics of Jürgen Habermas* (Berkeley: University of California Press, 1994).

53. About the relationship between social analysis and reflections on an ideal society in his writings see Habermas, *Vergangenheit als Zukunft: Das alte Deutschland im neuen Europa? Ein Gespräch mit Michael Haller* (Munich: Piper, 1993), 132–35.

54. See especially Habermas, "Historical Consciousness," 250, 255–56 and "Neohistorismus," 151–52; and Knowlton and Cates, *Forever*, 166.

55. Claussen, "Vergangenheit mit Zukunft: Über die Entstehung einer neuen deutschen Ideologie," in Eschenhagen, *Die neue deutsche Ideologie*, 7–30, 17; see also Lüdtke, "Einleitung," 16; and the excellent critique by Barbara Hahn and Peter Schöttler, "Jürgen Habermas und 'das ungetrübte Bewuatsein des Bruchs,'" in Gerstenberger and Schmidt, *Normalität*, 170–77. For a critique of Habermas's concept

of postnational identity from a Hegelian perspective see Shaun Gallagher, "The *Historikerstreit* and the Critique of Nationalism," *History of European Ideas* 16 (1993): 921–26. For a critique of Habermas's concept of modernity see Mario Biagioli, "Science, Modernity, and the 'Final Solution,'" in Friedlander, *Probing*, 185–205, 194–99.

56. See in this respect also Lutz Niethammer, who argued: "Both projects in philosophical politics mistakenly assume that the case of the Federal Republic fits current global societal tendencies and they also overestimate the power of philosophical consciousness" ("Konjunkturen und Konkurrenzen kollektiver Identität: Ideologie, Infrastruktur und Gedächnis in der Zeitgeschichte," *Prokla* 96 [1994]: 378–99).

57. Wolfram Schütte quoted after Kaes, *Hitler*, 183.

58. On the Fischer Debate see John A. Moses, *The Politics of Illusion: The Fischer-Controversy in German Historiography* (London: Prior, 1975); Wolfgang Jäger, *Historische Forschung und politische Kultur in Deutschland: Die Debatte 1914–1980 über den Ausbruch des Ersten Weltkrieges* (Göttingen: Vandenhoek & Ruprecht, 1984); and Arnold Sywottek, "Die Fischer-Kontroverse: Ein Beitrag zur Entwicklung des politisch-historischen Bewuatseins in der Bundesrepublik," in *Deutschland in der Weltpolitik des 19. und 20. Jahrhunderts*, ed. Imanuel Geiss and Bernd Jürgen Wendt (Düsseldorf: Bertelsmann, 1973), 19–47; and especially the account by Fischer's student Imanuel Geiss, "Die Fischer-Kontroverse: Ein kritischer Beitrag zum Verhältnis zwischen Historiographie und Politik in der Bundesrepublik," in *Studien über Geschichte und Geschichtswissenschaft* (Frankfurt am Main: Suhrkamp, 1972), 108–98.

59. Most recently Geiss, *Habermas-Kontroverse*, 14–16. However, Volker Berghahn has shown that by 1980 Fischer's thesis had not found its way into the applicable surveys and handbooks on German and European history of the twentieth century; see Berghahn, "Die Fischerkontroverse—15 Jahre danach," *Geschichte und Gesellschaft* 6 (1980): 403–19. Apparently little has changed since 1980. The most recent survey, Klaus Hildebrand's *Das vergangene Reich: Deutsche Außenpolitik von Bismarck bis Hitler* (Stuttgart: Deutsche Verlagsanstalt, 1995), also dismisses most of Fischer's arguments.

60. On the postwar historiography see Georg Iggers, *The German Conception of History: The National Tradition of Historical Thought from Herder to the Present*, rev. ed. (Middletown CT: Wesleyan University Press, 1983), 252–64; and Winfried Schulze, *Deutsche Geschichtswissenschaft nach 1945* (Munich: Oldenbourg, 1989), 46–76.

61. On the concept of totalitarianism see Kershaw, *Nazi Dictatorship*, 20–23, 30–35; Karl Dietrich Bracher, *Zeitgeschichtliche Kontroversen: Um Faschismus, Totalitarismus, Demokratie* (Munich: Piper, 1984), 34–62; and especially Uwe Backes and Eckhard Jesse, *Totalitarismus, Extremismus, Terrorismus* (Opladen: Leske & Budrich, 1984), 47–102.

62. For the development of the paradigm of social history in the Federal Republic see Georg G. Iggers, *New Directions in European Historiography*, rev. ed. (Middletown CT: Wesleyan University Press, 1984), 90–122; Iggers, *Geschichtswissen-*

schaft, 54–63; and Iggers, introduction to *The Social History of Politics* (Dover NH: Berg, 1985), 1–48.

63. Otto Dov Kulka, "Singularity and Its Relativization: Changing Views in German Historiography on National Socialism and the 'Final Solution,'" *Yad Vashem Studies* 19 (1988): 151. On the study and representation of the Holocaust in West German historiography see also Kulka, "Major Trends and Tendencies in German Historiography on National Socialism and the 'Jewish Question,'" *Leo Beack Yearbook* 30 (1985): 215–42; Christopher Browning, "Approaches to the 'Final Solution' in German Historiography of the Last Two Decades," in *The Historiography of the Holocaust Period*, ed. Yisrael Gutman and Gideon Greif (Jerusalem: Yad Vashem, 1988); and Konrad Kwiet, "Judenverfolgung und Judenvernichtung im Dritten Reich: Ein historiographischer Überblick," in Diner, *Nationalsozialismus*, 237–64.

64. On the *Sonderweg* debate see Jürgen Kocka, "German History before Hitler: The Debate about the German *Sonderweg*," *Journal of Contemporary History* 23 (1988): 3–16; Helga Grebing, *Der deutsche Sonderweg in Europa 1806–1945: Eine Kritik* (Stuttgart: Kohlhammer, 1986); Bernd Faulenbach, "Eine Variante europäischer Normalität? Zur neusten Diskussion über den 'deutschen Weg' im 19. und 20. Jahrhundert," *Tel Aviver Jahrbuch für deutsche Geschichte* 16 (1987): 285–309; and Institut für Zeitgeschichte, ed., *Deutscher Sonderweg—Mythos oder Realität?* (Munich: Oldenbourg, 1982).

65. The essay that coined the terms "structuralist" and "intentionalist," "Intention and Explanation: A Current Controversy about the Interpretation of National Socialism," is now more easily available in Timothy Mason's collected essays, *Nazism, Fascism, and the Working Class*, ed. Jane Caplan (Cambridge: Cambridge University Press, 1995), 212–30. On the debate between structuralists and intentionalists see also Saul Friedlander, "From Anti-Semitism to Extermination: A Historiographical Study of Nazi Policies toward the Jews and an Essay in Interpretation," in François Furet, *Unanswered Questions: Nazi Germany and the Genocide of the Jews* (New York: Schocken, 1989), 3–31; Christopher Browning, "Beyond 'Intentionalism' and 'Functionalism': The Decision for the Final Solution Reconsidered," in *The Path to Genocide: Esays on Launching the Final Solution* (Cambridge: Cambridge University Press, 1992), 86–121; and Kershaw, *Nazi Dictatorship*, 82–106.

66. What remains from the former consensus is Eberhard Jäckel's explicit definition "that the National-Socialist murder of the Jews was unique because never before had a nation with the authority of its leader decided and announced that it would kill off as completely as possible a particular group of humans, including old people, women, children, and infants, and actually put this decision into practice, using all the governmental power at its disposal" (in Knowlton and Cates, *Forever*, 76). During and after the Historians' Debate the historians on the Left somewhat helplessly reiterated this formula, hoping to be able to restore the former tacit agreement. For that purpose, they mistakenly treated the highly abstract notion of uniqueness as a factual statement—see for instance Wehler, *Entsorgung*, 100.

67. This applies especially to the work of Rainer Zitelmann. See for example Zitelmann, *Hitler: Selbstverständnis eines Revolutionärs* (Stuttgart: Klett, 1987).

For a critique of Zitelmann's work see Kansteiner, "Emplotment," 81–85; and Stefan Berger, "Historians and Nation-Building in Germany after Reunification," *Past and Present* 148 (1995): 197–98.

68. Helga Grebing, "Deutsche Vergangenheit und politische Moral," *Niemandsland* 1 (1987): 6; and especially Hennig, *Zum Historikerstreit*, 83–102.

69. Sybelle Hübner-Funk, "Die 'Hitlerjugend'-Generation: Umstrittenes Objekt und streitbares Subjekt der deutschen Zeitgeschichte," *Prokla* 20 (1990): 85–86.

70. Karl Mannheim, "Das Problem der Generationen," in *Wissenssoziologie: Auswahl aus dem Werk* (Berlin: Luchterhand, 1964), 509–65, esp. 541–55.

71. The notion about the grace of late birth was first developed by the liberal journalist Günter Gaus (see epigraph). Later the idea was adopted and transformed by Helmut Kohl, also a member of this political generation. However, Kohl's interpretation of the phrase is more accurately translated as "the privilege of late birth," a privilege that he successfully employed in foreign policy and media events, most notably during his visit to Israel in 1984. The interesting "career" of the phrase, wandering from the moderate left to the moderate right of the political spectrum nicely symbolizes the particular perspective on the Nazi period shared by many members of the Hitler-Youth Generation.

72. There have been various approaches to the study of the Hitler-Youth Generation in postwar West German sociology and historiography. In his classical study of 1957 Helmut Schelsky focuses on postwar (West) German youth between 1945 and 1955; he calls this the skeptical generation. Since he defines youth as the age group between fourteen and twenty-five, he deals with those born from 1920 through 1945. However, Schelsky avoids any clear dividing lines and allows for a lot of overlap between the skeptical generation and its predecessor, the "political youth," whose members joined the youth organizations of the parties of the Weimar Republic beginning in the early 1920s. For the definitions see Schelsky, *Die skeptische Generation: Eine Soziologie der deutschen Jugend* (Düsseldorf: Eugen Diedrichs, 1957), 5, 57, 66–67, 87. The historian Rolf Schörken defines the Hitler-Youth Generation as the male age groups born between 1921 and 1929; he further divides his group into three subcategories: those born between 1921 and 1925–26, many of whom served as soldiers in World War II; those born between 1926 and 1928, the so-called *Flakhelfergeneration*, adolescents who staffed the anti-aircraft defense in the last years of the war; and those born in 1929, who were not drafted into the anti-aircraft units but were called up for other supportive duties. Schörken adds that for women the dividing line was 1926; women who were nineteen or older in 1944 had to support the "war effort" in various positions; see Schörken, *Jugend 1945: Politisches Denken und Lebensgeschichte* (Frankfurt: Fischer, 1994), 10–15. The *Flakhelfergeneration* is most closely analyzed in Heinz Bude, *Deutsche Karrieren: Lebenskonstruktionen sozialer Aufsteiger aus der Flakhelfer-Generation* (Frankfurt: Suhrkamp, 1987). Bude also highlights the different experiences of the various age groups within the Hitler-Youth Generation; see Bude, *Bilanz der Nachfolge: Die Bundesrepublik und der Nationalsozialismus* (Frankfurt: Suhrkamp, 1992), 81. Eike Hennig divides the age groups in question into two distinct generations: the war generation, comprising those born between 1920 and 1927; and the generation of Germany's postwar reconstruction, consisting of those born from 1928 through

1935. See Hennig, *Zum Historikerstreit*, 90–91. For our limited purposes Sibylle Hübner-Funk's general definition (cited above) suffices. On the Hitler-Youth Generation see also Gabriele Rosenthal, ed., *Die Hitlerjugend-Generation: Biographische Verarbeitung als Vergangenheitsbewältigung* (Essen: Blaue Eule, 1986).

72. Schelsky, *Die skeptische Generation: Eine Soziologie der deutschen Jugend* (Düsseldorf: Eugen Diedrichs, 1957), 84–95.

73. Mannheim, "Generationen," 537.

74. For the definition of "sites of memory" see Pierre Nora, "Between Memory and History: Les Lieux de Mémoire," *Representations* 26 (1989): 7–24.

75. For Assmann's definition of cultural and communicative memory see Assmann, "Collective Memory and Cultural Idenity," *New German Critique* 65 (1995): 125–33; quotes are from 126 and 130; see also Assmann, "Die Katastrophe des Vergessens: Das Deuteronomium als Paradigma kultureller Mnemotechnik," in *Mnemosyne: Formen und Funktionen der kulturellen Erinnerung*, ed. Aleida Assmann and Dietrich Harth (Frankfurt am Main: Fischer, 1991), 337–55; and especially Assmann, *Das kulturelle Gedächtnis: Schrift, Erinnerung und politische Identität* (Munich: Beck, 1992), 48–66.

76. Lutz Niethammer, "Diesseits des 'Floating Gap': Das kollektive Gedächtnis und die Konstruktion von Identität im wissenschaftlichen Diskurs," in *Generation und Gedächtnis: Erinnerungen und kollektive Identitäten*, ed. Kristin Platt and Mihran Dabag (Opladen: Leske und Budrich, 1995), 25–50; see also Niethammer, "Konjunkturen."

77. Notice the absence in the debate of historians like Lutz Niethammer, Klaus Tenfelde, Alf Lüdtke, and Detlev Peukert.

78. Kaes, *Hitler*, 196

79. Berger, "Historians," 213; for a post-unification endorsement of the category of national history in conjunction with a critical assessment of the social history of the Bielefeld School, see for example Harold James, *Vom Historikerstreit zum Historikerschweigen* (Berlin: Siedler, 1993).

80. Friedrich Nietzsche, *The Use and Abuse of History* (Indianapolis IN: Bobbs-Merrill, 1957); Maurice Halbwachs, *The Collective Memory* (New York: Harper and Row, 1980); Halbwachs, *On Collective Memory* (Chicago: University of Chicago Press, 1992); Pierre Nora, *Les Lieux de mémoire*, vols. 1–3 (Paris: Gallimard, 1984–1992); Nora, "Between Memory and History"; Yosef Yerushalmi, *Zakhor: Jewish History and Jewish Memory* (Seattle: University of Washington Press, 1982); and Jacques LeGoff, *History and Memory* (New York: Columbia University Press, 1992). For a good introduction to the topic of social memory see James Fentress and Chris Wickham, *Social Memory* (Oxford: Blackwell, 1992). An interesting interdisciplinary approach from the perspectives of oral history and cognitive psychology is developed in Jaclyn Jeffrey and Glenace Edwall, eds., *Memory and History: Essays on Recalling and Interpreting Experience* (Lanham MD: University Press of America, 1994). The dichotomy between history and memory has been explored with regard to Yerushalmi's *Zakhor* by Amos Funkenstein, "Collective Memory and Historical Consciousness," *History and Memory* 1 (1989): 5–26; and David Myers, "Remembering Zakhor: A Super-Commentary," *History and Memory* 4 (1992): 129–42; see also Michael Roth, *The Ironist's Cage: Memory, Trauma, and the Construction of*

History (New York: Columbia University Press, 1995). In this context, Aleida Assmann has recently suggested replacing the history/memory divide with a differentiation between functional memories, which cast particular aspects of the past in narrative formats for academic as well as nonacademic purposes, and storage memory, which contains all kinds of unsystematized, non-narrativized, amorphous recollections of the past. See Assmann, "Funktionsgedächtnis und Speichergedächnis: Zwei Modi der Erinnerung," in Platt and Dabag, *Generation*, 169–85.

81. See for a recent example Yael Zerubavel, *Recovered Roots: Collective Memory and the Making of Israeli National Tradition* (Chicago: University of Chicago Press, 1995).

82. For the press coverage of the recycling of Jenninger's speech see Arno Widmann, "Ignatz Bubis und die Jenninger-Rede," *Die Zeit*, 8 December 1995; "Gedenkreden: 'Falsches Bild,'" *Der Spiegel* 49 (1995); "Trauer oder Pflichterfüllung: Bubis wiederholte die umstrittene Jenninger-Rede," *die tageszeitung*, 1 December 1995. Only *die tageszeitung* gave the news a prominent place in its coverage.

Robert J. Soucy

The Debate over French Fascism

Among the most highly contested issues that have separated histo-rians of French fascism are whether French fascist writers and move-ments in the 1920s and 1930s were more Left than Right, more radical than conservative, more revolutionary than reactionary, more social-ist than capitalist, more populist than elitist, and more plebeian than bourgeois. Related to these questions is whether important sections of the traditional Right were complicit with fascism during the interwar period or immune to its appeal. Did many French conservatives share fascism's basic values and goals during the Depression era, as William Irvine has argued; or is it true, as Paul Sérant has claimed for France, that "to pretend to establish a kinship between fascism and traditional [conservative] doctrines would be in vain"?[1] Finally, did fascism have a numerically significant following in France in the 1930s, or was it lim-ited to a few dozen writers and intellectuals who, however fascinating they might be to students of French literary and intellectual history, had only a minuscule influence on the French populaton in general and were therefore politically insignificant.

Historians of French fascism have split into two generally opposed schools regarding these issues. One school, which includes such French scholars as René Rémond, Serge Berstein, Philippe Burrin, and Jean-Paul Brunet, as well as the American Eugen Weber and the Israeli Zeev Sternhell, have underscored the left-wing elements in French fas-cism, characterizing it as a highly anticonservative, antiestablishmen-tarian, antibourgeois phenomenon. For this school, large right-wing paramilitary movements like the Jeunesses Patriotes and the Croix de Feu—and even the highly anti-Semitic Action Française—were too socially and economically conservative to be fascist.

In 1954 and again in 1968 René Rémond characterized French fas-cism as a socially revolutionary movement that was fundamentally at odds with traditional French conservatism. "Fascism dreams only of overthrow," wrote Rémond. "The Right wants to be reassured and aspires after stability." Indeed, according to Rémond, fascism descended from the Jacobinism of the French Revolution of 1789:

it is clear that fascism does not have much in common with political and social conservatism: it is only by abusing the term that one can confuse it with "reaction." The two notions are, in fact, irreducible. Nothing is so refractory to the seductions of fascism than the "classical" rights. . . . [The traditional Right] was born of reaction against the principles of 1789. . . . Whereas fascism does not renounce Revolution. It assumes it: its existence and its content imply the principles of 1789. Fascism . . . ascribes the origins of power to the same foundation as democracy: the sovereignty of the people. . . . Conservative traditionalism and fascism thus recognize two contrary foundations of power: tradition, unique source of legitimacy, and the popular will, free for fascism to falsify.[2]

As for Pierre Taittinger's blue shirts, the Jeunesses Patriotes, they were Bonapartists, not fascists.

In 1964 the American historian Eugen Weber went even further. Fascism, he maintained, was not only Jacobin but socialist. In contrast to more humanitarian, pacifistic, and internationalistic forms of socialism, fascist socialism was opportunistic, utilitarian, and nationalistic. Thus, to identify it with reaction was "wide of the mark." "While social reaction and social thoughtlessness have made their contributions to fascism, we have seen that fascist doctrines and the fascist temper are far from reactionary in themselves."[3]

Weber argued, therefore, that the reactionary Action Française was not fascist because its leader, Charles Maurras, abhorred socialism and broke with men like George Valois and Robert Brasillach when, according to Weber, they became too leftist. On the other hand, Weber had no difficulty categorizing as fascist Georges Valois's Faisceau ("communists came to join them," Weber noted) and Marcel Bucard's Franciste party (which, Weber said, "drew both its elements and its spirit from the Left"). For Weber, Colonel de La Rocque's Croix de Feu—which was the largest and fastest growing political movement on the French right between 1936 and 1939—was more Right than Left, more conservative than fascist. According to Weber, La Rocque was "a respectable, law-abiding man" and members of the Croix de Feu "simply do not qualify as anything more than patriotic conservatives." In his latest book, *The Hollow Years* (1994), Weber describes La Rocque as "a soldier respectful of republican institutions and the law." Thus, Weber concludes, "the fascist menace in France was slight" and France "never turned to fascism."[4]

In 1964 Weber did consider Jacques Doriot's Parti Populaire Français (which had some fifty thousand members in 1937) to be fascist, partly because many of its original rank-and-file were former Communists:

"they evidently thought to find [salvation] in the forceful man who proposed to tear away the disfiguring mask of capitalism."[5] Weber also characterized Marcel Déat's Neo-Socialist movement as fascist, observing that Déat drew his followers "chiefly from the ranks of the academic and journalistic Left." For Weber, fascism was a movement of young and deracinated radicals rather than of mature and established conservatives:

One cannot take great risks, run the chance of scandal or arrest, be available for anything at all hours, if the thought of career or mortgage or an income holds one back. Only the very poor, the very young (also perhaps the very rich, but there are few of those and even fewer who want to change the order from which they benefit), can qualify for revolutionary action, as opposed to writing or talk; and they envisage it quite often as a way of ceasing to be nonentities or to be poor.[6]

Nevertheless, Weber was more willing than Rémond to acknowledge the appeal of fascism to some social and economic conservatives in the 1930s. Indeed, despite his original characterization of fascism as a form of neosocialism and his denial therefore that the Action Française was fascist, Weber stated that whereas Déat's party drew its inspiration and cadres from the Left, "most of the [other French fascist parties] drew theirs either from the Right or from the sort of authoritarian opportunism we tend to associate with the 'fascist temperament.'"[7]

However, in emphasizing the importance of the fascist "temperament" by describing fascism as a kind of "fever," and in declaring that fascism was "neither Right nor Left," Weber downgraded the rational economic interests fascists and conservatives had in common. For, according to Weber, by rejecting theory in favor of practice, fascism "relies largely on the attractions of that 'fever.'"[8] Thus, he portrayed even right-wing fascists as driven more by irrational feelings than by a desire to defend class advantages, more by misguided "romanticism" than by well-guided materialism. "Fascism," he wrote, "offered to the men of the Right what communism offered to those on the left: [what Robert Brasillach has described as] 'the banners of revolution, the exaltation of the clan, the prestige of the leader, of his militias and his standards.'"[9] Weber returns to this theme in *The Hollow Years*, where he says that in moments of distress fascism appeals to "sections of the Right with which it shares some ideological affinities, to disillusioned members of the Left who appreciate enthusiasm and activism over substance, and to nonconformists in general who reject bourgeois materialism, egoism, rationalism, and hedonism for more heroic, more theatrical, and less pedestrian utopias."[10]

In contrast to Weber, Ernst Nolte described fascism as deeply reactionary, as an "anti-emancipatory" movement whose fundamental aim was to defeat Marxism. Nolte maintained that the reactionary Action Française was not only fascist, but originated many ideas later adopted by German Nazism. At the same time, Nolte argued that while fascism was opposed to Communism in its ends, it was similar to Communism in its means.[11] By 1969, however, Nolte's interpretation of fascism, at least of Italian fascism, had grown closer to Weber's. In *Fascist Movements* Nolte concluded that some of Mussolini's early followers were quite left-wing in their goals, albeit in a syndicalist rather than a Marxist way, and that they were socialists and proletarians who had a far greater affinity for fascism than did supporters of capitalism.[12]

The scholar who has gone the furthest in insisting on the left-wing sources of fascism, especially of French fascism, is Zeev Sternhell. Indeed, Sternhell has contended that "in many respects, one can write the history of fascism as that of an incessant attempt to revise Marxism, of a permanent effort toward neo-socialism." Although Sternhell has also described fascism as "neither Right nor Left," it is its leftism that he underscores. According to Sternhell, fascism launched an "assault upon capitalism" and aimed at a "socialism for all." In France, "real, authentic fascism was always born on the Left, never on the Right," while in Italy fascism was "an unprecedented war machine against the bourgeois order," which is why "so many men of the Left slid toward fascism during the interwar period."[13] Consequently, Sternhell denied that the socially and economically conservative Croix de Feu was fascist—as did two other leading scholars of French fascism, Philippe Burrin and Pierre Milza.[14]

The Canadian historian William Irvine has called those scholars who emphasize the Jacobin, socialist, left-wing nature of French fascism—and who therefore deny that the Croix de Feu was fascist—the "consensus" school of interpreters of French fascism, inasmuch as they have dominated most scholarship on the subject since World War II.

In recent years, a few historians and sociologists have challenged the consensus school: William Irvine, Sam Goodfellow, Michel Dobry, Jacques Julliard, and myself. In contrast to the consensus school, these scholars maintain that most French fascists (what I have called "mainstream" fascists) had much in common with French conservatism, that what they advocated was in fact an authoritarian brand of French conservatism, and that only a small minority of leftists went over to fascism during the interwar period. Mainstream fascism, they contend, was overwhelmingly right-wing, not left-wing, including Colonel de La Rocque's Croix de Feu, a movement that by 1938 had between seven hundred thousand and 1.2 million party members (more than the Nazi party in Germany had in 1932, the year before it came to power) and whose party membership in 1938 was larger than that of the French Communist and Socialist parties combined. If one adds to Croix de Feu membership figures those of Doriot's Parti Populaire Français, the size of mainstream fascism in France was even greater. Nor do anticonsensus historians see Doriot's party as seriously left-wing.

For William Irvine, there is something odd about the consensus school's portraying fascism and conservatism as mutually exclusive. Irvine writes: "The notion that fascists cannot consort with 'liberals' or 'conservatives' is surely a fiction unique to France. No one, for example, has ever suggested that the presence of liberal politicians such as Vittorio Orlando and Antonio Salandra on the 1924 fascist electoral ticket renders Mussolini's movement less fascist."[15] Irvine also disputes Philippe Burrin's notion that Colonel de La Rocque simply does not fit the typical fascist profile. According to Burrin, "Nothing about La Rocque, his past as an officer, his social origins, the circles in which he moved, resembled that of a fascist leader of déclassé, marginal, or modest origins and expert in the agitation and manipulation of crowds."[16] Irvine replies:

The assumptions here are more than a little problematic. La Rocque is very different from Mussolini and Hitler, although social origins may be the least important of differences. But Hitler and Mussolini were also very different from one another. Moreover, it is not clear to what degree the fascist qualities of a movement can be derived from its leader. Certainly it would be quite wrong to suggest that ex-army officers with social contacts among the *bonne bourgeoisie* are refractory to fascism. Such elements were notoriously present in National Socialism and, above all, in Italian Fascism.[17]

Why, Irvine wonders, have Burrin and other consensus scholars been so invested in denying that the Croix de Feu was fascist? Irvine's answer:

If the Croix de Feu can be shown to have been fascist, then two principal tenets of the French historiography of fascism collapse. It would no longer be possible to argue, in the tradition established by René Rémond forty years ago, that French fascism was the work of an isolated minority. Nor would it be possible to maintain . . . as Zeev Sternhell has done, that fascism was omnipresent in France but only among dissident members of the Left seeking to revise Marxism. A serious scholarly examination of the Croix de Feu might reveal that French fascism was both widespread and clearly on the political Right.[18]

Another Canadian historian, John Bingham, has since added: "The principle reason we know so little about the Croix de Feu . . . is that Rémond long ago decided it was not fascist."[19]

Like Irvine, the British historian Kevin Passmore, who has researched Croix de Feu activities in Lyon, and the American historian

Sam Goodfellow, who has researched Croix de Feu activities in Alsace, also consider the organization fascist.[20] For anticonsensus scholars, most French fascism was not only socially and economically conservative but also antiliberal, antidemocratic, paramilitary, devoted to mass politics, and highly nationalistic—the last characteristic fueling its hatred of internationalists (whether they were Marxists, freemasons, or unassimilated Jews) and of anyone else who rejected the "traditional" values of the French Right. The Croix de Feu was no exception.

In my own work, I have argued that the Croix de Feu, like several other French fascist movements of the interwar period, was hostile to proletarian class struggle, working-class indiscipline, and political, social, and economic democracy—as well as to socialist and liberal "hedonism," skepticism, and humanitarianism (which La Rocque called "sentimentalism"). The Croix de Feu hated the Popular Front in 1936 and joined the political backlash against it. As Colonel de La Rocque later admitted, the reason he did not try to overthrow the Popular Front by force in 1936 was not because he was a law-abiding citizen respectful of republican institutions, but because, given the Popular Front's control of the police and the military and the power of the mass organizations of the Left, he lacked enough paramilitary muscle to do so.[21]

To find the socially conservative Croix de Feu fascist, however, does not mean that all French fascist movements were right-wing. I agree with Sternhell and other consensus historians that there were some French fascist movements in the 1930s, particularly Marcel Déat's Neo-Socialist and Gaston Bergery's Common Front parties, that were genuinely left-wing in their goals (at least until 1940, when they turned sharply rightward). Where I disagree with Sternhell is on the political importance he attributes to these movements. Compared to such right-wing French fascist movements as the Faisceau, the Jeunesses Patriotes, the Croix de Feu, and the Parti Populaire Français, Déat's and Bergery's movements were minor affairs. They were also overwhelmingly rejected by followers of the French Socialist and Communist parties of the era.

One can tell much about the nature of French fascism from the enemies it hated. For most French fascists, the enemy was not only the Communists and the socialists, but also political democrats and liberal "fellow-travelers" who allowed the Marxist threat to exist in the first place. For most French fascists, anti-Marxism, anti-democracy, and anti-liberalism went hand in hand: to permanently defeat Marxism one had to defeat the others as well. French fascists, who never came to power in France and who therefore were never in a position to impose a "totalitarian" solution from above, floated a number of plans during the interwar period for constitutional revisions that, by allowing corporatist assemblies to undermine electoral democracy, would have greatly disempowered the political Left. French fascists did not advocate the sovereignty of the people; on the contrary, they repeatedly sought to negate the will of the majority so that upper-class elites could control government policy. Prior to 1936 (when the Jewish Léon Blum led the Popular Front to victory), most French fascists were much more focused on class issues than on racial issues. Indeed, their leaders accepted right-wing Jews into their movements; the anti-Semitic Action Française and the Solidarité Française were exceptions, not the rule.

This raises another issue in the debate over French fascism: whether only movements that were anti-Semitic should be considered fascist. Some consensus historians—René Rémond and Jacques Nobécourt, for example—in denying that the Croix de Feu was fascist, point out that Colonel de La Rocque publicly disavowed anti-Semitism in the 1930s.[22] But this is proof of nonfascism only if one assumes that all fascism was anti-Semitic. German fascism was indeed anti-Semitic, but Italian fascism was not—at least not until 1938, when Mussolini struck a military alliance with Hitler.

In an article titled "Italian Jews and Fascism," published in 1969, an American historian, Michael LeDeen, notes that during its first fourteen years the fascist regime in Italy repeatedly denounced anti-Semitism. It was not until 1938, to appease Hitler, that anti-Semitic legislation was adopted in Italy. From the early 1920s through the mid-1930s, Mussolini (who counted several Jews among his political associates, and had for a time a Jewish mistress, Margherita Sarfatti) publicly rejected anti-Semitism, declaring that "in Italy there is absolutely no difference between a Jew and non-Jew in all fields, in religion, in politics, in the military, in economics."[23] In May 1929, the Duce declared before the Italian parliament: "We respect [the] sacred character of Rome. But it is ridiculous to think, as has been said, that the synagogues must be closed. . . . The Jews have been in Rome from the times of the Kings . . . there were 50,000 at the time of Augustus, and they asked to cry on the corpse of Julius Caesar. They will remain undisturbed."[24] Not only did the Italian fascist regime defend the rights of Jewish communities in Italy; it arranged that public examinations not fall on Jewish holidays. In February 1929, the Duce's son-in-law and soon-to-be foreign minister, Costanzo Ciano, visited the synagogue of Livorno and declared that there were too few Jews in Italy.

Immediately after Hitler came to power in Germany, Mussolini let it be known that he was sympathetic to the plight of German Jews and would do all he could to help them. By the late 1930s, more than ten thousand Jews had fled to Italy to avoid racial persecution in Germany and Austria. The Zionist Nachum Sokolov, after talks with the Duce, praised his human qualities, told him that "true Jews have never fought against you," and announced that Italian fascism was immune to anti-Semitism. As LeDeen notes, "these words, tantamount to a Zionist endorsement of the Fascist regime, were echoed in Jewish periodicals all over the world."[25] In the autumn of 1933, a group of American Jewish publications named Mussolini among twelve Christians who had been most outstanding in their opposition to anti-Semitism.[26]

Perhaps most shocking to post-Holocaust minds was the rush of many Italian Jews to join the Fascist Party. By 1922 some 750 Jews had become members, by 1928 1,770 more, and by 1933 another 4,800 had been added. As LeDeen observes, what seems absurd today seemed reasonable then:

What [Italian Jews] saw . . . was that over the first decade of Fascist rule [in Italy] the situation of Jews got better and better. They were consequently behaving pragmatically when they supported a government which not only improved their legal status but also became one of the foremost advocates of the Zionist cause in Europe. . . . By the middle of the 1930s, Mussolini was the darling of European Zionists as well as a hero to most Italian Jews.[27]

That anti-Semitic articles occasionally appeared in Italian newspapers (government control of the press, says LeDeen, was far from complete) and that Mussolini himself attacked Jews who were anti-fascist were greatly outweighed by the influence of Judeophiles in the Italian government, such as Italo Balbo, and by the repeated condemnations in the fascist press of Hitler's racism and anti-Semitism. LeDeen writes: "With very few exceptions [before 1938], the Italian press had nothing but scathing epithets for the prophet of Aryanism in the North."[28]

Moreover, as Robert Paxton and Michel Marrus have shown in *Vichy France and the Jews*, even after Mussolini joined the Axis and even as late as 1943, fascist Italy remained a haven for Jews escaping Vichy France. When fascist Italy invaded eight French départements in 1940, it refused, as late as 1942, to allow anti-Jewish measures to be applied to its occupation zone and defended foreign as well as Italian Jews in the zone. One German administrative officer in France described this Italian attitude as "revolting."[29] Thus it is inaccurate to equate all fascism at all times with anti-Semitism. Otherwise, one would have to say that Mussolini was not a fascist before 1938—or that Colonel de La Rocque and Jacques Doriot were not fascists before 1936, because until then they had both welcomed right-wing Jews into their movements.

Another misconception that has distorted the debate over French fascism is the notion that all French fascists were pro-German and collaborated with the Nazis during the Second World War, and that if one were not and did not, especially if one served in the French Resistance during the war, one was not a fascist. Jacques Nobécourt, for example, cites the fact that Colonel de La Rocque went over to the Resistance in 1942 as proof that La Rocque was not fascist.[30] Yet the evidence is overwhelming that during the 1920s and 1930s most French fascists were just as nationalistic toward their country as Hitler was toward his.[31]

Moreover, even during the Second World War when some French fascists subordinated their nationalism to Hitler's crusade against Bolshevism, not all French fascists collaborated with the Germans. Philippe Barrès, who in 1933 had called upon French integral nationalists to save France the way Hitler had saved Germany, chose in 1940 to serve under De Gaulle in London. Eugène Deloncle, one of the leaders of France's major right-wing terrorist organization of the 1930s, the Cagoule, was involved in a plot to assassinate Hitler and died in 1944 shooting at Gestapo agents who had come to arrest him. Another Cagoulard of the 1930s, François Duclos, joined De Gaulle in 1940, later parachuted into France and founded the famous Saint-Jacques branch of the French Resistance. When after the war he stood trial for his earlier terrorist activities in the Cagoule, he wore the Cross of the Liberation, the Croix de Guerre, the Medal of the Resistance, and the Military Cross. As one journalist who attended the trial remarked, Duclos was "naturally acquitted."[32]

Many French fascists in Alsace during the German Occupation, as Sam Goodfellow writes, were "willing to ally with the English, the Gaullists, or even the Communists, if, as one of them put it, 'these people will be able to rid us of the Boche.'"[33] None of this nationalistic behavior during the war made these individuals any less fascist prior to 1940, when they were also highly nationalistic. Bertrand de Jouvenel, for example, may not have collaborated with the Germans during the Occupation, but this hardly made him an antifascist in 1938 when he praised Mussolini as a "New Augustus."

Another false standard by which to judge whether a movement was fascist is whether it espoused totalitarianism under all political circumstances. Eugen Weber, Serge Berstein, and other historians have employed the term "totalitarian" to distinguish fascism from movements like the Croix de Feu, which, they argue, was in the 1930s too un-totalitarian to be fascist.[34] Yet Hitler and Mussolini behaved much differently before they came to power than they did afterward, and even in the first two years after they came to power they were much less totalitarian than they later became. As an electoral politician between 1930 and 1933, Hitler promised to defend Christians, not persecute them; to liberate workers, not exploit them; to avoid war, not start a war; to curtail Jews, not exterminate them (in 1935 some Germans even regarded Hitler as a "moderate" on the Jewish question). As late as 1936, Hitler often sounded more like Salazar of Portugal than the fanatical tyrant he proved to be. Mussolini, as Charles Maier has shown, also sang a more moderate tune before he came to power (at least toward parliamentary conservatives), and even after he came to power he was far more "totalitarian" toward the Left than toward the Right.[35] Similarly, to argue that Colonel de La Rocque was not fascist because he never tried to overthrow the Third Republic by force between 1933 and 1940 ignores the fact that Hitler, having learned his lesson from the disastrous Munich *putsch* of 1924, did not attempt to overthrow the Weimar Republic by force between 1924 and 1933.

Historians who require fascists before they come to power to behave like fascists after they come to power simply ignore the many expedient compromises both Hitler and Mussolini made before they came to power. As Michel Dobry observes, historians who apply such an ahistorical model to French political movements "demand of the radical Right not only that it define itself with more clarity than original fascism—Italian—but that it undertake everything immediately and openly."[36] Thus, to expect Colonel de La Rocque to show all his cards before he came to power would be to expect of him what Hitler and Mussolini never did. Nor should it be forgotten that neither La Rocque nor any other French fascist leader came to power in the 1930s, and therefore never had the opportunity Hitler and Mussolini had to show how ruthless he could be—although La Rocque's call under the Vichy regime for the "extirpation of contaminated elements" in French society is no small indication.[37]

Another issue in the debate over French fascism has to do with the extent of French fascism in the 1930s—that is, with the degree of its mass appeal or lack thereof. In 1954 René Rémond argued that France was largely immune to fascism during the interwar period, that the fascism that did emerge in France was "imported" from abroad, and that since French political culture was firmly rooted in longstanding democratic traditions fascism was never attractive to more than a few insignificant or ephemeral fringe groups.[38] In 1982, however, responding to new scholarship to the contrary, Rémond revised this view, declaring that it would be wrong to claim that France had "in no way known the temptation of fascism"—although he continued to insist that the popular Croix de Feu was not fascist.[39] Nevertheless, as late as 1984, Serge Berstein continued to assert that France had been "impermeable" to fascism during the interwar period and that, with the exception of Doriot's Parti Populaire Français, founded by former Communists, fascism's appeal in France had remained feeble.[40]

Berstein took this position in a review of Zeev Sternhell's *Neither Right nor Left*, Sternhell being the foremost interpreter of French fascism in Europe to take the opposite position.[41] Indeed, Sternhell, an Israeli and a graduate of the École des Sciences Politiques in Paris, maintained that French intellectual life had been so permeated with fascist ideas that a large number of French intellectuals were "fascists without knowing it."[42] It is noteworthy that Sternhell's editor, Bernard-Henry Lévy, has published a book claiming that French political discourse is full of fascist ideas (he even calls fascism "the French ideology")—although, unlike Sternhell, Lévy blames the political Right and the political Left equally.[43]

Even though Sternhell echoed the consensus school in emphasizing the "socialist" characteristics of French fascism, he was sharply attacked by some consensus historians for denying that France was allergic to fascism in the 1930s. In some respects, the reaction of French scholars to Sternhell's works is reminiscent of some of the harsh responses originally directed at Robert Paxton's *Vichy France*, in which Paxton suggested that during the German Occupation France was a nation more of collaborators than of resisters.[44] Sternhell himself has commented on the storm of criticism aroused by his writings. He agreed with one interviewer that he had particularly shocked the French public with his claim that prior to the First World War France had been the birthplace of fascist ideology and that during the 1930s fascist ideas had been widespread in France, especially in French intellectual circles.

It has been truly a very rough affair. But the reticences, the resistance, and the criticisms stem from two essential causes. First, there is a certain effort at repression; there is a problem of the collective unconscious, a refusal to cope with the disagreeable side of history. France is the France of the French Revolution of 1789, it is the liberal and democratic republic, the open society. People refuse to admit that France had also secreted a political culture antipodal to the revolutionary and rationalist tradition of the eighteenth century. People refuse to admit that there has been another side to the nation's history. The most striking thing is the refusal to conceive of Vichy as something other than an accident, a parenthesis, or a regime imposed by the occupier.[45]

As Michel Dobry has observed, what Sternhell violated was the assumption, shared not only by most of the French public but also by most French historians and political scientists, that France had always been immune to fascism—"la thèse immunitaire" (the immunity thesis) Dobry calls it. (I myself recall encountering evidence of the popularity of this thesis when I took my family to France in 1969. Both my children came home from their first day at school, each having gone to a different French school, to inform me that they had been asked by their new classmates what their father was doing in France. When they said that he was researching French fascism they were told that was silly, since there had never been any such thing as French fascism.) For Michel Dobry, however, French historians' denial of the past appeal of fascism in France was remarkable. Those who made such denials, he said, not only displayed a "surprising amnesia" about the crisis democracy had undergone in France in the 1930s; they had also, in their reactions to Sternhell's writings, revealed "a passion which . . . appears to be the most certain indication that a sensitive point has been touched on questions that are not exclusively methodological."[46]

In October 1983, Sternhell even had to stand trial in a French court when Bertrand de Jouvenel, who had supported Doriot's party in the late 1930s and whom Sternhell suggested had collaborated with the Germans during the Second World War, sued Sternhell for defamation. Sternhell was fined one franc. He was cleared of all charges regarding his "opinions" as to the fascist nature of de Jouvenel's ideas, but he was found guilty of accusing de Jouvenel of actual behavior during the war that was fascist—that is, according to the court, collaborationist. Following the verdict, de Jouvenel's lawyer, Henri Coukroun, commented: "We had demanded the symbolic franc, and we got it. The essential and most serious thing was having the attitude of my client during the Occupation put in doubt. For that Sternhell has been condemned. I am therefore satisfied." Sternhell commented: "What I learned from this process is that on the terrain of ideas everything is permitted, but one does not have the right to touch persons. One can speak of fascism but not of fascists. On a personal level, I will never forgive those who have questioned my honor, my good faith, my integrity as a professional historian. Never."[47] One indication of the passions aroused by this trial was the fatal heart attack suffered by Raymond Aron as he was leaving the court building. Aron, the famous liberal philosopher and *Le Figaro* columnist who had taken on Sartre in his book, *The Opium of the Intellectuals*, had spoken at the trial in defense of de Jouvenel, berating Sternhell for having written an "ahistorical" work that had failed to put de Jouvenel's previous "state of mind" within its proper historical context.[48]

Six months later, the historian Serge Berstein also took aim at Sternhell, although in this case it was France he was defending, not de Jouvenel. In his review of Sternhell's *Neither Right nor Left*, Berstein returned to Rémond's original position that fascist ideas had been imported from abroad and had never received much support in France. He cited Rémond's comment that old democratic habits had created "efficacious barriers" to "irrational" movements like fascism. According to Berstein, French fascism had never appealed to more than a "marginal" minority. If some intellectuals were attracted to fascism, they were "less numerous" than Sternhell believed, their success was "ephemeral," and they were unable to obliterate "the profundity of democratic culture in France."[49]

Berstein did concede that one sizeable French political party in the 1930s, the Parti Populaire Français, led by the former Communist Jacques Doriot, was fascist—with its "symmetrical rejection of capitalism and bolshevism," its "totalitarian practices," and its "exacerbated cult of the leader." Nevertheless, Berstein concluded that the general appeal of fascism remained weak in France, as indicated by the fact that by 1939 Doriot's party was in decline and was revived during the Occupation only with German help. Thus Berstein agreed with the remark of one of Doriot's biographers that "if the Parti Populaire Français was fascist, France was not." As for the Croix de Feu, Berstein asserted that it was not fascist because it proposed nothing that was "incompatible with [French] national traditions."[50] For Berstein, then, Sternhell was mistaken to argue that France had a significant fascist tradition.

In contrast to Berstein, two other French scholars, Jacques Julliard and Michel Winock, commended Sternhell for having performed an important service for French scholarship. According to Julliard, Sternhell has played "the glass-breaking role formerly held by Robert Paxton regarding Vichy." "French historiography," Julliard wrote, "often approaches subjects of contemporary history with so much caution and timidity that the intervention of foreign historians is necessary so that problems considered taboo will be openly discussed."[51] Winock added that prior to Sternhell's books, French historians had written only of a national allergy to fascism and had even practiced an "autocensorship" on the subject.[52]

While they credited him for his contributions, Julliard and Winock faulted Sternhell for neglecting the political and social history of fascism. Winock described Sternhell's *Neither Right nor Left* as a "pure history of ideas" "without direct relation to events." Winock wrote: "In search of the platonic idea of fascism, [Sternhell] fails to analyze the conditions of its eventual rise in France."[53] Julliard criticized Sternhell for asserting that in France fascist ideology had come closest to "the ideal type, to the 'idea' of fascism in the platonic sense of the term" precisely because it "never passed the stage of theory and never suffered the inevitable compromises" that it did in Italy and Germany. Julliard considered this approach to be a form of historical idealism that divorced fascism from its historical context, "artificially separat[ing] fascist ideology from fascism itself." He noted that "all the proceedings of recent historiography tend, by contrast, to privilege the study of practice in relation to that of discourse, at the very least to not take the latter for ready cash."[54]

Julliard and Winock also criticized Sternhell for largely ignoring the major French fascist organizations and intellectuals of the 1930s in favor of less sizeable movements and less influential intellectuals whose origins were on the Left. As a result, Winock wrote, Sternhell "quickly passes over vulgar fascism," that of the paramilitary nationalist leagues, of Doriot's party, of the Cagoulards, and of the Croix de Feu in order to focus on the ideas of the Belgian socialist Henri de Man, the French neosocialist Marcel Déat, and the writings of others who proposed "a socialism without a proletariat." Julliard regretted not only that Sternhell displayed little interest in the mass organizations of the extreme Right, but also that he "totally pass[ed] over in silence" such leading French fascist intellectuals of the period as Pierre Drieu La Rochelle and Robert Brasillach (whose politics in the 1930s, I have argued, were firmly on the Right) in order to concentrate on certain articles in the left-wing Catholic review *Esprit* or on certain writings of the young Pierre Mendès-France.[55]

Although I have been critical of Sternhell on similar grounds and have attempted to avoid such criticism of my own works on French fascism by combining intellectual history with political and social history and by placing the ebbs and flows of French fascism within their immediate historical contexts, I have not pleased everybody, any more than Sternhell has. In July 1995 Gilles de La Rocque, the son of Colonel de La Rocque, took me to task in a letter to the French newspaper *Le Monde* for not agreeing with a large number of French historians and journalists who deny that the Croix de Feu was fascist. Gilles de La Rocque also accused me of manipulating texts in a way that suggested that his father had collaborated with the Germans when he had not. My partial reply to the latter charge can be found in a subsequent issue of *Le Monde*.[56]

I have also been criticized by Eugen Weber, Julian Jackson, and John Bingham, who all agree that in my book on French fascism between 1924 and 1933, I did not discuss fascist organizations so much as I did conservative or centrist groups that were not fascist: the Action Française, the Légion, the Jeunesses Patriotes, and the Faisceau. Bingham writes: "far from being fascist revolutionaries, Soucy shows that [the members of these movements] espoused traditional economic programs. These conclusions lead one to suspect, with Julian Jackson, that Soucy's book is not really about fascism." Bingham adds: "Soucy's definition of fascism as an essentially conservative phenomenon cannot account for its more radical social aspects; indeed, the more radical the group, the further from Soucy's definition it gets."[57] Eugen Weber wondered in his review of my book whether what I called fascism might not better be called Bonapartism.[58] Thus by assuming that fascism had to be socially and economically "radical," these scholars were able define out of existence even the fascism of Georges Valois's Faisceau—a movement that called itself fascist, wore fascist uniforms, and employed the fascist salute.

Bingham also challenged some of my conclusions on the grounds that they were based on the "dubious" records of the French police.[59] In doing so, he referred to a related criticism John Sweets made of one of my books in his 1988 historiographical essay on the debate over French fascism, collaborationism, and the Resistance. Sweets wrote:

> Soucy's method of citing police reports leads to a more general objection to his interpretation of the significance of French fascism. As those who have done research with French police reports know, these vary considerably in terms of their origins—from different types of police (Sûreté, Renseignements généreaux, Corps urbaine, etc.)—closeness to events, and reliability. Thus, Soucy's reference only to Archives Nationales file numbers and dates of origin of the documents is not very informative, unless one has ready access to the Archives. I mention this, in particular, because one would like to know what sort of documents are being used to support the author's estimation of the size of various fascist movements. Eugen Weber has noted that "the Sûreté took most of its figures from statements made by the organizations themselves," leading to inflated claims concerning membership, and other writers have recognized the difficulty of establishing precise head counts.[60]

I replied at some length, in my most recent book on French fascism, to the matter of using French police reports of the 1930s, pointing out among other things that historians of both the consensus and the anticonsensus schools have mined these "dubious" reports with rich results, including such scholars as Eugen Weber, Philippe Burrin, Paul Mazgaj, Jean-Paul Brunet, Alan Douglas, Stewart Doty, Paul Jankowski, William Irvine, Kevin Passmore, and Sam Goodfellow.[61] Indeed, in the same article in which Sweets questions my use of French police reports, he himself cites such reports in support of some of his own generalizatons.[62] Historians, of course, do need to exercise discernment in evaluating the credibility of any report, a discernment that applies to local as well as national police reports, since greater proximity does not necessarily mean greater reliability. At the same time, to associate police reporting in France in the 1930s with that of J. Edgar Hoover's ideologically monolithic FBI in the United States would be to err in the opposite direction. Certainly, French fascist propagandists had far more reason to distort the truth than did informers reporting to the French police or French police reporting to their superiors, especially to a succession of ideologically diverse French Ministers of the Interior.[63] If used prudently, French police reports of the 1930s remain an invaluable means of penetrating the façade of French fascism and revealing some of its most important inner workings, including the major financial backing of its organizations.

Eugen Weber's remark that the French police took most of their membership figures for fascist organizations from the organizations themselves ignores police reports to the Minister of the Interior that challenged such inflated claims and provided their own much lower estimates.[64] No one disputes that fascist leaders often exaggerated the size of their movements. Of course, Sweets is right when he notes the difficulty of arriving at "precise" head counts, but this is a problem with all estimates. However, to say, as the French historian Philippe Machefer has, that the Parti Social Français (PSF), the new name for the Croix de Feu after 1936, had between seven hundred thousand and 1.2 million party members in 1937 is quite different from saying that it had between two and three hundred party members. Machefer's estimate may be imprecise, but it is not silly. In discussing the size of the PSF's party membership, William Irvine has put it as well as anyone:

The actual number may never be known, but by any standard the membership of the PSF was large and dynamic. The records of the local newspapers dealing with the activities of the PSF sections are consistent only with a very large membership. [The same is true] for the size of its provincial rallies. Remember too that political participation in France is low compared to, say, Germany—all parties, from the Socialists to the Right, are a fraction of the size of their German counterparts. So, in this context, even 700,000 (an absolute minimum I would think) is simply gigantic.[65]

Debates over the value of police reports and other sources are no small matter, since ultimately it is the power of the evidence that determines the superiority of one interpretation over another, not simply the interpretation itself, no matter how ideologically satisfying or theoretically "brilliant" it may be. To conclude from the debate over French fascism that one interpretation is as good as another would be to indulge in the worst kind of radical deconstructionism or intellectual relativism. For historians at least, evidence still counts. This is why local, in-depth research in recent years by such scholars as Paul Jankowski, Sam Goodfellow, and Kevin Passmore into the social realities of French fascist movements in Marseille, Alsace, and Lyon have been so important, disproving with impressive evidence less substantiated generalizatons of the past.[66]

The debate over French fascism has not been limited to assessments of various movements and writers of the 1920s and 1930s; a number of fascist ideas and attitudes reemerged under the Vichy regime, as well as in more recent years within Jean-Marie Le Pen's Front National. The conflicting historical interpretations of Robert Paxton and John Sweets over whether France under the German Occupation was more a nation of collaborators than a nation of resisters is only one aspect of that debate.[67] Here too the assumption has often gone unchallenged that for a French person not to have collaborated with the Nazis after 1940 is proof that he or she was not fascist before 1940—which has led some historians to further assume that a lack of large numbers of active collaborationists after 1940 is proof of a lack of large numbers of active French fascists before 1940. What these assumptions ignore is that many nationalistic French fascists of the 1930s may have found fascism much less attractive in the 1940s when it became associated with German soldiers occupying French soil, ordering French people about, and plundering the French economy. The differing historical contexts need to be taken into account.

A fascinating extension of the debate over the Vichy period is Henry Rousso's *The Vichy Syndrome*, which questions how various sectors of postwar public opinion in France, including influential postwar French historians and journalists, have preferred to remember the Vichy years. Rousso shows how following the Second World War those who had been Pétainists, Gaullists, or Communists during the war tended, each in their own way, to "forget" or repress certain politically inconvenient memories on behalf of their own sanitized and politically expedient versions of the past. For Rousso memory can be a "structuring of forgetfulness," which in this case derived from the "Franco-French civil war" between rightists and leftists that tore France apart from the victory of the Popular Front of 1936 to the end of the Vichy regime in 1944. Rousso writes: "The memory of Vichy, the conflicting representations of the regime, have been shaped by the same antagonistic values that led to the Vichy crisis itself."[68] A more recent addition to the discussion of the Vichy syndrome is John Hellman's exposé in the fall 1955 issue of *French Historical Studies*—an article sure to anger a good many Catholic historians of Vichy whom Hellman accuses, among other things, of reserving certain archives under their control for scholars sympathetic to their cause, including the archives of the Croix de Feu.[69] This is one of the most important articles written on the historiography of Vichy in recent years.

The debate over French fascism also extends chronologically backward to the possible existence of proto-fascist ideas and movements prior to the First World War, with their origins in the Boulanger and Dreyfus Affairs of the late nineteenth century. Robert Byrnes, Stephen Wilson, Ernst Nolte, Zeev Sternhell, C. Stewart Doty, Peter Rutkoff, William Irvine, Steve Englund, Jack Roth, Patrick Hutton, Paul Mazgaj, and myself are only a few of the historians who have written on the subject.[70] Here again, the question has been raised as to whether French fascist movements, or in this case their precursors, were more Left than Right. Paul Mazgaj, for example, in a historiographical essay on the origins of the radical Right in France, has faulted me for describing Maurice Barrès during the Boulanger Affair as far more conservative than revolutionary, as someone who was long on socialist rhetoric but short on socialist substance. By taking non-Marxist definitions of socialism in the 1880s as their standard (to be for child labor laws, for example, was considered by some people at the time to be "socialist"), Mazgaj agrees with Zeev Sternhell, Patrick Hutton, and others that Barrès was leftist.[71]

Whatever disagreements continue to exist among scholars about the nature of French fascism, one thing seems certain: French fascism did not begin with what I have called the "first wave" between 1924 and 1926, nor did it end with what I have called the "second wave" between 1933 and 1939. Nor should one conclude that French fascism has appeared only in one form—that, for example, the Parti Populaire Français was fascist but not the Croix de Feu. Eugen Weber was quite right many years ago when he observed that there was not just one brand of fascism in Europe, but "varieties" of fascism, a concept that should be applied to fascist movements within nations as well as to fascist movements that differ from nation to nation.

It also seems clear that when political circumstances change, fascism changes, adapting to new situations, privileging certain fascist ideas over others, downgrading those that are less expedient. In 1932, for example, Adolf Hitler, following the advice of his campaign manager, Joseph Goebbels, temporarily muted his anti-Semitism to improve his electoral chances. Nor did Hitler begin exterminating Jews until the Second World War provided him with sufficient cover (and countries like the United States and Great Britain refused to accept more than a few Jewish refugees).

Different circumstances can also spur fascists to replace old scapegoats with new ones. As Richard Wolin has pointed out, with the collapse of Communism in Eastern Europe and the Soviet Union in the 1990s, the radical Right in Western Europe has found new enemies to hate: Algerian, Turkish, Vietnamese, and other immigrants.[72] With Marxists and liberal "fellow-travelers" no longer credible bogeymen, with the "Judeo-Bolshevik" menace no longer perceived as so menacing, some fascists have turned elsewhere for unifying targets.

Indeed, one wonders whether managers of the new global economy who, at least in the West, seem to be presently reducing the standard of living of the many while increasing that of the few, will be tempted, like some politically beleaguered businessmen in France in the 1930s, to finance right-wing authoritarian propaganda that will divert social resentments away from themselves and toward new scapegoats. Should another major economic crisis occur one day, will a new set of "aliens" replace Marxists, liberals, and Jews in fascist demonology? Only partially, I think, since presumably such a crisis would lead to a revival of the political Left and therefore to another conservative back-lash whose extreme Right would be quick to return to some familiar themes of the past. Fascist opportunism exists, but so too do fascist traditions—now more than a hundred years old—whose ideas remain available to those inclined to employ them.

Notes

1. William Irvine, *French Conservatism in Crisis: The Republican Federation of France in the 1930s* (Baton Rouge: Louisiana State University Press, 1979); Paul Sérant, *Le Romantisme fasciste* (Paris: Fasquelle, 1954), 12.

2. René Rémond, *La Droite en France de la première restauration à la Vème république* (Paris: Aubier, 1968), 213–15, 218.

3. Eugen Weber, "Nationalism, Socialism, and National Socialism in France," *French Historical Studies* 2, no. 3 (spring 1962): 296; Weber, *Varieties of Fascism* (New York, 1964), 133–36, 139–41.

4. Eugen Weber, *The Hollow Years: France in the 1930s* (New York: W. W. Norton, 1994), 119, 140, 141.

5. Weber, *Varieties of Fascism*, 133–34, 136.

6. Weber, *Varieties of Fascism*, 140.

7. Weber, *Varieties of Fascism*, 137.

8. Weber, *Varieties of Fascism*, 141.

9. Weber, *Varieties of Fascism*, 138.

10. Weber, *The Hollow Years*, 119.

11. Ernst Nolte, *Three Faces of Fascism* (New York: Holt, Rinehart and Winston, 1966), 20–21.

12. Ernst Nolte, *Les Mouvements fascistes* (Paris: Calmann-Levy, 1969), 75–76.

13. Zeev Sternhell, *Ni droite ni gauche: L'Idéologie fasciste en France* (Paris: Seuil, 1983), 34; Sternhell, *Naissance de l'idéologie française* (Paris: Fayard, 1989), 45, 305, 317; Sternhell, "Precursors of Fascism in France," in *Who Were the Fascists?* ed. Stein Larsen (Bergen: Universitetforlaget, 1980), 496.

14. Sternhell, "Precursors of Fascism in France," 495; Philippe Burrin, *La Dérive fasciste* (Paris: Seuil, 1986), 192; Pierre Milza, *Fascisme française* (Paris: Flammarion, 1987), 133–41.

15. William Irvine, "Fascism in France and the Strange Case of the Croix de Feu," *Journal of Modern History* 63 (June 1991): 277, 278.

16. Burrin, *La Dérive fasciste*, 192.

17. Irvine, "Croix de Feu," 273.

18. Irvine, "Croix de Feu," 294.

19. John Bingham, "Defining French Fascism, Finding Fascists in France," *Canadian Journal of History/Annales canadiennes d'histoire* 29 (December 1994): 537.

20. Kevin Passmore, "The Croix de Feu, Bonapartism, National Populism, or Fascism?" *French History* 9, no. 2 (1995), and *From Liberalism to Fascism: The Right in a French Province, 1928–1939* (Cambridge: Cambridge University Press, 1997), 219–45; Sam Goodfellow, "Fascist or Conservative? The Croix de Feu/Parti Social Français in Alsace," paper presented at the French Historical Society Meeting, Chico, California, 1993.

21. Robert Soucy, *French Fascism*, 172; Colonel de La Rocque, *Disciplines d'Action* (Clermont-Ferrand: Editions du "Petit Journal," 1941), 29–30.

22. René Rémond, *Notre siècle, 1918–1988* (Paris: Fayard, 1989), 105, 216; Jacques Nobécourt, "Le Pen et La Rocque," *Le Monde*, 8–9 May 1988.

23. Benito Mussolini, cited in Michael A. LeDeen, "Italian Jews and Fascism," *Judaism: A Quarterly of Jewish Life and Thought* 18, no. 3 (summer 1969): 281.

24. LeDeen, "Italian Jews," 287.

25. LeDeen, "Italian Jews," 286.

26. Marrus and Paxton, *Vichy France and the Jews*, 316.

27. LeDeen, "Italian Jews," 282.

28. LeDeen, "Italian Jews," 289.

29. Marrus and Paxton, *Vichy France and the Jews*, 147, 305, 307, 315, 317, 364.

30. Nobécourt, "Le Pen et La Rocque."

31. Soucy, *French Fascism*, 23–24, 66, 82–83, 97–98, 102, 122, 223, 251–52.

32. Philippe Bourdrel, "Le Complot de la Cagoule," *Candide*, 25 January–1 February 1962.

33. Sam Goodfellow, "The French Radical Right in Alsace, 1924–1945," paper presented at the French Historical Society conference, Columbus, Ohio, 31 March 1990.

34. Weber, *The Hollow Years*, 119; Serge Berstein, "La France des années trente allergique au fascisme," *XXe Siècle* 2 (April 1984): 83, 89, 92–94.

35. Charles Maier, *Recasting Bourgeois Europe* (Princeton NJ: Princeton University Press, 1975), 324, 339, 347, 348; see also Denis Mack Smith, "The Theory and Practice of Fascism," in *Fascism: An Anthology*, ed. Nathaneal Greene (New York: Thomas Y. Crowell, 1968), 88–95.

36. Michel Dobry, "Février 1934 et la découverte de l'allergie de la société française à la 'Révolution fasciste,'" *Revue Française de Sociologie* 30 (July–December 1989): 511–13.

37. La Rocque, *Disciplines d'action*, 146.

38. René Rémond, *La Droite en France de 1815 à nos jours* (Paris: Aubier, 1954), 12.

39. René Rémond, *Les Droites en France* (Paris: Aubier, 1982), 206–7.

40. Serge Berstein, "La France des années trente," 83, 89, 92–94.

41. Sternhell, *Ni droite ni gauche*; Sternhell, *Naissance de l'idéologie fasciste*; Sternhell, *Droite révolutionnaire, 1885–1914: Les Origines française du fascisme* (Paris: Seuil, 1978).

42. Sternhell, *Ni droite ni gauche*, 311.

43. Bernard-Henri Lévy, *L'Idéologie française* (Paris: Grasset, 1981), 18–19, 27.

44. See summary of this criticism in Henry Rousso, *Le Syndrome de Vichy de 1944 à nos jours* (Paris: Seuil, 1987), 288–97.

45. Zeev Sternhell, quoted in Marco Diani and Michela Nacci, "Fascisme: Idéologie française et intellectuels européens. Entretiens avec Zeev Sternhell," *Contemporary French Civilization* 14, no. 2 (winter–spring 1990): 52.

46. Dobry, "Février 1934," 512–13.

47. Pierre Assouline, "Enquête sur un historien condamné pour diffamation," *L'Histoire* 68 (June 1984): 101.

48. Assouline, "Enquête," 99.

49. Berstein, "France des années trentes," 83, 89, 92–94.

50. Berstein, "France des années trentes," 94.

51. Jacques Julliard, "Sur un fascisme imaginaire: À propos d'un livre de Zeev Sternhell," *Annales. E.S.V.* 39, no. 4 (July–August 1984): 849.

52. Michel Winock, "Fascisme à la française ou fascisme introuvable?" *Le Débat* 25 (May 1983): 35.

53. Winock, "Fascisme," 42.

54. Julliard, "Fascisme imaginaire," 850–52, 859.

55. Winock, "Fascisme," 38; Julliard, "Fascisme imaginaire," 851–52. For more on the Sternhell controversy, see António Costa Pinta, "Fascist Ideology Revisited: Zeev Sternhell and his Critics," *European History Quarterly* 16 (1986): 465–83; Robert Wohl, "French Fascism both Right and Left: Reflections on the Sternhell Controversy," *Journal of Modern History* 63 (March 1991): 91–98; and Robert O. Paxton, "Radicals. The Birth of Fascist Ideology: From Cultural Rebellion to Political Revolution," *The New York Review of Books*, 23 June 1994, 51–54.

56. Gilles de La Rocque, "Correspondance. Fascism Made in France (suite)," *Le Monde*, 21 July 1995; Robert Soucy, "Correspondance. Fascism Made in France," *Le Monde*, 18 August 1995.

57. Bingham, "Defining French Fascism," 532, 538.

58. Eugen Weber, "Review of Robert Soucy's *French Fascism: The First Wave, 1924–33*," *American Historical Review* 91 (1986): 1217–18.

59. Bingham, "Defining French Fascism," 532.

60. John Sweets, "Hold that Pendulum! Redefining Fascism, Collaborationism, and Resistance in France," *French Historical Studies* 15, no. 4 (fall 1988): 739.

61. Soucy, *French Fascism*, 11, 323–24.

62. Sweets, "Hold that Pendulum!" 754, 747.

63. Soucy, *French Fascism*, 11, 323–24.

64. See for example Pierre Taittinger's claim that the Jeunesses Patriotes had 130,000 members in 1928 and 200,000 in 1929, compared to the French police's estimate of 102,000 in 1929. Taittinger, quoted in Jean Philippet, *Les Jeunesses Patriotes et Pierre Taittinger, 1924–1940* (Paris: Bibliothèque de l'Ecole des Sciences Politiques, 1957), 133 vs. Archives Nationales, Paris, F7 13232, 3 June 1929. See also Soucy, *French Fascism*, 61, 111, 114.

65. William Irvine, letter to Robert Soucy, 18 January 1990.

66. Paul Jankowski, *Communism and Collaboration: Simon Sabiani and Politics in Marseille, 1919–1944* (New Haven CT: Yale University Press, 1989); Sam

Goodfellow, "Fascism in Alsace, 1918–1945," Ph.D. thesis, Indiana University, 1991; Kevin Passmore, "The French Third Republic: Stalemate Society or Cradle of Fascism?" *French History* 7, no. 4 (1993); Passmore, "The Right and the Extreme Right in the Department of the Rhône, 1928–1939," Ph.D. thesis, Warwick University, 1992.

67. Paxton, *Vichy France: Old Guard and New Order*; John Sweets, *Choices in Vichy France*. See also my review of this book in the *Journal of Modern History* 60, no. 1 (March 1988): 167–69. Robert O. Paxton, "Vichy Fifty Years Later," *Proceedings of the Western Society for French History* 21 (1994): 233–43; John Dupont, "Robert Paxton: France's American Expert on Vichy," *International Herald-Tribune*, 21 October 1994; and Gordon, *Collaboratonism in France*.

68. Rousso, *Vichy Syndrome*, 300.

69. John Hellman, "Wounding Memories: Mitterand, Moulin, Touvier, and the Divine Half-Lie of Resistance," *French Historical Studies* 19, no. 2 (fall 1995): 461–86.

70. See Paul Mazgaj, "The Origins of the French Radical Right: A Historiographical Essay," *French Historical Studies* 15, no. 2 (fall 1987): 287–315; Zeev Sternhell, *Maurice Barrès et le nationalisme français* (Paris: Armand Colin, 1972); Robert Soucy, *Fascism in France: The Case of Maurice Barrès* (Berkeley: University of California Press, 1972); Sternhell, *Droite révolutionnaire*; C. Stewart Doty, *From Cultural Rebellion to Counterrevolution: The Politics of Maurice Barrès* (Athens: Ohio University Press, 1976); Paul Mazgaj, *The Action Française and Revolutionary Syndicalism* (Chapel Hill: University of North Carolina Press, 1979); Peter Rutkoff, *Revanche & Revision: The League of Patriots and the Origins of the Radical Right in France* (Athens: Ohio University Press, 1981); Steve Englund, "The Origin of Oppositional Nationalism in France (1881–1889)," Ph.D. dissertation, Princeton University, 1981; William Irvine, *The Boulanger Affair Reconsidered* (New York: Oxford University Press, 1989); Nolte, *Three Faces of Fascism*; Robert Byrnes, *Antisemitism in Modern France* (New York: Howard Fertig, 1969); Roth, *Cult of Violence*; Stephen Wilson, *Ideology and Experience: Antisemitism in France at the Time of the Dreyfus Affair* (London and Ontario: Fairleigh Dickinson University Press and Associated University Presses, 1982); Michel Winock, *Edouard Drumont and Cie: Antisémitisme et fascisme en France* (Paris: Seuil, 1982).

71. Mazgaj, "Origins," 300–301.

72. Richard Wolin, "Mussolini's Ghost: Europe and the Specter of Fascism," *Tikkun* (July–August 1994): 13–16, 76.

Bertram M. Gordon

World War II France Half a Century After

In July 1995, half a century after the Second World War, French President Jacques Chirac's public apology for France's complicity with Nazi German political and racial persecution during the German occupation once again drew public attention to the war years. Chirac's statement reinforced the impact of the 1994 public disclosures and media discussions of then President François Mitterrand's Vichy activities and his repeated refusal to assign any responsibility to the Republic for French involvement in the Holocaust. Not surprisingly, the contrasting actions of the two French presidents focused attention on ways in which World War II and its recollections influenced French history during the fifty years that followed the war.[1] This attention was maintained in 1996 and 1997 by government initiatives to make restitution, where possible, to the Occupation victims of art and apartment expropriation. An appellate court ruling in January 1997 to try former Vichy Secretary General of the Gironde Prefecture Maurice Papon for crimes against humanity also contributed to a focusing of attention on the wartime years.[2] In February 1997, the news magazine *Le Point* published a story asserting that Michel Junot, an aide from 1977 through 1995 to Jacques Chirac, then Mayor of Paris, had served as subprefect in Pithiviers, in the Loiret, under Vichy and in this capacity had helped maintain order in French concentration camps from which Jews were later deported to Auschwitz.[3] These events, together with the election of three National Front mayors in France in 1995, plus an enhanced visibility of the European Right in the form of the National Alliance in Italy, the Freedom Party in Austria, and right-wing manifestations in reunified Germany and the former Soviet Union and East Bloc countries, made retrospective views of the war years the foci of considerable historical discussion in France and elsewhere.

Suggesting that fascism, in terms of scandal, revision, and ideology, has somehow returned in Europe since 1980 raises the question of whether 1980 was a turning point in the history of the European

Right.[4] This essay, therefore, examines whether 1980, or by extension the late 1970s and early 1980s, did in fact mark a significant turning point in French retrospective views of their wartime past. The answer to this question is mixed. The year 1980 does not appear to stand out in the continuing French reassessments of their wartime past, but there were several shifts in the late 1970s and early 1980s that set the stage for what has been a modest but real alteration in historical perspective concerning the war, limited largely, however, to the political, academic, and journalistic community. Accordingly, this article first examines the historians' debates relating to World War II France in the period since the late 1970s, and then develops an approach to place not only the World War II years, but also the French recollections of them, into historical perspective.

The Historians' Debate in the 1980s and 1990s

The year 1979 was marked by the emergence of a "New Right" in France, though the term goes back at least to 1947, when *nouvelle Droite* was used in reference to the Parti Républicain de la Liberté, which was seen as a continuation of the interwar leagues in defense of urban capitalist rather than agrarian interests.[5] Two years after the election of Mitterrand and the Socialists in 1981, Jean Marie Le Pen's National Front, in what is sometimes called its "breakthrough," emerged from political marginality by placing several of its members on the Dreux city council.[6] The enhanced strength of the National Front after 1983 follows a twentieth-century French pattern of Leftist governments offering opportunities to movements of the Right, exemplified by the relative successes of the Faisceau under the Cartel des Gauches during the mid-1920s, and the Croix de Feu and Parti Populaire Français under the administration of the Popular Front in 1936. Together with the rise of the National Front came a decline in the strength of the French Communist party, followed by the end of the cold war in Europe and the reunification of Germany, all factors in the reassessment of French views of the Second World War taking place as the generation that fought the war dies off.[7] Indeed, the French publication statistics dealing with World War II show a moderate (if somewhat irregular) growth, with higher rates of publication on the war during the late 1980s and early 1990s than at any time since interest peaked in the mid-1940s. Doctoral dissertations on World War II have also become more numerous during the 1980s, related perhaps to the opening of official archives to historians in 1979.[8]

Often the *post facto* naming of historical periods based on present-day perspectives that highlight selected characteristics taken out of

their historical context obscures more than clarifies historical process. "Antiquity," "Medieval," "Renaissance," "Modern," and "Postmodern" exemplify terms that have engendered arcane historical controversies, often to the detriment of the understanding of historical
process. Since the 1970s, the French wartime experience has been
summarized by terms such as "mode rétro" and, more recently and frequently, "Vichy syndrome." "Mode rétro" gained a certain currency
during the 1970s, when it was used by Pascal Ory, among others, and
"Vichy syndrome" was selected by Henry Rousso as the title of a book
that was first published in 1987 in France and has since structured
much of the discussion of how the French see their wartime past.[9]
These terms have become metaphors for a supposedly agonized postwar France somehow attempting to reconcile itself to wartime French
collaboration with Nazi genocide. Images of Vichy as "syndrome" and
France as "obsessional" in wrestling with guilt for collaboration with
the Nazis have been used to assemble a model of a virtually unique
postwar French retrospective fixation with the Vichy years.

In an article entitled "The 'Vichy Syndrome' Problem in History,"
which appeared as part of a forum devoted to the Vichy syndrome
thesis in the fall 1995 issue of *French Historical Studies*, I examined
the pattern of publishing on Vichy and World War II in France since
1940.[10] There I suggested that terms such as "mode rétro" and "Vichy
syndrome" were not necessarily inappropriate, but that they needed to
be understood in a broader historical context than has been common
in the usage since the late 1980s. In reality, French history shows a continuing pattern of syndromes à la Vichy or *modes rétro* following military defeat, betrayal, collaboration, retribution, and subsequent re-
evaluation.[11] These types of events, dating from Vercingétorix through
Jean le Bon and Sedan, to name just a few, have often been used as symbols whose meanings take on a life of their own, transcending their
real significance in the long-term history of France. A glimpse at the
historical literature covering the years 1940–44, drawn from the larger
survey in the "'Vichy Syndrome' Problem in History" article, shows
an extensive literature on World War II France all the way back to 1940.
Many of these reinterpretations take the World War II experience out
of the French historical context, bestowing on it significance more related to issues at the time of writing than to the World War II experience itself. It is also important to emphasize that French reassessments of World War II have been and continue to be influenced by
other countries, as historians writing in English or German are translated and read in France, and become part of the continuing dialogue
there. Significant examples include the work of Stanley Hoffmann,

Eberhard Jäckel's *Frankreich in Hitlers Europa*, and Robert O. Paxton's *Vichy France: Old Guard and New Order.*[12]

The mid-1970s produced Pascal Ory's argument for a mythical "rétro satanique" image of the collaborators, created by what he called a "résistancialisme établi," attempting to deny the reality of wartime French collaboration with the Germans.[13] Discussion of a racial or "neo-pagan" New Right was especially marked in the pages of *Figaro-Magazine* in 1979. Raoul Girardet argued that the case of Charles de Gaulle showed that not all rightists favored Vichy, and François Nourissier suggested that the creative spirits who joined the Resistance were generally on the Left.[14] Most of the "New Right's" argumentation, however, did not specifically evoke Vichy. Insofar as World War II was discussed, the focus was more on the racial aspects of Nazi thought in Germany. "New Right" spokesmen such as Alain de Benoist sought to distance themselves from the traditionalist or Christian Right they identified with Vichy.[15]

By the beginning of the 1980s, a long and varied sequence of argumentation had been established about Vichy and its subsequent effects on France. This sequence was not dramatically altered even with the partial opening of the French archives in 1979. My own study, published in 1980, examined the wartime French collaboration as a manifestation of the historical French Right and a source of retrospective interest for a small number of *nostalgiques*, attracted to the adventures of the collaboration militants.[16] In 1981, Paxton and Michael Marrus published *Vichy France and the Jews*, which emphasized Vichy's autonomous role in the Holocaust and placed Vichy anti-Semitism in the context of a French reaction against refugees, often Jewish, that had intensified during the late 1930s.[17] The sequence of literature dealing with World War II shows no dramatic shifts in argumentation accompanying the emergence of the "New Right" in 1979, the election of the Socialists in 1981, or the "breakthrough" of the National Front in 1983. Indeed, Rousso noted that from 1978 through 1987 "the tide [of historical discussion of Vichy] seemed to be ebbing."[18] In 1983 and immediately thereafter, historical controversy in France focused more on Zeev Sternhell's *Ni droite ni gauche*—which traced the development of European fascism to late-nineteenth- and early-twentieth-century French thinkers such as Maurice Barrès, Georges Sorel, and Charles Maurras—than on France in World War II.[19]

French retrospective views of World War II were colored by the events surrounding Klaus Barbie, the former Lyon Nazi Gestapo chief, extradited from Bolivia to France in 1983 and convicted there four years later on charges of crimes against humanity. With the expulsion of Barbie from Bolivia in 1983, French Jews began researching more intensively the history of the Holocaust in France. In *The Children of Izieu*, published in 1984, attorney Serge Klarsfeld, a Nazi hunter and historian eager to elucidate the entire history of Vichy's complicity in the extermination of the Jews, examined the deportation of Jewish children from the town of Izieu, a crime of which Barbie was accused. The deportation of the Izieu children was a crime against humanity, Klarsfeld argued, rather than a war crime, as the children had represented no threat to the safety of the German occupation forces.[20] It is this quality of the Barbie story upon which Klarsfeld, Marek Halter, and other leaders of the Jewish community focused, emphasizing the educational role of the trial. Six months before the start of the Barbie trial, Bernard-Henri Lévy was quoted to the effect that "What my generation learned was what the Germans did to us. We were taught that foreign doctrines were implanted here. But, in fact, we had our very own fascism, a fascism in the colors of France."[21]

In 1986, examining another aspect of homegrown French fascism, Philippe Burrin published a study of the appeal of fascism to specific elements of the interwar French Left. Studying the careers of Jacques Doriot, Marcel Déat, and Gaston Bergery, Burrin highlighted the fact that not all wartime collaborators had their political origins on the Right. As in the case of Mussolini, Burrin suggested that despite the significant differences between fascism on the one hand and Socialism and Communism on the other, it was easier for a worker activist than for a liberal activist to become a fascist militant. French militants of the Left shared with their fascist confreres, according to Burrin, an activist spirit of political engagement aimed against the elites that governed their society.[22] As the Barbie trial unfolded in 1987, Jacques Chirac, then prime minister, called upon the French to use it to educate themselves about their history in World War II, while Klarsfeld and others worked to have French history textbooks rewritten to reflect local collaboration with the Nazis.[23]

Rousso's *Le Syndrome de Vichy*, which appeared in 1987, the year of Barbie's trial, described a perceived Vichy syndrome that emphasized, more than a historical curiosity about the events of World War II in France, the moral issues of collaboration. Arguing that the French viewed their wartime experience with guilt and shame, the Vichy syndrome thesis claimed a uniqueness to the experience of Vichy in postwar France. The French, Rousso wrote, had been "obsessed with the memory of Vichy and the Occupation."[24] He also referred to a "mode rétro," which he called "the forties revival [which] played an essential role in the history of the Vichy syndrome," starting with the film *The Sorrow and the Pity* in 1971 and abating by 1978.[25] During the late

1980s and early 1990s, Vichy syndrome arguments, emphasizing the topicality of and preoccupation with the war years, were taken up by writers both inside and outside France.[26] Not all academic historians viewed the Vichy experience in totally negative terms. In 1990, François-Georges Dreyfus prefaced a lengthy study of the four-year period by arguing against what he called the "Manichaean" views that had depicted the Vichy government as all good or all bad. He evoked as his model Robert Aron's 1954 *Histoire de Vichy*, which Dreyfus saw as having been balanced in its judgments, following neither the Right in one-sided praise of Marshal Philippe Pétain and Pierre Laval nor the Left in excessive support of de Gaulle, the Resistance, and the Communists. Aron had pointed the direction; all that remained, according to Dreyfus, who gave his book the same title Aron had used, was to fill in the gaps that had resulted from Aron's inability to consult all the relevant archives.[27] Concluding that Vichy had opposed Republican ideals of liberty and equality, had collaborated with Nazi Germany, and had fought against the Resistance, Dreyfus, however, argued that Vichy had in fact represented a real antiparliamentarian and anticommunist France, opposed to war in 1939. Vichy had also given a group of technocrats, brought into the government of Admiral François Darlan, a chance to try to modernize France, a direction subsequently resumed under the Fifth Republic. Most importantly, perhaps, Dreyfus argued that Vichy's collaboration with the Germans, at least until Laval's return to office in April 1942, had been a ruse to deceive the Germans, who at the time had appeared all-powerful, and to save as much as possible for France; and that even after Laval's return to power, France was spared a worse fate by the presence of the Vichy government.[28] Dreyfus's approach echoed earlier arguments that had portrayed Vichy as France's shield against the Germans under occupation conditions and de Gaulle as her sword for subsequent use. Not surprisingly in view of the work of Paxton, Marrus, and others who focused on Vichy's role in the deportation of the Jews, and coming on the heels of the Barbie trial, Dreyfus's book intensified the controversies Rousso had described.[29]

Discussion of the wartime period turned in the early 1990s to the rediscovery in September 1991 of Vichy's *fichier juif*, a census of Jews later used for roundups and deportation. A document whose history and even existence had engendered controversy since the late 1940s, the *fichier juif* was found in the War Veterans Archives by Serge Klarsfeld. The 1992 acquittal of former Milicien Paul Touvier in the Paris Court of Appeals also focused the attention of historians and political commentators on the war years. The court argued that Touvier's complicity in the crimes of which he had been accused had not been established, and dropped most of the charges against him. However, it ruled that on one count, the execution of seven hostages at Rillieux-la-Pape following the assassination of Vichy Minister of Information Philippe Henriot, Touvier's guilt had, indeed, been proven. Particularly vexing to many, however, was the court's going on to state that the Rillieux murders had been a war crime rather than a crime against humanity. According to the court, the Rillieux crime had been committed on behalf of Vichy, which was not, it argued—as contrasted to Nazi Germany—a government that had practiced "ideological hegemony." French law, however, required "ideological hegemony" to convict for crimes against humanity.[30] In its ruling on Rillieux, the court had effectively exonerated Vichy of all wartime guilt concerning racial persecution.

Syndrome and "mode rétro" arguments followed the April 1992 Touvier exoneration. Tony Judt regretted an incompleteness in the "moral cartography of France's recent past."[31] Alan Morris broadened the *rétro* argument to an "all-embracing . . . remarkable renewal of interest in, and extensive re-evaluation of, the wartime occupation of France by Adolf Hitler's Germany."[32] Meanwhile, the April 1992 Touvier verdict was appealed, and in November of that year the Criminal Chamber of the High Court of Appeals ordered that the former Milicien be retried for his role in the Rillieux incident. While the Touvier affair continued to draw attention to the history of the Jews under the Occupation, Annette Kahn, in a book on the *fichier juif*, suggested that the arrest of Klaus Barbie in 1983 had contributed to an increase in French compassion toward victims of the Holocaust and a greater desire to investigate its history.[33] Nowhere was the syndrome argument presented more clearly than in a 1993 special issue of the *Annales* devoted to Vichy and the Holocaust. Describing the French recollection of the war years as "trauma," Lucette Valensi argued that Vichy itself had been tried in French public opinion but its specific responsibility in collaborating with the German genocide against the Jews had not. The French, she wrote, needed a "Vergangenheitsbewältigung," an overcoming of a past that, she stated, "remains present today in the collective memory."[34]

In June 1993, former Vichy Secretary General for the Police René Bousquet, then awaiting trial on charges of crimes committed against humanity, was murdered by an apparent publicity seeker. Several days thereafter, Paul Webster, suggesting among other things that General de Gaulle was a collaborator "who allied with Vichyists to oppose the Communists at the liberation," called the wartime period France's "filthiest hour." Claiming that there was "an excessive amount of information" regarding France during World War II, Webster wrote that "not a day goes by without magazine investigations, broadcast inquiries, public meetings or the dedication of a new anti-Vichy memorial or museum."[35] In 1994, Peter Carrier claimed an "unprecedented public awareness of Vichy France" following the 1992 Touvier decision, the fiftieth anniversary of the Vélodrôme d'Hiver roundup of Jews later that year, and the assassination of Bousquet.[36]

In April 1994, the appeal of the Touvier decision of two years earlier was heard by the Assizes Court of Versailles. This time, Touvier was convicted, his role in the Rillieux murders judged a crime against humanity. That same month, the periodical *Autrement* published a book, titled *Oublier nos crimes*, in which a group of contributors debated the specificity of French crimes, especially those committed by Vichy.[37] In the *Autrement* book, Alfred Grosser recalled that the Republic had set up internment camps even before the defeat of 1940 and suggested that these had been insufficiently discussed in French historiography. He also wanted more attention paid to the role of the wartime French police, who had blindly obeyed orders, he maintained, whatever the source of the authority. In the German occupation zone they had unquestioningly followed Nazi orders to arrest Jews, whereas in the Italian zone they had just as adamantly followed orders not to. Indicating that opinions had shifted at least somewhat over time, however, Grosser found the French public in the early 1990s more receptive to information about the role of the police than they had been twenty years earlier.[38]

Grosser also found a greater willingness on the part of at least some within the French Catholic community, led by the periodical *La Croix* and Cardinal Albert Decourtray, to discuss past Catholic anti-Semitism, a willingness he did not see in the German Catholic Church or in Pope John Paul II.[39] Decourtray's concern was undoubtedly intensified by revelations of the hiding of Touvier by Church officials during the years prior to his arrest in 1989. Decourtray had at the time ordered an investigation of the Church's role in the affair, which did in fact show complicity by some within the Church, if not by the official Church as an entity.[40] In addition to the role of the Church in the war, Grosser discussed the communists, especially historians under their influence who wished to whitewash the history of the gulags. If Bernard Notin could be denied a teaching post at the University of Lyon for having argued outside the university that the Holocaust did not happen, Grosser asked, what should be thought of historians who for decades after the war not only denied the existence of Soviet crimes but also labeled as "fascists" those who had brought these crimes to public attention?[41] François Bédarida warned against not only the kind of revision that denied the reality of the Holocaust, but also a "soft" revisionism, notably the assertion made in 1993 by Thierry Wolton to the effect that

Resistance leader Jean Moulin's entourage had been contaminated by contacts with the Soviet KGB.[42] Another contributor to the *Autrement* book, Sonia Combe, accused Archives Nationales authorities of trying to conceal Vichy's *fichier juif* in order to impede the investigations of those accused of crimes against humanity, such as Touvier, Bousquet, and Papon.[43]

Two books in the late summer of 1994 continued to draw attention to the Vichy years. Pierre Péan's *Une Jeunesse française: François Mitterrand 1934–1947*, examined then President Mitterrand's service at Vichy prior to his joining the Resistance in 1943, and highlighted his longtime relationship with Bousquet, which continued until at least 1986.[44] Shortly thereafter came the publication of *Vichy: Un Passé qui ne passe pas*, by Rousso in collaboration with Éric Conan. This book restated the theme of France's "obsession" with her Vichy past. Now worried that a "dangerous evolution" would blind the French to more pressing issues of the present and future, its authors regretted that a "common discourse on that period [Vichy] sweeps along increasingly in drifts and threatens to empty into a dead end."[45] Having argued so strongly for the existence of a Vichy syndrome, Rousso, along with Conan, now suggested that its emphasis on "Judeocentrism" had so disoriented French perceptions of their wartime past that the entire history of the Occupation was being seen solely in terms of Vichy's anti-Semitism and the Holocaust, thereby marginalizing the Resistance.[46] The Péan and Conan-Rousso books were followed in late 1994 by *Mémoires à deux voix*, written by Mitterrand and Elie Wiesel, in which the then President continued to defend his own wartime and postwar activities, justifying his longstanding relationship with Bousquet, whose crimes, he argued, had been revealed only by "recent historiography."[47]

In 1995, *Le Monde* reviewed three books on World War II France in January, six more in June, and an additional three in July. These included Philippe Burrin's *La France à l'heure allemande*, Renée Poznanski's *Être juif en France pendant la seconde guerre mondiale*, and *L'Esprit de résistance* by Serge Ravanel. The fiftieth anniversary of the end of the war and the trial of Marshal Pétain occasioned several studies of the Marshal.[48] In *La France à l'heure allemande*, Burrin focused on the impact of the Occupation on the lives of different social strata of the French. He noted that most of the French had not believed in collaboration and, especially after 1942, had eagerly awaited the Liberation. Paradoxically, he stated, a growing awareness during the past twenty years of Pétain's popularity had led to a strengthened "culture of suspicion" with regard to French behavior during the wartime years.[49] Reviewing Burrin's book, Olivier Wieviorka suggested that despite an "avalanche" of books on the Vichy years, in focusing on the behavior of the French more than that of their leaders, Burrin had succeeded in casting new light on the subject.[50] In her book, *Vivre et survivre en France, 1939–1947*, which also studied the daily life of the French, Dominique Veillon took a broader view of the war period, starting with the *drôle de guerre* of 1939–40 and extending through the Liberation, France's participation in the final defeat of the Axis in late 1944 and 1945, and the immediate postwar era of purges and reconstruction. Veillon's more extended perspective allowed her to show how the peasants, whom she saw as the big winners during the Occupation, suffered afterward when renewed mechanization of agriculture led to an intensified rural exodus.[51]

Reviewing five new books on the war years in September 1995, Sarah Fishman saw "a series of interlocking myths" still surrounding Vichy. The myths Fishman enumerated (but without documentation) were: (1) that all Vichy's policies originated with "the depraved mind" of Laval, (2) that some "well-meaning intellectuals," after having been seduced by Pétain's "comforting rhetoric," quickly came to their senses, and (3) that forty million Frenchmen and women resisted the Germans.[52] The same issue of *French Historical Studies* that carried my " 'Vichy Syndrome' Problem in History" also featured in its forum on Vichy articles by John Hellman and Pierre Nora. As Grosser had in *Autrement*, Hellman addressed both communist and Catholic memory of the Occupation, though he emphasized the latter. Hellman concluded that prior to the war, French Catholics such as Touvier, the Esprit and Uriage groups, and Mitterrand had all agreed that some action had been needed to purge France of what they considered "non-French" elements. Accordingly, they had all supported Vichy. Whatever moral judgments might be made of their wartime actions, Hellman argued, they had all wished to be remembered as resisters and so had distorted the historical record of the war years. "Certain obtuse refusals to come to terms with the facts about the past," in Hellman's words, "are jolting, less understandable, and, as Henry Rousso suggests, cannot 'pass.' They can be as suggestive and troubling as the facts themselves."[53]

In his contribution to the *French Historical Studies* forum, Pierre Nora saw Rousso's work as a repeated indicator of future directions of historical research about World War II France. In 1987, Rousso's *Syndrome de Vichy*, according to Nora, had been the harbinger of a wave of historical attention that emphasized the qualitative uniqueness of the Holocaust and the French complicity with it. Seven years later, in *Vichy un passé*, Nora again saw the direction for future study. Rousso and Conan, according to Nora, had now called for a more balanced view of the French past. The recent studies by Poznanski, Burrin, and others, he argued, had again made a prophet of Rousso.[54]

Whether Nora was correct in his view that more balanced depictions of World War II France were the order of the day remains to be seen. In a book described as based on "the new American cultural" and "poststructuralist history," Francine Muel-Dreyfus offered a model in which Vichy represented an "eternal feminine," constructed by a male hierarchy in which women were seen as the "other." This perspective, according to Françoise Thébaud, risked obscuring the chronology of the wartime period and deflecting attention away from the ways in which the laws of Vichy were applied. Perhaps Muel-Dreyfus's argument that Vichy represented a "sociological tragedy," according to Thébaud, gave too little credit to the women of France, who might not have been so easily duped.[55] If Thébaud implied that women in France were more resistant to the message of the Nazis and Vichy than Muel-Dreyfus would have one believe, Douglas Porch leaned the other way with regard to the French as a whole. In contrast to the communists, who claimed 70,000 Resistance martyrs, Porch held that fewer than 350 had been executed by the Nazis as Resistance fighters. He also suggested that many of those in France who helped Allied prisoners escape were in fact motivated by five-thousand-dollar payments from the Allies (fifty thousand dollars at today's rates), rather than by the Resistance cause. Writing about Porch's book, *The French Secret Services*, Bernard D. Kaplan held that "the romantic image of selfless French men and women in berets and leather jackets blowing up bridges and ambushing columns of German soldiers on lonely country roads has become one of the most persistent wartime legends." Their own knowledge that the Resistance story was a "Big Lie," invented by de Gaulle and the communists, according to Kaplan, led the French to become "extremely tough customers." Kaplan quoted the former American ambassador to France, Charles Bohlen, as having said: "The French have never forgiven us for liberating them."[56]

The *French Historical Studies* forum and the books by Muel-Dreyfus and Porch, along with the related commentaries, were but examples of the controversy and passion occasioned by Vichy both within and outside France. Reactions to the revelations of Mitterrand's Vichy activity and to Chirac's apology for French crimes in World War II showed the fervor with which the Vichy syndrome thesis in its various forms was argued in books, articles, and professional meetings. The death of Mitterrand, in January 1996, and the publication of Georges-Marc Benhamou's *Le Dernier Mitterrand* later in the year, again called attention to the wartime years. In conversations with Benhamou, the former President was clearly thinking about history's judgment of his Vichy activities of 1942–43.[57]

After Mitterrand's death, historians continued to examine previously obscure aspects of the French past, such as the joint Franco-German enterprises formed during the Occupation. According to an article by Annie Lacroix-Riz, these joint enterprises included a partially French firm, Durferrit-Sofumi, associated with the German company Degesch, a branch of IG Farben, which produced the Zyklon B gas used in the extermination camps. A member of the French communist party, Lacroix-Riz asserted that to French businessmen who had been compromised with the Germans, the occupant had "only changed uniforms" after the Liberation. These businessmen had turned immediately afterward to collaboration with the Americans. Extending Paul Webster's 1993 argument that de Gaulle had allied with Vichyists to oppose the communists at the liberation, Lacroix-Riz also contended that the English and Americans had made sure Germany was supplied through neutral countries with the materiel needed to prolong the war against the Soviet Union. When her article, "Les Élites françaises et la collaboration économique," was turned down by the periodical *Études et documents*, Lacroix-Riz claimed to have been the victim of censorship.[58] In another, related sensitive area, the involvement of L'Oréal perfume company's boss, Eugène Schueller, with the interwar right-wing Cagoule and the wartime collaborationist Mouvement Social Révolutionnaire of Eugène Deloncle, was addressed in a book by Michel Bar-Zohar, published in the United States and France in late 1996.[59] Although the ties between L'Oréal and the Cagoule, and later the MSR, had long been known, the interwar and postwar involvement of the young Mitterrand with Schueller and his aides had received little publicity.[60] In another retrospective domain, the use of East European archives, opened after 1989, to help locate, after more than fifty years, the legal inheritors of property taken from Jews during the Occupation, focused attention on the methodology of genealogical study and may have had the indirect consequence of popularizing this branch of historical study.[61]

The War and the Debate in Historical Perspective

The intensity of the arguments about France in World War II has subordinated some critical questions that historians need to ask: namely, whether available data support the syndrome argumentation articulated in the metaphorical language of obsession, *rétro*, trauma, and hyperesthesia, or whether the use of such terms has confused rather than clarified the historical record. Do the data suggest a significant shift in the retrospective argumentation in the early 1980s about France in World War II? The quantitative analyses of French publications about the wartime years in my "'Vichy Syndrome' Problem in History" article suggest a moderate but not dramatic increase in argumentation in the early 1980s.[62] From the advent of the Vichy government in 1940, book publications on World War II, as a proportion of the total, peak in 1945 and 1946, when the press had been newly freed from the restrictions of the Occupation and when the purge trials of leading Vichy officials were capturing people's interest. Then they decline steadily to a nadir in the mid-1950s. The figures belie claims made for a surge of "mode rétro" interest in the Occupation during the 1970s. During the 1980s, the figures are a little higher than for the three previous decades. They rise and fall with a slightly upward pattern through the early 1990s. At no time, however, does the proportion of books published on World War II return to the peaks of the mid-1940s. In addition, the shifting subcategories under the main entries represent largely war stories of campaigns, battles, and battlefields rather than shame, malaise, or trauma focusing on Vichy, the collaboration, and the Holocaust. As recently as 1993, the listings showed far more titles dealing with resistance movements and "campaigns and battles," belying the argument in *Vichy un passé* that the Resistance has been a neglected field of study in recent years in France.[63]

The sequences in the *Bibliographie annuelle de l'histoire de France* (*BAHF*), which started publication in 1953 and began listing titles under the Second World War only in 1964, confirms the longer book series for the period it covers. In 1969 the *BAHF* began to offer subheadings, the largest of which were: (a) military operations, (b) German occupation, and (c) Resistance. The *BAHF* shows an increase in the proportions of World War II listings since the mid-1960s, as does the longer book series, but no significant turn around 1980. Its listings consistently relate more to fighting and resistance than to guilt, trauma, or malaise, again bringing into question the claim that the Resistance is a neglected subject for historians in France. For 1992, the last year included in my "'Vichy Syndrome' Problem in History" series, only 20 of 527 entries listed were under "Deportation," and there were no subheadings specifically for the concentration camps or the plight of the French Jews under Vichy.[64] In 1993, the *BAHF* figures for articles on World War II actually declined slightly to 448, of which 24 were listed under "Deportation."[65] The *BAHF* does not include articles from *Le Monde Juif*, the only periodical devoted exclusively to the history of the Jews in World War II, and although inclusion of such articles might increase its percentage for World War II, it remains to be shown whether they would significantly change the proportions over time, which is fundamental for a historical assessment of interest in World War II. It is equally unclear whether the listings from *Le Monde Juif* would affect the internal subdivisions within the BAHF category of World War II.[66]

Another useful series is the sequence of articles on World War II published in the magazine *L'Histoire*, a reflection of what is sometimes called "popular" history. The proportion of World War II topic articles in the *L'Histoire* sequence from the beginning of publication in May 1978 through 1991 show a pattern similar to the book and BAHF data, with no significant shift after 1980. Articles on World War II in *L'Histoire* peaked in frequency in the years 1979, 1985, and 1990. Rousso notes that the years 1985 and 1990 included special issues marking the fortieth anniversary of the end of the war and the fiftieth anniversary of the inception of the Vichy government, respectively, but there is no discernible upward or downward movement for the entire period 1978 through 1991.[67] In this magazine that reflects popular interests in history in France, there is no appreciable increase that would mark an exacerbated obsession through the 1980s and early 1990s. The entire run of 2,310 articles contains only 9 references to anti-Semitism, 3 to deportation, 2 to genocide, and 1 each for war crimes and concentration camps.

Although the quantitative data do not indicate a significant shift after 1980 regarding French interest in the World War II period, it is reasonable to address the qualitative significance of any of the specific books or articles that appear on the lists. One event or publication might conceivably have had a greater historical impact than all the statistics regarding the thousands of books and articles published through the years. Two possible examples have been suggested, of which one, the 1978 *L'Express* interview with Louis Darquier (also known as Darquier de Pellepoix), might potentially explain a shift in retrospective interest in the war after 1980. The former head of Vichy's Office for Jewish Affairs, Darquier claimed that only lice had been gassed at Auschwitz. A former deportee wrote a letter thanking *L'Express* for publishing the Darquier interview and, thereby, "having awoken the entire country."[68] Accusing Bousquet of playing a central role in the roundup of Jews, Darquier helped instigate the move to try the former police minister on charges of crimes against humanity. Darquier did not say anything previously unknown in France about Bousquet's Vichy role, but he refocused attention on questions some had previously thought closed.[69] The affair, however, engaged primarily journalists and politicians, as well as Masonic, deportee, and jurist organizations. Publication of the Darquier interview did not materially affect the publication sequences, nor is there evidence that the interview substantially changed French opinion about the war years.

The second possible resonance of a qualitative argument relates to the media attention given Mitterrand's discussion of his Vichy past during the summer of 1994; accordingly, it applies less to the argument that the 1980s saw a dramatic change in French reaction to the war. Following the publication of Péan's *Une Jeunesse française*, Mitterrand discussed his wartime activities in an hour-and-a-half-long interview on France 2 national television with Jean-Pierre Elkabbach.[70] Whereas Mitterrand's interview with Elkabbach was watched by more viewers than normal for a French television program, it still scored less well than the competing police mystery show "Navarro."[71] Historians debated the Péan book, together with Mitterrand's televised statements and the question of Vichy in general, but by the second half of 1995, with Mitterrand out of office and France preoccupied with nuclear weapons testing and government workers' strikes, interest in the former president's Vichy years had noticeably waned. Despite renewed scrutiny of Mitterrand's wartime activities following his death in January 1996, most attention was directed elsewhere. Robert Tombs, for example, summarized Mitterrand's legacy for France with only passing mention of the war years.[72] Indeed, both President Chirac and *Le Monde* suggested that with the death of Mitterrand had come the end of an era. For *Le Monde*, the former president's death marked the passing of a century. More specifically, the newspaper argued, his death "closed for France—definitively—the postwar period [la page de l'après-guerre]."[73] By implication, Mitterrand's longtime political adversary President Chirac agreed. Announcing his predecessor's death on French television, Chirac stated that in a fifty-year-long public career Mitterrand had "married his century."[74] Chirac's 1995 apology on behalf of the French state for crimes committed by Vichy, however, intended perhaps to close fully the postwar era, may have had the opposite effect by contributing to the initiatives to return art and apartments taken during the Occupation, and to the court ruling to try Papon.

Although the events since Chirac's apology may have prolonged for a few more years the "après-guerre," the passing of the wartime generation has changed and will continue to alter, if not defuse, the passions of historical debate about France in World War II. However, just as the various French publication series regarding World War II show that arguments for shifting *modes rétro* or syndromes that turn on one event, whether Darquier's 1978 interview, a "return" of fascism in 1980, or Mitterrand's retrospective admissions of 1994, are too narrowly conceived, the effects of Chirac's apology in 1995 and Mitterrand's death in 1996 must also be viewed in historical perspective. The same is likely to hold for the trial of Papon, promised "as soon as possible."[75] Dating and measuring French revisions and reassessments of World War II must be placed into a larger context of French history in which problems of defeat, collaboration, and the persecution of minorities began long before World War II. René Rémond has observed that such reappraisals and reorderings after periods of national disunity have occurred repeatedly in French history.[76]

A pattern of collaboration and retribution can be seen dating back to Caesar and Vercingétorix, though in an enumeration Hélène Dupuy goes back to Cain and Abel.[77] The history of the late sixth- and early-seventh-century Merovingians includes repeated instances of betrayal by the queens Frédégonde and Brunehaut that produced half a century of fratricidal war. Subsequent episodes of retribution, purges, doubt, and guilt include the betrayal of Charlemagne's forces by Ganelon at the 778 Roncesvaux battle and the capture of King Jean le Bon in 1356 and his betrayal of French interests to the English.[78] In an essay, *Icon Animorum*, written by John Barclay of Scotland and published in Latin in 1612 in both London and Paris, the French are depicted as valiant horsemen, but incapable of follow-through and unable to win wars.[79] The defection of the Count of Artois, youngest brother of King Louis XVI, and the attempted flight of the king himself during the Revolutionary era contributed to the overthrow of the monarchy. Talleyrand betrayed Napoleon to the Allies but escaped punishment when, after Waterloo, Louis XVIII returned from exile to reign with the émigrés of 1789 "in the baggage of the foreigners." A desire for expiation after the 1870 defeat at Sedan and the Paris Communard revolt the following year produced the Sacré Cœur cathedral in Paris. During the Dreyfus Affair of the 1890s, France was again engulfed in accusations of treason and collaboration that called into question the identity and role of the army in Republican France and the role of the Jewish community there. In fact, retrospective visions of the Dreyfus Affair are a good model for the French reinterpretations of World War II. In words similar to those sometimes used to describe Vichy, the Dreyfus Affair has been said to be always present.[80] The recollection of both the Dreyfus Affair and the Second World War spark occasional moral responses, often connected to the anniversaries of specific events, but with no dramatic popular surge. "Dreyfus Affair" entries in the long-term book publications series, at least for the postwar years, show a pattern similar to the World War II references, though the numbers are smaller.[81]

The paradigm of betrayal, collaboration, and revision intensified in the twentieth century with the accession of the Bolsheviks to power in Russia and their relationship with the French communist party, which gave an added dimension to the pattern after 1917.[82] In January 1940, seventy communists, who after the August 1939 Nazi-Soviet pact had called for opposition to the Anglo-French war against Germany, were removed from the French Parliament by the Édouard Daladier government. Reviled by Vichy after the German invasion of the Soviet Union in June 1941, they were treated as Resistance heroes for their subsequent role in fighting the Germans. The most obvious target for Vichyite accusations of dereliction of duty and treason was General de Gaulle, condemned to death under Vichy for having fled France to continue anti-Nazi resistance from London. During the Occupation, the Riom trial, which was opened in February 1942 by the Vichy government, was intended to try leaders of the Third Republic, notably Daladier, Léon Blum, and Paul Reynaud, for having instigated the war by anti-German collaboration with the English. The trial was hastily suspended under German pressure when it turned to the issue of French preparedness rather than responsibility for the war. In the literary world, well-known collaborators included Georges Simenon, the Belgian native and widely read mystery writer who served from 1940 through 1942 as commissioner for Belgian refugees in La Rochelle. As conditions worsened with the German occupation of the southern zone in November 1942, Simenon indicated he wished only to take advantage of whatever opportunities the situation offered.[83] Not surprisingly, when the tables turned with the Liberation in 1944, purges, chastisement, and subsequent revision were again on the agenda. The writer Paul Morand, an ambassador under Vichy, was silenced after 1945 and died in 1976, yet his work regained popularity several years later.[84] Paul Malaguti, a member of the collaborationist Parti Populaire Français paramilitary squads, involved in a Gestapo massacre of resisters on 15 August 1944 in Cannes, was condemned to death in absentia on 20 March 1945. In March 1992, however, his name headed the National Front's list of candidates for the regional elections in the Loiret.[85]

The revision and reassessment in the shifting French perspectives of Morand and Malaguti, to name just two examples, have been paralleled in other European countries and around the world. Two military barracks in Bavaria, which had been named by the *Bundeswehr* for Nazi generals, were ordered renamed in November 1995 by the German ministry of defense.[86] In Italy, the pro-Fascist Movimento Sociale Italiano, under the new name of the National Alliance, arguing that it had no desire to return to the Mussolini era, participated in the 1994 government of Silvio Berlusconi and subsequently rejoined the opposition. In September 1995, Rome's leftist mayor, saying he was attempting to promote reconciliation, decided to name a street there for Giuseppe Bottai, a fascist leader known for virulent anti-Semitism in the Mussolini era. Under pressure from critics, the mayor later rescinded his initiative.[87] Aware that, at least at times in the fascist era, there had been a national consensus in support of Mussolini, Italians were divided as to whether the time had come to integrate the fascist period into their national history. For the young, however, according to Paolo Flores d'Arcais, director of the periodical *Micromega*, May 1968, the antifascist resistance, and the Roman Empire all belonged to the same distant past. Meanwhile, National Alliance leader Gianfranco Fini had been applauded at a party for *L'Unità*, the newspaper of the ex-communists. Everyone in Italy, wrote Sophie Gherardi in *Le Monde*, was " 'post' something."[88]

A controversy over betrayal and collaboration, less prolonged but not unlike that over Vichy, also developed in Britain relating to the Channel Islands occupied by Germany during the war. Reviewing Madeleine Bunting's *The Model Occupation: The Channel Islands under German Rule 1940–1945*, Linda Holt critiqued Bunting's claim that during and after the occupation Channel Islanders had been guilty of denying the plight of victims, for which they were to bear some responsibility. According to Holt, Bunting had turned the entire wartime history of the islands into a morality play. In language paralleling the suggestion in *Vichy un passé* that the French were now focusing too heavily on wartime guilt, Holt argued that Bunting and others were using the Channel Islands story as a "justification of their disenchantment with the myths of Britishness which their parents' generation helped to create" and "an expiatory narrative for the guilt engendered by the Holocaust."[89] The Channel Islands' experience, according to *Le Monde* correspondent Patrice de Beer, was summed up in the title of Jean-Yves Ruaux's *Vichy-sur-Manche: les Anglo-Normandes sous l'Occupation*, published in 1994. According to de Beer, the history of English collaboration with the German occupation authorities on the islands struck a nerve because it called into question the "grandeur" symbolized by Winston Churchill and still offered by British "Euroskeptics" as justification for their remaining aloof from the presumably less morally pure Continental states, with their wartime histories of treason and collaboration.[90] Parallel arguments concerned American wartime collaboration with Vichy, and by extension with Nazi Germany, which surfaced early in 1996 when United States Secretary of State Warren Christopher planted a tree in honor of Varian Fry at Jerusalem's Yad Vashem memorial to the Holocaust. Christopher noted that Fry, the representative of the private American Emergency Rescue Committee, had spent thirteen months in 1940 and 1941 helping some four thousand Jews escape from occupied France. The American consulate in Marseilles had confiscated his passport in an attempt to stop

Fry's rescue work, and eventually the Vichy government had expelled him. Publicly regretting the consulate's action, Christopher called for Fry's work to become better known in America.[91] Revisions in perspectives on betrayal and collaboration elsewhere included the public rehabilitation in India of Subhas Chandra Bose, who, after meeting Hitler, organized an Indian armed force to fight alongside the Japanese in World War II.[92] Closer to home, several prominent Swiss banks were accused in late 1996 of having accepted property stolen by the Nazis in occupied Europe, France included. The banks were charged with having failed to return much of it to its legal owners after the war. Following bitter exchanges with critics both in Switzerland and abroad, the Swiss agreed to set up a restitution system in which the American, British, and French governments were to participate. As in France, the affair incited revision in the way some Swiss saw their country's wartime record, which contributed also to the French reassessments of the wartime years.[93]

The recent cases outside France highlight the limitations in perspective of historical visions of Vichy restricted to the French metropole between 1940 and 1944. Most historians have paid insufficient attention to the reality of Vichy as part of a larger reorganization of Europe, orchestrated and dominated by Germany. The years from the Munich accords of 1938 through the reorientation of European politics in the late 1940s mark an era of failed German domination of Europe, which subsequently yielded to the European Coal and Steel Community and ultimately to the European Union.[94] Of course, Franco-German collaboration in the era of the ECSC and the European Union was very different from that of 1940 through 1944. For many in France and elsewhere in Europe, however, one form of collaboration was followed by another. As Grosser hinted in *Oublier nos crimes*, the numbers of Europeans who turned their allegiance from Nazi Germany to Stalinist Russia, at least through 1989, will probably never be known. Questions of betrayal and reassessment were reopened by the end of the cold war in Central Europe, which also reintroduced the possibility of a German-dominated Europe, this time in the form of the Union. French and other European retrospectives on World War II will increasingly reflect the evolving Union, and consensus among the European countries is far from achieved. Reassessments of Vichy will need to study the entire World War II collaboration paradigm, which extends at least through 1989 for the former Soviet satellites of Central and Eastern Europe.[95]

As Paolo Flores d'Arcais noted for the young Italians, the French also appear to be more interested in contemporary issues, such as the erosion of socialism, the regeneration of capitalism, economic dislocations, relations with a reunited Germany, and the place of France in Europe and the world.[96] The writing of history reflects concerns with the present, but as the quantitative publications data do not support the argument that France is obsessed with her Vichy past, the data explain neither any revisionary shift that might have occurred around 1980 nor why arguments for the presence of a Vichy syndrome, obsession, or trauma appeared in the late 1980s and early 1990s. The reasons for the arguments made by politicians, journalists, and historians in publications such as *Le Monde* or *Le Nouvel Observateur*, or in recent issues of journals such as the *Annales* or *Autrement*, must be sought outside the lists of publications about the war. That these retrospective arguments may reflect present-day open or hidden agendas was, perhaps, best said by Michael Marrus. Reviewing Asher Cohen's *Persécutions et sauvetages*, a study of the Jews under the Occupation that appeared in 1994, Marrus noted that it "will probably disappoint readers seeking fresh indictments or new reasons to accuse the French."[97]

Substantial evidence, even beyond the publications series, calls into question the extent of any Vichy syndrome or *mode rétro* among the French population. Polls taken during the 1970s and 1980s showed continuing differences between politicians preoccupied with Vichy and the Occupation in parliamentary debates and a more indifferent public. A French poll taken in May 1987, before Barbie walked out of his trial, while he and his lawyers were still hinting at spectacular courtroom revelations about the war years, indicated that only 51 percent of the French population planned to follow the trial closely. Interest declined even further after Barbie stopped appearing in court.[98] More recently, the court appearances of Touvier in 1992 and 1994 evoked relatively little interest outside narrow judicial circles.[99]

Despite evidence to the contrary, many historians continue to see France in an obsessional or traumatic relationship with her wartime past. Among those who emphasize French fixations on the war period, Zeev Sternhell in 1994 called Vichy "this past that refuses to pass" and Lothar Baier wrote of the Vichy years "which appear curiously more present than ever." In words similar to those of Lucette Valensi, Tony Judt wrote that France had to "assumer son passé national."[100] Replying to my "'Vichy Syndrome' Problem in History," Rousso cited the recent work of Burrin, Poznanski, and Veillon to suggest, along with Pierre Nora, that the current phase of the Vichy syndrome is characterized by a "delirium" (*délire*).[101] He presented the view of a Vichy syndrome concerning the totality of French society ("qui concerne l'ensemble de la société française"), in contrast to the German *Historikerstreit* of the 1980s, which he saw as limited to the historians' community.[102] At the August–September 1995 International Congress of

Historical Sciences in Montréal Rousso continued to maintain that France was obsessed with her Vichy past, and cited the Touvier affair and demands for official state apologies for Vichy crimes as examples of an "acceleration" of this obsession.[103] Arguing that the memory of Vichy is "central" to French political life, he maintained, if not deepened, his position regarding the role of the syndrome in French history and in defining French identity.[104]

Undoubtedly, France has seen a shift in the way her wartime past is remembered, with more emphasis upon the role of Vichy in abetting the Holocaust. Attention to the Jews as victims has increased. The limited and fading impact of Mitterrand's 1994 justifications of his Vichy career, the muted response to Chirac's apology on behalf of the French State in 1995, and the lessened attention paid the war years on the occasion of Mitterrand's death in 1996, however, confirm the publications series in their indication of a less than obsessional interest on the part of the French in their World War II past. None of this, however, is to deny the real shifts that have occurred in Vichy revision argumentation shown by the data in the 1980s and 1990s as compared with the 1950s through the 1970s, even if it is difficult to see a turning point in or around 1980.[105] Half a century after the war, the trials of Barbie and Touvier, the assassination of Bousquet, and, more recently, property restitution initiatives, the Papon case, and a possible Junot "affair" to follow, together with continuing reassessments of the wartime experience in France—specifically of Vichy, the collaboration, and the Jews—continue to be of interest, indeed passion, to many in the French political, academic, and journalistic community.[106]

The second half of the 1990s may yet bring the turning of the page in French retrospective visions of the war years, a closing of the "après-guerre" period that *Le Monde* had foreseen with the death of Mitterrand. Government moves to compensate the victims of art and apartment confiscations during the Occupation gave practical effect to Chirac's 1995 apology and highlighted the mostly Jewish victims—ironic in the light of the fears of an increased "Judeocentrism" that Conan and Rousso worried might divert the French from more pressing present-day needs.[107] Revelations of Junot's Occupation-era activities make it less certain as of early 1997, though still probable, that the Papon case will be the last of the postwar purge trials in France. During an interview in March 1996, while hearings were being held to determine whether his case should go before an appeals court, Papon denied all wrongdoing. Arguing that he had held a minor post devoid all power of initiative in matters relating to the Jews, he claimed to be an innocent scapegoat for those who wished to try the Vichy government. Echoing the earlier arguments of François-Georges Dreyfus and others who had seen

Vichy as a shield protecting the French from even harsher treatment at the hands of the Germans, Papon insisted that he had surreptitiously undermined the wartime anti-Jewish policies and that he had, in fact, saved at least 139 Jews from deportation. Because of his successful postwar political career, however, he was being targeted for retribution, he claimed, by American Jews of German extraction and by the Anti-Defamation League in the United States. Their agenda, according to Papon, was to help whitewash Germany of guilt in the Holocaust by blaming other countries, notably the French. Accordingly, he continued, they were helping to fund Serge Klarsfeld and others making the case against him.[108] Annette Lévy-Willard, who interviewed Papon, wrote, however, that in contrast to his claim that lists of Jews had been given to the Germans by a Jewish organization, it had been his own service that had provided them. His claim not to have known the destination of deported Jews was also false, she wrote.[109] Following the ruling that he was to stand trial on charges of crimes against humanity, Papon argued that facts had been falsified by the prosecution in what he claimed was to be a political trial, behind which he saw the machinations of the French communists, "gauchistes," unnamed "high foreign institutions," eager "to implicate France in the Holocaust," and high functionaries within the French government who wanted to silence him, presumably because of embarrassing information he possessed as President Georges Pompidou's appointed National Treasurer of the Gaullist UDR (Union des Démocrates pour la République) in the 1970s. Papon claimed he was being framed like Captain Alfred Dreyfus. When pressed for details about the foreign conspiracy he saw working against him, Papon replied, "Ask New York."[110]

Even if followed by other related events or "affairs," the trial of the eighty-six-year-old Papon is likely to become the last act of the "après-guerre," which may produce ripple effects as current attempts at moral, if not material, restitution to surviving victims of the Holocaust run their course.[111] With more being learned about the Second World War period from East European sources and the interlude of Vichy growing increasingly remote, parallels with Jean le Bon, the Count of Artois, and others involved in the long-term French collaboration problem become increasingly clear. As with the Dreyfus Affair, Vichy will be increasingly historicized—that is, seen as an event in a long French sequence of defeat, collaboration, and retribution.[112]

The eventual historicization of the wartime period should not, however, diminish the awareness of the enormity of the persecutions committed then.[113] If the historical significance of the wartime crimes is to be understood, however, the crimes must be understood in a long-term historical perspective that examines not only the war years but also the ways in which they have been seen in France and elsewhere. It has not been demonstrated that terms such as "mode rétro," "Vichy syndrome," "obsession," and "delirium" as currently used have contributed to the needed historical clarity. Rather, when we examine French history, it is evident that France's northeastern border, the one Hexagonal boundary lacking a natural frontier, has been the repeated source of political instability in France, whether occasioned by the French spilling into Germany or the reverse, from the time of Louis XIV. Under the revolutionary government of the 1790s and Napoleon, the French took the entire Left Bank of the Rhine, but were unable to hold it beyond 1814. The German victory of 1870–71 failed to settle the frontier, which again became a battlefield in 1914. Victorious in 1918, the French were no more successful in resolving the northeast border problem than the victorious Germans had been in 1871. Hitler's victory in 1940 was even more short-term than Bismarck's in 1871. Today the French eastern linguistic frontier, passing through Switzerland and Belgium, is still not clearly defined, as witness the angry reaction in Belgium to a Paris meeting devoted to "la Wallonie française" and presided over by a member of France's Constitutional Council.[114] Europe remains in a process of re-formation with Franco-German relations at the core, evidenced in the moves toward a common European currency and the joint Franco-German security initiatives announced in 1997 by President Chirac and Chancellor Helmut Kohl.[115] More than half a century after World War II, if terms such as "syndrome" and "mode rétro" are used in historical analysis, they should at least reflect the long-term perspective of geography, war, betrayal, defeat, collaboration, purges, and subsequent retrospective revision and reassessment that have played so characteristic a role in French history.

Notes

1. President Chirac created a special committee, attached to his office, devoted to the memory of World War II and of all of France's "contemporary" wars. See Pascale Robert-Diard, "Le Chef de l'État crée un 'haute conseil de la mémoire combattante,'" *Le Monde*, 10 January 1997, 7. Reporting on Chirac's public apology in 1995, Tony Judt argued that French intellectuals had been silent about French complicity in the Holocaust. See his "French War Stories," *New York Times*, 19 July 1995, A15. For a dissenting view, see Kevin Anderson, "French Intellectuals Wanted Truth Told," *New York Times*, 23 July 1995, 14E.

2. See the editorial linking the stolen art and the trial of Papon, "Entre vertu et habilité," *Le Monde*, 28 January 1997, 16. For the investigation of the wartime expropriation of the apartments of Parisian Jews, see Christine Garin, "L'Enquête sur les annexions de logements juifs au domaine privé parisienne est à peine commencé," *Le Monde*, 29 January 1997, 30. The legal concept of crimes against humanity is dis-

cussed in Bertram M. Gordon, "Collaboration, Retribution, and Crimes against Humanity: The Touvier, Bousquet, and Papon Affairs," *Contemporary French Civilization* 19, no. 2 (fall 1995), 251–53.

3. Régis Guyotat, "Des Documents mettant en cause Michel Junot pour son rôle dans la déportation des juifs," *Le Monde*, 2–3 February 1997, 24.

4. See, for example, reference to "the troubling return of fascism throughout the Western world in the last fifteen years," in the flyer describing "Fascism's Return: Scandal, Revision, and Ideology since 1980," a conference held at Texas A&M University, 10–11 November 1995.

5. Jean Labasse, *Hommes de droite, hommes de gauche* (Paris: Économie et Humanisme, 1947), 39, 95–96.

6. See Bertram M. Gordon, "How French Right Broke From Margins," *New York Times*, 20 June 1995, A18.

7. For the linking of Jean-Marie Le Pen and the National Front with Vichy, with the argument that Le Pen is "obsessed with the 1940s," see Rousso, *Vichy Syndrome*, 197. Other writers in France have also linked their concern with the National Front with a retrospective interest in Vichy. For example, see Rita Thalmann, *La Mise au pas: Idéologie et stratégie sécuritaire dans la France occupée* (Paris: Fayard, 1991), 9–10; also Jean-François Sirinelli and Éric Vigne, "Des Droites et du politique," in *Histoire des Droites en France*, ed. Sirinelli (Paris: Gallimard, 1992), 1:iii.

8. The suggestion was made by Rémy Handourtzel and Cyril Buffet, *La Collaboration . . . gauche aussi* (Paris: Perrin, 1989), 23–24. Robert Tombs noted in 1994 that the Second World War stimulated more research by historians than any other period in French history except for the Revolution. See Tombs, "The Dark Years," *Times Literary Supplement*, 28 January 1994, 9.

9. Pascal Ory, *Les Collaborateurs 1940–1945* (Paris: Seuil, 1976), 9; Henry Rousso, *Le Syndrome de Vichy, 1944–198...* (Paris: Seuil, 1987).

10. Bertram M. Gordon, "The 'Vichy Syndrome' Problem in History," *French Historical Studies* 19, no. 2 (fall 1995): 495–518.

11. Bertram M. Gordon, "Afterword: Who Are the Guilty and Should They Be Tried?" in Golsan, *Memory, the Holocaust, and French Justice*, 193.

12. See Stanley Hoffmann, "The Vichy Circle of French Conservatives," in *Decline or Renewal? France since the 1930s* (New York: Viking, 1974), a translation of an updated version of his "Aspects du régime de Vichy," which appeared in the *Revue Française de Science Politique* in March 1956. See also his "Collaborationism in France during World War II," *Journal of Modern History* 40 (September 1968); Eberhard Jäckel, *Frankreich in Hitlers Europa. Die Deutsche Frankreichpolitik im zweiten Weltkrieg* (Stuttgart: Deutsche Verlags-Anstalt, 1966); and Robert O. Paxton, *Vichy France: Old Guard and New Order, 1940–1944* (New York: Alfred A. Knopf, 1972).

13. Ory, *Les Collaborateurs*, 9. See also Gordon, "Vichy Syndrome," 501, n.29.

14. Raoul Girardet, "D'Innombrables étrangetés," and François Nourissier, "Deux simples réflexions," in *La Droite aujourd'hui*, ed. Jean-Pierre Apparu (Paris: Albin Michel, 1979), 77 and 87, respectively.

15. See for example Mona Ozouf and Jean-Paul Enthoven, "Quand la Droite pense," *Le Nouvel Observateur*, 2 July 1979, 37–38.

16. Gordon, *Collaborationism in France*, 354.

17. Marrus and Paxton, *Vichy France and the Jews*, xiii. This book was first published as *Vichy et les juifs* (Paris: Calmann-Lévy, 1981).

18. Rousso, *Vichy Syndrome*, 235.

19. Jacques Julliard, "Sur un fascisme imaginaire: À propos d'un livre de Zeev Sternhell," *Annales Économies Sociétés Civilisations* 39, no. 4 (July–August 1984): 850.

20. Éric Conan, "Affaire Moulin: À qui profite Caluire?" *L'Express*, 15 May 1987, 26. On the Izieu deportation, see Paul Lewis, "Lyons Trial Hears of Dead Children," *New York Times*, 28 May 1987, 6.

21. Quoted in Judith Miller, "Erasing the Past: Europe's Amnesia about the Holocaust," *New York Times Magazine*, 16 November 1986, 40.

22. Philippe Burrin, *La Dérive fasciste. Doriot, Déat, Bergery, 1933–1945* (Paris: Seuil, 1986), 451–52.

23. For Klarsfeld, see Miller, "Erasing the Past," 40. Chirac's request that French classes teach about the Holocaust while the trial was going on is discussed in "On Trial at Last, Barbie Withdraws From French Court," *Martyrdom and Resistance*, May–June 1987, 16.

24. Rousso, *Vichy Syndrome*, 5–6 and 272. See also Gordon, "Vichy Syndrome," 502.

25. Rousso, *Vichy Syndrome*, 131. See also p. 1, where he writes that the "mode rétro" was one of the influences that had stimulated his interest in how the wartime period was remembered in France.

26. For examples, see Gordon, "Vichy Syndrome," 503.

27. François-Georges Dreyfus, *Histoire de Vichy* (Paris: Perrin, 1990), 11.

28. Dreyfus, *Histoire*, 781–83.

29. For earlier "sword and shield" arguments, see Gordon, "Vichy Syndrome," 498–99.

30. A fuller discussion of the Touvier trial may be found in Gordon, "Collaboration," 257–58.

31. Judt argued that the Vichy elites trained at Uriage between 1940 and 1942 were "monsters." See his "Here be Monsters," *Times Literary Supplement*, 17 April 1992, 9.

32. Alan Morris, *Collaboration and Resistance Reviewed: Writers and the Mode Rétro in Post-Gaullist France* (New York and Oxford: Berg, 1992), 1.

33. Annette Kahn, *Le Fichier* (Paris: Robert Laffont, 1993), 152.

34. Lucette Valensi, "Présence du passé, lenteur de l'histoire," *Annales Économies Sociétés Civilisations* 48 (May–June 1993): 496.

35. Paul Webster, "France Haunted by Its Filthiest Hour," *The Observer*, 13 June 1993, 13.

36. Peter Carrier, "Vichy France," *Modern & Contemporary France*, n.s. 2, no. 3 (1994): 322.

37. Suzanne Citron, "Au Tableau noir de notre histoire," in *Oublier nos crimes, L'Amnésie nationale: une spécificité française?* ed. Dimitri Nicolaïdis, *Autrement*, Série Mutations, vol. 144 (Paris: Autrement, 1994), 137.

38. "La Morale de l'histoire. Table ronde avec François Bédarida, Alfred Grosser et Pierre Vidal-Naquet," in *Oublier nos crimes*, 214–15.

39. *Oublier nos crimes*, 219.

40. René Rémond et al., *Paul Touvier et l'Église* (Paris: Fayard, 1992), 10–11.

41. Grosser, "Table Ronde," in *Oublier nos crimes*, 219.

42. François Bédarida, in *Oublier nos crimes*, 222. See also Thierry Wolton, *Le Grand recruitement* (Paris: Grasset, 1993) and the discussion in Éric Conan and Henry Rousso, *Vichy: Un Passé qui ne passe pas* (Paris: Fayard, 1994), 222–23.

43. Sonia Combe, "L'Archive du crime," in *Oublier nos crimes*, 140. See also Bédarida, "La Conscience française entre mémoire et savoir," Combe, "Vichy, les archives et les historiens 'raisonnables,'" and Odile Krakovitch and Caroline Obert, "Pour des archives ouvertes," all in *Le Monde*: 19 January 1995, 19; 31 January 1995, 18; and 27 May 1995, 11, respectively.

44. Pierre Péan, *Une Jeunesse Française: François Mitterrand 1934–1947* (Paris: Fayard, 1994), 7. In support of Péan's comments, see also Emmanuel Faux, Thomas Legrand, and Gilles Perez, *La Main droite de Dieu: Enquête sur François Mitterrand et l'extrême droite* (Paris: Seuil, 1994), 103. On Mitterrand and Bousquet, see especially Péan, *Jeunesse française*, 315–16.

45. Conan and Rousso, *Vichy*, 30.

46. Conan and Rousso, *Vichy*, 269, 286.

47. François Mitterrand and Elie Wiesel, *Mémoire à deux voix* (Paris: Odile Jacob, 1995), 107–8. See also "Des Fautes qui ont conduit à des crimes," *Le Monde*, 11 April 1995, 10.

48. See Nicolas Weill, "Comportements des années noires," *Le Monde*, 20 January 1995, ix; Jean Planchais, "Le Temps des ambiguïtés" and "Toulouse entre francs-tireurs et politiques," and Weill, "Fascisme made in France," all in *Le Monde*: 2 June 1995, xi (the first two), vii (the last one); and Weill, "Les 'ratés' du procès Pétain," *Le Monde*, 21 July 1995, 14.

49. Philippe Burrin, *La France à l'heure allemande 1940–1944* (Paris: Seuil, 1995), 471.

50. Olivier Wieviorka, "Review of Burrin, *La France à l'heure allemande 1940–1944*," *Vingtième Siècle* 48 (October–December 1995): 167.

51. Dominique Veillon, *Vivre et survivre en France, 1939–1947* (Paris: Payot, 1995), 320.

52. Sarah Fishman, "The Power of Myth: Five Recent Works on Vichy France," *Journal of Modern History* 67, no. 3 (September 1995): 666.

53. John Hellman, "Wounding Memories: Mitterrand, Moulin, Touvier, and the Divine Half-Lie of Resistance," *French Historical Studies* 19, no. 2 (fall 1995): 486.

54. Pierre Nora, "Le Syndrome, son passé, son avenir," *French Historical Studies* 19, no. 2 (fall 1995): 492.

55. Françoise Thébaud, "Vichy, la défaite des femmes," *Le Monde*, 5 January 1996, i. This article reviews Francine Muel-Dreyfus, *Vichy et l'éternel féminin* (Paris: Seuil, 1995).

56. Bernard D. Kaplan, "French Resistance Deemed More Myth Than Reality," *San Francisco Examiner*, 28 January 1996, A8.

57. Following Mitterrand's death, *Le Monde* republished two articles by Edwy Plenel pertaining to the 1994 "revelations" of the former president's Vichy activities. See Plenel, "Les Secrets de jeunesse d'un président," 2 September 1994, and "Trou de mémoire," 14 September 1994, in "La Mort de François Mitterrand," special section, *Le Monde*, 12 January 1996, sec. III. See also Georges-Marc Benhamou, *Le Dernier Mitterrand* (Paris: Plon, 1996) and Rafaële Rivais, "François Mitterrand avait 'confiance dans le jugement de l'Histoire,'" *Le Monde*, 7 January 1997, 6.

58. Nicolas Weill, "Des Entreprises françaises au service de l'Allemagne nazie," *Le Monde*, 11 October 1996, 1 and 15. For Webster, see above, note 35.

59. Michel Bar-Zohar, *Bitter Scent: The Case of L'Oréal, Nazis, and the Arab Boycott* (New York: New American Library/Dutton, 1996); translated into French as *Une Histoire sans fard: L'Oréal, des années sombres au boycott arabe* (Paris: Fayard, 1997). See also Florence Noiville, "L'Oréal, une histoire au parfum de soufre," *Le Monde*, 17 January 1997, X.

60. For Schueller and the MSR, see Gordon, *Collaborationism in France*, 71–72 and 206–7; and "The Condottieri of the Collaboration: Mouvement Social Révolutionnaire," *Journal of Contemporary History* 10, no. 2 (April 1975), 261–82.

61. Philippe Dagen, "Un Généalogiste sur les traces des héritiers oubliés," *Le Monde*, 4 February 1997, 9.

62. For the figures, see Gordon, "Vichy Syndrome," 507.

63. Conan and Rousso, *Vichy*, 211–12.

64. Gordon, "Vichy Syndrome," 510.

65. *Bibliographie annuelle de l'histoire de France* (Paris: C.N.R.S., 1993).

66. The objection concerning *Le Monde Juif* was raised in Rousso's response to the three contributions to the *French Historical Studies* forum on Vichy. See Rousso, "Le Syndrome de l'historien," *French Historical Studies* 19, no. 2 (fall 1995): 520.

67. Rousso, "Syndrome de l'historien," 521.

68. Rousso, *Vichy Syndrome*, 142.

69. Gordon, "Collaboration," 258–59. See also Pascale Froment, *René Bousquet* (Paris: Stock, 1994), 228; and Stanley Hoffmann and Robert Paxton in "Symposium on Mitterrand's Past," *French Politics and Society* 13, no. 1 (winter 1995): 10 and 20, respectively.

70. See Sylvie Pierre-Brossolette, "Mitterrand rattrapé par l'histoire," *L'Express*, 22 September 1994, 8–9.

71. "'Navarro' a fait mieux que François Mitterrand," *Le Monde*, 15 September 1994, 15.

72. Robert Tombs, "The Brilliant Second, Mitterrand and the Strains of the Franco-German Alliance," *Times Literary Supplement*, 19 January 1996, 6–7.

73. J.-M. C., "La Fin du siécle," *Le Monde*, 10 January 1996, 1.

74. "Jacques Chirac: 'Respect pour l'homme d'État et admiration pour l'homme privé,'" *Le Monde*, 10 January 1996, 2.

75. Maurice Peyrot, "Maurice Papon sera le second Français jugé pour crimes contre l'humanité," *Le Monde*, 25 January 1997, 8.

76. See René Rémond, "Introduction," in Fondation Nationale des Sciences Politiques, *Le Gouvernement de Vichy, 1940–1942* (Paris: Armand Colin, 1972), 7.

77. Hélène Dupuy, "Aux origines du mythe," in *Oublier nos crimes*, 160.

78. See Bertram M. Gordon, "The Morphology of the Collaborator: The French Case," *Journal of European Studies* 23 (March–June 1993): 6; and Pascal Balmand, *Histoire de la France* (Paris: Hatier, 1992), 98–99.

79. Marc Fumaroli, "A Scottish Voltaire: John Barclay and the Character of Nations," *Times Literary Supplement*, 19 January 1996, 16.

80. The Dreyfus Affair "ne cessera jamais d'être d'actualité," in the words of Eric Cahm, *L'Affaire Dreyfus: Histoire, politique et société* (Paris: Le Livre de Poche, 1994), cited in Michael Burns, Review, *Modern & Contemporary France*, n.s. 3, no. 4 (1995): 472.

81. Gordon, "Vichy Syndrome," 515.

82. See, for example, the open letter of 1925 from Charles Maurras to Abraham Schrameck, who was Jewish and served as Interior Minister with the moderate leftist Cartel des Gauches cabinet; in Jean-Luc Pinol, "1919–1958, Le Temps des droites," in Sirinelli, *Histoire des droites en France*, 1:304–5. See also Yves-Marie Hilaire, "1900–1945, L'Ancrage des idéologies," in Sirinelli, *Histoire des droites en France*, 1:535.

83. Patricia Highsmith, "Desperate Connections," *Times Literary Supplement*, 17 April 1992, 4.

84. Gordon, "Morphology," 2.

85. Gordon, "Morphology," 2.

86. "Military Barracks Honoring Nazi Generals Are Renamed," *The Week in Germany*, 17 November 1995, 6.

87. Sophie Gherardi, "Les Ambivalences de la mémoire italienne," *Le Monde*, 29 September 1995, 1.

88. Gherardi, "Les Ambivalences," 18.

89. Linda Holt, "Our Dear Channel Islands," *London Review of Books* 17, no. 10 (25 May 1995): 9–11.

90. Patrice de Beer, " 'L'Occupation modèle' de Jersey et de Guernsey," *Le Monde*, 10 May 1995, 19.

91. Serge Schemann, "In Israel, a Day to Plant Trees and Rebuild a Forest," *New York Times*, 6 February 1996, A6.

92. John F. Burns, "India Rehabilitates Wartime Leader Who Fought for Japan," *New York Times*, 24 January 1997, A7.

93. For a good summary of the Swiss bank affair and reevaluations of Swiss wartime neutrality, see Alan Cowell, "Swiss Beginning to Question Image of Heroism in the War," *New York Times*, 8 February 1997, A1 and A5.

94. Specific parallels in wartime and postwar Franco-German collaboration are examined in Bertram M. Gordon, "Frontiers in the Vichy Mind and Contemporary French Views of France in the European Union: Differences and Continuities," in *L'Établissement des frontières en Europe après les deux guerres mondiales/The Establishment of European Frontiers after the Two World Wars*, ed. Christian Baechler and Carole Fink (Berne: Peter Lang, 1996), 281–99.

95. Attempts to bring European school history texts into agreement on the historical significance of the war are discussed in "Le Manuel d'histoire sous surveillance," in Conseil Régional de Basse-Normandie, *Caen*, 20 Mai 1995, Le Devoir de

mémoire, la tentation de l'oubli (Caen: Conseil Régional de Basse-Normandie, 1995), 12–13.

96. Representative of the present concerns of the French over the Germans may be the remark of Paris radio commentator Philippe Aubert: "We hate them [the Germans] with their silver Mercedes cars. Didn't we win the war? It's unbearable. . . . We would really prefer it if they were poor and unhappy." This was quoted by Stephen Kinzer, "Best of Gibes, Wurst of. . . ," *New York Times*, 16 January 1994, 4E. For a more recent discussion of the challenges France faced from Germany and the globalization of a new fin-de-siécle economic order, see François Rachline, "Le Monde dans la France," *Le Monde*, 16 January 1997, 13.

97. Michael Marrus, "Vichy and the Jews," *Times Literary Supplement*, 28 January 1994, 10. More examples of syndrome-type arguments in France are offered in Gordon, "Vichy Syndrome," 516, n.84.

98. Jean-Marc Théolleyre, "La Justice doit l'emporter sur l'oubli," *Le Monde*, 2 May 1987, reprinted in "Le Procés de Klaus Barbie," *Special Edition*, July 1987 (Paris: Le Monde, 1987), 8. See also William Echikson, "In France, 'The Trial of the Decade' Fizzles," *Christian Science Monitor*, 18 May 1987, 10.

99. Gordon, "Vichy Syndrome," 513.

100. See, respectively, Zeev Sternhell, "Ce Passé qui refuse de passer," Lothar Baier, "Un Acharnement déconcertant," and Tony Judt, "Entre le tabou et l'obsession," all in *Le Monde*, 21 September 1994, 8–9.

101. Rousso, "Syndrome de l'historien," 525.

102. Rousso, "Syndrome de l'historien," 523.

103. Henry Rousso, "La France inconsolable ou le deuil perpétuel des années noires," 1945: Consequences and Sequels of the Second World War, special issue of *Bulletin du Comité international d'histoire de la Deuxiéme Guerre mondiale* 27/28 (1995): 331.

104. Rousso, "France inconsolable," 326.

105. A similar progression in the quantity of histories, especially by survivors, of the Nazi concentration camps has been noted in Germany. See John Rutledge, post on H-German, H-Net List on German History, 20 July 1995.

106. For reactions to the announcement that Papon would be tried, see " 'Comme tout procés politique, les jeux sont faits d'avance,' " *Le Monde*, 25 January 1997, 8.

107. See above, note 45.

108. " 'Je suis le bouc émissaire d'un complot politique,' Papon expose sa défense à 'Libération': Il n'était qu'un exécutant sécondaire et un 'spectateur impuissant,' " *Libération*, 6 March 1996, 7–8.

109. Annette Lévy-Willard, "La 'Sérénité' d'un ambitieux: Sans remords, Papon minimise son rôle et n'hésite pas à mentir," *Libération*, 6 March 1996, 6.

110. " 'Les Jeux sont faits," 8; and Roger Cohen, "Accused French Ex-Official Says Jews Aided Nazi Deportations," *New York Times*, 30 January 1997, A7. The Papon affair is more extensively discussed in Gordon, "Afterword: Who Are the Guilty and Should They Be Tried?" in *The Holocaust in France Today*, ed. Golsan, 179–98; also Pascale Nivelle, "Le Renvoi en cour d'assises de l'ancien fonctionnaire de Vichy va être examiné, Après quinze ans de procédure, la dernière ligne droite du dossier Papon," *Libération*, 6 March 1996, 6–7; and Peyrot, "Maurice Papon sera le second

Français jugé pour crimes contre l'humanité" and Laurent Greilsamer, "Un Col blanc de la collaboration, exécutant scrupuleux d'un projet criminel," both in *Le Monde*, 25 January 1997, 8.

111. Henri Hajdenberg, president of CRIF (Conseil représentatif des institutions juives de France), made it clear that he and his organization wanted moral rather than financial indemnification for the losses suffered more than fifty years earlier. See Jean-Louis Saux, "M. Hajdenberg exclut toute indemnisation globale," *Le Monde*, 4 February 1997, 9.

112. Examples of the historicization process at work regarding wartime France are the historical dictionaries appearing that are devoted to the period: for example, Jean-Pierre Azéma and François Bédarida, eds., *1938–1948, Les Années de tourmente, de Munich à Prague, Dictionnaire Critique* (Paris: Flammarion, 1995) and Bertram M. Gordon, ed., *Historical Dictionary of World War II France: The Occupation, Vichy and the Resistance, 1938–1946* (Westport CT: Greenwood, forthcoming).

113. An example of attempts to maintain the enormity of the Nazi crimes in occupied France present in today's world, in addition to the work of Klarsfeld and others in France, was the photography show, "French Children of the Holocaust: A Memorial Exhibition," staged in New York; see Anne Roiphe, "Holocaust's Children, One by One by One," *New York Times*, 7 February 1997, B1 and B26.

114. See Luc Rosenzweig, "La Sortie parisienne des 'rattachistes' wallons," *Le Monde*, 22 January 1997, 31; Gordon, "Frontiers in the Vichy Mind," in Baechler and Fink, *L'Établissement des frontières en Europe après les deux guerres mondiales*, 285.

115. See "Concept commun franco-allemand en matière de sécurité et de défense," *Le Monde*, 30 January 1997, 12–13.

Richard J. Golsan

History and the Responsibility of Memory: *Vichy: Un Passé qui ne passe pas* and the Trial of Paul Touvier

In 1987 the young French historian Henry Rousso published his now-classic study, *Le Syndrome de Vichy de 1944 à nos jours*,[1] a work that carefully dissected the troubled memory of the Vichy period as it manifested itself in political, social, and judicial controversies in postwar France. Rather than receding peacefully into the past, Rousso argued, the dark years of the Occupation continued to haunt the nation. The Vichy past was, as he described it, a "corpse [that] was still warm," a specter that could still affect electoral campaigns, provoke governmental and judicial scandals, and even shape conflicting discourses surrounding events as disparate as the Algerian crisis in the 1950s and 1960s and the student revolts of May 1968.

As it turned out, *Le Syndrome de Vichy* was not simply a history in progress but in many ways a prophetic work that would define the parameters of a growing national malaise still alive in France today. After 1987 the troubled memory of the Occupation provoked scandal after scandal, involving at various times the judicial system, the Catholic Church, and members of the government. All of these scandals, moreover, were covered in depth by the media.[2] In September 1994, the "Vichy Syndrome"—now a widely acknowledged national "malady" affecting nearly every phase of French public life—reached the office of the president of the Republic itself. Revelations in Pierre Péan's *Une Jeunesse française: François Mitterrand 1934–1947* concerning the extent of Mitterrand's Vichy past and his postwar friendship with René Bousquet, the former head of Vichy police charged with crimes against humanity in 1989, forced Mitterrand to go on national television to explain that past and justify his friendship with Bousquet. By most accounts, few were satisfied with the president's explanations.[3]

Precisely at the moment of the irruption of *l'Affaire Mitterrand*, Rousso, now an influential public figure in his own right, coauthored a new book entitled *Vichy: Un Passé qui ne passe pas*.[4] The book called, in effect, for a moratorium on public debate and controversy surrounding the Occupation. Rousso and his coauthor, Eric Conan, argued that the nation's "duty" to remember the past through public scandals played out in the press and on television was leading not to an authentic understanding of historical realities or the shouldering of responsibility for that past, but to a media circus in which "pseudo-disclosures" obscured rather than clarified the truth concerning the events and issues themselves. Having dispatched the Gaullist Myth of Resistance, the Vichy Syndrome in its most recent manifestations risked bending the truth in the opposite direction by painting a portrait of a collaborationist France where only a few heroic individuals resisted and the rest went along with Vichy and the Nazis.[5]

Rousso and Conan also argued that this obsessive focus on the past allowed the nation to avoid dealing with the troubling and more pressing realities of the present, a view shared by other French intellectuals including Tzvetan Todorov and Alain Finkielkraut. In an essay denouncing France's obsession with Vichy and its indifference when faced with the horrors of ethnic cleansing in the former Yugoslavia, Finkielkraut bitterly noted that "past errors have made us forget present ones."[6] The memory of Vichy, in other words, was less what Todorov has labeled an "exemplary memory"—one that teaches us to be vigilant and act in the name of justice in the present—than what he describes as a "literal memory"—an obsessive and ultimately destructive preoccupation from which we learn nothing.[7]

Reactions to the stand taken by Rousso and Conan were generally favorable. Many journalists and historians described the book as "courageous" and "necessary." In an essay published recently in the United States, Pierre Nora lauded *Vichy: Un Passé qui ne passe pas* and asserted that Rousso and Conan should be "congratulated" for what he described as their *véhémente mise en garde*.[8]

Despite praise such as this, however, the central premise of the book and the polemical stance taken by the authors raise a number of historical, historiographical, and even political concerns. I would like to look briefly at these broader issues before testing the central thesis of the book in the context of one of the most controversial recent "flare-ups" of the Vichy Syndrome, the trial for crimes against humanity of Paul Touvier in spring 1994.

It is worth noting at the outset that what Pierre Nora describes as the *véhémente mise en garde* contained in *Vichy: Un Passé qui ne passe pas* could hardly avoid close scrutiny, given the events transpiring in France at the moment of the book's publication. Rousso and Conan's call for a moratorium on media extravaganzas focusing on the worst aspects of the Vichy past must certainly have seemed incongruous at a time when Mitterrand's Vichy involvements and friendship with Bousquet were all the news. In another sense, however, given these circumstances, Rousso and Conan's message could not have been more timely. Despite the spectacular nature of the "revelations" concerning Mitterrand's past, the news was in fact old news: the disclosures were for the most part merely further examples of the "pseudo-disclosures" Rousso and Conan had denounced. Mitterrand's links to Bousquet had already been widely noted in the early 1990s in media coverage of the legal and judicial imbroglio attendant upon efforts to bring Bousquet to trial on charges of crimes against humanity.[9] Moreover, Mitterrand's Vichy past, and even his friendship with former members of the 1930s right-wing terrorist group the Cagoule, had been trumpeted earlier in extreme right-wing periodicals including *Le Choc du mois*.[10] So, depending on one's perspective, Rousso and Conan's message could appear either completely anachronistic or remarkably timely.

By suggesting that the events occurring at the moment of publication of *Vichy: Un Passé qui ne passe pas* make the book's central thesis appear all the more controversial, I do not mean to suggest that the position taken by its authors and the tone they adopt are any the less polemical or, ultimately, problematic. As Nora remarks in his comments on it, the book is clearly more judgmental concerning the events it describes than the earlier *Syndrome de Vichy*, to the point of making Nora wonder—facetiously, no doubt—if the two books were authored by the same person.[11] But it is not simply the message and tone of the book that make it provocative. The title is to all appearances borrowed from an (in)famous polemic by Ernst Nolte, "The Past that Will Not Pass," penned during the Historians' Debate in Germany in the mid-1980s. In that essay, Nolte had sought, through a series of highly dubious claims and comparisons, to "normalize" Germany's Nazi past and deemphasize the Holocaust by challenging its uniqueness and raising the possibility of its having been inspired by non-German, "Asian" sources. While Rousso and Conan certainly were not seeking to "normalize" Vichy or rationalize its crimes in any way, their choice of titles must have shocked those aware of Nolte's positions and struck some as deliberately inflammatory.

These issues aside, *Vichy: Un Passé qui ne passe pas* raised a number of other concerns, historiographical and political, that are not bound so explicitly to the moment. Among these is the nature of historical writing itself. In *Apologie pour l'histoire ou Métier d'historien*, Marc Bloch criticizes what he describes as the "satanic enemy of history: the mania of judgment."[12] Is it, in fact, the historian's duty to pass judgment on his subject matter, or should he maintain a more detached and "objective perspective"? As Tzvetan Todorov (among others) has argued recently, it is doubtful if such objectivity is even possible. Using Bloch's example of Robespierre, Todorov wonders if one can even discuss the architect of the Terror without reference to one's own value judgments. As Todorov frames the question: "Can one say anything sensible about [Robespierre] without deciding whether he was a bloody dictator or the liberator of a people?"[13] The judgments brought to bear do not, of course, have to be as divergent as those suggested by Todorov in the example just cited, and Rousso and Conan's attitudes toward the phenomenon they criticize and especially the individual events they analyze are certainly more nuanced than the contrasting attitudes toward Robespierre. But even generally balanced and well grounded judgments such as theirs, when expressed polemically, may adversely affect the reception of their work. *Vichy: Un Passé qui ne passe pas*, it would appear, is already remembered more for its polemical stance than for the events it analyzes. Rightly or wrongly, it is unlikely to have the lasting impact of *Le Syndrome de Vichy*.

If issues such as these are of abiding interest to historians, other issues raised by Rousso and Conan's critique of France's "duty to memory" are of broader historical and political concern. Among those who would defuse the scandal surrounding the Occupation and "normalize" the Vichy past are historians, lawyers, politicians, and even judges whose various writings and pronouncements seek to rehabilitate Vichy by defending its actions or obscuring the realities of the regime through distortions, dubious comparisons, and other means. To cite only one example here (several more will be noted in the discussion of the Touvier case), one of the "historical" studies of Vichy published in 1990 was Sorbonne Professor François-Georges Dreyfus's *Histoire de Vichy*.[14] Dreyfus's eight-hundred-page book sought to exculpate Vichy by reviving Robert Aron's "shield" thesis of Vichy as protector of the nation and challenging the specificity of Vichy xenophobia by discussing Third Republican anti-Semitism and anticommunism under the heading "Vichy before Vichy." The fact that the book was favorably reviewed by the extreme right-wing press should come as no surprise, nor should the fact that many of those involved in "normalizing" the Vichy past are active sympathizers and supporters of Jean-Marie Le Pen's National Front. The struggle over the Vichy past and its interpretation, it would appear, is also linked to a struggle over the present.[15]

Given Rousso and Conan's general skepticism concerning France's obsessive preoccupation with its Vichy past, it is not surprising that they would have serious reservations about the trial for crimes against humanity of Paul Touvier, which took place in Versailles in March and April 1994. For many, the trial represented the opportunity to "reconstitute [the nation's] collective memory" and "inform [its] youth while provoking the latter's interest and developing its critical sense."[16] But for Rousso and Conan, these potential benefits—at best optimistic and at worst illusory—were outweighed by other considerations and perspectives that cast serious doubts on the entire proceedings. In general terms, the circumstances of the trial itself—an old man standing trial for events committed fifty years earlier on behalf of a political regime long since defeated and disgraced—raised a number of important questions:

> Could one pass judgment so long after the events themselves? Was it possible, cloistered in the courtroom, to reimmerse oneself in the context of the period, to evaluate retrospectively the realities of the situation? How could one reconcile the exigencies of justice by satisfying on the one hand the demands of the victims or their descendants while at the same time observing the necessary detachment from the period of history in question? Could one condemn the criminality of particular political regimes in passing judgment on individuals who were not necessarily representative of what one wished to denounce? Could one undo without risks that which the wartime generation had repaired not without difficulty after 1944: the national fabric as it applied both to society and to the minds of the French people?[17]

The concerns noted in the passage just cited were not the only ones raised by Rousso and Conan in relation to the Touvier trial, nor were they of necessity the most significant historical and legal issues raised by the case itself. To discuss these issues, we must first sketch in the background of the trial by examining briefly the lengthy and complicated history of *l'affaire Touvier*, which had received considerable media attention and stirred troubling memories for the French for more than twenty years. A consideration of the history of the affair is, of course, also necessary before any final assessment of the pedagogical and historical importance of the Touvier trial can be undertaken.

The trial of Paul Touvier was the culmination of almost fifty years of police investigations, manhunts, and miscues, controversial judicial decisions, and high-level negotiations between representatives of the Catholic Church and the French government, all punctuated by periodic media extravaganzas. Although ultimately a banal and vicious individual, Touvier had assumed almost mythic proportions in the public imagination by the time he was tried in spring 1994. The singer Jacques Brel, in fact, had even written a song inspired by his plight.[18] Born in 1915, Touvier was raised in a large lower-middle-class family in the small town of Chambéry not far from Lyons. The family was reactionary Catholic and profoundly nationalistic. Touvier's father, tyrannical by nature, was rabidly anti-Semitic and anglophobic, and a religious fanatic to boot. An ascetic *manqué* who cultivated friendships with local priests, Touvier senior also claimed that he performed his conjugal duty only in order to create more servants for God. Touvier's mother died bearing her eleventh child, which she had conceived against her doctor's orders.[19]

Paul Touvier's youth was completely unremarkable. A mediocre student, he went to work as a railway clerk; when war came in 1939, he went into the army. Suspected of desertion in June 1940, he was briefly imprisoned and then released. Back in Chambéry in July, he joined Vichy's veteran organization, the Légion des Combattants, and quickly became the local commander. As the war progressed and the Vichy regime became increasingly dominated by overtly fascistic elements, the Légion des Combattants became increasingly militant, evolving finally in January 1943 into the Milice, a paramilitary police force created primarily to combat France's "internal enemies"—resisters and Jews.[20] Touvier followed the organization in its evolution, continuing to climb the ranks until he was placed in charge of Milice intelligence in Lyons. In his new capacity as head of the so-called Second Service, Touvier quickly earned a reputation for brutality and profiteering. He confiscated apartments and cars owned formerly by Jews, and ordered raids, executions, and deportations of Jews and Resistance fighters.[21] On 29 June 1944, Touvier ordered the execution of seven Jewish hostages at the cemetery of Rillieux-la-Pape to avenge the assassination by the Resistance the day before of Vichy's Minister of Propaganda, Philippe Henriot. For this crime and this crime alone, Touvier would finally stand trial for crimes against humanity in 1994.

Following the liberation of Lyons from the Germans in September 1944 and with the help of a priest friendly to the Milice, Touvier fled the city and began a life in hiding given over largely to petty crime and, reportedly, occasional extreme right-wing political activity.[22] During his long *cavale*, or flight from justice, Touvier was regularly assisted by priests whom he, like his father before him, sought to cultivate. So successful was Touvier at ingratiating himself with Catholic clerics that he eventually acquired friends well up in the Church hierarchy. These well-placed friends would eventually secure a pardon for Touvier from President Georges Pompidou in 1971, an event to which I shall return shortly.

In order to understand how Touvier could be tried for crimes against humanity in 1994 after receiving a presidential pardon more than twenty years earlier, it is necessary to examine the legal history and complexities of the Touvier case in some detail. In 1946 and 1947, Touvier was convicted of treason and "intelligence with the enemy" and condemned to death, first by a court in Lyons and a year later by another court in his native Chambéry. In 1967, twenty years after the last of these convictions, according to the statute of limitations Touvier was for all intents and purposes a free man. But due to a peculiar feature of French law known as *peines accessoires* "accessory penalties," even after the statute of limitations had run out on Touvier's crimes, he could not return to the region where the crimes had been committed nor claim his inheritance from his father in Chambéry. It was to lift these sanctions alone that President Pompidou, lobbied for years by high Church officials who misrepresented their protégé, granted his pardon. (Moreover, from the numerous accounts of the pardon and in testimony concerning the pardon given at the trial, it is clear that Church officials presented Touvier as a victim of injustice, and considerably downplayed the extent and nature of his crimes.)

When the presidential pardon for Touvier was revealed in a national magazine article that also enumerated Touvier's crimes during the Occupation, the Touvier affair became a public scandal.[23] Protests were organized, and Touvier and even Pompidou himself were denounced in the press. In a belated effort at damage control, Pompidou called a press conference in September 1972 in which he asserted his belief that the time for national reconciliation had come where the Occupation was concerned, and that it was necessary to "draw a veil over the past."[24]

Pompidou's assertions fell on deaf ears. Public outcry continued, and Touvier, fearing for his life, went into hiding again. In November 1973 the legal stakes in the Touvier affair changed completely. The children of two of Touvier's Jewish victims, one of whose father had been murdered at the cemetery of Rillieux-la-Pape, brought charges of crimes against humanity against Touvier in a court in Lyons.

In order to appreciate the magnitude of the changes brought about by these new charges, it is necessary to look briefly at the general definition of crimes against humanity and especially the history of its codification in French law. Defined by the international Military Tribunal in London in 1945 as "murder, extermination, enslavement, deportation, and other inhumane acts committed against any civilian population, before or during the war, or persecution on political, racial, or religious grounds . . . whether or not in violation of domestic law of the country where perpetrated,"[25] crimes against humanity were first incorporated in French law in 1964. No explicit definition was codified at that time; the law simply cited the 1945 International Tribunal definition just given. What was crucial, however, was that these crimes were declared imprescriptible—that is, no statute of limitations applied to them. Therefore Touvier and others involved in the persecution of the Jews, most notably Klaus Barbie, could be tried, as it turned out, even up to fifty years after the crimes themselves had been committed.

Under the pressure of events, the definition of crimes against humanity laws in France underwent significant and highly controversial changes. Before the trial of Klaus Barbie, and as a result of demands made by former members of the Resistance who wished to see Barbie's crimes against their fellows punished, the definition of crimes against humanity was modified in at least two significant ways. First, the definition was revised to include "inhuman acts" committed not only against individuals because of their appurtenance to a particular racial or religious group, but also against those who fought against the perpetrators of these crimes, namely the Resistance in their struggle against the Nazis. Second, the new law also defined the type of government in whose name such crimes were committed as one "practicing a politics of ideological hegemony."[26] As we shall see, this last qualification was to have a profound impact on highly controversial legal decisions concerning the Touvier case in the early 1990s.

In the meantime, the original charges of crimes against humanity lodged against Touvier in 1973 were to have an extraordinary history themselves. Passed from court to court, the charges were declared by numerous examining magistrates and judges to be beyond their jurisdiction. Some questioned the legitimacy of incorporating the Nuremburg statutes concerning crimes against humanity into French law. The question was referred finally to the Ministry of Foreign Affairs; the answer came back in the affirmative.[27] At issue, apart from a reticence to try Frenchmen for such heinous crimes, were concerns regarding the imprescriptibility of these crimes. In Touvier's case and others as well, some were uneasy applying retroactively the 1964 law, and its later modifications, to crimes committed many years before.[28] Besides, in general terms, many wondered if it would be fair to try a man for crimes committed so long ago, when after all, he might have changed entirely.

Despite legal obstacles and the more philosophical reservations expressed by some, Touvier was finally indicted for crimes against humanity in June 1981. It would take eight more years for the national police to locate and arrest him. Touvier, who had been hiding in a succession of monasteries, was finally captured in a right-wing *intégriste* monastery in Nice in 1989.[29] After more than forty years, it appeared that Touvier would at last stand trial for crimes he had committed as a young member of the Milice during the Occupation.

The examining magistrate having completed his work and submitted his report to the court for prosecution, it came as a stunning surprise when in April 1992 the criminal chamber of the Paris Court of Appeals dropped all charges against Touvier. The three judges writing the decision found the evidence and testimony assembled against Touvier inadequate. More importantly, they rejected the notion that crimes against humanity could be committed on behalf of the Vichy regime, since, in their view, the regime was not one that practiced a policy of "ideological hegemony" as prescribed in the 1985 law, but rather one lacking a unified ideological core. For the appeals court judges, Vichy embodied an eclectic mix, a "constellation," of "good intentions" and "political animosities." Despite its own traditionalist views, the judges asserted, Vichy tolerated other views as well. Finally, in the most shocking part of their decision, the judges argued that Vichy was not in essence anti-Semitic because there had never been "an official proclamation that the Jew was the enemy of the state." Besides, they concluded, none of Pétain's speeches contained "anti-Semitic pronouncements." As an agent of such a regime, by definition Touvier could not be guilty of crimes against humanity. The most memorable aspect of the April 1992 decision, apart from the storm of controversy it provoked in the media, the government, and the halls of justice themselves,[30] was the fact that the judges chose to rewrite the history of Vichy and to exonerate it in ideological terms. Their assessment of the historical and political realities at issue was breathtakingly ill-informed—indeed, Rousso and Conan noted that any history student would have flunked his or her exam for arguing as the judges did.[31] Moreover, the decision was clearly geared not only toward exoneration, but toward rehabilitation.[32] Very few were surprised, in fact, when the reactionary politics of the judges themselves came to light.[33]

Given the extraordinary tendentiousness of the appeals court's opinion, it is not surprising that its verdict was partially overturned by a higher court in November of the same year. But while the higher court's reversal paved the way, finally, for Touvier's trial for crimes against humanity, the nature of the decision further muddied the historical waters. The higher court determined that there was sufficient evidence to try Touvier for ordering the murders of seven Jews at the cemetery of Rillieux-la-Pape, especially since Touvier had confessed to these crimes himself.[34] But the higher court then declined to overturn the appeals court's assessment of the Vichy government as a regime not practicing a policy of ideological hegemony, not wishing to indulge in the rewriting of history in its own right. What this meant, in essence, was that Touvier could be tried and convicted of crimes against humanity if he could be shown, in whatever fashion, to have acted on behalf of Nazi Germany, whose status as a nation practicing a policy of ideological hegemony was never in doubt. On the other hand, if he could convince the court that he had been acting on Vichy's behalf, then the Rillieux murders could no longer be defined as crimes against humanity and Touvier would walk.

The ironies and frustrations of the situation created by the higher court's decision were manifold. In their comments on the decision and its implications, Rousso and Conan note that it is "a very strange form of incrimination which punishes complicity but not the act itself" (134). More troubling still was the fact that by definition the trial could not really accomplish what many hoped it would, which was to pass judgment on the brutal realities of Vichy's own anti-Semitism, since Vichy was, in a legal sense, out of bounds to begin with. Finally, in order to secure Touvier's conviction, prosecutors would be obliged to distort history once again by arguing that Touvier had acted on orders issued by the Germans, which, a good deal of evidence suggested, was not in fact the case. Many of those called to testify did in fact contradict their own earlier testimony to the examining magistrate and in other contexts in which they had attributed Touvier's crimes to Vichy, stating under oath on the stand that they now believed he had acted on behalf of the Nazis.

Such reversals may be attributed to the fact that the witnesses in question believed, for any number of reasons, that an acquittal would be the worst outcome imaginable.[35] During the course of the trial itself, as it turned out, it was one of the prosecution lawyers, Arno Klarsfeld, who denounced the hypocrisy of such distortions of the truth in no uncertain terms.[36] How could one teach a lesson about history, he argued, if one was willing to distort history to make the point?

When the trial finally did get underway at the Yvelines court at Versailles in March 1994, one Parisian newspaper announced that the "trial for memory"[37] was about to begin, but the characterization was clearly vexed, not only as a result of the legal decisions leading up to the trial, but as a result of events and statements made immediately preceding the start of the deliberations themselves. If the trial, even indirectly, was intended to recall Vichy's role in the persecution of the Jews and the Final Solution, the conservative mayor of Versailles, André Damien, wanted no part of it; he refused to provide a room at the Town Hall for a public exhibition commemorating "Le temps des rafles," the "time of the roundups."[38] Moreover, Touvier's lawyer, Jacques Trémolet de Villers, not content to make a case exonerating his client for the crimes committed, indulged in some historical revisionism of his own. Choosing analogies many found not only provocative but obscene, Trémolet painted his man both as the victim of a massive ideological conspiracy and as a modern-day saint interested not in murdering Jews, but rather in saving as many as he could.[39] According to Trémolet, Touvier was this century's Alfred Dreyfus,[40] victimized by the full weight of a government and media conspiracy. Moreover, his actions vis-à-vis the murders at the Rillieux cemetery were more akin to those of a Schindler than a Klaus Barbie. According to the version of events that justified this comparison, the Germans had originally demanded that one hundred hostages be executed to avenge Henriot's murder. Touvier's superior in the Milice had reduced the number to thirty, and Touvier, concerned only with saving as many Jewish lives as he could, succeeded in reducing the number of victims to seven, a mere fraction of the original hundred supposedly exacted by the Germans.

As the trial proceeded, it became quite clear to attentive observers that all of these historical analogies and versions of the past were either groundless or fictitious. Unlike Dreyfus, Touvier was not an innocent and honorable man railroaded by powerful figures behind the scenes, but a devious liar who had in fact duped and misled others in his efforts to avoid punishment for any number of crimes.[41] The comparison with Schindler was even more spurious, as several revelations during the trial would confirm. First, Touvier had not succeeded in saving some ninety hypothetical Jewish victims from the more voracious Germans, since it now appeared that no German order calling for the execution of one hundred Jews after the murder of Henriot had ever been issued.[42] Moreover, when the executions of the seven hostages did occur, Touvier chose to save not one of the Jewish hostages he had had rounded up, but a non-Jewish Resistance member who was about to be taken along with them to the cemetery at Rillieux.[43] Any doubts about Touvier's anti-Semitism, then or in the more recent past, were put to rest when pages from Touvier's journal from the 1980s were read to the court. In the so-called "green notebooks," Touvier vented his considerable spleen on politicians, movie stars, and other public figures whom he denounced as "kikes" and, in many instances, as members of modern-day Jewish conspiracies and cabals.

The collapse of the "Schindler defense" did not, however, prevent Touvier's lawyer Trémolet from continuing in his attempt to reshape history to serve his own ends. When distinguished historians including René Rémond and the American Robert Paxton were called to testify about the nature of Vichy ideology and the politics of the regime, Trémolet challenged their testimony, arguing that new interpretations of Vichy could displace theirs at any time, and that history, after all, was largely just a "matter of opinion." This enraged those present, sensitive as they were to le négationnisme—the French version of the Holocaust denial—but it fit nicely with the view of history of the accused, who, among other things, could see no difference between his service to Vichy during the war and that of his brother, who was a Gaullist. Their patriotism, Touvier asserted, was "the same thing."[44]

When the twelve-member panel of judges and jurors brought back their verdict of guilty in mid-April, not all the French felt a sense of catharsis or even satisfaction. For many, despite all the sound and fury, the trial had in reality not proven constructive. Assessing the historical impact of the trial just after its conclusion in the Parisian daily *Libération*, Rousso, anticipating the view he later shared with Conan in *Vichy: Un Passé qui ne passe pas*, asserted that historians had "learned very little" in factual terms during the proceedings.[45] As a result of the legal and juridical contortions leading up to the trial and making it possible in the first place, in the aftermath of Touvier's conviction legal experts questioned whether crimes against humanity could even exist in a juridical sense, given the pressures imposed on the law by the entire affair.[46] Such pessimistic assessments only seemed to add historical and legal weight to more philosophical musings by the president of the Republic himself. During the last stages of the trial Olivier Wieviorka published a book of interviews with leading political figures who had been in the Resistance. Among them was François Mitterrand, who along with other comments on Touvier and the prospect of his trial had wondered if such an event fifty years after the fact had any meaning, since the accused was now "just an old man." Besides, Mitterrand concluded, in a statement that now appears much less disinterested than it did at the time, "One cannot sustain oneself forever on memories and rancor."[47]

It is appropriate at this point to return to the broader issue raised at the outset of this essay: did the nation's duty to memory as exemplified in the court proceedings against Touvier serve to inform the public and contribute in the long run to curing the Vichy Syndrome, or did it merely distort history without really contributing to a meaningful resolution of the debate over the Vichy past? For Rousso and Conan, the latter was in fact the case. They pointed to many of the concerns raised above, especially the violence done to historical truth: "Historical truth had difficulty finding its proper place, caught as it was between the imperious exigencies of memory, the sophisms of law placed at the mercy of political considerations, and the logic of the ritual of the Assizes court."[48] Rousso and Conan also lamented the fact that in their view the press had further distorted history by turning Touvier into a "French Eichmann," thus attributing to his person a symbolic weight that his pettiness and insignificance could hardly sustain.[49]

More troubling still, perhaps, is that events following the conclusion of the trial and the appearance of Conan and Rousso's book confirm that historical revisionism coupled with an inability to confront the historical realities of the Pétain regime are still symptomatic among many of the French, including François Mitterrand. During his national television interview intended to defuse the scandal produced by Péan's biography, Mitterrand's comments confirmed that he either failed to understand the realities of Vichy or worse, refused to acknowledge them. Vichy's anti-Semitic laws, he asserted, were only directed at foreign Jews, a claim that was blatantly false. In a more general context, Mitterrand simply refused to acknowledge an indigenous and vicious French anti-Semitism, the kind that resulted in the forced wearing by Jews of the Yellow Star during the latter part of the Occupation and still clearly informed the attitudes of the likes of Paul Touvier. Finally, in statements that apparently shocked the French public more than anything else, Mitterrand praised his former friend René Bousquet as a man of "exceptional stature," even though in his capacity as head of Vichy police Bousquet had been responsible for implementing the Final Solution in France.[50] Bousquet, in fact, would have stood trial for crimes against humanity like Touvier if he had not been gunned down in his Paris apartment by Christian Didier—a crazed publicity seeker who had earlier tried to kill Klaus Barbie—in the summer of 1993. So outraged were many by Mitterrand's past and his televised self-justification that some, including the philosopher André Glucksmann, compared the affair to Watergate and praised the Americans for their courage in ridding themselves of a corrupt and compromised leader, something the French failed to do in the case of Mitterrand. The circumstances of the two events were in reality hardly comparable, but for Glucksmann Mitterrand's blindness where Vichy was concerned was symptomatic of a broader and more dangerous complacency toward fanatical and murderous extremisms. Glucksmann noted that it was Mitterrand who encouraged the sale of arms to the Hutus in Rwanda, arms that would later be used in the 1994 genocide of the Tutsis.[51]

Glucksmann's comments, of course, take us a long way from the memory of Vichy, but they do remind us that the stakes involved in France's duty to memory are certainly not without political implications in the present. Following Touvier's conviction, the trial of another and more famous collaborator, Philippe Pétain, became the subject of revisionist readings, in the form of new monographs on the topic or reprints of earlier books favorable to the Marshal and denouncing the injustice of his 1945 trial. One of the authors of these revisionist readings was the lawyer Jean-Marc Varault, a right-wing zealot with links to Le Pen's National Front and, not coincidentally, the defense attorney for the last man charged with crimes against humanity for his actions during the Occupation, Maurice Papon.[52]

Lest this litany of recent flare-ups of the Vichy Syndrome, coupled with the Touvier trial, suggest that France is in fact incapable of understanding or dealing with its Vichy past, it is important to add a few observations that point to a more optimistic conclusion than that offered by Rousso and Conan. First, it is also true that the Touvier trial and verdict did reveal the man for what he was, a vengeful and vicious anti-Semite and, in that capacity, a loyal and valued functionary of the Vichy regime. Moreover, it would certainly be impossible henceforth to present him as a Dreyfus, a Schindler, or an innocent Christian martyr of any sort. History was no longer a "matter of opinion," at least where the character of the accused was concerned.

It is also possible that the controversy surrounding Mitterrand's past, representing as it did perhaps the apogee of the Vichy Syndrome, would have been less significant had not the public been recently and repeatedly reminded of the brutalities of Vichy and the horrors of anti-Semitism and the Final Solution by daily reports from the Versailles courts in all the media. For while Mitterrand still entertained illusions concerning Vichy anti-Semitism and agents of the Holocaust like Bousquet, the volume and vociferousness of public reaction to Mitterrand's televised interview, *pace* Glucksmann, suggested that most of the French did not.[53]

But the most encouraging evidence of the nation's comprehension of the past and its willingness to act responsibly toward that past is President Jacques Chirac's acknowledgment, in summer 1995, of Vichy's culpability. On the fifty-third anniversary of the Velodrome d'Hiver roundups, Chirac publicly recognized Vichy anti-Semitism and the nation's obligation to assume responsibility for the regime.[54] If the scandal and controversy surrounding the person of Paul Touvier and his trial for crimes against humanity, and other events like it, encouraged Chirac to make the statement he made, then perhaps these scandals have served memory and truth and have not, after all, been in vain.

Notes

1. *Le Syndrome de Vichy de 1944 à nos jours* was originally published in 1987 by Editions du Seuil. A second, updated edition appeared in 1990. The book appeared in English translation under the title *The Vichy Syndrome: History and Memory in France since 1944* (Cambridge: Harvard University Press, 1991).

2. The Vichy Syndrome as described by Rousso and others has been discussed and analyzed in the press, on radio and television, and in the cinema. In this sense it diverges sharply from the Historian's Debate in Germany, which, as Wulf Kansteiner notes in his essay here, was played out largely within the confines of the press.

3. For a discussion of reactions to Mitterrand's Vichy past and his friendship with Bousquet, see my "Reflections on Mitterrand's *Années Noires: Une Jeunesse Française*," Contemporary French Civilization 19, no. 2 (1995): 292–311.

4. Eric Conan and Henry Rousso, *Vichy: Un Passé qui ne passe pas* (Paris: Fayard, 1994). A paperback edition with an afterword by the authors was published in the

Folio series in 1996. A translation of the updated edition is forthcoming from Dartmouth and the University Press of New England.

5. Stanley Hoffman had earlier labeled the myth of an abjectly collaborationist France the "Lacombe Lucien myth," after Louis Malle's famous film by that name. See Stanley Hoffman, "Cinquante ans après, quelques conclusions essentielles," *Esprit* 181 (May 1992): 38–42.

6. Alain Finkielkraut, *Comment peut-on être croate?* (Paris: Gallimard, 1992), 69.

7. Tzvetan Todorov, *Les Abus de la mémoire* (Paris: Arléa, 1995), 28–33.

8. Pierre Nora, "Le Syndrome, son passé, son avenir," *French Historical Studies* 19, no. 2 (fall 1995): 489.

9. For details of the Bousquet affair and Mitterrand's links to Bousquet, see Golsan, *Memory, the Holocaust, and French Justice*.

10. See *Le Choc du mois* 42–43 (July–August 1991): 6–19.

11. Pierre Nora, "Le Syndrome," 489.

12. Quoted in Tzvetan Todorov, *The Morals of History*, trans. Alyson Waters (Minneapolis: University of Minnesota Press, 1995), xi.

13. Todorov, *Morals of History*, xix.

14. François-Georges Dreyfus, *Histoire de Vichy* (Paris: Perrin, 1990).

15. It is of course widely known that many former Vichyites are linked to Le Pen's National Front. See the essays by Gordon and Flood here.

16. These reasons for the trial of Touvier are given in the pamphlet by P. Quentin and P. Bataille, "Paul Touvier devant ses juges" (Paris: Ligue Internationale contre le Racisme et l'Antisémitisme, 1994).

17. Conan and Rousso, *Vichy,* 111–12.

18. At the time of Touvier's trial, Brel's widow wrote a letter to the court insisting that Touvier had misrepresented himself to Brel and his family. Brel's wife thought he was a "defrocked priest." See Ted Morgan, "The Last War Criminal: The Trial of Paul Touvier," *The New York Times Magazine,* 22 May 1994, 45.

19. Details of Touvier's family background and upbringing are discussed in René Rémond et al., *Touvier et l'église* (Pars: Fayard, 1992), 29–60.

20. The most thorough account of the history of the Milice is Jacques Delperrié de Bayac, *Histoire de la Milice 1918–1945* (Paris: Fayard, 1969). The book was referred to frequently during the course of the trial itself.

21. In *Touvier, histoire du procès* (Paris: Julliard, 1995), 88, Alain Jakubowicz and René Raffin note that at least part of Touvier's involvement in the Légion and then in the Milice was motivated by financial considerations. They report that his salary jumped from seven hundred to seven thousand francs a month in moving from the SNCF to the Milice.

22. Jakubowicz and Raffin report that in July 1947 Touvier was picked up by police on suspicion of belonging to the *plan bleu* group, which they describe as "an essentially anti-communist conspiracy . . . whose purpose was to bring to power in France an authoritarian regime" (*Touvier, histoire,* 31). Conspirators included right-wing veterans and former Resistance members, as well as certain elements in the army. The plot was exposed and dismantled not long after its inception.

23. The pardon was revealed by Jacques Dérogy in "Exclusif: *L'Express* a trouvé le bourreau de Lyons," *L'Express,* 5 June 1972.

24. For details of the Pompidou pardon and the events leading up to it, see Rousso, *Vichy Syndrome*, 114–26.

25. Quoted in Michael Reisman and Chris T. Antoniou, eds., *The Laws of War: A Comprehensive Collection of Primary Documents on International Laws Governing Armed Conflict* (New York: Vintage Books, 1994), 319.

26. The changes in the law as described here are taken from Conan and Rousso, *Vichy*, 130–31.

27. For a brief summary of these judicial decisions, see Jacques Trémolet de Villers, *Paul Touvier est innocent* (Paris: Éditions Dominique Martin Morin, 1990), 27–28.

28. In *La Face cachée du procès Barbie* (Paris: Samuel Tastet, 1983), 12–13, Barbie's lawyer Jacques Vergès underscores one of the reasons many in France might have felt uncomfortable applying laws such as the crimes against humanity statutes retroactively: the most recent example in French history of laws being applied retroactively was in cases brought before Vichy's infamous Sections Spéciales.

29. Support for Touvier among reactionary Catholics was not limited to asylum in *intégriste* monasteries. Police investigations revealed that Touvier had for some time been receiving financial support from the Ordre des Chevaliers Notre-Dame, among whose members were former collaborators and Pétainists. The lay person responsible for the Paris chapter, Jean-Pierre Lefèvre, was a former member of the Waffen ss. See Jakubowicz and Raffin, *Touvier, histoire*, 33–34.

30. For a detailed discussion of public reaction to the April 1992 decision, see my introduction in Golsan, *Memory, the Holocaust, and French Justice*, 37–38.

31. Conan and Rousso, *Vichy*, 132.

32. For detailed discussions of the April 1992 decision and its implications, see especially Jean-Denis Bredin, "The Touvier Affair: History and Justice Abused," and Tzvetan Todorov, "The Touvier Affair," in Golsan, *Memory, the Holocaust, and French Justice*. See also Théo Klein, *Oublier Vichy? A propos de l'arrêt Touvier* (Paris: Criterion, 1992).

33. See "La Justice 'révise' l'histoire de Pétain et de Vichy," *Le Canard enchaîné*, 15 April 1992.

34. See Touvier's pamphlet, *Mes Crimes contre l'humanité*, 16–18.

35. One of those who changed his testimony was Jacques Delarue, a magistrate who had originally recommended against Pompidou's pardon of Touvier in 1971. Rousso reports that in a conversation after the trial, Delarue justified his reversal by saying that for a man of his generation, the prospect of a Touvier acquittal was "intolerable." Conan and Rousso, *Vichy*, 170.

36. Klarsfeld, the son of Serge Klarsfeld, the famous lawyer and historian of the Holocaust, was actually one of several lawyers representing different plaintiffs at the trial. These lawyers, known as lawyers for "civil parties," were present along with a prosecutor appointed by the state at the Touvier trial. Arno Klarsfeld is especially hard on Jacques Delarue. For his account of the trial and his denunciation of Delarue, see A. Klarsfeld, *Touvier, un crime français* (Paris: Fayard, 1994), esp. 66–70.

37. See *Libération*, 17 March 1994.

38. Jakubowicz and Raffin, *Touvier, histoire*, 75.

39. See especially Trémolet's characterization of Touvier in *Paul Touvier est innocent.*

40. Jakubowicz and Raffin, *Touvier, histoire*, 51.

41. A recently published novel, *The Statement* by Brian Moore (New York: Dutton, 1996), captures Touvier's deviousness and dishonesty better than any factual discussion of Touvier I have encountered.

42. The "Schindler defense" was decimated primarily by Arno Klarsfeld, who, through careful documentation, demonstrated convincingly German indifference to the idea of avenging Henriot, especially by the means suggested by Touvier. Besides, he argued, Henriot was a hero to the Milice in particular, since he was their vocal supporter and a member. That the members of the Milice took Henriot's death as a personal affront is suggested by numerous other reprisals carried out in other towns after Henriot's murder. See Klarsfeld, *Touvier*, 75–76.

43. The testimony of this survivor, Louis Goudard, is reported in Golsan, *Memory, the Holocaust, and French Justice*, 138–41.

44. See Jakubowicz and Raffin, *Touvier, histoire*, 83.

45. See Henry Rousso, "What Historians Will Retain from the Last Trial of the Purge," in Golsan, *Memory, the Holocaust, and French Justice*, 163.

46. See Christian Guery, "Une Interrogation après le procès Touvier: Le Crime contre l'humanité, existe-t-il?" *Le Genre humain* 28 (autumn 1994): 119–37.

47. Quoted in Olivier Wieviorka, *Nous entrerons dans la carrière: De la Résistance à l'exercice du pouvoir* (Paris: Seuil, 1994), 315.

48. Conan and Rousso, *Vichy*, 170.

49. Apart from expressing a distrust of the press that is somewhat excessive (Rousso, after all, covered the trial for *Libération*), the comparison with Eichmann is itself misleading for a number of reasons. The first is that Touvier's arrogance and the intensity of his hatred of Jews as revealed at the trial is hardly indicative of the "banality of evil" associated with the name of Eichmann as a result of Hannah Arendt's study. Moreover, Touvier was a Frenchman tried in a French court, which as I hope to have shown, helped create a number of obstacles to the trial not present in the Eichman case. Finally, historical comparisons of this sort are always dangerous, as Charles Maier has brilliantly demonstrated in his study of the German Historians' Debate, *The Unmasterable Past: History, Holocaust, and German National Memory* (Cambridge: Harvard University Press, 1988).

50. For a brief and precise account of Bousquet's role in carrying out the Final Solution in France and his reasons for participating in the undertaking, see Annette Lévy-Willard's interview with Robert Paxton in Golsan, *Memory, the Holocaust, and French Justice*, 53–60.

51. André Glucksman, *De Gaulle, où es-tu?* (Paris: Lattès, 1995), 201–30.

52. Jean-Marc Varault, *Le Procès Pétain* (Paris: Perrin, 1995). In his book Varault blames "Jewish memory" for distorting the memory and historical realities of Vichy, and notes that this view is shared by Rousso and Conan in *Vichy*, 26. The most interesting and best written of the books recently reissued that laud Pétain and express hostility toward his trial is Jules Roy's *Le Grand Naufrage: Chronique du procès Pétain* (Paris: Albin Michel, 1995). The book is dedicated to, among others, "all those who thought they were serving their country in serving Pétain."

53. As if to add insult to injury, in April 1995 Mitterrand published a book of conversations between himself and Nobel Prize winner and Holocaust survivor Elie Wiesel in which he reiterated his strongly favorable impression of Bousquet and announced that he had "no regrets and no remorse" concerning his friendship with the former head of Vichy police. He concluded, "I am at peace with myself." See *Mémoire à deux voix* (Paris: Odile Jacob, 1995), 102–11. For a sampling of the public outcry, see especially the numerous articles in *Le Monde* in the days following the televised interview.

54. For an excellent discussion of Chirac's address and its implications, see Conan and Rousso's afterword in the Folio edition of *Vichy*, 444–57.

Lynn A. Higgins

The Barbie Affair and the Trials of Memory

The French Ministry of the Interior houses an office called the Département du Déminage. The *démineurs* form a select group of explosives technicians whose job it is to make about eleven thousand stops at citizens' homes each year in response to reports of buried bombs, land mines, grenades, and other wartime detritus that still surfaces from time to time in farms and back yards, country lanes and urban green spaces. Despite these efforts, an estimated 12 million unexploded shells remain in the vicinity of Verdun, and millions of bombs from the Second World War remain buried around Normandy and Brittany. Not surprisingly, this is dangerous work: since the department was established in 1946, 18 million artillery shells have been collected, along with 10 million grenades, six hundred thousand aerial bombs, and as many underwater mines. Six hundred thirty *démineurs* have died in the line of duty. In 1991 alone, thirty-six farmers were killed when their machinery hit unexploded shells.[1]

The story of the *démineurs* is almost too literal to be allegorical. Multiple layers of wartime traumas still lie unexploded under the surface of the French soil and consciousness. The wars of decolonization, two World Wars, even the Franco-Prussian War continue to claim one "casualty of the peace" after another.[2] The heroic *démineurs* make a brief appearance in Bertrand Tavernier's 1989 film *La Vie et rien d'autre* (Life and nothing but). In this fiction feature set in 1920, a farmer tilling his field comes upon a buried shell and sends someone hurrying to fetch the explosives experts. Shortly afterward, the film's protagonists hear an explosion. "What was that?" asks the woman (Sabine Azéma), to which the officer (Philippe Noiret) responds: "A layer of memories" [*Un gisement de souvenirs*].

More than one layer of that mined territory was on view during the 1987 trial of Klaus Barbie. What is apt about the image of *déminage* is the way remains from a series of wars lie hidden together, so that when you dig, you never know which stratum you will unearth. Excavating for one set of memories, you might very well get blown away by another explosive layer.[3] Henry Rousso, as is now well known, identifies four stages in the evolution of French memory (and representation) of the Vichy period, beginning with the "unfinished mourning" of the immediate postwar period (1944 to 1954). From 1954 to 1971 there followed a period of "repressions." The years 1971–74 marked what Rousso calls the "broken mirror" phase during which the Gaullist myth of a united Resistance began to lose its coherence. Since 1974, the country has been immersed in a period of "obsession," particularly with an awakening of Jewish memory and the recognition of the Shoah. While the 1987 trial of Klaus Barbie fell within—and is a direct result of—the most recent "obsessions" phase of memory, I want first to draw attention to the fact that Rousso locates the turning point from mourning to repression in 1954. That year put an end to wartime rationing and ushered in a new era of prosperity. It also marked the end of the *Épuration*. That 1954 also saw France's military defeat at Dien Bien Phu and the beginning of the "undeclared war" in Algeria is far from coincidental, however, as Rousso acknowledges, remarking that "Other hatreds supplanted those of World War II."[4]

I want to investigate the possibility of what might be called, though it remains more amorphous, an incipient Algeria syndrome in French memory, superimposed upon the Vichy one but with syncopated rhythms. As historians like Benjamin Stora have pointed out, memories of the conflict in Algeria have been, if anything, more repressed than those of the Occupation. There has been no collective (even if false) consensus corresponding to Gaullist Resistancialism, and there is no official commemoration of the conflict. Since Algeria was not a colony but rather part of France, its administration came under the Ministry of the Interior, and thus technically the hostilities did not even constitute a war. The conflict in Algeria was officially an "opération de maintien de l'ordre," initially carried out by the police until it was handed over to the army. The undeclared war referred to as "les événements," as "la guerre sans nom," or even more suggestively as "la guerre qui ne veut pas dire son nom"[5] was fought by soldiers who even today do not enjoy full official veteran status or benefits. So while those who have gone in quest of the true Occupation—such as Henry Rousso and Marcel Ophuls in his *Le Chagrin et la pitié*—have had to cut through tangles of myth and countermyth, lies and evasions, those seeking to understand the Algerian "question" have had to confront a wall of euphemism, silence, and taboo.[6]

I believe one of the reasons for the extraordinary anxieties and conflicts of opinion surrounding Klaus Barbie was that as a public ceremony, his 1987 trial functioned as a vector (Rousso) or site (Pierre

Nora[7]) of more than one repressed memory. Thanks largely to the media theatrics of Barbie's chief lawyer, Maître Jacques Vergès, memories of the Algerian experience contributed to shaping the way the defense was conducted and consequently the way the Occupation was remembered. My purpose is not to provoke a competition of memories or to displace the Occupation or Barbie's atrocities (although this was indeed Vergès's strategy). I simply observe that there is more than one skeleton in the closet (or grenade in the back yard), and from there delineate ways in which two "gisements de souvenirs"—the Occupation and Algeria—have been intertwined, each shaping the way the other has been remembered and represented. Even without Vergès, given the configurations of the collective imaginary, the Barbie trial would still have functioned as a metaphor—or an alibi—for other trials that never took place.

Born in 1913, son of an embittered Verdun veteran, Nikolaus Barbie made his way to leadership positions in the Hitler Youth, joined the Nazi party, served in the infantry, and then worked for the ss in Amsterdam before being assigned in 1942 to root out the Resistance in Lyon, just as the Final Solution was being implemented and anti-Resistance repressions and reprisals were being intensified. He presided over Gestapo raids on the Lyon Union Générale des Israélites de France (UGIF) and then signed the report as officer in charge of the 6 April 1943 roundup of Jewish children at their refuge in Izieu. The children all died at Auschwitz. At Caluire on 21 June 1943 he arrested Jean Moulin, the emissary sent into occupied France by de Gaulle to unify the Resistance. Moulin was tortured by Barbie and died in prison. Barbie is also held responsible for the August 1944 massacres in the Lyon suburbs of Bron and St. Genis Laval.

By the time of the 1947 and 1950 acquittals of René Hardy for the betrayal of Moulin, Barbie was working as an anticommunist agent for the U.S. Counter-Intelligence Corps. In 1951 a network of sympathizers and anticommunists helped him escape to South America, where as Klaus Altmann he became a wealthy shipping magnate and supported fascist causes around the globe. France convicted Barbie in absentia and sentenced him to death in 1952 and 1954. Following a decade of activism by Nazi-hunters Serge and Beate Klarsfeld and others, the man who had been known as the "Butcher of Lyon" was finally located in Bolivia and, under somewhat dubious circumstances, was extradited to Lyon in 1983. In 1987 he was tried and convicted of crimes against humanity and sentenced to life in prison, where he died of cancer in September 1991.

The task of formulating the charges against Barbie took several years and generated much acrimonious debate. Resistance veterans and deportees wanted Barbie held accountable for the murder of Moulin. Jewish organizations such as the local Jewish Congress (CRIF) wanted to bring the Holocaust to trial at last. However, Judge Christian Riss, responsible for preparing the case for the prosecution, insisted on charging Barbie with specific crimes for which an airtight case could be constructed. From an initial list of eight major atrocities, therefore, Riss was forced to eliminate war crimes whose statute of limitations had expired,[8] crimes for which many potential witnesses had died and thus for which complete and credible evidence could not be presented, and crimes (such as the murder of Jean Moulin) covered by the trials of 1952 and 1954. Barbie was finally charged with the arrest, deportation, and massacre of fifty-five Jews, including fifty-two children, from a children's refuge in Izieu outside Lyon. The one non-Jewish child present had been allowed to escape. Barbie had signed the telegram reporting on and taking responsibility for the roundup.[9]

From the beginning, the trial was a focus of controversies. Some— such as Raymond Aron—saw in the trial a definitive indictment of the whole Nazi program. Others—such as Simone Veil and Alain Finkielkraut—felt the trial trivialized Nazism and diluted the specificity of the Holocaust. Some anticipated renewed hostility about divisions within the Resistance, particularly those that might have led to betrayal of Moulin. The bitterness of these divisions had been fueled by repeated trials and acquittals of Hardy, by suits and countersuits, and then by memoirs published by Hardy and others. Some feared revelations concerning long-buried acts of collaboration. The governing Socialist Party may well have wished to keep its own skeletons in the closet, since many former collaborators occupied public positions, some posing as honored veterans of the Resistance. Still others might have worried about the excesses of the *Épuration*. For example, Vergès subpoenaed writer and filmmaker Marguerite Duras, on the grounds that she had published a semi-autobiographical story recounting the torture of a *collabo* by Resistance members at the Liberation. Barbie's lawyer fueled all these fears with his strategy of politicizing the trial by comparing Nazi crimes to more recent atrocities, particularly those committed during France's colonial wars. It is no surprise, then, that the Barbie "trial" quickly became the Barbie "Affair."

Vergès proceeded by means of what he called the "procès de rupture," or strategy of disruption. The lawyer himself became the main actor (and I use the word advisedly) in the trial through his attempts to use the judiciary as an arena for political confrontation. In his many books, Vergès describes his techniques for executing an *arroseur-arrosé* about-face in which the defense becomes the prosecution, and a criminal proceeding is transformed into a political trial and a media spectacle. The goal is no longer to produce a verdict, but to sway public opinion and exert political pressure on the government. The aim is less to judge an individual for specific crimes than to precipitate a sort of back-door referendum. Vergès ably juggled two incompatible strategies, making them complementary. To those who saw Barbie as a symbol of Nazism in general, he rejoined that his client was one sick old man who could not, he claimed, be proved guilty of the specific charges brought against him. To those who identified Barbie as the Butcher of Lyon, the response, delivered to intimidate, was that that Germans were not the only army that had committed atrocities and genocide while occupying a foreign territory. Vergès exploited his awareness that, as he put it, "The Barbie trial is a mirror. It reflects all the ambiguities of the Occupation."[10] I would rather amend this statement to emphasize that the trial reflected the ambiguities of remembering the Occupation.

Even without the likes of a Vergès, then, one of these ambiguities is that it is inevitably remembered through the traumas of decolonization. Moreover, the interaction between the two sets of memories has been further complicated by a series of amnesty laws enacted with reference to the two historical periods. At the end of World War II in France, there were forty thousand individuals in prison for acts of collaboration. After the amnesties of 1947, 1951, and 1953, only nineteen remained. By 1964 there were none. Three amnesty laws, each more inclusive than the last, constituted, to use the official term, an "oubli juridique"—a legally imposed forgetting, an officially enforceable amnesia covering (in both senses) the Dark Years.[11] In similar fashion, amnesties of 1964 and 1967 freed from exile or prison those accused of atrocities in Algeria and helped others to avoid prosecution. In France, amnesty has particularly acute effects on participants, scholars, and the general public because not only is it impossible to indict individuals for crimes covered by the laws, but it is illegal, in certain circumstances, even to mention them.[12] Passage of these laws has thus been a major political victory for the extreme Right, which benefitted from the silence imposed on continuities between Vichy and certain proponents of l'Algérie française. Thus for example has Jean-Marie Le Pen won several lawsuits against the press—notably against the newspaper *Libération*—for suggesting that he might have been guilty of acts of torture in Algeria. As a result, amnesty takes over where wartime censorship leaves off; both terms are to be understood in both their political and their psychic extensions.

Early in the preparation of the Barbie dossier, Vergès wondered rhetorically why the French government had taken so long to bring Barbie to justice. In particular, Vergès wanted to know why France waited until 1964 to adopt the Nuremberg definition of crimes against humanity, including abolishing statutes of limitation. He answers his own rhetorical question by observing that amnesties for crimes committed during the Algerian conflict were put into place first. While this configuration of events has made it possible to "forget" (officially, at least) some of the more horrifying faces of both periods, it has become difficult to remember one without conjuring up the other. Furthermore, the amnesty dilemma makes it possible to displace memories from one site onto the other.

Maître Vergès arrived at the Barbie trial with a lot of baggage. His acceptance of Barbie's invitation to defend him was a surprise to many because of the lawyer's previous association with trials surrounding France's colonial conflicts. In 1954 he had risen to the defense of communist militants who disrupted the departure of trains full of conscripts bound for Algeria. It was also he who in 1961 defended the Jeanson network, those "porteurs de valise" who gave aid to the Algerian independence movement and who supported the "droit à l'insoumission" of young French draft resisters.[13] It was Vergès, too, who defended Algerian revolutionary and terrorist Djamila Boupacha (and then married her), who took on the case of the "Affaire des foulards" and many other highly-publicized cases on behalf of Algerian militants and immigrants. During the Barbie trial itself, he announced he would represent an Algerian family bringing charges of crimes against humanity on behalf of their father, who had been tortured by French soldiers. Relentlessly, he has constructed and then driven home an analogy comparing the German Occupation of France with the French presence in Algeria.

In his 1989 *Remembering in Vain: The Klaus Barbie Trial and Crimes Against Humanity*,[14] Alain Finkielkraut puts forth an eloquent condemnation of the way the Barbie trial was handled. Appearing too in Marcel Ophuls's 1988 film, *Hotel Terminus: The Life and Times of Klaus Barbie*, Finkielkraut expresses his disappointment that the focus has been on the verdict and not on uncovering the truth. He particularly deplored the way the trial blurred the boundaries between disparate historical contexts and events, undercutting the specificity of individual crimes. Finkielkraut is right, of course, and yet Vergès's strategy could only succeed if the fears and guilts were available to be exploited, and the analogy, while seriously flawed, was nevertheless already rooted in memory, however repressed those memories might be. Despite their opposing perspectives and divergent frames of reference, Vergès and Finkielkraut agree that the Barbie trial was bound to fail as justice or as a commemorative ceremony because the venue of a national court belies the concept, introduced at Nuremburg, of a united humanity against which the crimes were committed.

The persistence and force of the analogy can be appreciated if we examine a selection of imaginative works, especially films, in which the two dark memories—the Occupation and Algeria—are contrasted and interwoven. What can these cultural objects tell us about the discursive context in which the Barbie trial unfolded? What already-circulating issues and anxieties might the "Affair" have provoked, and how were these expressed? What categories of thought and memory gave the trial its resonance?

The discourses used by the Left to describe the Algerian conflict had from the start been linked polemically to representations of the Occupation. The 1958 return to power of de Gaulle—a Phoenix act that repeated the one of 1940—made the comparison inevitable. Even before the amnesty laws, official and unofficial censorship made it likely that the war in Algeria would find indirect expression, and representations of the Occupation provided a convenient screen or alibi. I will cite only a few of the more vivid examples from the early period.

The impact of Alain Resnais's 1955 film *Nuit et Brouillard* (Night and fog) remains powerful today. The narration of Auschwitz is retrospective, but the film's concluding message makes the comparison with the present all but explicit:

Who among us . . . will warn us when the new executioners arrive? Is their face very different from our own? We who imagine that hope can be rekindled in the wake of that image that fades away, as if a cure were possible for the plague of the concentration camps. We who pretend to believe that all of this belongs to a single time and a single country. And who do not think to look around us.

This trope whereby memories from the past are brought into uncomfortable parallel with events of the present is a common narrative device in many New Wave films, such as *Hiroshima mon amour* (1959) and even *Last Year at Marienbad* (1961). Though structured by irony, however, this is no modernist conceit; rather, it is a thinly veiled insistence that atrocities recur, while people occupy varying roles.[15]

In 1961, Marguerite Duras published an article in *France-Observateur* titled "Les Deux Ghettos." The piece builds its editorial polemic by juxtaposing two interviews: one with a survivor of the Warsaw ghetto, a second with an Algerian immigrant working in Paris. The two voices echo uncannily, as each recounts the painful realization of having been designated as Other, the humiliating restrictions, the debilitating fear that ensued, and the precautions taken to placate and remain inconspicuous. The Algerian avoids wearing neck scarves or anything that could be used to strangle him. He says his companions compare themselves to Jews during the Occupation.[16]

By 1963, there was some relaxation in the censorship of news and cultural production imposed during the Algerian conflict. Films such as Godard's *Le Petit soldat* (filmed in 1960, but suppressed until 1963) and Marker's *La Jetée* (1962) that evoked torture were no longer denied distribution permits, and issues of journals that talked about Algeria were confiscated less frequently. In that year, Resnais's *Muriel: Le Temps d'un retour* deliberately weaves together memories of World War II and of the war in Algeria: the story of a couple separated in 1940 and reunited twenty years later is braided together with another story about the woman's nephew, who has just returned from Algeria. Both men have something to hide, and their secrets forge an analogy between them: Alphonse may have been a collaborator who fled to Algeria after the war, and "Muriel" is the name Bernard gives to a young Algerian woman whose torture and death he witnessed. Muriel herself is never seen, and Bernard insists that her story cannot be told. All that remains of her—the only means by which she can be read in the film— is the way Bernard is haunted by these repressed memories.

That *Muriel*'s director and screenwriter were similarly haunted by memories of the Second World War should not surprise us: Resnais served in the army in Germany during the immediate postwar Occupation there, and Jean Cayrol was himself a concentration-camp survivor. Less obvious is that the two would bring forth these memories in the context of the more recent national debacle. But as historian Isabelle Lambert explains about acts of torture witnessed by French soldiers in Algeria, "These torture scenes will provoke the young draftees, raised in a France still discovering the horrors of Nazism, to make certain rapprochements: the image of the Second World War ss agent comes to be superimposed, consciously or not, on that of the French soldier of today."

Decades later, the comparison still holds, as Lambert continues: "Twenty years later, such analogies are numerous. They are incontrovertibly among the causes of the voluntary collective amnesia surrounding the Algerian war. One gets the impression that, twenty years later, the war in Algeria can only be expressed by comparison with the Second World War."[17] And Anne Donadey puts a slightly different slant on the question when she wonders "whether the emphasis on the Second World War in French public life, the media, and education, and on the literary scene, in the past twenty years is not due in part to a displacement, a 'Freudian slip': what is being silenced (the Algerian war) resurfaces as an excess of speech about a previous war."[18]

The behavior of Jacques Vergès himself is driven by just such a displacement, as can be seen in the light of a 1960 incident. In the morning of 30 September 1960, issue number 173–74 of *Les Temps Modernes* was peremptorily seized by the police and distribution prevented, until the journal agreed to suppress eighty pages containing four articles witnessing to atrocities committed against Algerians. Among these was an article by Vergès titled "Le Génocide en Algérie," described as a collection of documents with names, places, and dates, about assassinatons of Algerians by French officers. Not only was Vergès forbidden to publish his article; he was soon removed from the Jeanson case in the courts. He was later able to refer to the article (which has a certain weight, having never appeared), and *Les Temps Modernes* got away with inserting a note "explaining" the missing pages.[19] However one might deplore Vergès's strategy of bringing Algeria to the fore in the Barbie trial, it is not unreasonable, I think, to understand this strategy in terms of the obstacles he had encountered in making atrocities against Algerians visible in the courts and in the press of 1960. He himself makes the connection repeatedly.

The logic of this conflation of two memories is brought into further relief if one compares two films that seem similar in their content, goals, and form, though they are separated by twenty years: Marcel Ophuls's 1971 *Le Chagrin et la pitié* about the Occupation, and Bertrand Tavernier's 1992 *La Guerre sans nom* (The undeclared war) about France's Algerian conflict. Ophuls's four-hour film, subtitled "Chronique d'une ville française sous l'Occupation," consists mostly of interviews with individuals—famous, infamous, and obscure— who spent the Occupation in Clermont-Ferrand, near Vichy. The film also includes archival photographs, newsreel footage, advertisements, and other recognizable documentary material from the period. Tavernier's film, which could (but doesn't) have an analogous subtitle, is also four hours in length and was also made approximately thirty years after the events it evokes. This film is composed of interviews with former conscripts from the Grenoble area who fought in Algeria between 1954 and 1962.[20] Grenoble was chosen because it was the site of a mass protest demonstration (on 18 May 1956) during which wives and girlfriends, parents and friends blocked the railroad tracks in an attempt to prevent the departure of train convoys full of conscripts. As in *Le Chagrin*, many points of view are represented: Patrick Rotman conducted interviews with demonstrators, counterdemonstrators, and bystanders, and Tavernier filmed these conversations and others with parachutists, members of alpine patrols, border engineering brigades, and urban counterterrorists, ordinary soldiers all.

It is as if Tavernier sought to provoke a shift in sensibility and a shocked reevaluation similar to what occurred in 1971 and again in

1981 at the release and final televised screening of *Le Chagrin*.[21] And indeed the film did provoke strong reactions. Although *La Guerre sans nom* was not widely reviewed and journalists systematically stayed away, Tavernier's film was a tremendous and immediate success, especially among veterans, who found their experience articulated for the first time. Tavernier and Rotman traveled around France to present their work and to participate in after-show conversations that were as emotional as the film itself. *La Guerre sans nom* may have been instrumental in provoking a small political shift as well. Although public discussion of that war is still largely taboo in France, shortly after the film's release President Mitterrand received a delegation of Algerian war veterans, and three government ministers—two of whom had seen Tavernier's film—officially commemorated the Franco-Algerian ceasefire of 1962 for the first time with a visit to the Arc de Triomphe.[22]

And yet there are significant differences between the two films, because there are differences in the ways the two wars had been remembered before the films appeared. Unlike Ophuls's film, no period newsreels, offical documentary or explanatory material of any kind, nor even any recognizable public figures appear in *La Guerre sans nom*. This riveting and moving work includes only interviewees' personal memories and souvenirs (photos, letters, a piece of shrapnel in one case) and songs from the period. Also unlike Ophuls's documentary, which is divided into two "chapters"—"L'Effondrement" and "Le Choix"—*La Guerre sans nom* flows loosely from topic to topic, from witness to witness, doubling back on itself and repeating key points in different voices. There is no overall conceptual framework or mythography, only a very general chronology to move the collective story along. The film begins with accounts of the 1956 demonstration and proceeds through memories of departure, arrival in Algeria, homesickness, fear, descriptions of different types of military tasks and operations, and issues like torture and the treatment of the harkis, and ends with the soldiers' experiences upon their return to France.

In other words, despite the compelling topic, Tavernier—who has shown himself elsewhere to be a consummate storyteller—refuses to impose any overarching story or interpretation. Compared to the grand historical panorama of Ophuls's film, the drama of *La Guerre sans nom* is to be found in the individual testimonies, not in any overall narrative it constructs or revises. Personal anecdotes and individual accounts intersect only thematically, through compilation. In fact, the book drawn from the same interviews proceeds by parataxis, each chapter addressing a single topic through the biography of one or two former soldiers. This is not because Ophuls is more didactic or Tavernier a lesser cinéaste—far from it. Rather, the difference is elucidated when one observes that a canonical cast of "characters" for a World War II genre film already existed, so that Ophuls was able to interview at least one of each: a Grand Résistant, more obscure Resistance heroes, collaborators, a *femme tondue*, military officers, and politicians, not to mention recognizable positions such as Catholic Resistance, communist Resistance, cowardly bystander, and so on. Those categories got transferred by analogy in some instances to Algeria, where they didn't apply, but even where this is not the case, in *La Guerre sans nom*, each man is his own category, and the viewer experiences both the excitement and the confusion of an encounter with unprocessed data and raw emotions. History here remains a collection of individual memories. In short, there could be no narrative strategy of demystification here, because there is no coherent public discourse— heroic or otherwise—to demystify, no counterpart of Resistancialism. No clear factions appear, and no passionate interpretations clash. The only unity that emerges is an overwhelming sadness and an uphill struggle against what Stora calls "la fabrication de l'oubli."[23]

One reason for this silence is often cited by the veterans themselves. They held their tongues because they resented and feared being compared to Nazis. Many of the soldiers are haunted by the Occupation and make explicit comparisons.

CAMILLO PIVANO: We had suffered during the war with the Germans; I wouldn't have wanted it to be said that France was the same.

ROBERT ANDRE: After all, torture or no torture, for me there's no such thing as a clean war, a dirty war. I was nine in 1944 when I saw unhappy young Germans in the Rhone valley; they'd been shot, they were left stripped to the waist with bare feet, their identity papers on their chests.[25]

ALAIN BOEUF (whose grandfather was in the Resistance): Often the image came spontaneously to my mind that in Algeria, we were the occupying troops and that the resisters were on the other side. The Algerian fighters were like the Resistance was for us in 1939–45; they had gone underground. Here the resistants fought the invader, and there, for the Algerians, the invader was us.[26]

ÉTIENNE BOULANGER (a conscientious objector who spent two years in a military prison for desertion): During the earlier war, as we saw in the maquis, there were Germans who deserted. They were the ones who were right.[27]

SERAPHIN BERTHIER (a right-winger who still believes in l'Algérie française, about the day of the cease-fire): I was a child when Paris was liberated. This was the same thing.[28]

The German Occupation of France, still fresh in memory, is the frame of reference here and elsewhere in the interviews. As a result, one story that does get told in *La Guerre sans nom* about the French disaster in Algeria is the largely unsuccessful struggle to historicize, to give the Algerian experience its own voice and field of memory in the face of an overwhelming and oppressive analogy.[29]

There are nevertheless signs in other films about the conflict in Algeria that this more recent war might come out from hiding, claim its specificity, and forge its own imaginative discourse. One recurrent topos that deserves attention is the use of what Susan Sontag called "illness as metaphor." Sontag has explored the mythologies and fears associated with tuberculosis, cancer, and in a later book, AIDS.[30] At least three films employ a cancer metaphor more extensive than (but related to) Resnais's "peste concentrationnaire." It is comparable to (but distinguishable from) the leprosy that invades Duras's portraits of decomposing colonial life in Indochina as depicted in *India Song* and in her novels. It appeared first in Agnès Varda's 1963 *Cléo de 5 à 7*, the story of a brief encounter between a soldier on leave who must soon return to combat in Algeria and a young singer (Cléo) awaiting results of her medical tests. That film ends with the soldier's departure and Cléo's discovery that she has cancer. While not an explicit comparison, the juxtaposition makes a clear commentary on the diseased nature of the conflict that had just ended and its effect on the national health.

Pierre Schoendoerffer's 1977 *Le Crabe-tambour* makes the same juxtaposition with similar aims: a Merchant Marine commander suffering from lung cancer makes one last expedition across the frozen Atlantic. During that voyage, he reminisces with the ship's doctor about his own navy service in Algeria and the doctor's in Indochina. This past, which we must piece together from flashbacks, was dominated by a former comrade of both, one Wilsdorf, known as the *crabe-tambour*. As fragments of the two men's memories fall into place, we learn that the commander is eaten away from within not only by his illness, but by his regret about a promise he made to Wilsdorf and was then unable to keep. The two had been in opposite camps at the aborted 1961 putsch of the Generals in Algeria. Wilsdorf was dishonorably discharged from the navy for his participation in the military rebellion, and the commander had promised he too would end his career. His dying wish is to find Wilsdorf, now captain of a fishing vessel. At the film's end, we know that the commander will die as much as a consequence of his shameful memories as of his cancer.

Finally, Brigitte Rouan's *Outremer* (1990)[31] is the story—told in three convergent flashbacks—of three *pied-noir* sisters facing the end of their family's Algerian idyll. Zon, the sister whose story is told first and thus serves as frame of reference for the other two, dies of cancer. At first the family thinks she is pregnant, but they finally realize otherwise. "J'ai un crabe dans le ventre," she tells a sister-in-law who speaks no French and thus cannot really hear her explanation.[32] She dies as well of longing for her navy husband, missing in action, and of the wasting disease of what will later be portrayed retrospectively by the film as a whole as the lost paradise of "overseas" life—what has widely been dubbed "la nostalgérie."

The cancer metaphor Sontag delineates startlingly evokes France's mythical relation to Algeria. Sontag describes how images surrounding cancer speak of civil strife—a body at war with itself—creating a site where military and medical discourses converge. Cancer is a disease of space, she says, and thus of geography, travel, and imperialism. Cells "colonize" from an original site to far locales.[33] The disease is understood to be "invasive," and so must be treated by means of "aggressive" counterattack. In addition—and here is its historical specificity—I think cancer is also a metaphor endemic to cold war mythology. Unlike tuberculosis, to which Sontag compares it, cancer is an invisible but potentially omnipresent enemy. It advances thanks to stealth and a conspiracy of internal subversives, threatening to overpower the system (body, body politic) from within. The enemy is unseen but everywhere, and its methods are those of guerrilla warfare; it infiltrates by means of "cells" until it launches an attack in a new place. Like a guilty memory, it moves in silence and secrecy, feeding projection and a paranoid world view. The protagonist of *Le Crabe-tambour* makes a voyage to the heart of that darkness, a trial whose accused turns out ultimately to be himself.

Curiously, while military language is used to describe cancer and its treatment, one can also discern the reverse: a medical metaphor in a military "operation." Just as a "disorder" must be treated "aggressively," so a civil dis-order (as in Algeria) provoked in response an "opération de maintien de l'ordre." Moreover, until quite recently, cancer was taboo and thus diagnoses were kept hidden, euphemized. A disease without a name. A "guerre sans nom."

Outside the cinema, those who opposed the French presence in Algeria used a related image to publicize atrocities (particularly torture) committed there by the police and by the army, atrocities that quickly spread to the treatment of many Algerian immigrés at the hands of Parisian police. The political practice of torture, especially its spread to the metropole, was commonly referred to by opponents of the war as "la gangrène."[34] Gangrene shares some of cancer's metaphoric properties: it too is a disease of space and colonization. But although it spreads, its source is known. It is not fatal, but it can lead to mutilation or amputation, a severing of a part of the self.

Sontag also points to some of the dangers of a rhetoric that metaphorizes disease. In addition to the unnecessary burden such associations inflict on those afflicted with the illness, Sontag identifies attempts to justify extreme and punitive forms of attack (such as, for example, torture) on the grounds that the society is diseased. "To describe a phenomenon as a cancer is an incitement to violence," she asserts. "The use of cancer in political discourse encourages fatalism and justifies 'severe' measures . . . cancer metaphors are in themselves implicitly genocidal."[35] Since the colonial system itself is now frequently compared to a disease, mythologies of illness help us understand how decolonization was being experienced as a mythical event in the psychic life of a nation.

Two forces felt as threats to French identity today directly evoke these Algerian memories and were, not surprisingly, foregrounded in the Barbie affair: the presence of foreigners, and torture. It was perhaps inevitable, then, that the Barbie trial could only be viewed through the haze of more recent memories.

Exacerbated by economic ills, immigration is the most volatile political issue in France today, in large part because, as can be readily seen by the discourse circulating around it, it touches on a painful "gisement de souvenirs." The issue evoked the Occupation when, for example, those opposed to new laws debated in 1993 compared them to the anti-Semitic policies of the Vichy government, and Interior Minister Charles Pasqua to René Bousquet.[36] New laws imposed restrictions on the open-door policy put into place just after the Liberation, and, as Ronald Koven points out, "this is the first time since the end of the Second World War that a foreign presence in France has become the leading item on the national agenda."[37] The issue also evokes France's colonial history, because the primary targets of the new restrictions are immigrants from France's former North African territories. ("Maghrébin," "Nord-Africain," "Arabe" are all code words for "Algerian.") It is widely suggested that the virulence of the debate derives from unforgotten rancor and a desire to avenge the French expulsion from Algeria. During the Barbie trial, Erna Paris reports, the restrooms in the Lyon courtroom were covered with anti-Arab graffiti.

Torture is the indigestible memory of Nazism and of Algeria. This is the crime that defines the line between war crimes and crimes against humanity, and it was on this basis that many hoped the murder of Jean Moulin might originally have been included in the prosecution's case against Barbie. Cumulative cases of torture are what make genocide describable. But as Pierre Vidal-Naquet points out, in the French world view, torture is by definition carried out by foreigners. Speaking of torture under Vichy, he writes: "While everyone was outraged by these methods, everyone also thought that we were dealing with a specifically foreign institution, and that France, nation of the Rights of Man, had not known since 1789 and would not reacquaint itself after 1945 with any cases of torture."[38] During the Algerian war, revelations about French military torture in Algeria and of immigrants by Parisian police (la gangrène) were thus toxic to the sense of national identity and purpose. Such revelations undercut the ideology justifying colonialism, predicated on the assumption that the colonizer is exporting Civilization and Enlightenment. Given this cognitive dissonance, it is not surprising that the topic was taboo. Vidal-Naquet shows examples where, when not censored entirely, the word "torture" is handled with typographical kid gloves, put between quotation marks, as we speak of an "alleged" crime. So much so that the use of quotes spread to accounts of Vichy, as in a 1961 *Paris-Presse* description of a man "whose father had been 'tortured' by the Germans. Quotation marks for the Gestapo!" exclaims Vidal-Naquet.[39] The title of his book—*La Torture dans la république*—is meant to be an oxymoron or to suggest a foreign body, like a cancer, within the nation.

Both François Mitterrand and Jean-Marie Le Pen have tapped into the national propensity for commemorating the Occupation while passing over the Algerian period in silence. Among Mitterrand's first ceremonial acts as president were his visit to the maquis where he had worked in the Resistance and a visit to Jean Moulin's tomb. His terms as minister of interior and minister of justice during the Algerian conflict are not commemorated. Le Pen's Resistance activities are almost certainly apocryphal, and thanks to the amnesties, it is now against the law to refer to his "alleged" stint as a *parachutiste* in an "interrogation center" in Algeria.[40]

That the Occupation and the Algerian conflict are still linked in the public imagination means, as I hope to have suggested, that the memories of both will continue to be distorted. It also means that the two in tandem are susceptible to renewed repression. A moment in *Hotel Terminus* demonstrates how this might occur. Among Ophuls's interviewees was one Albert Rosset, head of the Lyon Front National and friend of Le Pen. In the course of the interview, Ophuls asks Rosset an ostensibly hypothetical question whose carefully formulated conditional construction avoids infringing the amnesty law and risking a libel suit: "If Le Pen practiced torture in Algeria," Ophuls asks, "would you say he did this under orders from his superiors?" "Of course," answers Rosset, falling into the trap. "But it's the same case with Barbie!" exclaims a triumphant Ophuls. Realizing what has happened, Rosset's confident posturing collapses. "It's a trick question," he whines. And besides, he adds dismissively, putting the lid on both memories, it's a very old story. "C'est une très vieille histoire."

Notes

I would like to thank Richard J. Golsan, whose relentless encouragement induced me to pursue this topic; Marianne Hirsch and Leo Spitzer, who invited me to speak about Marcel Ophuls's documentary film, *Hotel Terminus: The Life and Times of Klaus Barbie*, in their course on the Holocaust; Jean-Pierre Davoine and Michèle Villard in Lyon, who made the trial and the city's history vivid for me; and Roland L. Higgins, who watched the films with me and illuminated many puzzling moments. Translations are my own unless otherwise specified.

1. Donovan Webster, "Out There Is a Bomb with Your Name: The Soldiers Moved On. The War Moved On. The Bombs Stayed," *Smithsonian Magazine*, February 1994, 26–37. France's plight is only a small part of a worldwide crisis: according to a recent *Newsweek* report, 110 million active mines scattered in sixty-four countries claim some two thousand victims a month. And the work of *déminage* becomes increasingly desperate: in 1994 alone, 2 million new mines were planted, twenty times as many as were removed. In April of 1996, representatives of fifty nations met in Geneva to debate ways to address this "plague of mines." "Buried Terror," *Newsweek*, 8 April 1996, 24–27.

2. *Newsweek*, "Buried Terror," 24, referring to deaths and injuries caused by explosion of mines remaining after the war is over. The article appeared in the context of the international convention in Geneva organized to address the problem of civilian casualties of land mines remaining after wars in many countries around the world.

3. Given the literally buried wars, it is not surprising to find a number of buried manuscripts as well: Marguerite Duras's *La Douleur* (Paris: Minuit, 1985), Alain Robbe-Grillet's *Un Régicide* (Paris: J'ai lu, 1978), and Lucie Aubrac's *Ils partiront dans l'ivresse* (Paris: Seuil, 1984) are all about World War II, and all were supposedly written during the Occupation and published many years later.

4. Rousso, *Vichy Syndrome*, 60.

5. Patrick Rotman and Bertrand Tavernier, *La Guerre sans nom: Les Appelés d'Algérie 54–62* (Paris: Seuil, 1992), 24.

6. See Benjamin Stora, *La Gangrène et l'oubli: La Mémoire de la guerre d'Algérie* (Paris: Éditions de la Découverte, 1992). Anne Donadey applies the term "Algeria Syndrome" to processes of unfinished mourning as these relate to anti-Arab racism in France today. See her "'Une Certaine Idée de la France': The Algeria Syndrome and Struggles over 'French' Identity," in *Identity Papers: Contested Nationhood in Twentieth-Century France*, ed. Steven Ungar and Tom Conley (Minneapolis: University of Minnesota Press, 1996), 215–32.

7. Pierre Nora, *Les Lieux de mémoire* (Paris: Gallimard, 1984).

8. France abolished the statute of limitations for crimes against humanity in 1964.

9. For detailed accounts of the Barbie trial and the events that led up to it, see Ladislas de Hoyos, *Klaus Barbie*, trans. Nicholas Courtin (London: W. H. Allen, 1985); Ted Morgan, *An Uncertain Hour: The French, the Germans, the Jews, the Klaus Barbie Trial, and the City of Lyon, 1940–1945* (New York: William Morrow, 1990); Erna Paris, *Unhealed Wounds: France and the Klaus Barbie Affair* (New York: Grove Press, 1985).

10. Jacques Vergès, *La Face cachée du procès Barbie* (Paris: Samuel Tastet, 1983), 66.

11. Rousso, *Vichy Syndrome*, 53–54.

12. For example, as they appear in the *Journal Officiel de la République Française*, Law 64–1269 of 23 December 1964, Law 66–396 of 17 June 1966, and Law 68–697 of 312 July 1968—all Amnesty laws pertaining to "les événements d'Algérie"—contain wording specifying that (as for example in the second law listed above) "Il est interdit à toute personne en ayant eu connaissance dans l'exercice de ses fonctions, de rappeler sous quelque forme que ce soit, ou de laisser subsister dans tout document quelconque, les condamnations pénales, les sanctions disciplinaires ou professionnelles et les déchéances effacées par l'amnistie." [It is forbidden for anyone having had official knowledge of them to refer in any form or to allow to remain in whatever form in any document of any kind the convictions, the disciplinary or professional sanctions, or the penalties *erased* by this amnesty—italics mine].

13. See Hervé Hamon and Patrick Rotman, *Les Porteurs de valise: La Résistance française à la guerre d'Algérie* (Paris: Albin Michel, 1979).

14. Finkielkraut, *Remembering in Vain*. Originally published as *La Mémoire Vaine: Du Crime contre l'humanité* (Paris: Gallimard, 1989).

15. As I have shown elsewhere, much fiction from the Algerian war period concerns World War II and has as a subtext, buried to varying depths, the then-current situation in Algeria. Others, such as *Marienbad*, eschew historical content altogether while retaining the device of parallel events in the present and past. See Higgins, *New Novel, New Wave, New Politics.*

16. Marguerite Duras, *Outside: Papiers d'un jour* (Paris: P.O.L., 1984), 150–61.

17. Isabelle Lambert, "Vingt ans aprés," in *La Guerre d'Algérie et les Français*, ed. Jean-Pierre Rioux (Paris: Fayard, 1990), 557.

18. Donadey, "Algeria Syndrome," 217. I have made a related point in *New Novel, New Wave, New Politics.*

19. *Les Temps Modernes*, 173–74 (October 1960): 392.

20. The film's actual subtitle is "Les Appelés et rappelés d'Algérie 1954–1962." A book containing much material from the interviews was published shortly after the film was released. See Patrick Rotman and Bertrand Tavernier, *La Guerre sans nom: Les Appelés d'Algérie 1954–62* (Paris: Seuil, 1992).

21. Ophuls's film inaugurated Rousso's "broken mirror" phase. Even the imagery is evocative in Tavernier's film: memories of both historical moments are informed (or guilt is figured) by the belief that one could have changed history if only one could have prevented the trains from leaving.

22. Information about the film's release and reception is garnered from Bertrand Tavernier, "I Wake Up, Dreaming: A Journal for 1992," in *Projections: A Forum for Film Makers*, no. 2, ed. John Boorman and Walter Donohue (London: Faber and Faber, 1993), 252–378.

23. Stora, *Gangrène et l'oubli*, 304.

24. Rotman and Tavernier, *La Guerre sans nom*, 66. Pivano nevertheless uses the analogy himself when he refers to a sadistic soldier he encountered as "un nostalgique d'Hitler" (67).

25. Rotman and Tavernier, *La Guerre sans nom*, 131.

26. Rotman and Tavernier, *La Guerre sans nom*, 174, 184.

27. Rotman and Tavernier, *La Guerre sans nom*, 216.

28. Rotman and Tavernier, *La Guerre sans nom*, 291.

29. This difference between the two documentaries is confirmed by juxtaposing the two histories of memory, Rousso's *Le Syndrôme de Vichy* and Benjamin Stora's *La Gangrène et l'oubli*. Rousso's work, like Ophuls's, is a labor of revision and reinterpretation. The memory of the Occupation has become visible as a "syndrome" that can be tightly periodized, and Rousso's analyses achieve a level of synthesis impossible so far in studies of Algeria. In contrast, Stora's book is an admirable and passionate work of archeology. But the vectors of memory he identifies and documents have not coalesced into an official story that can be either recounted or demystified.

30. Susan Sontag, *Illness as Metaphor* (New York: Farrar, Straus & Giroux, 1978) and AIDS *and Its Metaphors* (New York: Farrar, Straus & Giroux, 1988).

31. For a perceptive analysis of *Le Crabe-tambour* and *Outremer*, see Naomi Greene, "Empire as Myth and Memory," in *Cinema, Colonialism, Postcolonialism,* ed. Dina Sherzer (Austin: University of Texas Press), 103–19.

32. It is worth noting that many testimonies in *La Guerre sans nom* complain that although they had tried to tell their story, others had been unable or unwilling to listen. The same observation has often been made by Holocaust survivors.

33. Sontag, *Illness as Metaphor*, 14, 63, 65.

34. See Pierre Vidal-Naquet, *La Torture dans la République: Essai d'histoire et de politique contemporaine* (Paris: Minuit, 1962, reissued in 1982), and Stora, *Gangrène et l'oubli.*

35. Sontag, *Illness as Metaphor*, 81.

36. Louis Pauwels, "Ils devraient tout de même cesser d'être absurdes," *Le Figaro Magazine*, 3 July 1993, 15.

37. Ronald Koven, "Muslim Immigrants and French Nationalists," *Society* 29 (May–June 1992): 25.

38. Vidal-Naquet, *La Torture*, 18.

39. Vidal-Naquet, *La Torture*, 163–64.

40. See Gilles Bresson and Christian Lionet, *Le Pen: Biographie* (Paris: Seuil, 1994) for what little can be said about the matter.

Elliot Neaman

Ernst Jünger's Millennium:
Bad Citizens for the New Century

In front of the Pompidou Center in Paris stands an ultramodern clock, the Génitron, counting down, with nuclear precision, the seconds, minutes, and hours until the last day of this millennium on 31 December 2000. Peter Sloterdijk, his philosophical finger always on the pulse of *Zeitgeist*, calls the clock a "messianic calendar, developed to cheer up Europeans threatened by exhaustion, to celebrate the end of the millennium like an advent."[1] Sloterdijk is right to point to the postmodern hunger for merging the sacred and the profane, exemplified best by the slightly giddy, but also angst-ridden anticipation of the day when our newspapers will carry the date with three gaping zeros. After the parousia failed to materialize in year "M" of the Roman calendar, it dawns upon us to ask the second time around, what are we actually waiting for? Counting the numbers for whom? A redeemer who has missed his announced return by another thousand years?

Ernst Jünger's work, now a century in the making, steps into this void and provides metaphysically and theologically oriented readers with a new set of signposts for an age now experiencing, according to Jünger's admirers, a metamorphosis of the gods (*Gestaltwandel der Götter*).[2] Like Hegel's philosophy of history, Jünger's oeuvre portends to uncover the occult meaning of time's passage, in abstraction from empirical content, situating human activity in relation to cosmic design or purpose. The contemporary interest in his work, across the ideological spectrum I will argue, has much to do with the enticing diagnosis of a putative end to the bourgeois epoch, a variant of the "end of history."

Some wish to see in the cultural apotheosis of Jünger, which reached new heights when he turned one hundred years old in March of 1995, a sign of German repression of the past, or even worse, a fascist cultural onslaught.[3] Here one is reminded of the story of the smuggler who came every week to the Austrian-German border on bicycle, arousing the suspicions of the guards. After repeated searches of his belongings, no contraband, no merchandise of any kind was found. They remained skeptical, but never found out the man was in fact a smuggler—of bicycles. Like the purloined letter always open to view, Jünger's literary engagement reaches back across a long century of Germany's darkest and brightest years, and critics still passionately disagree about the significance of his work.

In general, much confusion reigns in the academy about the status of "fascist intellectuals," especially in regard to the radical conservatives of the Weimar era and the residual influence of their thought on German culture after 1945. One could construct a list of "fascist intellectuals," which might arguably include, for example, Oswald Spengler, Alfred Rosenberg, Alfred Bauemler, Ernst Kriek, Martin Heidegger, and Ernst Jünger. Which commonalities, beyond the most vague generalities, would be meaningful? Were not Mussolini and Hitler—certainly the former more than the latter, but each in their own way— "intellectuals?"

Undoubtedly all these men were attracted to some aspects of fascism. From their published writings, "fascist texts" might easily be isolated and identified. One might compare, for example, the inaugural addresses of Bauemler, Krieck, and Heidegger at Berlin, Frankfurt, and Freiburg respectively, all made in May 1933.[4] One could easily mark out the contours of their respective fantasies about the coming National Socialist Revolution, a heroic, mythopoetical projection soon disappointing even its own progenitors. One would attain more theoretical complexity and concrete historical configurations by comparing Ernst Jünger's *The Worker* and Oswald Spengler's *Year of Decision*, both written in late 1932, both quasi-blueprints for a nationalist revolution architected by a technocratic elite.[5] Here one encounters a serious problem in the reception history, for both works construct anthropologies of social space, the "form" of the worker, or the "destiny" of Prussian socialism that were never taken seriously by the National Socialists. The rupture between idea and reality in all these examples contains a double ambiguity, with opposing moral connotations: the "fascist idea" was never realized, therefore it was either purer and therefore historically legitimate, or inversely, even more totalitarian and ruthless than real National Socialism.[6]

We are still far from possessing a clear definition of the *fascist idea*. We can more confidently draw meaningful boundaries around a Marxist, liberal, or conservative idea, given the myriad complexities, exceptions, and shades of differences that apply in any intellectual taxonomic system. One might have to be satisfied with Wittgenstein's notion of "family resemblances" when treating the group characteristics of Weimar's radical conservatives.

Bad Citizens: Jünger as a Weimar Radical

Jünger's place along the ideological spectrum of Weimar politics has always been a matter of dispute. In the scholarly literature, this is the most avidly studied period of Jünger's life.[7] A recurrent and unresolved tension in this reception is the profound imbalance between Jünger's underdeveloped concept of the political and his highly rarefied, original, and resonant aesthetic explorations of modernity. His nationalist political writings of the 1920s were derivative—a mixture of Barrès-inspired blood and soil romantic nationalism and populist scorn for the Versailles Treaty and the Weimar government's policy of fulfilling the Allied demands. By contrast, Ernst Niekisch's so-called National Bolshevism was more original and politically astute, though unrealizable to a large degree because of the widespread fear of communism among the German middle classes. Ernst von Solomon's soldierly nationalism better reflected the mentality of the Front Generation. Carl Schmitt's genealogical explorations of legal concepts were infinitely more complex than Jünger's highly evocative, but conceptually vague catch-phrases such as "total mobilization" or "planetary technology."

Jünger was heavily involved in the political activities of the national-revolutionary movement. After leaving the army in 1923, his first political publication was an essay in the Nazi newspaper *Völkischer Beobachter* praising the National Socialists for offering a dictatorship close to the "mystique of blood" of the German people.[8] His exclusive and elitist self-consciousness made it impossible, however, for him to join the party, and he moved from one front soldier organization to another, finally abandoning political activity by 1930. In line with the role of the dandy he self-consciously played, politics, in this case right-wing politics, were a means to provoke and ridicule bourgeois society. Thus it is not surprising that he associated with those writers on the Left, most notably Erich Mühsam, Ernst Toller, and Bertolt Brecht, who also wanted to *scandaliser les bourgeois*.[9] Jünger was most comfortable alone or in the company of eccentrics and outsiders. His best friends in the Berlin days were Carl Schmitt, Arnold Bronnen, Ernst Niekisch, and the surrealist painter Alfred Kubin.[10] He spent his days as a flaneur on the streets of Berlin, visiting old books shops and antiquariats, nights sitting in his small apartment on the Holenzollenstrasse, reading and writing or gazing into a microscope. Ernst Niekisch described the place as dark and dingy, lined with old leather volumes and hundreds of jars of gooey blue-green biological specimens.[11]

This strange atmosphere pervades *The Adventurous Heart*, a brilliant and foreboding set of nocturnal observations that easily rank with the best examples of surrealist literature of the 1920s.[12] On these pages, Jünger indulged in what would become a lifelong preoccupation with the aesthetics of horror. His first teachers in this endeavor were the surrealist artists. The book contained a phantasmagoria of scientific and poetic vignettes, a collage of wild associations and deathly, ghostly images recalling the war-inspired art of painters like René Magritte, de Chirico, Yves Tanguy, Salvador Dali, and Max Ernst.[13]

Goebbels was eager to promote Jünger as a poster boy for National Socialism, and was bitterly disappointed after reading the book, especially in comparison to Jünger's front generation odyssey *In Storms of Steel*, which he described as a "war gospel, cruelly great." Goebbels now disdained him as another member of the demoralizing critical intelligence, a "writer, closed off from life, just ink, literature!"[14] He was not the only one to feel alienated from the previously adulated writer. The National Bolshevik Ernst von Solomon wrote that the publication of *The Adventurous Heart* precipitated the first "painful separation" of Jünger from the ideals of the front generation.[15] At about this time, Jünger began to speculate about hidden apocalyptic forces and magical realms of the imagination that no longer spoke to the immediate political interests of the disaffected soldiers. The intellectual gap between Jünger and the veterans' movement became even wider with the publication of the metaphysically-laden *The Worker* in fall 1932.

Jünger was originally attracted to the revolutionary thrust of National Socialism. He entered the political arena as a spokesperson for a new, nonreactionary nationalism. But he became disgruntled when the Nazis began to court the masses for votes like any other political party and cut deals with the traditional conservatives. For Jünger's sense of heroic idealism, the Nazi movement came to rest on the support of—in his eyes—an unbridled, plebeian mass of the petit bourgeoisie.[16] He derisively equated the political phenomenon of mass parties with "typical nineteenth-century movements" led by demagogues and charlatans.[17] He didn't like Hitler's fanatical anti-Semitism or his crusade against the East, which explains Jünger's ideological affinity to Niekisch, Edgar Jung, and the National Bolsheviks. They were working toward a more thorough social revolution, one that would combine Leninist vanguardism with Prussian hierarchy and order. On the other hand, the National Bolshevik position was too collectivist and not radical enough for Jünger's anarcho-martial hostility to bourgeois society. Jünger dreamed up his own anarcho-fascist state in which the spirit of steel-jawed, clear-eyed soldier-workers reigned. Jünger's vision also upset the traditional Right, which still held to reactionary ideas, including monarchism, in the 1920s. The radical modernity of *The Worker* made Jünger suspect in the eyes of *völkisch* conservatives, a "left-winger from the Right."[18]

In fact, many National Bolshevist intellectuals viewed *The Worker* as dangerously close to communism, mistrusting its "apoliticism."[19] Niekisch equated the planetary domination of *The Worker* with the dictatorship of the proletariat.[20] Fritz Elsholz criticized the book in a National Bolshevik weekly, *Der Nationale Sozialist*, writing that it represented "a horrible temptation" for National Bolsheviks, "a neo-fascist, state-capitalist experiment in the style of Herrn von Schleicher."[21]

In the essay *The Total Mobilization*, Jünger drew from the lessons of the First World War, contemplating the rise of communism in Russia and fascism in Italy. Not only had the old monarchies been swept away, but the gradual intrusion into every aspect of society of the war effort also meant the bell had tolled for the old bourgeois elites and their liberal ideology. Jünger explained the rise of fascism and communism, but also Zionism and "Americanism," as a result of the opposing forces of frenetic technology, breaking down all old forms of life, and nationalism, which restores a sense of orientation in the midst of chaos. He prophetically saw National Socialism as a "grotesque, half-barbarian" mirror image of the machines it opposed, bound to end as a "naive cult of technology." Nationalism and socialism function as "two great millstones, between which progress, the rest of the old world and finally these two forces themselves will be crushed." This denigration of the mass movements built on the twin pillars of nationalism and socialism was hardly the stuff on which the Nazis could build. But Jünger had his own formula for the German Revolution. In the end he spoke opaquely of the coming "new supremacy" (*neue Herrschaft*), a mobilization of Germans facing themselves, "a stronger power than the war."[22]

The Worker was written as the Weimar Republic was in its death throes. The antibourgeois stance of the soldier, so prominent in Jünger's works up until this point, was transformed into the heroic Worker, a being Jünger asserted was incapable of freedom, and could therefore do without it. The inner logic of the book sought to turn the German defeat of 1918 into a proleptic victory. It was a sophisticated version of the stab-in-the-back legend: Jünger's hatred of the Third Estate and liberalism reflected the soldierly resentment of the civilians who supposedly snatched defeat from the hands of victory. If the Germans are "bad citizens" in the democratic bourgeois sense, as the first lines of the book blast out like a clarion,[23] then the "logical" alternative would be the establishment of a new world order led by the German soldier-worker state.

The Worker was Jünger's most proto-fascist book. It was a Right-Hegelian representation of the Worker that, in conscious opposition to the proletariat of Karl Marx's *Das Kapital*, seeks to get at the essence of labor through a phenomenology of automation. Jünger described all spheres of life in the modern world as having been organized through the principle (or Gestalt) of the worker toward ever-increasing predictability, efficiency, and discipline. Evoking Goethe, Jünger used Gestalt as a metaphysical concept to denote the all-encompassing reality prior to individual appearances.[24]

Jünger's analysis (in contrast, for example, to Max Weber's) was an almost optimistic affirmation of the death of nineteenth-century liberalism and the establishment of an authoritarian soldier-worker state, ruled by Nietzschean supermen who would build an autotelic society of steel-nerved automatons. In this work, Jünger valorized the potent mixture of nationalism and socialism. He specifically called for a "young and ruthless leadership" to lead the way to a new state, built on the dual pillars of nationalism and socialism, where "military discipline" and "labor duty" would be implemented "from top to bottom."[25]

Jünger's views on technology, urban life, and modern progress were antithetical to the beliefs cherished by Weimar's many *völkisch* movements. For Jünger, the glorification of the countryside and old "Germanic" values and traditions was simply outmoded.[26] German nationalism had to reject both antitechnological escapism and liberal internationalism. Jünger's interpretation of technology was both "modern" and "reactionary" because he welcomed modern machine culture as a replacement for both humanistic culture and enlightened individualism. He advocated a resolute break with the past, an idea at odds with the sentimental nostalgia of the Right. Jünger's embrace of technology as a growing planetary power borrowed themes from Oswald Spengler's prophecy of the return of caesarism, and from Karl Haushofer's widely read books on geopolitics.

From Spengler Jünger also borrowed organic and vitalist metaphors of the birth and death of cultural periods: amid the death throes of the Age of the Bourgeois, the Age of the Worker is born. For Jünger, the "bourgeois" age—the epoch of the war veterans' parents—was one of striving for security and order behind a façade of transparency and Enlightenment rationality. The Worker was trained to destroy and create new forms of life, whereas the bourgeois wanted to ban all pain from life. Pain was for Jünger an "elementary" power shattering the substance of bourgeois illusions of order and progress during the First World War.[27] Jünger predicted that the vitalistic energy of the elementary powers unleashed by the war would not be forced back into the genie's bottle, but would lead to "new orders not calculated to reduce danger, but rather born through a marriage of danger and life."[28]

The imaginative force of Jünger's apocalyptic visions, achieved by collapsing human history into a speck of what he calls *Erd-Geschichte* (geological history), has tempted Jünger's readers to consider him more a prophet than an author. In spite of a number of intriguing twists and turns along the ideological way, Jünger has, from the beginning, offered a critique of Enlightenment humanism drawn from the experience of the crisis of the German state after 1918. For Jünger the electoral system of mass politics and the public sphere of Weimar were not only fraudulent, but also distortions of supposedly deeper, elementary forces of nature. This conceptualization of politics and nature as holistic and organic—a "deeper Enlightenment" and a denigration of "bourgeois" politics—has had a fatal attraction for certain intellectuals of the Left in post-1968 Germany. Richard Wolin has described a parallel phenomenon across the Rhine as the "antihumanism discourse" of French intellectuals.[29] In Germany, the fault line that best explains how leftist radicals of the 1960s became "spiritual reactionaries" of the 1980s runs along the divide of *Zivilizationskritik* in the Jünger tradition. My thesis is that in the course of the 1960s a new intellectual synthesis was forged, bearing fruit finally in the 1980s: the Frankfurt School critique of both consumer capitalism and the logic of Western rationalism merged with radical conservative antimodernism into a postmodern critique from the Right of Western civilization, liberalism, democracy, and market capitalism. Added to this heady mixture was a trendy and disingenuous revision of the historical significance of National Socialism, the valorization of German *différance*, and the affirmation of uniqueness of nation and *Volk*. I want to give support for these claims by turning to the cultural politics of the resurgence of the New Right in Germany since 1989 as it has intersected with the public persona of Jünger and the ongoing debates about his now century-old work.

The German New Right

After the constitutional enlargement of Germany in 1990, neo-Nazi attacks on foreigners made world headlines for several years. The firebombings of asylum housing in Mölln, Solingen, and Rostock, close to a thousand physical assaults on foreigners, the desecration of Jewish cemeteries, and the media attention given to Swastika-bearing, drunken skinheads marching through the streets of German cities all contributed to nervous questioning about German democracy. It appears now that these events can be attributed to the birth trauma of the New Federal Republic, rather than a long-term structural weakness of German democratic institutions.[30] Ingo Hasselbach, the former East German leader of the most prominent neofascist political party, Nationale Alternative, has written critically of his engagement in the neo-Nazi

scene, providing added empirical evidence to the thesis, long argued
about neo-Nazi youth politics in the West, that the attraction of fascism for juveniles had much to do with extemporaneous anti-authori-
tarianism.[31] Neo-Nazi youths rarely have more than the most superfi-
cial knowledge of historical fascism, and what information they do
have comes from Holocaust denier literature.

Much less attention, both from the mainstream media and from
scholars, has been paid to the more interesting and possibly more ominous political realignment of a large number of German intellectuals
from Left to Right, and the emergence of an articulate, youthful New
Right.[32] As the self-proclaimed heirs of the Conservative Revolution,
the New Right that has emerged since 1989 is a diverse group of intellectuals united more by what they oppose than by any concrete political vision for the future. Politically they can be placed somewhere on
the spectrum between the ruling Christian Democrats and the various
neo-Nazi parties (such as Gerhrad Frey's German People's Union).
Some found a home in Franz Schönhuber's Republikaner party, but
since the fortunes of that party have waned, they are again in search of
a new political constellation.

The "newness" of the New Right supposedly consists in its demarcation from both postwar neo-Nazism and older forms of conservatism. It is a chic, updated version of conservatism transcending the social-democratic consensus of the major political parties. The New
Right sees itself locked in a "cultural battle" with the liberal cultural
elite of the old Federal Republic.[33] In its self-understanding the New
Right is a generational revolt against the Left of the Federal Republic,
in particular against the generation of 1968, the aging "Apo-Opas"
whose ideas are viewed as anachronistic, frozen in dogma, and who are
allegedly ensconced comfortably in positions of power in the media,
education, and other cultural and political institutions.[34] But the
"Generation of 1989" also sees itself as having transcended the politics
of the "Generation of Yalta," the founders of the Federal Republic, and
in particular Konrad Adenauer, who "sacrificed" East Germany and
the chance for unification in order to anchor West Germany firmly under the tutelage of the United States and its allies. The New Right
questions the utility and wisdom of Germany's ties to the West in the
changed international situation after unification.[35]

The self-image of the generation of 1989 is one of Young Turks: ener-
getic, radical young men with a mission to save Germany. Rejecting
the image of stuffy conservatism, the New Right sees itself as an avant
garde for disillusioned leftists, whose "conversion" they actively prop-
agate. As Heimo Schwilk, born in 1952, asserted in an interview:

The German intellectual who comes over to the camp of the 89ers is following an existential need to avoid being buried under the old concepts. The year 1989—and this will soon be clear to all intellectuals—has given an entirely new foundation to our intellectual and political reality. This epochal caesura worked like a catalyst, making the conversion of many intellectuals possible.[36]

I want to emphasize here that the much vaunted and seemingly fashionable claims about the disappearance of a viable distinction between Left and Right—propagated by, for example, Alain de Benoist in France and the journal *Telos* in the United States—can be explained for the German case much better with another dichotomy, simply put between pro-West and anti-West positions along a broad spectrum of economic, political, ecological, legal, and social issues. By "West" I mean here modern industrial capitalism and a life-world dominated by global technology. The subjection of Western capitalism to a cultural critique is itself a product of Western rationalism, but fundamental opposition to its most basic premises usually involves a more radical rejection of pluralism, the market economy, and the inevitable compromises of a democratic political decision-making process. Hans Jonas, for example, the eco-pacifist author of *Prinzip Verantwortung*, pleaded quite openly in the 1980s for a kind of green tyranny, against the existing democracy of West Germany, because, as he put it in a *Spiegel* interview from 1992, in its current form democracy is not capable of "rolling back the monstrous hedonism of modern pleasure-seeking culture [*Genusskultur*—almost untranslatable]."[37] When the attacks on liberal democracy from a Left-libertarian vantage point seem hollow and outdated, as they do to many European radicals, it is not surprising to see much searching among the ruins of the German Ideology on the Right, especially when the Right is now offering an increasingly sophisticated critique of American consumer culture, and an interpretation of capitalism as an enemy of *Heimat*, the environment, and a supposedly endangered high German culture. This form of cultural nationalism seems to offer the best explanation of the attraction of the "ideas of 1989."

One can trace various ideological currents that come together in the political waters of the new Right, among them French "ethno-pluralism," Heideggerian antimodernism, Schmittian "strong-state" theory, and the various writings of "spiritual reactionaries."[38] Jünger can be considered one of the most important inspirations of this form of national romanticism. He influenced authors who, beginning in the early 1970s, bewailed the effects of "Americanization" (i.e., Hollywood, Coca-Cola, pop music, consumerism, etc.) on German culture. An early exponent of this trend was the filmmaker Hans Jürgen Syberberg, whose post-unification book *On Misfortune and Fortune of the Arts in Germany after the Last War* was openly anti-Semitic. Syberberg blames the lack of a specifically German culture after 1945 on a "Jewish Left aesthetic" in an "unholy alliance" with "throwaway products like punk, pop and junk."[39] Syberberg does not seem called upon to give a reason why punk or pop should be considered aesthetically Jewish, nor does he understand that punk and pop are self-ironically marketed as junk.

Another Jünger-epigon, following Syberberg in bewailing the state of German culture, is the playwright Botho Strauss. In a recent laudation he wrote that "the epoch of postwar German literature will only have passed when it has been generally accepted that it was dominated for forty years by the work of Ernst Jünger."[40] Hyperbole aside, Strauss's early work was hailed by critics in the late 1970s and early 1980s as revolutionary and innovative, but he recently infuriated them by publishing a number of scathing critiques of German society from a romantic-nationalist point of view.[41] For Strauss, Jünger represents a conservative version of postmodernism, a return to myth, magic, and deification of language, beneath the flat rationality of the Enlightenment and far from the noise of the public sphere. Strauss hails this as an "art of the future."[42]

Strauss's latest provocation of German political correctness occurred after the publication in *Der Spiegel* in 1992 of the culturally despairing essay "Swelling Tragedy."[43] Strauss analyzed the rise of neo-Nazism in Germany, blaming the Left, particularly the generation of 1968, for having created a moral and intellectual vacuum that prepared the social space for revolt by the current younger generation against a supposedly hypocritical antifascism. Strauss also defended the traditions of the intellectual Right in Germany and lashed out against the culture of West Germany because of its supposed debasement through television and commercialism. Most disturbingly, while claiming to abhor all forms of anti-Semitism, Strauss wrote that racism and xenophobia can be thought of as cult rituals that "originally had sacred, order-creating meaning." The writer implied that the hatred of foreigners, like the sacrificial victims of the Bronze Age, could have a cathartic, positive effect on society by unloading aggression on one concentrated victim.

In both Germany and France the New Right attempts to attract young intellectuals by occupying the traditional themes of the Left and giving the old issues a new twist. The Munich publishing group of Mathes & Seitz, for example, has been instrumental in translating the French avant garde, from Georges Batailles to Jean-François Lyotard and Michel Foucault.[44] The poststructuralist discourse on power, consumerism, and bourgeois society can easily be turned into an elitist and reactionary critique of present society.

The late Heiner Müller is another good example of a tightrope walker on the fraying ideological divide between Right and Left. A travel-privileged East German dissident who considered the West as dictatorial as the East, Müller found Jünger's habitus congenial to his own anti-authoritarian, antibourgeois anarchism. From his autobiography, it becomes clear that Müller admired Jünger's absolute independence and contrarian, iconoclastic ability to shock and dismay his enemies.[45] In a series of interviews given in the early 1990s, Müller indulged in metahistorical speculations and abstruse comparisons that are clearly inspired by the kinds of provocative observations Jünger repeatedly made in his diaries, which are still being published.[46] In his obituary, Wolf Biermann aptly summarized Müller's lifelong attempt to perform a balancing act between the demands of authoritarian socialism and his own apocalyptic imagination with the observation: "He stood with one leg on the shoulder of Brecht, with the other on the shoulder of Ernst Jünger: a wobbly clown number in the ideology circus."[47]

History and German Memory

German history and German identity as contested ideological fields have also informed the politics of the new Right. Jünger's writings provide another weapon in the arsenal of the neo-Revisionists, a term that refers to historians who aggressively take the side of Ernst Nolte and, to a lesser extent, Andreas Hillgruber, Thomas Nipperdey, and Michael Stürmer in the Historians' Debate of the 1980s. The stakes in this debate have been raised by the claim that a new nationalist paradigm frees German historians from relating all of German history to the National Socialist era, either in an anticipatory or a consequential sense. The most prominent among this group are Rainer Zitelmann, Karlheinz Weismman, Michael Wolffsohn, Ansgar Graw, and Karl-Eckhard Hahn.[48] Besides questioning Germany's political and economic ties to the West, much of this work questions the singularity of the Holocaust and the centrality of racism for the Nazi regime. Germany is often cast in the role of a victim of geography and the plans of other European powers to oppose German hegemony on the European continent. National Socialism is seen ultimately as a consequence of four centuries of obstruction and interference in Germany's attempt to exercise its national ambitions, the most important example of which was French and English "intransigence" after World War I. This interpretation of German history does not deny the extermination of the Jews, but it recasts the origins, causes, and outcome of the world wars as a set of purely strategic moves on the chess board of world politics, recapitulating Hitler's own world-view. The Holocaust is reduced to a marginal side effect of Hitler's geopolitics.

The first self-named revisionists were a group of American historians in the 1920s, who argued that Germany had been falsely accused of igniting the war. Most prominent among this group were Harry Elmer Barnes and Sidney B. Fay. The revisionists accused the allies of diverting attention from their own complicity in the origins of the war by laying all the blame on Germany. Although this argument can be forged into a scholarly thesis, the problem is that the modern Holocaust deniers have used this line of reasoning to equate the war guilt question in 1945 to 1918. They charge, for example, that Roosevelt was in the tow of Jewish interests who had pushed him into declaring war on the Germans. According to this way of thinking Pearl Harbor was a diversion because the Roosevelt administration needed something to draw public attention away from the failures of the New Deal. A number of revisionists after World War II, including Barnes, Charles Tansill, and Austin App, argued that Hitler was a good and benign leader who did not want to invade Poland; that all sides in the war were equally devious and thus equally guilty; and so forth. The concentration camps had barely been liberated when revisionists began to charge that the photographs and reports had only been circulated to instill feelings of vengeance in the American public. By 1950 the foundation had been laid not only for those who would seek to relativize the Holocaust, but also for those who claimed the Holocaust was a hoax. Virtually all the revisionists' charges have been reiterated by the deniers. But it is important to note that the revisionists after World War II did not deny that the atrocities happened. They argued, like Jünger did after the war, that all participants were equally guilty of committing atrocities.[49] This is essentially the line taken by the neorevisionists, who in the German context have also added a strident defense of German cultural nationalism. They argue that the period of two German states between 1949 and 1990 was the exception in German history, rather than the twelve years of National Socialist rule.[50] Neo-Revisionists argue for a return to "normality," meaning that the German nation should once again be ethnically, culturally, linguistically, and politically defined inside her "historic" borders—that is, as "Mitteleuropa." They are also interested in proving that the Allies committed "war crimes," such as intentionally allowing Germans to starve or be killed after the defeat in 1945. This literature, once the speciality of bitter ex-Nazi officials who wrote historical apologies for small right-wing publishers, has moved progressively closer to the mainstream since 1989.[51]

The Link to 1950s Radical Conservatism

For radical conservatives, the attempt to "normalize" the course of German history necessarily involves confronting the history of German conservatism, especially in its prewar radical phase. After the establishment of the Federal Republic in 1949, Jünger wrote a series of important essays aimed at correcting the view that the Weimar German Right was complicitous in the rise of National Socialism. For Jünger, the National Conservatives of the 1920s were the German version of Trotskyists who had lost the political battle while retaining the purity of their ideas.[52] After the war, a central concept in this discourse was nihilism, about which Jünger and Heidegger corresponded often in the 1950s.[53] For both men, the discourse on nihilism was a conceptual means of elevating fascism to a world-historical battle for the preservation of occidental culture from the twin threats of American and Bolshevik hypertechnological productivism.[54] The National Socialists had fallen prey to the same technological drive for power they had initially intended to overcome. For Heidegger and Jünger the nihilism of planetary technology posed an even greater threat to Germany, since as a defeated nation it was even less capable of defending its culture.

Whereas Heidegger sought solace in the stance of *Gelassenheit*, a course correction of his politically fatal decisionist stand of the 1930s, Jünger's solution for nihilism was what he called a forest walk (*Der Waldgang*). The *Waldgänger* is a form of resistance not simply against technology or the bourgeois world, but more directly against historical guilt. Jünger realized that the central problem for postwar Germany was the crime of the gas chambers, for which there was no statute of limitations. Thus the German "goes into the forest," hibernates where there is a "well-sheltered hiding place, a secure refuge."[55] In Jünger's metaphorical wordplay, Germany is the proscribed international outlaw (in ancient Iceland the ostracized were sent into the forest). Resistance, legal or illegal, is the way out of isolation, of breaking the spell of collective guilt. "The German has to think about it," he wrote, "after his defeat the intention was to deprive him of his rights forever, to enslave him, to destroy him by distributing his property."[56] In response the *Waldgänger* goes underground, fights as a partisan.

The *Waldgänger* knows the munition depots, the hiding places of the oppressed, the minorities who are waiting for their moment. He fights the little war along the railway lines and supply routes, threatens the bridges, cables and depots. On his account one has to disperse the troops, multiply the guard posts. The *Waldgänger* takes care of surveillance, sabotage and the spreading of news to the population. He goes underground and becomes anonymous and then appears again when the enemy shows a sign of weakness. He causes repeated outbreaks of violence, instigates nightly panic.[57]

These kinds of images give sustenance to the radical conservative's desire to throw off the straitjacket of foreign expectations of good behavior by Germans on the world stage, encapsulated in the *cri du coeur* "I allow myself the revolt."[58] For the Right, mastering the past is self-defeating, self-hating, and unnecessary.[59] Far from "liberating" the Germans from Nazism, the Allies imposed a new regime of forced Americanization, and according to this world-view, committed war crimes as heinous as those of the National Socialists by allowing the formerly occupied Eastern European states to take revenge on the fleeing German population.[60] Jünger saw little difference between the Nazis and the victorious Allies as imposers of a foreign ideology. He argued that postwar reeducation efforts were an exercise in national humiliation and refused to fill out the obligatory questionnaires. Fifty years later the issue was rejoined in a debate on the meaning of the defeat in 1945. In the summer of 1995, a group of New Right historians launched an appeal "Against Forgetting" that recapitulated exactly Jünger's oft-repeated assertions about the sham idea of liberation from Nazism. The 8th of May was a paradox, the appeal reads, because on that day "we were redeemed and destroyed" at the same time. What has become forgotten, these historians tell us, is that

This day was not only the end of the National Socialist regime of terror, but was also the beginning of a terror against the exiles in the east and the beginning of the separation of our country. A history that is silent represses or relativizes these truths, cannot be the basis for the self-understanding of a Self-Confident nation, which we Germans must become in the family of European nations, in order that comparable catastrophes are avoided.[61]

If Germany, on the cusp of the twentieth century, has become again a "self-confident nation," (whatever this psychological metaphor means), the question remains, how will the legacy—the memory, the traces of the experience of fascism in the collective national psyche—play itself out in the new millennium? To advance the argument proposed at the beginning of this essay, I think it would be wrong to see the celebration, rediscovery, and reconstitution of radical conservative figures like Jünger as a "return" of fascism, whether one thinks in aesthetic, moral, or political terms. The current interest in the Weimar radical Right—whether it be the politics of Heidegger or Schmitt, or the aesthetics of Jünger and Gottfried Benn—cannot be related, I contend, to a desire to whisk elements of fascism into contemporary cultural discourse; rather, they are inspired by the way these intellectuals analyzed the defeat of fascism and their complicity in—or their "resistance" to—its rise. This renewed interest is not coincidentally tied to a widespread disillusionment with the rigid Marxist understanding of fascism by the German Left and a post-1968 search for a historical analysis that could explain the defeat of fascism and the cul-de-sac of Soviet communism, as well as the increasing globalization of capitalism, which seems to be creating in Europe a standardized, increasingly petrified and all-powerful commodity culture of sameness. The only diagnosis for mass culture along these lines has been offered by the Right under the rubric of *posthistoire*.[62]

Europe at the End of History

Cultural modernism has witnessed at least three disparate and sometimes contradictory attempts to conceptualize the "end" of history: (a) as the emancipation from historical determinism and the Hegelian march toward freedom; (b) as cultural paralysis; or (c) as the discursive negation of "history." In ideological terms, the first is the liberal/neoliberal, the second the radical conservative, and the third the postmodern variant.

Radical conservative pessimism might be seen as a polar opposite of liberal triumphalism, while postmodern skepticism seems to negate any affirmative stance altogether. But rather than seeing the liberal, conservative, and postmodern variants as heterogeneous, I would argue that they possess in common certain eschatological tropes that display a consistent ambiguity toward cultural modernism. A disquietude of varying degree expresses itself in regard to the homogenization of culture and power structures of social formation (in other words, the gradual disappearance of alterity and the obsession with social control). Even Fukuyama in *The End of History* is as nervous as postmodernists about the absence in the modern world of ideals worth fighting and dying for. In other words, with all due respect to the differences in approach, the theme of exhaustion can be traced like a wandering thread through the fabric of most *posthistoire* cultural criticism.[63] Ernst Junger's *posthistoire* vision can be read in this context as as a diagnosis of the end of authentic European culture, encapsulated in the metaphor of the sinking ship, the *Titanic*: "The individual does not stand alone anymore in society like a tree in the forest; rather, he or she is like the passenger in a fast-moving vehicle, what we might call the *Titanic*, or also the *Leviathan*."[64]

In the German context, the *Titanic* was fascism and Hitler's state was the *Leviathan*. When the fascist experiment failed, the radical conservatives of Weimar had to situate themselves, and their heterodox versions of antibourgeois revolt, in relation to that failure. The decisive moment in Jünger's confrontation with the Nazi regime came after the launching of the Russian offensive in June 1941 and the entrance of the United States into the war against Japan and Germany in December. As a military strategist, Jünger realized that in the long run Germany could not win the war against the logistical and material superiority of the Soviet Union, Britain, and the United States. His reaction was to begin thinking about the postwar situation and the defeat of fascism, even as the German army stood on the doorstep of Moscow and Leningrad. These ideas were written down in *The Peace*, which might be considered one of the founding documents of the postfascist conservative attempt to come to terms with Germany's failed revolution from the Right.

Jünger regarded the core of the problem as the rise of nationalist ideologies, borrowing Spengler's phrase, the "red and white terror"[65] that could not be contained by the democracies established in the wake of World War I. In his view, these nation-states would be replaced, in the post-World War II era, by new empires. He prophesied a drive toward greater unities, particularly a united Europe, as a necessary outcome of the war. On the surface, there is little that is new or particularly controversial in these arguments. Like many others, Jünger foresaw that Europe's only chance of economic and political recovery lay in extensive integration and unity. The contention that the source of the two world wars lay in the rise of mass nationalistic ideologies was a standard conservative argument found, for example, in Friedrich Meinecke's *The German Catastrophe of 1946*.[66]

On another level, though, Jünger was describing the end of the revolutionary period that began in 1918. He views *The Worker* as a historical subject looking forward, and its transformation into a "post"-historical entity who looks back into history living off its reserves. The stress on unity, authority, and "organic" freedom seemed to favor the national liberal principles of the Bismarckian state extended to Europe:

The United States of Europe must incorporate the principles of unity and diversity: in this combination the two main trends which democracy has assumed in our time must be reconciled—that of the authoritarian and that of the liberal state. There is good reason for both; but life cannot be either entirely disciplined or completely dominated by free will. It is rather a question of distinguishing the levels appropriate to each.[67]

The authoritarian state is appropriate where "men and things can be organized technically," but "freedom must have control where the organic processes are the rule."[68] For Jünger, the state must possess wide powers to run society, technologically and logistically, like an army. Only within the strong shell of the state is there room for freedom, the essay asserts. Jünger did not have in mind the freedom of more democratic political institutions, which historically are often crushed by strong states, and certainly not the protection of universal, individual rights. Quite the contrary, "organic" freedom meant liberty informed by "custom, rule and habit." In mirroring his own development, Jünger recasts the *Worker* as a deradicalized subject, a reconciliation with history: "At the same time the figure of the Worker, losing its titanic cast, will reveal new aspects of itself—then it will be seen what relation it bears to tradition, creation, happiness and religion."[69]

The range of meanings evoked by the word "peace" in this essay is not complete if understood merely as the opposite of war. Jünger argued that modern technology and ideology had corrupted both the practice of war and the making of peace. The experience of total war led him to believe that peace was just "power dressed up in a phrase."[70] Thus the "loss of its titanic cast" (see quote above) revealed the end of the revolutionary era, in both fascist and bolshevist versions, and the inauguration of a period of stagnancy of European culture after those social experiments had failed. This ontotheological version of historical progress becomes clear if one reads the metaphor of "peaceful waters" in the following passage not as connoting harmony, but literally as suggesting waters that do not run, that must eventually stagnate: "The Peace will have achieved its aims when the forces which are given over to total mobilization are freed for creation. Then the heroic age of the worker will have achieved its fulfillment—the age which was also the age of revolutions. The angry torrent has hollowed out the bed in which peaceful waters run."[71] The "angry torrent" made the bed in which Europe has come to rest. Jünger conceived of the prewar era as a "world civil war," and a struggle for "vital spheres," suprahistorical and depersonalized categories.[72] According to this logic, the bourgeois world is somehow to blame for sending the nineteen-year-old Jünger into the bloodbaths of war and then for the national humiliations after 1918. World-historical forces are responsible for causing these European civil wars, and now all nations must benefit from the peace. This is the core of the argument: the equal distribution—or, one might say, the "socialization"—of war guilt: "We have seen the victims of this war. To their somber ranks all nations added their contingent. All shared the suffering and therefore the peace must bear fruit for them all. That is, this war must be won by all."[73]

If the causes of the world wars could be derived from the failure of world-historical figures to live up to their own ideals—Jünger uses the examples of Napoleon "spreading the seed, but not reaping the crops," and President Wilson, whose ideals were putatively reversed by the Treaty of Versailles—then everybody is cast in the role of the sufferers; the line between victim and victimized is effectively erased. This was Jünger's intention, and rhetorically he succeeded in cloaking a personal belief in the end of any possible meaningful historical movement (for instance, a version of fascism that could have "saved" Europe) in the kind of humanist prose that postwar deradicalized conservatism demanded.

Jünger's war diaries contain a series of meditations that directly confront the ontotheological significance of the Holocaust. From Jünger's excursion to the Russian front, we know that he had direct information about the atrocities being committed by the *Einsatztruppen*. In Paris he saw Jews being rounded up, and he freely admitted to knowing the extent of other atrocities being committed in the concentration camps.[74] But Jünger's cool distance from the events is evident here as well. As distasteful as the barbarism of the Nazis was to him, Jünger could not help but interpret the persecution of the Jews and others as part of a fated, "cosmological" scheme. Particularly in the last books of the war diaries, where Jünger contemplated the issue of German guilt, his search for metaphysical entities below the surface of events clouded the issues he claimed to be illuminating. The following example shows how theodicy could be appealed to as a way of minimizing the uniqueness of the Holocaust: "Was our persecution the last birth pang before the appearance of the second messiah, the paraclete, with whom the epoch of the spirit shall begin? It is impossible that such a sacrifice won't bear fruit."[75]

Jünger's question is troublesome because it provides a metaphysical justification for the suffering of the Holocaust, a kind of theodicy that survivors would vigorously disavow.[76] Also a recurring topic in the war diaries, Jünger interpreted death as the sole authentic experience of life, indeed as having a higher reality than life.[77] Thus what interested him about the Nazi mass murders was not the experience of death for those upon whom it was perpetrated, but the abstract historical significance of the method applied in committing the crime. In a commentary on the concentration camps he noted that death had become standardized, mechanized, and sanitized, like everything in the technical world.[78] He thereby linked the administration of death to the increasing technological perfection of the modern world, the "disinfection of the technical world."[79] In the final pages of the war diaries, Jünger varied this theme with a not-too-subtle attack on the thesis of collective guilt. The engineers of the atom bomb, mused Jünger, make Tamerlane and his atrocities look absolutely royal. Death becomes cheaper and responsibility untraceable when millions are killed. The advancement of technology brings with it a concomitant impoverishment of the world, because rational calculation takes precedence over the "higher" faculties of the imagination. Finally, the collective guilt assertion is just a mantle the Allies use to hide their real interests: "The thesis of collective guilt has two strands which run together. For the defeated it means: I have to stand for my brother and his guilt. It gives the victor an excuse for undifferentiated plundering. If the bow is pulled too tightly, the dangerous question arises whether the brother was really so unjust."[80]

The "end of history" implies that after the demise of European culture, intellectuals can only take stock of what has been handed down. Nothing significantly new will appear, as eclecticism in the arts, architecture, and literature will prevail. Moreover the individual, at the end of history, will be regulated, depersonalized, managed by increasingly intrusive systems of order. In the 1949 introduction to his war diaries, Jünger postulated that the Copernican quest for ordering the cosmos and the diary as a modern literary form fall together chronologically. They have in common "the bifurcation of mind from object, the author from the world."[81] Jünger regarded the exploration of the planet/cosmos, and the corresponding registration by literature, as essentially completed. *Posthistoire* thinkers had only to contemplate the stranded objects of history that have washed up onto the shore.[82]

In Jünger's "New Testament" (as he calls his postwar writings) the apocalypse was nearing as the planet entered a "new" timeless zone, "over the line" into a postnihilistic world. The construction and reception of this *posthistoire* mode of thought can best be traced in Jünger's political writings of the 1950s, written as a contribution to the postwar West German conservatives' attempts to orient themselves ideologically to the new geopolitical reality of attachment to the West, which had for so long been the cultural and political enemy. It fell upon Jünger and several other important postwar intellectuals to make sense of cultural modernity for a nation whose best minds had gone into exile and whose culture had fallen into barbarism under Nazi rule.

Friedrich Sieburg first described this condition for Germany in apocalyptic tones, as the "last days of humanity" and as a *Spätzeit* (late era), in his 1954 book *Die Lust am Untergang*.[83] In 1951, Giselher Wirsing, an important member of the Young Conservative TAT-Circle in the 1920s and early 1930s, also published a book dealing with the end of all possible revolutionary politics. He predicted a World Federation, similar in structure to Jünger's idea of the *Weltstaat*.[84] In the "Unity of the World," published in 1952, Carl Schmitt announced that the world lacked any viable political alternatives, as the two seemingly opposed blocs were united by the same messianic "belief" in progress and science: "East and West faith flow together here. Both claim to be the true humanitarians, the true democracies. Both also descend from the same source, the philosophy of history of the eighteenth and nineteenth centuries."[85]

Hans Freyer, the author of the programmatic *Revolution from the Right* in 1931, published a sociological study in 1955 arguing that the spread of technology would result in the elimination of cultural specificity, as "secondary systems" would gradually absorb all human societies and reduce them to subjects of meaningless technical rationality.[86] In the same vein, Arnold Gehlen, allegedly improvising on a concept from the nineteenth-century French philosopher Antoine A. Cournot, used the epithet *posthistoire* in 1963 as a sociological category, applying it to all of European civilization.[87] For Gehlen the "industrial-technical-scientistic" envelopment of the modern world meant that the Enlightenment had ended, but its consequences lived on. Human beings, being "instinct-poor," had to abandon the idea of emancipation and accept the protection of institutional, technical order.[88]

The elements of Jünger's *posthistoire* vision can be reconstructed as follows: the defeat of fascism brought the last heroic epoch in Europe to an end, the age of the Worker and the Soldier. What followed was retreat, hibernation, resistance to the rise of two technocratic superpowers and global mass culture. During this period, European culture was undermined by nihilism (a product of the French Enlightenment), the end of aristocratic society, the "Americanization" of world culture, and the suzerainty of technology. Fascism was the last heroic attempt to save Europe from this nihilistic envelopment by planetary technology, but plebeian, mass movements arose instead, intent on dominance and war by means of the same technology. The world wars were in truth European civil wars, caused by all, and peace should be shared by all. The term "peace" is a code in the radical conservative vocabulary for cultural stagnation and a new European empire, the homogeneous, dull and work-like European community, possibly even a world federation. The individual survives in this death of culture by living off the reserves, the stranded objects of past culture. The individual retreats into cultural hibernation.

The answer to nihilism is the rejection of the Allied imposition of historical guilt. The concentration camps were not the result of human agency, but rather the metahistorical transformation of life into a global workshop (*Werkstätttenlandschaft*). Heidegger and Jünger agreed on the connection between automation, modern culture, and nihilism, but they disagreed on the solution. For Jünger, the twentieth century would see a transition into a new, posthistorical age, beyond the current horizon of technological thinking, into the age of Aquarius and the return of the gods. Heidegger also thought only new cultural practices would "save" us, but he was less sanguine that this would happen. Jünger's eschatological vision promises redemption beyond the myths and ideologies of the twentieth century: here some of the original impulses and possibilities of the fascist revolt survive into a new age, but they are suffused in the milky rhetoric of titans, "absolute art," and the subordination of human history to "earth-history."[89]

Jünger's attempt to tie together, conceptually, the Holocaust and modernity was a cornerstone of his and other conservative reactionaries' interpretation of fascism and the destruction of Europe during the Second World War. The New Right has taken the cue from Jünger and updated the fascist rejection of Western culture to fit a plethora of current resentments. Today it is fashionable to see the bourgeois age as historically complete, and the quest to reevaluate the contours of postmodern society in its global aspects—the scarcity of work, the organization of leisure, the end of nature and science, the hyperreality of electronic communication and media, the bioscientific regulation of sexuality, the neopagan fragmentation of religion, and a host of other previously radical conservative themes—is well underway, though the original impetus for the *posthistoire* diagnosis is either unknown or willingly repressed.[90] All of which means the rise of an aggressive New Right and the widespread disillusionment with contemporary liberalism have more than passing affinities with the mood of the latest fin-de-siècle.

Notes

1. Peter Sloterdijk, "Nietzsche im Monsterpark," in Günter Figal and Heimo Schwilk, *Magie der Heiterkeit: Ernst Jünger zum Hundersten* (Stuttgart: Klett-Cotta, 1995), 117.

2. Rüdiger Safranski, "Der Wille zum Glauben oder die Wiederkehr der Götter," in Frugal and Schwilk, *Magie der Heiterkeit*, 252.

3. See, for example Mark Terkessidis, *Kulturkampf: Volk, Nation, der Westen und die neue Rechte* (Cologne: Kiepenheuer & Witsch, 1995).

4. See Hans Sluga, *Heidegger's Crisis: Philosophy and Politics in Nazi Germany* (Cambridge: Harvard University Press, 1993), 125–53.

5. *Der Arbeiter* was published in fall 1932, *Jahre der Entscheidung* (Munich: DTV, 1961) in summer 1933.

6. Armin Mohler is a good example of a proponent of the former, and Wolfgang Kämpfer of the latter. See Armin Mohler, *Liberalenbeschimpfung: Drei politische*

Traktate (Essen: Heitz & Höfkes, 1990) and Wolfgang Kämpfer, *Ernst Jünger* (Stuttgart: Metzler, 1981).

7. See Martin Meyer, *Ernst Jünger* (Munich: Hanser, 1993). For a good study in English, see Thomas Nevin, *Ernst Jünger and Germany: Into the Abyss, 1914–1945* (Durham NC: Duke University Press, 1996).

8. Ernst Jünger, "Revolution und Idee," *Völkischer Beobachter*, 23–24 September 1923.

9. Ernst Jünger, Strahlungen II, *Sämtliche Werke* (hereafter *sw*), vol. 3 (24 August 1945, 516–20).

10. Karl O. Paetel, *Ernst Jünger in Selbstzeugnissen und Bilddokumentation* (Hamburg: Rowohlt, 1962), 43. One of the few collections of Jünger's letters to be published was with Kubin, *Eine Begegnung: Briefwechsel* (Berlin: Propylaeen, 1975). On the importance of Kubin's influence on Jünger's style, see Heinz Beckman, "Die gemeinsamen Fische," *Literaturblatt/Rheinischer Merkur* 49 (5 December 1975).

11. Ernst Niekisch, *Erinnerungen eines deutschen Revolutionärs*, vol. 1 (Cologne: Verlag Wissenschaft und Politik, 1972), 192.

12. First published in 1929 and substantially revised in 1938, the title was derived from Louis Aragon's programmatic surrealist novel *Le Paysan de Paris*. Ernst Jünger, *Das Abenteurliche Herz: Aufzeichnugen bei Tag und Nacht* (Berlin: Frundsberg Verlag, 1929); *Das Abenteurliche Herz: Figuren und Cappricos* (Hamburg: Hanseatische Verlagsantalt, 1938).

13. See Sidra Stich, introduction to *Anxious Visions: Surrealist Art* (New York: Abbeville, 1990).

14. Elke Fröhlich, ed., *Die Tagebücher von Joseph Goebbels, Sämtliche Fragmente*, 4 vols. (Munich: Saur, 1987); see vol. 1, 13 January 1926 and 4 April 1929.

15. Ernst von Solomon, "Ich besuchte Ernst Jünger," *Die Welt*, 10 January 1950.

16. See Roger Woods, "Ernst Jünger and the Nature of Political Commitment" (Ph.D. Thesis, St. Johns College, Oxford, Trinity Term 1981). *Deutsches Literaturarchiv Marbach* (hereafter DLAM).

17. In the *Totale Mobilmachung*, Jünger wrote that mass parties, with their ideas of progress, constituted the "great people's church of the nineteenth century." *sw*, vol. 7, 122.

18. Discussion between Armin Mohler and Klaus Vondung on *Kulturreport*, narrated by Manfred Franke, NDR 11 August 1982; manuscript by German Werth, DLAM RFS:AA.

19. Otto-Ernst Shüddekopf, *National-Bolschewismus in Deutschland 1918–1933* (Frankfurt am Main: Ullstein, 1972), 252ff.

20. Shüddekopf, *National-Bolschewismus*, 251.

21. Shüddekopf, *National-Bolschewismus*, 252.

22. Ernst Jünger, *Die totale Mobilmachung*, 145–46.

23. Ernst Jünger, *Der Arbeiter*, *sw*, vol. 8, 17: "The domination of the Third Estate has never touched the inner core of Germany, which determines the power and fullness of life. Looking back at over a hundred years of German history, we can proudly say that we have been bad citizens."

24. "Gestalt—this is a word Goethe liked to use; it characterizes the effect behind the things, something all encompassing in any case. Thus I talked about the

Gestalt of the Worker, not as a representative of a class or an estate, but rather as a new titan, with creative and destructive effects." From Gertrud Fussenegger, "Der schöpferische Augenblick—ein Kurzschluss; Pressegespräch mit Ernst Jünger," *Süddeutsche Zeitung* (30–31 March 1985).

25. Jünger, *Der Arbeiter*, 217, 263, and passim.

26. See for example Ernst Jünger, "Grossstadt und Land," *Süddeutsche Monatshefte* (1926): 3–26.

27. "Über den Schmerz," in *sw*, vol. 7, esp. 174–81.

28. Jünger, *Der Arbeiter*, 63.

29. Richard Wolin, *Labyrinths: Explorations in the Critical History of Ideas* (Amherst: University of Massachusetts Press, 1995), 175–210.

30. As the asylum laws have been tightened, there has been a progressive reduction of violence against foreigners in Germany; there were 596 registered attacks in 1992, 284 in 1993, 80 in 1994, and 19 in 1995. The firebombing of an asylum house in Lübeck, as a result of which ten people died, at the end of January 1996 has still not been clarified, though all indications point to one of the residents of the house as the culprit. See "Die Lehre von Lübeck," *Die Zeit* 5 (2 February 1996): 1. The issue of Germany's democractic stability is still open to debate, of course. For a good discussion see "Unified Germany: Stabilizing Influence or Threat? A Symposium," *Partisan Review* 4 (fall 1995): 523–630.

31. See Ingo Hasselbach, *Führer-Ex: Memoirs of a Former Neo-Nazi* (New York: Random House, 1996); and Otto Plack, *Wie oft wird Hitler besiegt* (Frankfurt am Main: DTV, 1979). See also Richard Faber and Hajo Funke, *Rechtsextremismus* (Berlin: Hentrich, 1995), 96–156.

32. A recent exception is the short essay by Jacob Heilbrunn, "Germany's New Right," *Foreign Affairs* 75, no. 6 (November–December 1996): 80–98.

33. See Terkessidis, *Kulturkampf*, 37–72.

34. See Karlheinz Weissman, *"Rückruf in die Geschichte." Die deutsche Herausforderung: Alte Gefahren—Neue Chancen* (Frankfurt am Main: Ullstein, 1993), 42–50.

35. See the collection of essays *Westbindung: Chancen und Risiken für Deutschland*, ed. Rainer Zitelmann, Karlheinz Weissman, and Michael Grossheim (Frankfurt am Main: Ullstein, 1993), in particular Zitelmann's article, "Neutralitätsbestrebungen und Westorientierung," 173–93.

36. Wolfgang Fenske, interview with Heimo Schwilk, "Die Freiheit des Denkens zurückgewinnen," *Junge Freiheit*, 4 November 1994, 3.

37. Hans Jonas, "Dem Bösen Ende näher," in *Der Spiegel* 20 (1992): 92–107; quoted by Richard Herzinger and Hannes Stein, *Endzeitprohpeten oder die Offensive der Antiwestler* (Hamburg: Rowohlt, 1995), 81.

38. The term is used by Diedrich Diederichsen in "Spirituelle Reaktionäre und völkische Vernunftkritiker," in his essay collection *Freiheit macht arm: Das Leben nach dem Rock'n'Roll 1990–93* (Cologne: Kiepenheuer & Witsch, 1993). A version of this article was also published as "Spiritual Reactionaries After German Reunification: Syberberg, Foucault, and Others," *October* 62 (fall 1992): 65–83.

39. Hans Jürgen Syberberg, *Vom Unglück und Glück der Kunst in Deutschland nach dem letzten Krieg* (Munich: Mathes & Seitz, 1990), 14.

40. Botho Strauss, "Refrain einer tieferen Aufklärung," in Figal and Schwilk, *Magie der Heiterkeit*, 323.

41. See Claus Leggewie, *Druck von Rechts* (Munich: Beck, 1993), 115–19.

42. Botho Strauss, "Anschwellender Bocksgesang," *Der Spiegel* 6 (February 12, 1993): 324; reprinted in *Die Selbstbewusste Nation*, ed. Heimo Schwilk and Ulrich Schacht (Berlin: Ullstein, 1994), with reactions to Strauss from the intellectual Right.

43. Strauss, "Anschwellender Bocksgesang."

44. Diederichsen, "Spirituelle Reaktionäre."

45. See Heiner Müller, *Krieg ohne Schlacht: Leben in Zwei Diktaturen* (Cologne: Kiepenhauer & Witsch, 1994), 275–81.

46. Heiner Müller, *Jenseits der Nation* (Berlin: Rotbuch, 1991). See also Richard Herzinger, *Masken der Lebensrevolution: Vitalistische Zivilisations—und Humanismuskritik in Texten Heiner Müllers* (Munich: Fink Verlag, 1992).

47. Wolf Biermann, "Die Müller-Maschine," *Der Spiegel* 2 (8 January 1996): 159.

48. See Zitelmann et al., *Westbindung*.

49. See Ernst Jünger, "Der Friede," in *sw*, vol. 7, 195–99.

50. While the *Junge Freiheit* has published articles supporting Faurrisson and the "Leuchtner Report," editor Dieter Stein has often expressed his belief that the Right should not try to downplay or explain away the atrocities of the Third Reich. In a recent editorial he states flatly: "In order for the Third Reich not to be seen as the last word about German history, it is absolutely necesssary to recognize the criminal character of the National Socialist regime." See Stein, "Geschichte und nationale Identität," *Junge Freiheit* 7 (17 February 1995): 11.

51. For recent examples, see Joachim Hoffman, "Stalins Vernichtungskrieg," *Die Zeit* 46 (17 November 1995), and James Bacque's completely undocumented assertion that ten million Germans were killed through incarceration, hunger, or expulsion in *Verschwiegene Schuld: Die allierten Besatzungspolitik in Deutschland nach 1945*, trans. Hans-Ullrich Seebohm (Frankfurt am Main: Ullstein, 1995). See also Rudolf Augstein's demolition of the latest revisionist theses in regard to Stalin: "Die neue Thesen zum Russlandkrieg," *Der Spiegel* 6 (5 February 1996), 100–116.

52. See the inroduction by Armin Mohler to the revised *Die Konservative Revolution in Deutschland 1918–1932* (Darmstadt: Wissenschaftliche Buchgesellschaft, 1989), 6–10.

53. The letters are now in the German Literature Archive at Marbach but have not yet been made available to scholars. Armin Mohler discussed the letters with me in a general way when I visited him in November 1989.

54. See Michael E. Zimmerman, *Heidegger's Confrontation with Modernity: Technology, Politics, Art* (Bloomington: Indiana University Press, 1990).

55. Ernst Jünger, "Der Waldgang," in *sw*, vol. 7, 328.

56. Jünger, "Waldgang," 365.

57. Jünger, "Waldgang," 353.

58. The name of an anthology by the right-wing publishers Mathes & Seitz, *Ich gestatte mir die Revolte* (Munich: Mathes & Seitz, 1990).

59. The main arguments were made by Armin Mohler in *Vergangenheitsbewältigung* (Krefeld: Sinus, 1980).

60. See "Geflohen und vertrieben. Besetzt oder befreit. Kriegsgefangen. Besiegt," *Junge Freiheit* (5 May 1995): Special issue on the 8th of May.

61. "Paradoxie des 8. Mai," *Junge Freiheit* (5 May 1995): 16.

62. For an excellent overview of the subject in the postwar German context, see Lutz Niethammer, *Posthistoire: Has History Come to an End?* trans. Patrick Camiller (London: Verso, 1992).

63. One would therefore think it possible to construct a fourth version based on neo-Marxism. But Marxists tend to criticize all concepts of the end of history as bourgeois capitulation to systems, the marketplace, and commoditization of the life-world. See Perry Anderson, *A Zone of Engagement* (New York: Verso, 1992), 279–375.

64. Ernst Jünger, *sw*, vol. 7, 314.

65. Jünger, *sw*, 27. See Spengler, *Jahre der Entscheidung*, 33.

66. Friedrich Meinecke, *The German Catastrophe: Reflections and Recollections*, trans. Sidney B. Fay (Boston: Beacon, 1950). Originally published in German in 1946.

67. Jünger, *The Peace*, in *sw*, vol. 7, 224.

68. Jünger, *The Peace*, 224.

69. Jünger, *The Peace*, 57.

70. Ernst Jünger, "Ausgehend vom Brümmerhof," in *sw*, vol. 14, 128.

71. Jünger, *The Peace*, 222.

72. Jünger, *The Peace*, 211.

73. Jünger, *The Peace*, 207.

74. Walter Bargatzky, who kept Jünger informed of the plans of the German resistance, wrote in his memoirs: "Then the actual tragedy, genocide began. The French Jews are being transported to the east as well. Drancy and the camp at Compiègne have become stopping points on the way to Auschwitz. It is the summer of 1942. But even before we'd received the news that the Jews were being killed, systematically and en masse." See Walter Bargatzky, *Hotel Majestic: Ein Deutscher in Besetztem Frankreich* (Basel: Herder, 1987), 101.

75. Jünger, *Strahlungen II* (17 April 1945), 415. "War unsere Verfolgung nun die letzte Wehe vor dem Erscheinen des zweiten Messiahs, des Paraklet, mit dem das Zeitalters des Geistes beginnen soll? Es ist unmöglich, dass solche Opfer nicht Frucht tragen."

76. See for example Primo Levi, "Letters from Germans," in *The Drowned and the Saved*, trans. Raymond Rosenthal (New York: Summit Books, 1988), 167–97.

77. Jünger, *Strahlungen I*, 318, 322, 342, 355, 358; *Strahlungen II*, 401, 412, 422.

78. *Strahlungen II* (12 May 1945), 447–48.

79. *Strahlungen II* (12 May 1945), 447: "das Desinfizierte der technischen Welt." There are no hints of anti-Semitism in any of Jünger's published writings, with the exception of one short article in 1930. But after a thirty-year friendship, Jünger's translator, Henri Plard, broke off his relationship with the author because Jünger allegedly repeatedly defended Pierre Laval. Personal interview with Henri Plard, 7 March 1990.

80. *Strahlungen II* (20 August 1945), 509.

81. Preface to *Strahlungen I*, 12.

82. This image is taken from *Eumeswil* (1977), Jünger's most explicit *posthistoire* novel.

83. Friedrich Sieburg, *Die Lust am Untergang* (Hamburg: Rowohlt, 1954). See also the review by Otto Forst de Battaglia, in which Sieburg is compared to Karl Kraus, "Vom irdischen Katzenjammertal und von der Unlustseuche," *Der Standpunkt*, 21 January 1955.

84. Giselher Wirsing, *Schritt aus dem Nichts: Perspektiven am Ende der Revolution*, cited by Gotthard Montesi, "Mutationen der Menschheit," *Wort und Wahrheit* 7 (1952): 456–59.

85. Carl Schmitt, "Die Einheit der Welt," *Merkur* 1 (January 1952): 9.

86. Hans Freyer, *Theorie des gegenwärtigen Zeitalters* (Stuttgart: Deutsche Verlags-Anstalt, 1955); see Jerry Z. Muller, *The Other God That Failed* (Princeton NJ: Princeton University Press, 1987). 105–6. Freyer's systems analysis anticipated a much more sophisticated "theory of social systems" in the 1970s and currently enjoys a postmodern reception. See the special issue on Niklas Luhmann, *New German Critique* 61 (winter 1994), and the special issue "The Politics of Systems and Environments," *Cultural Critique* 30 (spring 1995).

87. Arnold Gehlen, "Über die Geburt der Freiheit aus der Entfremdung," in *Studien zur Anthropologie und Soziologie* (Berlin: Luchterhand, 1963), 246; cited in Niethammer, *Posthistoire*, 18.

88. Gehlen, *Studien*, 310 ff.

89. These terms come from an address Jünger gave to the Bienniale in Venice in 1990. Pierre Bourdieu was sufficiently outraged by what he called the "fascist speech" to sign an "Appeal to Vigilance" with sixteen hundred other French intellectuals, who in summer 1993 expressed their conviction that the democratic overtures of the Nouvelle Droite are not genuine. The document first appeared in *Le Monde* on 13 July, signed by Pierre Bourdieu, Jacques Derrida, and other notables, then exactly a year later by sixteen hundred other intellectuals. For a polemic against the appeal see Frank Adler, "Left Vigilance in France," *Telos* 98–99 (winter 1993–spring 1994): 23–33.

90. See Peter Sloterdijk, ed., *Vor der Jahrtausendwende: Berichte zur Lage der Zukunft*, 2 vols. (Frankfurt: Suhrkamp); Ludger Heidbrink, ed., *Entrauberte Zeit: Der melancholische Geist der Moderne* (Munich and Vienna: Hanser, 1997).

Reed Way Dasenbrock

Slouching toward Berlin:
Life in a Postfascist Culture

Let me begin by admitting that my title is provocative, but not, I think, needlessly so. The era in which we live has been repeatedly labeled as post. Postmodern, poststructuralist, postcolonial, post-Marxist, and even post-theory are a few of the labels in circulation for the current moment, and undoubtedly other "posts" are being put into circulation as I write. As a prefix, "post" is somewhere between hopelessly ambiguous and utterly oxymoronic: one claims the label "post"-anything only if one claims to have moved past that thing, yet the habit of defining something by reference to something one claims to have superseded implies a relationship, which further implies that the supersedence is not absolute. The claim to be "post" implies that one is not yet fully "post." So with all the leading contemporary "posts": poststructuralism, though presented initially as a sharp reversal of structuralism, can now easily be seen to be in important respects a continuation of it; postcolonial theorists now explicitly acknowledge that their object of study includes the colonial as well as the postcolonial period or world; and postmodernism stands in a close relation to the modernism it defines itself against. So too with my term postfascism: I use it to refer to a kinship we are particularly reluctant to acknowledge, but a kinship nonetheless. Some relatives are easier to acknowledge than others; this particular skeleton is just now, after fifty years, emerging from the closet named denial.

I want to make two claims here. Initially, I'd like to state them baldly and without supporting detail, and then take a somewhat roundabout route to provide that supporting detail. The first is that the era in Euro-American culture in which we find ourselves is described much more accurately by the term "postfascist" than by anything else, at least by any of the rival "posts" I have referred to. (I would certainly leave open the possibility that we are pre- or for that matter in the middle of a period best described in other terms, though we are unlikely to have a clear sense of what those terms are just yet.) The second point is that it has been the controversy over the political affiliation of central contemporary intellectuals—the scandal over Heidegger, over de Man, and over the implications of the writings of Derrida and others about both men—that has brought home the postfascist nature of our epoch most clearly. A final point, implicit in all this, is that coming to an understanding of the postfascist nature of much of our current thought might well make us see that there is nothing determined about any of this. There are other cultural logics we might embrace, and the important consequence of the various scandals over the past decade may well be a clarification of the choices that face us.

The Delegitimation of Modernism

Our story—and I am telling something of a story—begins with the observation that one of the central loci of academic activity from 1945 until the early 1970s could be called the legitimation or institutionalization of modernism. By Modernism, I refer to the great cultural achievements of the three decades from 1908 to 1939, largely created by a remarkable group of artists born in the 1880s, among whom might be named Joyce, Pound, Eliot, Stravinsky, Bartok, Picasso, and Le Corbusier, just to indicate a few reference points. Though Modernism was largely created before World War II, it was taken into the academy as an object of study largely in the postwar era. Hugh Kenner's "The Making of the Modernist Canon" provides a useful summary of how one influential canon-maker would tell the story, though of course the history of modernism in the various arts would have different nuances and inflections.[1] It is important to realize not just that most scholarly critics of modernism presented it in these decades as one of the key moments of Western civilization (the distinctive marker High Modernism working here implicitly to compare modernism to the Renaissance), but also that the advent of modernist studies in the academy went hand in hand with the advent of theorizing about the arts, as can be seen by the modernist affiliations of the New Critics in literature or of a figure like Clement Greenberg in the arts. And though the story I want to tell isn't my intellectual autobiography, or at least isn't just my intellectual autobiography, the moment at which I decided to become a specialist in modernist literature, which I can date to an independent study with Donald Theall my senior year at McGill, 1973–74, was a moment when to study modern literature seemed necessarily to entail studying modernism, the period of literary study with the highest prestige value or—as one might say today—the greatest "cultural capital." Things changed very quickly: when I arrived at Johns Hopkins just three years later, to study modernist literature with Hugh Kenner, the standard question asked by my fellow graduate students was "which one of Kenner's fascists" I was planning a dissertation on. It has taken me a long time to realize that this question—simply irritating at the time—was a straw in the wind, announcing the delegitimation of modernism as a field of study. The way the question was put shows that the issue of fascism was already lurking in the wings, but the advent of theory—particularly poststructuralist theory—played an equally important role.

Let me mention three key moments in what I am calling the delegitimation of modernism. The first is provided by Paul de Man's early and extremely influential essay, "Literary History and Literary Modernity," chapter 8 of *Blindness and Insight*. De Man's charge against modernism is a simple one, though hardly simply put: it is that the desire to be modern is itself not modern: "When [writers] assert their own modernity, they are bound to discover their dependence on similar assertions made by their literary predecessors; their claim to being a new beginning turns out to be the repetition of a claim that has already been made."[2] Or again, "The same fatal interplay governs the writer's attitude towards modernity: he cannot renounce the claim to being modern but also cannot resign himself to his dependence on predecessors—who for that matter, were caught in the same situation" (162). De Man refers therefore to the writer's "inability to be modern" (162). De Man's terminology varies between modernity and modernism, and his frame of reference includes earlier epitomes of Continental modernism, preeminently Baudelaire, Rimbaud, and Nietzsche, but these don't change the fact that his critique is broadly applicable to modernism no matter how one defines it.

Modernism comes across in de Man's account as something of a teenager, rebellious and unable to understand the origins of its own rebellion, naive in considering itself to have escaped something from which there is no escape. What it cannot escape is not so easy to name: it seems from the passages I have quoted as if it must be history, but in the final pages of the essay, de Man modulates somewhat surprisingly from a critique of modernism to a critique of structuralism. The critique is ultimately the same: just as modernism conceives of itself as self-sufficient, the structuralist account of literature treats it as self-sufficient, as taking "for granted the specificity of literature" (164). The problem with this assumption of self-sufficiency would seem to be that of an inside account, that it ignores context, but of course anyone hoping to find a simple critique of formalism in de Man will always be disappointed. The critique here is not one that assumes history as a stable outside to set against a modernist/formalist attempt to elide history, but rather the very notion of inside/outside. For de Man ends this essay with one of his famous epigrams, often quoted but not often reattached to its original context, "that the bases for historical knowledge are not empirical facts but written texts, even if these texts masquerade in the guise of wars and revolutions" (165). If modernism and structuralism alike are naive in believing that they can escape history, their problem for de Man is most deeply rooted in their notion of history, a notion we might call pretextualist. History is a text, de Man is proclaiming here in one of the most influential passages in all his work, and it is really the condition of textuality that is inescapable, since even wars and revolutions are ultimately revealed to be texts in de Man's account.

Obviously, this moment in de Man looks different after 1988 than before, but that's jumping ahead of the story. De Man's analysis of modernism was so influential, it seems to me now, because of the way it presents modernism and structuralism as comparably naive about history: this defines de Man's own position not just as poststructuralist, to use a label used often enough, but also postmodernist, to use a term less often applied to de Man. What I mean by postmodernist in this context is less the term as used in aesthetics in the 1970s, as descriptive of tendencies in art, music, and literature characteristic of the post-1945 period, than the sense dominant subsequently, in the 1980s, the sense associated with the work of Jean-François Lyotard, particularly *The Postmodern Condition*.

With the introduction of the work of Lyotard, the opposition modern/postmodern becomes more than simply a matter of the aesthetics of the pre- or rather interwar period and the postwar, though I think it never completely loses its connection to this. For Lyotard's critique of the modern and celebration of the postmodern stands in opposition to Jurgen Habermas's ringing defense of modernity. For Lyotard as well as for Habermas, modernity goes back a long way.[3] Modernity is represented in Lyotard's work by a belief in one of the "grand" or "metanarratives"; for Lyotard, the two essential grand narratives are those of "speculation and emancipation"[4]—the dreams of total knowledge and of total freedom. The problem with these narratives is less their content than their "totalizing" or absolute nature. Not allowing for alternatives to themselves, they become totalitarian, indeed terrorist in his terms, for forcing a single vision on us, for creating a kind of forced consensus. In contrast, the "postmodern" is marked by "incredulity towards metanarratives" (xxiv), by the replacement of one such grand narrative with "petits récits" expressed in a plurality of different language games that can coexist without one seeking domination over the others and thereby attaining the status of a grand or master narrative. Lyotard's call in the closing words of *The Postmodern Condition* is this: "Let us wage a war on totality; let us be witnesses to the unpresentable; let us activate the differences and save the honor of the name" (82).

Lyotard's grand narrative about grand narratives proceeds largely without reference to fascism; only one oblique reference to Heidegger brings in fascism in *The Postmodern Condition*. But for our purposes, one way of describing his description of modernism is that he describes it in terms perfectly applicable to fascism. For what is the dream of fascism but a dream of a collectivity, a community, sharing in common a single grand narrative about the fate of that collectivity? And what is the reality of fascism but the fact that in a modern society, such a consensus can only be achieved by terror, by driving out others, by reducing a plurality of language games to a single, prescribed linguistic code? Whether or not Lyotard's description holds true for modernity writ large, it holds true enough for fascism that his argument works to identify modernity itself with fascism, to make the fascist moment seem like the epitome of Modernism.

If an identification of fascism with Modernism is implicit in Lyotard's work, running underneath and helping to sustain the more overt project of delegitimizing modernism, that identification is perfectly overt in the work of Fredric Jameson, not coincidentally the person asked to write a foreword to the English-language translation of *The Postmodern Condition*. Jameson's work in this direction isn't neatly collected in one place, though the title of his book on Wyndham Lewis, *Fables of Aggression: Wyndham Lewis, the Modernist as Fascist*, is as direct a statement of the equation as one is likely to want.[5] Jameson, though influenced by Lyotard, obviously as a Marxist is unlikely to share Lyotard's critique of grand narratives, and indeed looking at the sequence of his books on modern culture, it is possible to discern a grand narrative in Jameson's work. I've described this at length elsewhere,[6] so let me briefly say that it is based on the perception of a homology between the three discrete arenas of economics, culture, and Marxist theory, and it presents these three arenas as moving through a tripartite historical sequence over the past century and a half: from the era of classical capitalism to imperialism (of which fascism is a distinct offshoot—here Jameson follows Hannah Arendt) to the period of "late Capitalism" in which we now find ourselves. Comparably, we have moved from the classical period of Marxism to the revisionary Marxism of the interwar period, with Gramsci and Adorno, and finally to the "late Marxism" of which Jameson himself is a representative. Finally, in the arena of culture, we begin with the classical age of realism, represented by Balzac, move to an era of modernism with close links to imperialism (in the case of Forster, discussed in "Modernism and Imperialism") and fascism (in the case of Lewis et al., discussed in *Fables of Aggression*), finally finding ourselves in the era of postmodernism, discussed at length in Jameson's long book of that title.

The fact that parallels exist for Jameson among these arenas doesn't necessarily identify them, for obviously Marxism in each of its stages stands in a critical relation to the forms of capitalism it analyzes and opposes. The question then becomes, does Jameson position the sequence of cultural epochs as critical vis-à-vis the stages of capital and therefore analogous to the stages of Marxism, or as complicitous with capital and therefore just as much the subject of critique as the stages of capital are? How is culture positioned in the titanic struggle between capital and revolution? The received account would, I think, see this relation as variable, as would Jameson, but the variability isn't exactly the same in the two accounts. The received myth about modernism is that it is opposed to the political structures of its time, while the received notion of postmodernism is that this oppositional stance has been greatly relaxed. Jameson reverses this, seeing a far greater oppositional (or utopian) nature to postmodernism, but everywhere presenting modernism as complicit with the political structures of imperialism and fascism.

If the net effect of this kind of analysis of modernism has been in large measure to delegitimize it, that is obviously only part of the story. What does this delegitimation legitimize in turn? Though clearly part of Jameson's agenda is a complex rehabilitation of "late Marxism" I won't detail here, the major beneficiaries of these theoretical critiques of modernism have been postmodernism and poststructuralism. De Man's critique of modernity as naive and blind to its own position positions that critique and the textualist vision of history that sustains it as sophisticated, as the source of insight; Lyotard's critique of totality and identification of totality with the modern constitutes a celebration of the postmodern, which he identifies with an absence of totalization; Jameson's work moves toward a complex endorsement of postmodernism as a source of resistance to the complicitous relation to imperialism and fascism he locates in Modernism.

It's not my concern here to enter into the cogency of these critiques of modernism and modernity: Lyotard's critique of grand narratives could obviously be employed in a critique of Jameson's grand narrative, for surely Jameson is guilty of a rather totalizing vision; but Lyotard's critique could just as easily be turned back on his own work. The Ezra Pound who borrowed the slogan "make it new" from an inscription found on a Chinese bathtub thirty-five hundred years ago was obviously not blind to the dialectical dependence on tradition found in modernism, so de Man's positioning of the modernists as blind to their own situation, leaving de Man to supply us with the needed insight, is obviously blind itself in important respects. But to the extent that points such as these were made during the 1970s and early 1980s, they had little effect in the critical debate. The consequence was not just the legitimation of a postmodern, poststructuralist current of literary theory; it was also the delegitimation of interest in modernist literature. Moreover, it was the delegitimation that enabled the legitimation. Modernist literature remained a possible topic of inquiry, but, as in Jameson's work, primarily as the subject of critique. A more interesting straw in the wind is that by and large even theorists who had earlier made much of their reputation working on modernist material—J. Hillis Miller comes to mind here—retreated from a detailed engagement with this body of work. A central part of that delegitimation was the modernist=fascist equation adumbrated by Lyotard and established by Jameson. Following on Jameson's work, the politics of modernism became a central issue, probably the central issue in modernist studies, and though defenses of such writers as Yeats and Pound on older lines were still published, the dominant tone of work on these writers was to see them as deeply engaged with fascist themes and politics. Since I have contributed to this, let me say quickly that in large measure this critical movement is right. My aim is not to dispute the existence of a connection between modernism and fascism; it is to think about where that connection leaves us. For de Man, for Lyotard, for Jameson, it leaves us, today, the postmodern, the poststructuralist safely removed from any association with fascism because we have developed a firm critique of modernism/fascism that clearly positions us on the far side. Unfortunately, as events of the last decade have revealed, it isn't so easy.

The Delegitimation of Postmodernism

In the late 1980s, the firm and accepted dominance of poststructuralist perspectives on the critical horizon was shaken by a series of scandals or "affairs," involving precisely the revelation of direct connections between the poststructuralist theorizing that had delegitimated modernism as fascist and the very forces and history of fascism it had sought to set itself apart from. In the United States, the central issue, of course, was the Paul de Man affair: the revelation after his death that de Man had written extensively for a number of collaborationist newspapers in occupied Belgium from 1940 to 1943 and that some of what he had written was explicitly pro-Nazi and anti-Semitic, while much of the rest can be read as assenting in—indeed collaborating with—the Nazi hegemony over Europe. A lot of ink has been spilled over the de

Man affair, and I've spilled a fair amount myself, so I won't delve back into this in detail here.[7]

But let me summarize what I see as the net effects of the de Man affair. The obvious short-term effect was that it worked to delegitimate deconstruction as the dominant mode of theorizing in favor of more historicist forms of poststructuralism. Put most crudely, if de Man and Derrida were the European imports of choice in 1985, Foucault, Althusser, Bourdieu, and others have proved decisively more influential in the development of what I have come to call the new thematics, the race-class-gender-sexual orientation criticism dominant today. More locally, but in keeping with this turn toward a more historical criticism, everyone committed to theory—put cynically, everyone who felt the need to have a position on the de Man question—began learning a good deal more than we had before about the political and intellectual origins of the poststructuralist theory we had taken for granted. Wars and revolutions may or may not, as de Man insisted, appear in the guise of texts, but what many of us began to ask was a different question: that is, what wars and revolutions were behind the texts we had taken for granted. This way of putting it, of course, assumes the inside-outside/text-context distinction textualist critics such as de Man had argued was naive; but that insistence, the insistence on de Man's part that "investigations into the actual historical existence of writers was a waste of time,"[8] of course looked rather different after the revelations about de Man. De Man had viewed the modernist attempt to escape history as naive and destined to fail, but after the revelations his own textualist insistence looked inevitably like an attempt to evade history, specifically his own history. The two don't seem in a relation of blindness and insight here; de Man was presumably not blind to his own situation, but it is hard to avoid the conclusion that he worked hard to blind others to it. Everyone who quoted de Man's critique of historical/contextual/biographical criticism so reverently over the last generation can therefore be criticized for precisely the same kind of blindness de Man accused modernism of.

The de Man affair, no matter how important in the psychic economy of American theorists of my generation, is ultimately minor compared to the parallel revelations about Heidegger that caused a parallel furor, focused in France, also in the late 1980s.[9] The difference in importance comes from two things. First, de Man, no matter how influential among American theorists, is not ultimately a figure of decisive importance in the history of twentieth-century thought; Heidegger is. More importantly, Heidegger's influence cuts a much greater swath across the contemporary spectrum than de Man's: if associating de Man with fascism allows non-deconstructive varieties of poststructuralism to take center stage, allows Foucault and Althusser to assume the mantle of master thinkers in place of de Man and Derrida, associating Heidegger with fascism does much more than that, since Heidegger has been a central influence on all these figures. The second point is that de Man, whatever one says about the wartime writings, was not a figure of any decisive importance in the history of fascism; Heidegger was. No one can sensibly argue that Paul de Man's 170 articles for *Le Soir* constituted a major historical event, but the role Heidegger played as Rector of Freiburg University did. A great deal more is at stake, therefore, when we turn to the question of Heidegger's relation to fascism, or more properly to Nazism, which is one reason why a veritable who's who of French intellectuals wrote not just articles, but whole books about Heidegger's relation to Nazism. The question at stake was fundamentally whether George Steiner was right in his epigram that poststructuralism represented the intellectual continuation of the German occupation of France.

The defenses of de Man and Heidegger, despite the differences in their situations, have essentially the same structure. There are two basic defenses: he wasn't really a fascist, and he wasn't always a fascist. The first aims at constructing a heterodox fascist in place of an orthodox one. So in the case of de Man, much has been made of his citation of Charles Peguy, his mention of Kafka, ironically his allusions to modern and modernist culture; in the case of Heidegger, of his own private sense of Nazism as opposed to the public sense. These are fairly flimsy defenses, since as I have argued in the case of de Man the very identification of a kind of modernism with a kind of fascism (largely Italian rather than German in orientation) allows us to read those references very differently and not as covertly antifascist.[10] In the case of Heidegger, it seems obvious enough from the biographical evidence gathered by Ott and Farias and others that whatever his private sense of Nazism, Heidegger was comfortable enough with the public sense that the distinction seems largely specious.[11]

The more serious point is the argument from temporal development: if indeed Heidegger's thought, as he himself argues, was marked by a great turning or *Kehre*, does that mean that the turn was away from that aspect of his thought that led him to support Nazism? The stakes here are enormous. For no one can question that in important respects all poststructuralist thought comes out of "French Heidegger," that starting with the "Letter on Humanism," Heidegger's influence on French thought was profound and that central themes of poststructuralism can be traced back to Heideggerean antihumanism.[12] This is not in dispute. Nor is it seriously in dispute that Heidegger's actions in the 1930s came from a deep philosophical commitment to Nazism. So the link in the chain that runs from fascism to Heidegger is basically conceded, as is the link in the chain that runs from Heidegger to poststructuralism. This would seem to make the case that "post-modern" thought is as deeply implicated in fascism as "modern" thought, except that the direct links are to different moments in Heidegger's life—to the 1930s on one side and to the postwar era on the other. The link in the chain that is under dispute is therefore the link between Heidegger and Heidegger. Is there a line of continuity between the postwar writing that was so influential and the pre- or interwar actions that were so disastrous? Is the *Kehre* a turn away from those actions, in which case the demarcation between the modern/fascist and the postmodern survives, or does talk of a turn not change the fundamental continuity between Heidegger the fascist and Heidegger the influence on the French, in which case the demarcation crumbles?

The theories of de Man and Derrida suggest, of course, that there can be no "fact of the matter" about this, that the detailed investigation into the chronology of Heidegger's publications and actions, the frenzied interpretive disputes over the key sentences in Heidegger's postwar writings about Nazi Germany, cannot obscure the fact that ultimately, our answer to this question will be less a matter of fact than a matter of narrative, of the kind of story we choose to tell. Furthermore, Derrida's work on contextualization and recontextualization would tell us that to have begun to ask questions such as these is in a sense to have answered them already. For if Derrida has taught us anything, it is that it is in the assignment of context that one assigns meaning. Poststructuralism controlled the terms in which it was represented and contextualized for a long time, controlled at the very least the dichotomizing of fascism (which it associated with modernism) as one thing, and poststructuralism as something else. No matter what conclusions one comes to about the question of the connection between contemporary "post" thought and the 1919–1945 era, the de Man and Heidegger controversies, simply because they pose the question, break the assumption that there can be no connection.

This hasn't stopped strenuous efforts by virtually every living figure in the poststructuralist pantheon, including Derrida, to prevent such a connection from being made. Of these, the most revealing because the most desperate is Philippe Lacoue-Labarthe's in *Heidegger, Art and Politics*; his argument is of particular interest because it engages the key issues more clearly than Derrida does in *Of Spirit* or Lyotard does in *Heidegger and "the jews"*.[13] In keeping with his French sense of Heidegger's work, Lacoue-Labarthe sees the "Letter on Humanism" as the key text of the post-turn phase. Moreover, he identifies with its critique of humanism, which everywhere resounds in French poststructuralist thought, from the respective perorations of Derrida's "The Ends of Man" to Foucault's *The Order of Things*.[14] It is in his critique of humanism that Heidegger escapes the Western philosophical tradition, moving to a properly "post-philosophical" position Lacoue-Labarthe endorses. This is also a turn away from Nazism in Lacoue-Labarthe's analysis, and this enables Lacoue-Labarthe to identify the post-positions as antifascist and to present the Fascist position as centrally implicated in the tradition of Western culture. Lacoue-Labarthe does this by identifying Nazism with humanism: "Nazism is a humanism insofar as it rests upon a determination of *humanitas* which is, in its view, more powerful—that is, more effective—than any other" (95). In my view, the best analysis of this astonishing passage comes from Richard Wolin, who writes appositely:

> The thought that deconstruction cannot think is that it is not humanism per se, but instead antihumanism in the guise of fascism, that has in our century led European civilization to the edge of the abyss. To contemplate this thought is structurally inadmissable since it risks the suggestion that fascism and deconstruction, *qua* variants of antihumanism, might secretly share certain value orientations; value orientations that pertain to the systematic denigration of "man," reason, and kindred liberal shibboleths.[15]

The only amendment I would make to Wolin's account here is that after the de Man and Heidegger controversies, the fact that certain value orientations are shared is no longer a secret.

I've written elsewhere that deconstruction as a movement did itself more damage in its attempt to deny de Man's fascism than the actual historical facts about de Man themselves could ever have done, and it seems to me possible to draw the same conclusion from the Heidegger wars. With friends like Lacoue-Labarthe, who needs enemies? The rhetorical desperation of Lacoue-Labarthe's prose, the fierce insistence that there can be no connection between a body of thought and a set of historical realities, is remarkable, and it shows not just what is at stake here but also what has to be denied. I don't wish to make a detailed excursion into the thickets of Heideggeran exegesis here, but it seems to me that the link in the chain between Heidegger and Heidegger is at least as strong as that between Nazism and Heidegger, or that between the Heidegger of the "Letter on Humanism" and the French Heideggereans who now so nervously and so confusedly defend him (or, rather, defend their borrowings from him). The net effect of the controversies over the last decade therefore has been twofold, in my judgment: first, to lay open to inspection the ways in which a fascist intellectual legacy has continued to be a major influence on the most contemporary and supposedly antifascist thought of our time; and second, in turn to open the possibility of a comparable delegitimation of poststructuralist thought comparable to the delegitimation of modernist thought accomplished by poststructuralism.

Let me say further that both delegitimations seem to be largely correct, if often rhetorically excessive in the way parricides have to be. If there is an uncanny resemblance between the totalizing grand narrative of modernity and the grand narrative of fascism, there is nevertheless also an uncanny resemblance between the themes of poststructuralism, the postmodern in Lyotard's vocabulary, and the imaginative themes of fascism: it is fascism as well as poststructuralism that urges us to move beyond the individualism and subjectivism of the humanist tradition, to see human beings as subjects produced by a larger collectivity; and it was central to the fascist project that there be no resistance to this process of "social construction." Fortunately, there was. Furthermore, it is fascism as well as poststructuralism that tells us that there is no truth, but rather that truth has to be relativized to the occasion and to the speaker. It is fascism as well as poststructuralism that celebrates the dissolution of the human individual into his or her collectivity. So if in important respects the postmodern critique of the modern has succeeded in associating the modern with the fascist, where it succeeded for a moment (but only for a moment) is in convincing us that the postmodern is beyond all these things, without substantial commerce with them. Postmodern theory is at least as implicated with fascism as modernist art is.

Where does this leave us? Those two things taken together leave us in an interesting impasse. For I take it for granted that the varieties of thought associated with the various "posts" represent the only serious challenge to modernist thought and art to have arisen in our century. If the 1908–39 period was the period of modernist art, the postwar period has been the period of postmodernist theory. I think little in the art identified as "postmodern" will withstand serious scrutiny and is likely to pass the test of time, but the work associated with poststructuralist thought has comparably provided the center of what serious culture is being created in Europe and America today—or, to put this slightly differently, what has been created in my lifetime.

The impasse I think we are in is summarized in my title: if the two major movements of twentieth-century culture are deeply compatible with and implicated in fascism, we live in a culture that can be described more accurately as postfascist than as post-anything else. The most vital new and innovative currents of European culture in this century have been currents associated not with Marxism or communism or with the struggle against fascism, but with fascism itself. The fact that this is an uncomfortable realization doesn't change this historical reality, nor is our resistance to this realization evidence of anything other than why we need to resist this realization. Moreover, it seems to me that our collective denial, our insistence on remaining in a state of illusion, is itself a problem, since it blocks our ability to confront our collective relation to fascism. In this country today, the themes of political discourse are moving steadily in a fascist direction. Let me cite just a few examples: the obsession with immigrants and racial others who are supposedly the cause of our problems; the obsession with sexual decadence; the idealization of the family as an antidote to both the evil without represented by immigrants and the evil within represented by homosexuality; and finally, the faith in a leader with a nonpolitical background who can somehow save us from our own decayed democratic procedures. The fact that Colin Powell declined to play the role of Duce in the last presidential election means that we may not be as close to the equivalent of 1922 or 1933 as we might have feared, but our collective faith in a figure like Powell is a deeply disturbing sign. Heidegger thought only a God could save us; thinking that a general can is a position more typical of a fascist political thematics. Furthermore, let us imagine a Rip Van Winkle who fell asleep in, say, August 1941 waking up today to find the British Empire gone, the Soviet Union dissolved into many different countries and communism discredited in virtually all of them, Europe moving toward unification under German hegemony, Italy with at least its vibrant north more prosperous than France or Britain, Japan the second largest economy in the world with what looks remarkably like an East Asia Co-Prosperity Sphere, and the United States quite content with all of these developments. Who would this Rip think had won the war? And what would he assume the role of the United States had been in the war?

Of course, I will freely admit more than a degree of overstatement in the previous paragraph, if you will grant in turn that there is a grain of truth in it. Commentators on the French scene have long argued that it was the myth of the resistance, or rather the myth that the resistance constituted the French response to the Germans, that kept the French for so long from seeing their own role in the war steadily and seeing it whole. I think there has been a comparable collective amnesia on the part of a broad range of intellectuals. I am not saying that we have been blind to our actual complicity with fascism; anyone born after 1945, as I was and I expect most of my readers were, is in any case safely out of that one. What we have been blind to is fascism's continuing complicity with us, to the impact it had on figures who continue to have an impact on us. After what I have called the delegitimation of modernism and the more recent beginning of a delegitimation of postmodernism, it seems to me that the issue of our commerce with fascism, of what I am calling the "postfascist" nature of our culture, is on the table in a way that means we can no longer evade the question. How we respond to this is another question, one too large for me to tackle here. Just as modernism is associated with fascism but not indissolubly so, so that that central modernist James Joyce not only escapes the fascist commitments of his fellow modernists but came up with the most compelling analysis—in *Ulysses*, twenty years before the Holocaust—of how cultural nationalism wes leading inexorably to anti-Semitism and fascism, so too there are comparable discriminations and dissociations to be made in terms of postmodern culture. This will be easier to see once the polemics of the past few years are behind us, and what this suggests is that one task in the coming years is not to reject modernism or postmodernism in toto but to sift and analyze, to realize that a critical analysis of the movements we have taken for granted is an urgent necessity.

Yet another move opens on the horizon, it seems to me. Though I have argued for modernist art and postmodern theory as the two most vital contributions to culture coming from Europe over the last century, I don't think 1908 to 1939 was the "age of modernism" or that the contemporary era is the "age of postmodernism" in the totalizing way Jameson implies. Lyotard's suspicion of grand narratives may be well taken here. An era is an abstraction after all, and a culture is a palimpsest made up of many different strands that date from different eras. It's common enough to lament our students' ignorance of history, of anything dating from before their births, which seem increasingly— indeed, preposterously—recent to me. But we need to think about some of the ways we may have contributed to that amnesia: this has been the era of theory, and most theorists consider 1960 the dark ages and 1900 prehistory in just the way our students do. In keeping with this, attention paid to women's literature, to gay and lesbian writing, to writing by minorities and writing from the postcolonial world, however valuable that attention might be as an antidote to previous neglect, is attention largely focused on contemporary literature, on the concerns of the present.[16] In this context, a little delegitimation of modern and contemporary culture may not in itself be a bad thing. Scholars of literature have traditionally conceived of their function as analogous to conservators and curators of art, concerned with preserving a heritage of the past for future generations to learn from. As we have shifted our focus from scholarship to theory, we have comparably moved away from the role of conservators, seeing that precisely as too conservative. Now that the politics of theory has been made somewhat more problematic, the door may be open to the possibility of finding a renewed value for that kind of conservation and cultural transmission. The old demands respect because it is old: this is a fundamental principle of human ethics and I think should be a more explicit part of our attitude toward culture as well. As a profession, we have relentlessly modernized, and it is not clear to me that this has been all to the good.

Moreover, there seems to me one perfectly good inheritance from the past that I think intellectuals in this country have done a great deal to weaken. I reveal my own political colors here, I suppose, when I say that Lyotard's posture of "incredulity" toward the grand narrative of "emancipation" seems to me bizarre, and clearly one of the places where the postmodern and the fascist are most closely aligned. I understand the problems involved with imposing grand narratives on others, the problem with manufacturing consensus. But these seem to me problems with the "grand" part of any grand narrative, not with the "narrative" part. If I understand it correctly, Lyotard's argument is not that we can dispense with narratives that structure our lives; it is that we need to be very careful about how those narratives begin to structure others without their full consent. But if we need a narrative, we cannot just spend all our time "waging war on totality"; we had better also spend some time thinking which "petit récit" we might want to live by. Though not wishing to terrorize you into a forced consensus, and in any case not having the power to do so, I want to suggest that intellectuals in the English-speaking world have our own traditions, which may sustain narratives we may indeed wish to endorse rather than maintain a critical stance toward, whether they be petite or grand. The liberal narrative of emancipation, based on a notion of a substantial self capable of making decisions autonomously and of escaping social determination, is so old-fashioned that I think it escapes what we might call the delegitimation crisis posed by the problems of a postfascist culture. It's so old-fashioned that we might bring it out of the closet and see if it might be an improvement on what we have been wearing. We might slouch toward Charlottesville instead of Berlin; at least we'd have a shorter walk.

Notes

1. Hugh Kenner, "The Making of the Modernist Canon," in *Canons*, ed. Robert von Hallberg (Chicago: University of Chicago Press, 1984), 363–75.

2. Paul de Man, *Blindness and Insight: Essays in the Rhetoric of Contemporary Criticism*, 2d ed. (Minneapolis: University of Minnesota Press, 1983), 161.

3. Habermas's defense of modernity is to be found in a number of his works, perhaps most notably in *The Philosophical Discourse of Modernity*. Recently, Louis Dupre's *Passage to Modernity: An Essay in the Hermeneutics of Nature and Culture* (New Haven CT: Yale University Press, 1993) has argued that the modernity/postmodernity debate looks different once one relocates the beginning of modernity—not in the eighteenth century, but in the fourteenth!

4. Jean-François Lyotard, *The Postmodern Condition: A Report on Knowledge*, trans. Geoff Bennington and Brian Massumi (Minneapolis: University of Minnesota Press, 1984), 38.

5. Works by Jameson drawn on in what follows include *Fables of Aggression: Wyndham Lewis, the Modernist as Fascist* (Berkeley: University of California Press, 1979); "Modernism and Imperialism," in *Nationalism, Colonialism, and Literature* (Minneapolis: University of Minnesota Press, 1990); and *Postmodernism; or, The Cultural Logic of Late Capitalism* (Durham NC: Duke University Press, 1991).

6. Reed Way Dasenbrock, "Fredric Jameson and the Dilemmas of Late Marxism," *Raritan* 11, no. 3 (winter 1992): 117–30.

7. My own writing on the affair can be found in Reed Way Dasenbrock, "Paul de Man: The Modernist as Fascist," in Golsan, *Fascism, Aesthetics, and Culture*, 229–41; and "Reading Demanians Reading de Man," *South Central Review* 11, no. 1 (spring 1994): 23–43. The central text in the controversy is *Responses: On Paul de Man's Wartime Journalism*, eds. Werner Hamacher, Neil Hertz, and Thomas Keenan (Lincoln: University of Nebraska Press, 1989).

8. De Man, *Blindness and Insight*, 35.

9. The proximate cause of the "Heidegger wars" in France was the publication in 1987 of Victor Farias's *Heidegger et le Nazisme* (Paris: Verdier, 1987); see Richard Wolin's "French Heidegger Wars," reprinted in *Labyrinths: Explorations in the Critical History of Ideas* (Amherst: University of Massachusetts Press, 1995), 142–61.

10. See Dasenbrock, "Paul de Man: The Modernist as Fascist."

11. Many of the important primary and secondary documents are included in Wolin, ed., *The Heidegger Controversy*; the most thorough single treatment of Heidegger's political involvements is probably Hugo Ott, *Martin Heidegger: A Political Life*, trans. Allan Blunden (New York: Basic Books, 1993).

12. Richard Wolin again has given us perhaps the best account of this in "Antihumanism in the Discourse of French Postwar Theory," in *Labyrinths*, 175–209.

13. Philippe Lacoue-Labarthe, *Heidegger, Art and Politics* (Oxford: Basil Blackwell, 1990); Jacques Derrida, *Of Spirit: Heidegger and the Question*, trans. Geoffrey Bennington and Rachel Bowlby (Chicago: University of Chicago Press, 1989); and Lyotard, *Heidegger and "the jews"*.

14. Jacques Derrida, "The Ends of Man," in *Margins of Philosophy*, trans. Alan Bass (Chicago: University of Chicago Press, 1982), 109–36; Michel Foucault, *The Order of Things: An Archaeology of the Human Sciences*, trans. Alan Sheridan (1970; New York: Vintage, 1973).

15. Richard Wolin, "Deconstruction at Auschwitz: Heidegger, de Man, and the New Revisionism," *South Central Review* 11, no. 1 (spring 1994): 19.

16. This point has been made by John Guillory in *Cultural Capital: The Problem of Literary Canon Formation* (Chicago: University of Chicago Press, 1993).

Thomas Sheehan

Friendly Fascism: Business as Usual in America's Backyard

I tremble for my country when I reflect that God is just. *Thomas Jefferson*

November, 1989. The war in El Salvador—America's longest and most expensive military engagement since Vietnam—had been dragging on for nine years.[1]

For Salvadorans the devastation was catastrophic. By the end of the war (January 1992) more than seventy-five thousand Salvadoran citizens—1.5 percent of the country's population—would be dead from the conflict, the majority murdered by right-wing death squads. The proportional equivalent within the United States would be 3.75 million American citizens dead: the combined populations of San Francisco, Dallas, Denver, St. Louis, Atlanta, and Washington DC. Of those cities, the last four would have had their entire populations wiped out by death squads.[2]

By fall 1989 it was the virtually unanimous opinion of the U.S. media that democracy had been restored to El Salvador. El Salvador had held five elections, sponsored and overseen by the United States and certified by the American media as free and fair. But the slaughter continued. Meanwhile, negotiations between Salvador's right-wing government and the Farabundo Martí National Liberation Front (FMLN) were dragging on. Everyone in El Salvador was weary of the war, most Americans had forgotten about it, and the U.S. Congress seemed to have lost all interest.

Then it happened.

Saturday, 11 November 1989, 8:00 P.M.: While Salvador's elite dined and danced at the lush El Camino Real Hotel—their bulletproof Jeeps outside and their armed guards nearby—suddenly the guerrillas were everywhere. Not out in the countryside where you usually found them—Chalatenango, Guazapa, Morazán—but all over the capital city, attacking the headquarters of the First Infantry Brigade, mortaring the

National Guard Headquarters, attacking the Presidential Palace and even the private home of Salvador's president, Alfredo Cristiani.

And they were not just attacking government positions; they were also holding large and heavily populated barrios in the northern and eastern sections of the capital city: Mejicanos, Zacamil, and Soyapango. Within hours up to three thousand guerrillas were deeply entrenched in nearly a third of San Salvador and were attacking the army in middle-class neighborhoods in the south and west of the city.[3]

The army, caught off guard and barely holding its own, declared a state of siege. As FMLN attacks continued through the weekend with no sign of abating, the chief of staff of El Salvador's High Command, Col. René Emilio Ponce, feared the game might be up. It was time for extraordinary measures.

On Monday, 13 November, Colonel Ponce, with the permission of President Cristiani, ordered soldiers of the Atlacatl Battalion, trained by U.S. Green Berets, to enter the campus of the Jesuit university, the University of Central America (UCA), in the southwest section of the capital city. Their mission was supposedly to search the Jesuits' residence for weapons and subversive material.[4]

Since the late 1970s the Jesuit university had been the target of frequent bombings and machine-gun attacks from right-wing groups. It was also the object of verbal attacks from the military. On 20 April 1989, the vice minister of defense, Col. Juan Orlando Zepeda, called the UCA "a refuge for terrorist leaders, where strategies are mapped out for attacks against Salvadorans."[5] Col. Inocente Montano, vice minister for public security, had also accused the Jesuits of being guerrilla leaders, if for no other reason than that Father Ignacio Ellacuría, the president of the university, was actively working for a negotiated solution to the nine-year conflict. When the 11 November offensive began, the army forced all Salvadoran radio stations to suspend their own broadcasting and to carry only the army's signal. The army then opened its channel to unnamed callers who voiced violent accusations against Ellacuría and even demands for his death.[6]

Born in Spain in 1930, Ellacuría had studied with the most famous Catholic theologian of the century, Karl Rahner, and had received his doctorate in philosophy under the renowned Spanish thinker Xavier Zubiri. He joined the UCA in the 1960s and became chairman of the philosophy department. From November 1979 on, he served as the UCA's president.[7]

Those were the years of growing repression in El Salvador, and Ellacuría was uncompromising in his denunciations of government and army injustices. Those were also the years when liberation theology was having its strongest effect in Latin America, and Ellacuría was one of its most powerful voices. None of this was lost on the U.S. State Department or the government of El Salvador.

The Atlacatl Battalion's search of the Jesuit living quarters on Monday, 13 November, turned up nothing subversive, nor was that its purpose. Rather, the soldiers took careful note of where each priest slept, and they positively identified the main object of the search, Ignacio Ellacuría, who had just returned from a trip to Europe. Ellacuría invited them to return the next day to look further, but they did not. Their search of the residence had nothing to do with searching for arms. It was reconnaissance for a mission they would carry out two days later.[8]

Intense fighting continued in the capital city, and by late Wednesday, 15 November, the situation was critical. Many Salvadoran military leaders were close to panic, and one American advisor compared the situation to the fall of Saigon.[9] At 6:30 P.M. Colonel Ponce and the High Command met at army headquarters with two dozen high-ranking officers to plan urgent strategy. The High Command decided to bomb guerrilla-held neighborhoods and attack them with tanks. They also decided to eliminate all known or presumed leftists and rebel sympathizers in sections of San Salvador still under army control—labor leaders, popular organizers, virtually anyone they considered suspicious.

That included the Jesuits. Colonel Ponce ordered Col. Guillermo Benavides, the head of the Military Academy and the man responsible for security in the university area, to have Ignacio Ellacuría murdered and to leave no witnesses. Benavides was to send the Atlacatl unit that had searched the priests' living quarters on Monday.

Colonel Ponce called President Cristiani to High Command headquarters to brief him on the army's decision to take extraordinary measures. Cristiani would remain with the commanders at military headquarters from around 11:00 P.M. until 2:00 A.M.—that is, throughout the period when the Jesuits were being murdered less than a mile away. Some think the High Command informed him of that operation too. Cristiani denies it.[10]

Back in his office at the Military Academy, Colonel Benavides chose Lt. Ricardo Espinoza and 2d Lt. Gonzalo Guevara to see that the murders were carried out. Accompanying them and overseeing the job would be Benavides's close collaborator, Lt. Yusshy Mendoza.[11]

Espinoza hand-picked a group of elite Atlacatl commandos to do the job. Just three days earlier these men had been receiving special training from thirteen U.S. Green Berets at Sitio del Niño, outside the capital city. The course included instruction in high-tech nighttime operations. To help in their mission to kill the Jesuits the commandos took with them the night-vision goggles of their American trainers.[12]

As midnight passed, the commandos, forty-seven in all, gathered by the gate of the Military Academy. The first wave left the grounds in two Ford pick-up trucks and drove to an assembly point in a residential neighborhood outside the west gate of the university. Minutes later they were joined by the remainder of their group.

The plan was laid out. Three hundred soldiers from another group would surround the university. Then the commandos would enter the campus and regroup near the priests' residence. Of those, seven would have a direct role in getting the Jesuits. Lieutenant Mendoza made it clear the key assassin would be commando Oscar Amaya, nicknamed "The Hangman." To make it seem the FMLN had committed the crimes, Amaya would use an AK-47 captured from the guerrillas.

About 1:00 A.M. the designated group forced the lock on the gate and entered the campus. The moon was out, and not all of the commandos needed night-vision goggles. They regrouped in a parking lot opposite the priests' residence and then spread out to surround the two-story building. The seven handpicked men forced their way in, some by scaling a low wall that marked off the garden. They then made their way through the same corridors they had searched two days before and ordered the priests out of the building and into the garden behind.

Oscar Amaya, carrying the AK-47, and Antonio Avalos, armed with an American-made M-16, forced the five Jesuits to lie face down on the grass:

> Ignacio Ellacuría, president of the university, distinguished professor of philosophy, honorary doctorates from Santa Clara University (1982) and Loyola University of Chicago (1986);
> Ignacio Martín-Baró, vice president of the university, professor of sociology, Ph.D., University of Chicago (1979);
> Segundo Montes, professor of sociology, chairman of the university's human rights institute (IDHUCA), just back from a human rights conference in Washington DC;
> Amando López, professor of theology, former president of the Jesuit university in Nicaragua; and
> Juan Ramón Moreno, spiritual director and professor of theology.

Espinoza and Mendoza, the two lieutenants in charge of the operation, seemed uneasy. They had their orders, but they also wanted to maintain personal deniability. They held back so that underlings would take responsibility for doing the job. Mendoza even left the scene with the excuse of searching for more subversives in the Jesuits' kitchen. Espinoza, from whom the soldiers awaited the order to kill, hovered in the background by the gate to the priests' residence.

Amaya and Avalos also seemed to balk at doing what was expected. Espinoza called Avalos over and, with intentional vagueness, asked, "When are you going to get on with it?" Avalos returned to his position and told Amaya, "Let's get on with it."

A second of silence. Then he and Amaya blasted away at the priests' heads, splattering their brains over the lawn and up onto the wall of the house.[13]

The soldiers had been ordered to leave no witnesses. In a building adjacent to the Jesuit residence they had found the priests' housekeeper, Elba Ramos, with her sixteen-year-old daughter Celina huddled in her arms. Commando Tomás Zarpate stood guard over them in their room. When he heard the blasts of fire outside, he shot them both until (in his own words) "they no longer groaned."[14]

At that point a sixth Jesuit, the frail, seventy-one-year-old Father Joaquín López y López, emerged into the garden, saw his murdered companions on the grass, and turned to go back in, telling the soldiers not to kill him. One of them shot him in the back and he fell into a room. Commando Angel Pérez decided to inspect the room. As he stepped over the bloodsoaked body, he felt Father López's feeble hand grope at his feet. Pérez stepped back and shot him four times.

Inside the building other soldiers were trashing the priests' offices, smashing windows, burning books, scattering documents. One of them found a briefcase containing five thousand dollars, a cash award for the UCA that Father Ellacuría had just brought back from Europe. The soldiers stole it.

Their job done, the commandos were leaving the scene when they heard moans from inside one of the rooms. It was the death rattles of Elba and Celina Ramos. The soldiers hesitated. They knew the women would soon die, but they had been ordered to leave no witnesses. They radioed the High Command and asked what to do. A direct order—from Colonel Zepeda, vice minister of defense, according to many—came back over the radio: *"Remátenlas"* (Finish them off). Commando José Sierra was sent back in. He found the two women lying in a pool of blood, still groaning. He finished them off.

The eight bodies were found at dawn. The High Command immediately charged the murders to the FMLN.

Later that afternoon, a sound truck from the Salvadoran Army's First Infantry Brigade passed in front of the offices of the archdiocese of San Salvador, proclaiming in Spanish, "Ellacuría and Martín-Baró are finished. We are going to continue killing Communists."[15]

Can one offer a definition of fascism that fits the topic of America's 1981–91 war in El Salvador? Or is one constrained to invoke, analogously, Justice Potter Stewart's dictum about hard-core pornography: "I can't define it, but I know it when I see it"?[16]

In the end we may be persuaded that our Central American War of 1981–91 was not an exercise in fascism *stricte dicta*—for surely the United States is not a fascist country, and neither the Reagan nor the Bush administration was a fascist regime. But if America's war in El Salvador was not an exercise in fascism, it will just have to do until the real thing comes along.[17]

This chapter is less about El Salvador than it is about the United States's role in that country. It is less about the murder of Ignacio Ellacuría and his companions than about what those murders stand for.

How could Ellacuría, this "incandescent intellectual of world reputation,"[18] who was regularly consulted by the U.S. embassy in El Salvador, who was a known and respected presence in the corridors of the U.S. Senate and House of Representatives, whose extensive writings on the Salvadoran situation were read and appreciated both in the State Department and the CIA—how could he and the best of his university faculty be murdered in cold blood by elite commandos armed and outfitted by the United States and trained by U.S. Special Forces? But weren't those commandos simply carrying out the orders of their superior officers, who themselves had been trained at Fort Benning, Georgia, and who served with the support and blessings of the U.S. embassy, the State Department, and the Pentagon?

And after the crime, how could the responsibility for the deaths of Ellacuría and his companions be covered up for months, and the perpetrators shielded, all with the knowledge and cooperation of the staff of the U.S. embassy and the U.S. Military Group in El Salvador?[19]

Perhaps the murder of Ignacio Ellacuría and his seven companions can tell us something of what the United States was about in the 1980s (the way the murder of Giacomo Matteotti laid bare what Italy was about in the 1920s): how the United States aided and abetted a systematically murderous Salvadoran regime, paid its bills, trained its killers, protected its criminals, covered its tracks, and, when it no longer needed that sorry country, abandoned it to its own fate.

The war in El Salvador was our war, and its dead are our dead, since with or without our consent, we Americans financed that bloody conflict, bankrolling the army and government of El Salvador to the tune of $6 billion (twice the cost of the Reagan-Bush adventure in Afghanistan[20]), training, arming, and advising not only El Salvador's regular soldiers but also the members of its paramilitary and security forces—

many of whom in fact operated as members of death squads—and even training them in how to torture.[21]

And it was our war because we not only paid for it, but also micromanaged its logistics. El Salvador's President Duarte complained about that very matter in an extended interview published in *Playboy* in 1984.

PLAYBOY: Do the American military advisers also tell you how to run the war?
DUARTE: This is the problem, no? The root of this problem is that the aid is given under such conditions that its use is really decided by the Americans and not by us. Decisions like how many planes or helicopters we buy, how we spend our money, how many trucks we need, how many bullets and of what caliber, how many pairs of boots and where our priorities should be—all of that. . . . And all the money is spent over there [in the United States]. We never see a penny of it, because everything arrives here already paid for.[22]

By calling this "our war" I refer not just to the overt conflict in El Salvador, but also to the secret war waged here at home against American citizens who opposed the Reagan administration's policies. The war at home included a nationwide and well-documented program of break-ins, FBI surveillance, and wiretaps carried out against groups and private individuals who exercised their First Amendment rights by protesting the financing and direction of the Central American war. I shall return to this later.

During the 1980s, Central America in general and El Salvador and Nicaragua in particular were a major focus of President Reagan's foreign policy. But the roots of this cathexis on Central America go back at least as far as President John F. Kennedy, who seemed to have discovered the cause of backwardness in the area. "Communism," he declared, "is the chief obstacle to economic development in the Central American region."[23]

To set things right, Kennedy in 1963 organized and chaired a summit of six Central American countries in Costa Rica, an event Allan Nairn, writing in 1984, described as the beginning of "a basic, bipartisan, institutional commitment on the part of six American Administrations—a commitment to guard the Salvadoran regime against the prospect that its people might organize in ways unfriendly to that regime or to the United States."[24]

The Costa Rican summit, which culminated in the "Declaration of San José" (19 March 1963), led to a series of subsequent meetings at which the minister of the interior of each of the Central American republics committed his country to setting up and coordinating "national security" programs. With the help of the CIA and AID, and under the direction of the U.S. State Department, each country would eventually reorganize its police and security forces to smoke out and eliminate people loosely defined as "subversives." In that regard, the crucial passage in the "Declaration of San José" states: "[T]he Presidents declare that in order to carry out their programs for social and economic betterment, it is essential to reinforce the measures to meet subversive aggression originating in the focal points of Communist agitation which Soviet imperialism may maintain in Cuba or in any other place in America."[25]

In El Salvador, an important product of that commitment was ORDEN (Organización Democrática Nacionalista) and ANSESAL (Agencía Nacional de Seguridad Salvadoreña), the combined intelligence network and death squad operation the United States began organizing there in the 1960s.[26] To lead ORDEN, the U.S. turned to the director of El Salvador's feared National Guard, Col. José Alberto Medrano, whom Jose Napoleón Duarte, the president of El Salvador from 1984 to 1988, would call "the father of the Death Squads, the chief assassin of them all."[27]

In 1983 Medrano acknowledged that his organization was the brainchild of the United States. ORDEN and ANSESAL, he said, "grew out of the State Department, the CIA, and the Green Berets during the time of Kennedy. We created these specialized agencies to fight the plans and actions of international Communism."[28]

The organization and training of the organization was supervised by Green Beret Col. Arthur Simons, who at the time was head of the 8th Special Forces Group in Panama. Colonel Simon had earlier served in Laos as a Special Forces commander and then at Fort Bragg as chief of staff at the Army Special Warfare Center. Simon sent Green Berets to El Salvador to train a team of Salvadoran commandos, including Col. Domingo Monterrosa, the man who would later be held responsible for the most horrible crime of the war, the 1981 massacre at El Mozote.

According to Amnesty International, the purpose of ORDEN was "to use clandestine terror against government opponents."[29] The U.S. embassy in El Salvador acknowledged the charges in a now declassified document dated 2 April 1979:

It has also been alleged that elements of ORDEN, either in conjunction with legally constituted security forces or acting on their own initiative, have taken violent, repressive actions against the church, campesino, and labor groups in the countryside.

According to Amnesty International findings, ORDEN was responsible for many of the most brutal human rights violations of the Molina period [Col. Arturo Molina, president 1972–77]—e.g., unexplained disappearances, assassinations of Catholic priests, murder of political opposition members, and beatings and intimidations at the polling places of voters seeking to cast a ballot for opposition parties.[30]

The cable also admitted the accuracy of the charges. However, it glossed over the issue with exquisite delicacy, referring to death squad operations simply as "surreptitious action" and expressing no particular concern about the matter: "Obviously the military government perceives a threat from a variety of groups and has undoubtedly tried on occasion to suppress such groups through surreptitious action. ORDEN forces have probably been used for this purpose in the past and may be utilized in certain instances again."[31]

According to its own self-description, ORDEN's goal was to ferret out suspected Communists among Salvador's rural poor. As Medrano put it, "You discover the Communist by the way he talks. Generally, he speaks against Yankee imperialism, he speaks against the oligarchy, he speaks against military men. We can spot them easily."[32] President Ford's ambassador to El Salvador, Ignacio E. Lozano Jr., explained this policy of discovering "Communists" everywhere: "I suppose to a large extent it is our own fault, because we in the United States made such a big thing about Communism as a real threat to Latin America for such a long period. If you are against [the ruling powers], or if you disapprove of what they are doing, they label you a Communist."[33]

ORDEN's central office, located within El Salvador's presidential palace, was staffed by eighty analysts whose job was to study reports from the countryside and pass them on to ANSESAL—with predictably lethal results. As former U.S. Ambassador to El Salvador Raul H. Castro revealed, the murders of suspected Communists were usually carried out by ORDEN death squads using the name "Mano Blanco" ("White Hand"). Updating the procedure into the 1980s, Colonel Medrano acknowledged, "In this revolutionary war, the enemy comes from our people. They don't have the rights of Geneva. They are traitors to the country. What can the troops do? When they find them, they kill them."[34]

ORDEN and its cognate paramilitary and military groups in El Salvador were little different from other death squads that functioned with U.S. supervision throughout Central America. In Honduras, for example, death squad operations were carried out by Army Battalion 3-16, commanded by Gen. Luis Alonso Discua Elvir with the support and supervision of CIA operatives. Battalion 3-16 has been charged with the torture and murder of hundreds of Hondurans during the 1980s when the United States used Honduras as the staging ground for its contra war against Nicaragua. More than twenty-five clandestine cemeteries, filled with the Battalion's victims, have since been discovered in that country. As the *New York Times* has reported, "Members of Battalion 3-16, including [General] Discua, got support and training from the American military and from the Central Intelligence Agency, which also paid officers as informants."[35]

Discua, having successfully defied arrest warrants for human rights abuses in his own country, has since been appointed to Honduras's diplomatic corps at the United Nations in New York City.

By 1979 much of Central America was in revolt. In July 1979 the Sandinistas overthrew the fifty-year dictatorship of the Somoza family; and on 10 January 1981, the week before Ronald Reagan was sworn in as president, revolution broke out in El Salvador.

Minuscule El Salvador, 150 miles long by 50 miles wide, is even today less a country than a fiefdom, where 2 percent of the population own 70 percent of the arable land, 20 percent earn less than two hundred dollars a year, and 60 percent are illiterate.[36] As with the more recent peasant uprising in Chiapas, the revolution in El Salvador was prompted by a desperate need for basic necessities like land, food, and respect for human rights.

Even José Napoleón Duarte, the Reagan administration's hand-picked candidate for the Salvadoran presidency and himself a fervent anticommunist, saw matters that way. Three weeks before Reagan took office, Duarte told a *New York Times* reporter why he thought the guerrillas were fighting the government: "Fifty years of lies, fifty years of injustice, fifty years of frustration. This is a history of people starving to death, living in misery. For fifty years the same people had all the power, all the money, all the jobs, all the education, all the opportunities."[37]

Add to that what a Rand Corporation report called the Salvadoran military's "almost uncanny ability to turn citizens into enemies" by "[equating] the government's critics with the enemy, repressing trade unionists, campesino leaders, opposition politicians, and student protesters with the same or more force than they use on the insurgents."[38]

In 1980 the State Department's Human Rights desk likewise viewed the problem as a matter of social injustice rather than external communist aggression. Patricia M. Derian, Assistant Secretary for Human Rights in the Carter administration, declared, "Those who study El Salvador know that the problem is home-grown and has been building to the present crisis for many years."[39] Robert White, U.S. ambassador to El Salvador from March 1980 until he was ousted by Reagan on 1 February 1981, concurred. "Whether Cuba existed or not, you would still have a revolutionary situation in El Salvador," he said in January 1981. "The revolution situation came about in El Salvador because he had one of the most selfish oligarchies the world has ever seen, combined with a corrupt security force."[40] Three years later, in testimony before the House Committee on Foreign Affairs, White asserted:

Any formulation of a national policy toward Central America must begin with the recognition that conditions in most of Central America justify recourse to revolution. This is especially true of El Salvador. Even the excesses of the despotic, venal Somoza clan in Nicaragua pale in comparison with the brutal, starvation existence imposed on the Salvadoran campesinos and workers by the economic and military elites.[41]

The Catholic Archbishop of San Salvador, Oscar Romero, identified El Salvador's problems with the unjust structures of the wealth in the country:

The cause of the evil here is the oligarchy, a small nucleus of families that does not care about the hunger of our people. . . . To maintain and increase their margin of profits, they repress the people. . . .

They are not yet used to seeing the face of a church converted to the poor. To raise the question of the rights of the poor is to call into question the whole established order. That is why they have no other category for us but that of subversives.[42]

He accused the oligarchy of "possessing the land that belongs to all Salvadorans" and advised:

Again, in the name of our people and our church, I call on them to hear the voice of God and joyously share their power and wealth with all, instead of provoking a civil war that will bathe us in blood. There is still time to take the rings from their fingers before they lose the hand. . . .

Let them share what they are and have. Let them not keep on silencing with violence the voice of those of us who offer this invitation. Let them not keep on killing those of us who are trying to achieve a more just sharing of the power and wealth of our country. I speak in the first person, because this week I received notice that I am on the list of those who are to be eliminated next week. But let it be known that no one can any longer kill the voice of justice.

Finally, on 23 March 1980, he appealed to the enlisted men of the army and security forces:

The campesinos you are killing are your own brothers and sisters. . . . No one has to obey an immoral law. It is time to take back your consciences and to obey them rather than sinful orders. . . . In the name of God and in the name of this suffering people whose cries rise to heaven each day more loudly, I beg you, I beseech you, I order you in the name of God: Stop the repression![43]

The next day Romero was murdered, shot in the chest while saying Mass. At his funeral six days later, Salvadoran Security Forces fired without warning on the crowd of mourners gathered on the cathedral steps. Thirty-nine people were killed, and more than two hundred wounded. Two days on later, 1 April 1980, the United States sent $5.7

million in riot control equipment to El Salvador—jeeps, communications equipment, and night-vision devices—in order (as an administration spokesman put it at the time) to strengthen the army's key role in reforms.

When Ronald Reagan took office in January 1981, he saw red in Central America. As he put it, "revolution has been exported to that area and by design."[44] An Administration White Paper published on 23 February 1981 called the revolution in El Salvador "a textbook case of indirect armed aggression by Communist powers through Cuba."[45]

For Mr. Reagan, El Salvador was part of a global, East-West struggle, and the problems of the country were caused not primarily by poverty and repression but by the encroachments of international communism. The FMLN rebels, in his view, "aren't just aiming at El Salvador but, I think, are aiming at the whole of Central and possibly later South America and, I'm sure, eventually North America."[46] In 1983 he warned a Joint Session of Congress: "If we cannot defend ourselves [in El Salvador] we cannot expect to prevail elsewhere. Our credibility would collapse, our alliances would crumble and the safety of our homeland would be put in jeopardy."[47]

This re-evocation of Richard Nixon's image of the United States as a "pitiful, helpless giant"[48] being made a fool of by Lilliputian Salvadoran rebels, apparently convinced many in the United States. During the ten years of the war the U.S. Treasury poured into El Salvador (a country that would fit inside Illinois seven times) an average of $1.5 million per day, thereby making that country the third largest recipient per capita of American foreign aid during the Reagan-Bush years. And it seemed that the Reagan Administration knew roughly as much about El Salvador in the 1980s as the Johnson Administration did about Indochina in the 1960s.[49]

The administration's 1981 White Paper had called El Salvador a "textbook case" of communist aggression through Cuba. However, both American and Salvadoran officials eventually acknowledged that they had no solid evidence in 1981 that Cuba or Nicaragua (not to mention the Soviet Union) were supplying military aid to the Salvadoran insurgents. In fact, by the end of 1983 the largest supplier of weapons to the Salvadoran guerrillas was President Reagan himself, since up to 20 percent of the light weaponry and ordinance he sent to the Salvadoran army was being captured by the FMLN in combat.[50]

The work of Father Ellacuría and other liberation theologians was a matter of great concern in Washington during the 1980s, not least in ultraconservative think tanks like the Council for Inter-American Security (CIS). In the spring of 1980, five CIS members authored the widely publicized "Santa Fe Report" for the Republican presidential candidate, Ronald Reagan.[51]

The fifty-three-page document, a blueprint for Central American policy in a new Republican administration, had considerable influence on the Reagan team. Three of its four authors went on to serve the Reagan administration: Lt. Gen. Gordon Sumner Jr. as special advisor to the assistant secretary of state for inter-American affairs; Roger Fontaine as a National Security Council Latin America specialist; and Lewis Tambs as a consultant to the National Security Council up to 1983, then as U.S. ambassador to Colombia from 1983 to 1985 and to Costa Rica from July 1985 to January 1987.[52]

Extraordinarily alarmist in tone and content, the Santa Fe Report demonstrated an enormous preoccupation with the specter of communism in Central America. It viewed the hemisphere as "penetrated by Soviet power." It saw the Caribbean as "spotted with Soviet surrogates and ringed with socialist states" and fast "becoming a Marxist-Leninist lake," and it deemed America to be "everywhere in retreat."[53]

In keeping with this apocalyptic vision, the report addressed not just the question of "External Military Threat" to the hemisphere but also "Internal Subversion." Accusing the Carter administration of neglecting communist expansion while overthrowing noncommunist regimes, the report went on to make a number of policy proposals regarding "Internal Subversion," among them the following:

Proposal 1: that the in-coming Republican administration distance itself from the Carter State Department's "policy of attacking anti-Communist governments for alleged human rights violations." . . .

Proposal 4: The United States must reject the mistaken assumption that one can easily locate and impose U.S. style democratic alternatives to authoritarian governments and the equally pervasive belief that change per se in such situations is inevitable, desirable, and in the American interest. This belief has induced the Carter Administration to participate actively in the toppling of non-Communist authoritarians while remaining passive in the face of Communist expansion.

Proposal 5: Human rights, which is a culturally and politically relative concept [sic] that the present Administration has used for intervention for political change in countries of this hemisphere, adversely affecting the peace, stability and security of the region, must be abandoned and replaced by a non-interventionist policy of political and ethical realism.

I save Proposal 3 for last:

U.S. foreign policy must begin to counter (not react against) liberation theology as it is utilized in Latin America by the "liberation theology" clergy.

The role of the church in Latin America is vital to the concept of political freedom. Unfortunately, Marxist-Leninist forces have utilized the church as a political weapon against private property and productive capitalism by infiltrating the religious community with ideas that are less Christian than Communist.[54]

As Father Ignacio Ellacuría was fond of pointing out, these were proposals the Reagan administration took to heart. Beginning in January 1981 the new team in the State Department shifted the driving force of its policy in the region from an emphasis on the "culturally and politically relative concept" of "human rights" to a focus on international communism.[55]

In one of its more cynical moves, the administration appointed as its assistant secretary of state for human rights none other than Elliot Abrams. William F. Buckley made the point when he recalled a conversation he had once had with Mr. Abrams about a hypothetical situation involving human rights: "'What would you do if you were told by the Secretary of State to cool it in your report on human rights in, say, Sri Lanka?' I asked him on television. Mr. Abrams said that what he would do would be to cool it."[56]

The administration also turned up the heat on liberation theology. Among other things, this resulted in the hearings on "Marxism and Christianity in Revolutionary Central America," held by the U.S. Senate's Subcommittee on Security and Terrorism, 18–19 October 1983. The sessions, chaired by ultraconservative senator Jeremiah Denton of Alabama, featured the testimony of right-wing contra supporters who made wild and unsubstantiated claims to the effect that liberation theologians preached that there was no God and that Jesus had never existed.[57] All of this might be quite humorous, were it not for the fact that people in Central America get murdered when such absurdities, sworn to under oath and appearing in the Congressional Record, are repeated in army barracks in places like El Salvador.

To take only one example: On 19 October 1983 the Subcommittee on Security and Terrorism heard one Miguel Bolaños-Hunter swear under oath that a Maryknoll sister, Maura Clarke, had run safehouses for Sandinista guerrillas during the Nicaraguan revolution and was so good at it that the communists sent her to El Salvador to continue her activities there.

As it turns out, Sister Maura Clarke was not in or even near Nicaragua during the revolution. She spent those three and a half years (from January 1977 through June 1980) entirely in the United States, interrupted by only a brief family visit to Ireland.

True, in August of 1980 her Maryknoll superiors sent Maura Clarke to El Salvador to help refugees who were fleeing army sweeps and death squad activities in the northern province of Chalatenango. After she had worked only a few weeks with the refugees, Col. Ricardo Peña Arbaiza, the commanding officer in nearby Chalatenango City, labeled Clarke and another sister "subversives" simply because they were working with the poor.[58] Shortly thereafter, on 2 December 1980, Maura Clarke and three other religious women were kidnapped, raped, and murdered by Salvadoran soldiers acting on higher orders.[59]

At the time of the murders Jeanne J. Kirkpatrick, President Reagan's appointee to be ambassador to the United Nations, characterized the four dead women as "leftists"—as if that justified or mitigated the crimes.[60] And Secretary of State Haig testified before Congress that the four women "may have tried to run a roadblock, or may have been perceived to be doing that, and there was an exchange of fire."

Note that phrase: "an exchange of fire." Mr. Haig was suggesting the nuns were shooting back at the soldiers, wild west fashion, after they had crashed their van through a military checkpoint—even though, as Secretary Haig well knew, the evidence showed that the nuns were first raped, and then shot point-blank, one of them in the chest and three of them in the back of the head.[61]

During the Iran-Contra hearings of 1987, Elliot Abrams was asked whether an earlier statement of his was not perhaps a lie. Abrams answered, "It depends what you mean by lying." He then went on to distinguish between lying and intentionally leaving a false impression.

In any case, whether it is lying or leaving a false impression, whether it is secretly murdering priests and nuns or blatantly massacring hundreds of peasants, whether it is actively burglarizing the offices of American citizens or merely spying on them—sooner or later, we are told, the truth will out. And so it has.

On 15 March 1993 the United Nations published its Truth Commission Report on El Salvador, detailing what happened and who was responsible for a dozen years of violence in El Salvador: massacres of peasants, the murder of the Jesuits, various "extrajudicial executions" and "enforced disappearances" (read: death squad murders), and so on.

Much if not all of the story is there. For example, the U.N. Report details how, during a three-day sweep through Morazán department (10–12 December 1981), Col. Domingo Monterrosa and his Atlacatl Battalion—"the pride of the U.S. military team in El Salvador"[62]—murdered at least 767 innocent civilians in and around the village of El Mozote. At least 207 of those victims were children under the age of five, and 32 of them were less than a year old. Soldiers of this elite, U.S.-trained battalion would be the ones to murder the Jesuits eight years later.[63]

The massacre at El Mozote happened just six weeks before President

Reagan was compelled by act of Congress—if he wanted Congress to continue military aid to El Salvador—to certify formally that the Salvadoran army was improving its respect for human rights.[64] Therefore, prominent U.S. officials, including Dean Hinton, U.S. ambassador to El Salvador from May 1981 to July 1983, and Thomas Enders, assistant secretary of state for inter-American affairs (the latter in sworn testimony before Congress) publicly denied that the incident had taken place. They did this despite solidly researched newspaper accounts of the massacre and notwithstanding the word of one of their own embassy officers, Todd Greentree, who reported back from Morazán that "there very probably had been a massacre."[65]

The evidence contradicting improvement in human rights was massive and would continue to mount. In the months following the slaughter at El Mozote, the Legal Trustee Office of the archdiocese of San Salvador verified that government forces or death squads had committed 2,334 political murders in the first four months of 1982. Two months later, Americas Watch reported that as of 1 July the number of victims had risen to 2,829. The Americas Watch report concluded: "The government of El Salvador deliberately engages in systematic political murder to advance its interests." Nonetheless, on 29 January 1982, and again on 29 July 1982, President Reagan officially certified improvement in the military's respect for human rights.[66]

The State Department also succeeded in hiding from Congress clear evidence of who had planned the assassination of Archbishop Oscar Romero in March 1980. Within months of the murder the U.S. embassy in San Salvador knew that Robert d'Aubuisson, a former major trained in the United States, had chaired the meeting at which participants vied for the privilege of killing the Archbishop. On 6 February 1984, former ambassador Robert White (who had been appointed by Carter in 1980 and fired by Reagan in 1981) testified before the House Foreign Affairs Committee that the Reagan administration knew but "chose to conceal the identity of Archbishop Romero's murderer." White made reference to cable traffic between the U.S. embassy and the State Department; if revealed, he said, this exchange would "finish the political fortunes of . . . d'Aubuisson."[67]

Ambassador White testified that

from the first days in office the Reagan White House knew—beyond any reasonable doubt—that Roberto d'Aubuisson planned and ordered the assassination of Archbishop Oscar Arnulfo Romero. In mid-November of 1980, a particularly brave and resourceful American diplomat made contact with a Salvadoran military officer who had participated in the plot to kill Archbishop Romero. This officer was present at the March 22nd meeting which resulted in the death of Archbishop Romero on March 24.

According to this eyewitness account, Roberto d'Aubuisson summoned a group of about twelve men to a safe house, presided over the meeting, announced the decision to assassinate the Archbishop and supervised the drawing of lots for the "honor" of carrying out the plot. The Salvadoran officer informant was disappointed that the luck of the draw had not favored him. He gave bullets from his gun to the officer selected in order that he might participate vicariously in the murder of the Archbishop.[68]

But the State Department neither released nor acted on the information. Instead it went on to broker a deal whereby d'Aubuisson became president of Salvador's Constituent Assembly in 1982. Moreover, Reagan officials actually denied they had any proof that d'Aubuisson was involved in the archbishop's murder. When Representative Thomas J. Tauke of Iowa petitioned the State Department for more information on the matter, he received a letter from the State Department declaring that the information about d'Aubuisson contained in the cables "is limited and incomplete and no definite conclusions regarding d'Aubuisson's involvement can be drawn from it."[69]

Years later the State Department declassified the cable in question. It was sent by White's successor at the embassy, Dean Hinton, to Secretary of State Alexander Haig on 21 December 1981. The text indicates unambiguously that d'Aubuisson had chaired the meeting to plan the murder of Archbishop Romero and that one of the accomplices in the crime, Walter Antonio Alvarez, was subsequently murdered "by unknown hands."[70]

[Note: The phrase "S-ENTIRE TEXT" may mean: "Secret—entire text." The term "REFTEL" may mean "Refer to telex." The device [.......] indicates lines or words that were blacked out when the document was declassified. I reproduce the document here with the same line breaks as in the original.]

P 211817Z DEC 81

FM AMEMBASSY SAN SALVADOR

TO SECSTATE WASHDC PRIORITY 7156

REF: SAN SALVADOR 8084 (80)

SUBJECT: ASSASSINATION OF ARCHBISHOP ROMERO

1. (S-ENTIRE TEXT).

2. [..

....

..........A MEETING CHAIRED BY MAJOR ROBERTO D'AUBUISSON

DURING WHICH THE MURDER OF ARCHBISHOP ROMERO WAS PLANNED

(REFTEL). [....................] DURING THE MEETING SOME

OF THE PARTICIPANTS DREW LOTS FOR THE PRIVILEGE OF KILLING

THE ARCHBISHOP. [..]

....

ASSASSIN) AS "WALTER [...........]

3. [.............] IDENTIFIED [...........................

.........] THE "WALTER" [................] AS WALTER ANTONIO
ALVAREZ. [..
....
....] ACCORDING TO PRESS
REPORTS SEVERAL GUNMEN TOOK ALVAREZ AWAY FROM A FOOTBALL GAME
ON SEPTEMBER 27, SHOT HIM SEVERAL TIMES AND LEFT HIS BODY ON
THE ROAD WHICH LEADS TO MARIONA PRISON. HE WAS 27 YEARS OLD AND
LEFT HIS WIFE, DINORA AND A SMALL SON.
4. [..
AC[................................] WE BELIEVE
IT IS HIGHLY LIKELY THAT THE ASSASSIN OF ROMERO IS NOW DEAD BY
UNKNOWN HANDS.
HINTON
SECRET73

Despite this information, the State Department was unable to draw
"definite conclusions regarding d'Aubuisson's involvement" in the
murder. But the United Nation's Truth Commission somehow managed to discover, in a mere eighteen months, what the State Department could not figure out in a dozen years. On 15 March 1993 the U.N.
Truth Commission Report declared:

The Commission finds the following:
   1. Former Major Roberto d'Aubuisson gave the order to assassinate the Archbishop and gave precise instructions to members of his security service, acting as a
"death squad," to organize and supervise the assassination.
   2. Captains Alvaro Saravia and Eduardo Avila, together with Fernando Sagrera
and Mario Molina, were actively involved in planning and carrying out the assassination.
   3. Amado Antonio Garay, the driver of former Captain Saravia, was assigned to
drive the gunman to the Chapel. . . .
   4. Walter Antonio "Musa" Alvarez, together with former Captain Saravia, was involved in paying the "fees" of the actual assassin. . . .
   Garay picked out a 1969 photograph of Mr. Héctor Antonio Regalado, with a
beard drawn on in, as being closest to his description of the gunman. After Saravia,
Regalado had been responsible for d'Aubuisson's personal security.[71]

The Reagan and Bush administrations covered up d'Aubuisson's
role in the murder because they wanted to work with him rather than
oust him. Former vice president Dan Quayle made the point in his
own breezy way. While acknowledging that d'Aubuisson had an "un-
savory reputation," Quayle writes: "Later in 1989 I met with d'Aubuisson himself, which gave fits to liberal commentators, but I didn't
care. He had influence, and if we were going to keep him in line, then
we had to talk to him."[72]
   Whether or not the Reagan-Bush administrations kept d'Aubuisson

in line, they certainly did work with him. D'Aubuisson had trained in the United States in 1970–71, both with the CIA and at the International Police Academy in Washington DC. (The academy was later shut down after a Congressional investigation revealed that it taught its clients how to torture.) As regards d'Aubuisson's work in El Salvador, the U.S. embassy and the State Department knew perfectly well that d'Aubuisson had helped found El Salvador's most active death squad, the Maximiliano Hernandez Martinez Anti-Communist Brigade (1979)[73]; that he had planned Archbishop Romero's murder (March 1980); that he had plotted a coup d'état against the Salvadoran government (May 1980); and that in June 1984 he had plotted to assassinate then U.S. Ambassador to El Salvador Thomas R. Pickering. (President Reagan personally dispatched Ambassador-at-Large Vernon Walters to El Salvador to warn d'Aubuisson not to carry out the assassination plot.)

The embassy in El Salvador and the State Department also knew the names of those who were paying for death squad murders. In his sworn testimony of 6 February 1984, former ambassador Robert White, recalling cables he had sent from El Salvador to the State Department from March of 1980 to January of 1981, publicly named the wealthy Salvadoran landowners who, having temporarily left their country for the safety of Miami, continued to fund the death squads in El Salvador: "these are the top leadership: [Enrique] Viera Altamirano, Luis Escalante, Arturo Muyshondt, the Salverría brothers (probably Julio and Juan Ricardo), and Roberto Edgardo Daglio. All are in Miami, hatch plots, hold constant meetings and communicate instructions to D'Aubuisson."[74]

But the American embassy and the State Department did nothing to bring d'Aubuisson and his handlers to justice. As a close friend and protégé of Senator Jesse Helms of North Carolina, d'Aubuisson frequently visited the United States, where his legal problems were taken care of by the Milwaukee law firm of O'Connor and Hannan, while the firm's Washington-based partner, Joseph Blatchford, handled public relations for d'Aubuisson in the nation's capital.[75] Back in El Salvador the State Department saw fit to invite him to such official functions as a private luncheon for U.N. Ambassador Jeanne Kirkpatrick (February 1983) and a Fourth of July celebration held at the embassy.[76]

Closer to home, another bit of truth (but only the tip of the iceberg) emerged on 27 January 1988, when a private citizens' group, the Center for Constitutional Rights in New York City, announced that it had broken through the FBI's code of secrecy and silence. Using the Freedom of Information Act, the Center had managed to pry loose 1,200 pages of documents the FBI had gathered by secret surveillance of more than two hundred groups of U.S. citizens over six years through wire-taps, undercover agents, and informants. These 1,200 pages represent only about one third of the complete file, which, as the FBI itself has disclosed, runs to 17 volumes and 3,756 pages. The FBI, it should be noted, vigorously denies that this surveillance was an exercise in ha-rassment designed to stifle dissent.[77]

The secret investigation began early in 1981, when CIA director William Casey decided El Salvador had become the latest battleground in the global contest between freedom and communism.[78] With Casey's encouragement, the FBI under William H. Webster (director, 1978–87) began spying on a citizen group that strongly opposed U.S. policy: the Committee in Solidarity with the People of El Salvador (CISPES). The FBI's goal was to discover whether CISPES was an agent of the Salva-doran guerrillas.[79] At the FBI's Washington headquarters the officers in charge of the surveillance were Oliver "Buck" Revell, executive assis-tant director of the FBI, and Ron Davenport, supervisory special agent, Salvadoran Terrorism Unit.

Even though the FBI found that CISPES was neither providing weap-ons to the Salvadoran rebels nor taking political direction from any "foreign principles," and thus supposedly ended the surveillance, the investigation was resumed in 1983 under the rubric of "counter-terror-ism." An apparently typical cable from the FBI's New Orleans office, dated 10 November 1983, reads:

[Two and a half lines blacked out] IT IS IMPERATIVE AT THIS TIME TO FORMULATE SOME PLAN OF ATTACK AGAINST CISPES AND SPECIFICALLY · AGAINST INDIVID-UALS, [thirty-one spaces blacked out] WHO DEFIANTLY DISPLAY THEIR CONTEMPT FOR THE U.S. GOVERNMENT BY MAKING SPEECHES AND PROPAGANDIZING THEIR CAUSE WHILE ASKING FOR POLITICAL ASYLUM.

NEW ORLEANS IS OF THE OPINION THAT DEPARTMENTS OF JUSTICE AND STATE SHOULD BE CONSULTED TO EXPLORE THE POSSIBILITY OF DEPORTING THESE INDI-VIDUALS OR AT BEST DENYING THEIR RE-ENTRY ONCE THEY LEAVE.[80]

It was in that year, 1983, that the FBI investigation began to widen into a policy of nationwide surveillance of such groups as the Mary-knoll Sisters, the Sanctuary Movement, the Chicago Interreligious Task Force, the Sisters of Mercy, Clergy and Laity Concerned, and U.S. Catholic Conference.[81]

The tactics of surveillance soon turned into active infiltration and included the assembling of a "Terrorist Photo Album" by Frank Va-relli, a contract operative in the FBI's Dallas office. As documented in the Congressional Record, the album contained pictures and political profiles of American citizens and foreigners, such as the following:

Maryknoll Sister Peggy Healy: The Terrorist Photo Album characterizes Sister Healy as one of the "frontrunners in preaching the Marxist-Leninist 'Liberation Theology,'" and lists her "Terrorist affiliation" as "Pro-Castro. Christian Socialist." The profile goes on: "In El Salvador as well as Nicaragua, the Maryknoll priests and nuns are guilty of aiding, protecting and supporting the Communist terrorists of the FDR-FMLN, [and] FSLN."

Representative Pat Schroeder: "She is openly working on behalf of the Sandinista Government in the US through the NNSNP [National Network in Solidarity with the Nicaraguan People] and CISPES."

Former ambassador to El Salvador Robert E. White: "He was very instrumental in the formation of CISPES in the US, and works very closely with Sandy Pollack (CPUSA)."

Archbishop Arturo Rivera y Damas: The "Terrorist affiliation" of the successor of Archbishop Oscar Romero is listed as "Socialist."[82]

The album goes on to characterize the "terrorist tendencies" of Representative Michael Barnes and Senators Christopher Dodd and Claiborne Pell, and mentions other "pro-Sandinista legislators" such as Ted Kennedy, Ron Dellums, and Edward Boland. Boland, of course, was the author of the Boland Amendment, the circumvention of which led to the Iran-Contra affair.[83]

In one sense such a photo album is truly funny. But this was the time when Lt. Col. Oliver North of the National Security Council was secretly working with the Federal Emergency Management Agency (FEMA) to draw up contingency plans to spy on political dissenters and even, as Ross Gelbspan of the *Boston Globe* has pointed out, "to arrange for the detention of hundreds of thousands of undocumented aliens in case of an unspecified national emergency . . . [and] the suspension of the Constitution under a number of scenarios, including a U.S. invasion of Nicaragua."[84]

The contingency plans relating to insurrection or national disturbances were worked out in meetings between North and Louis O. Guiffrida, director of FEMA, from 1982 to 1984. The martial law provisions of the plan, part of which was code-named Rex 84, were outlined in a 30 June 1982 memo written by deputy director of FEMA John Brinkerhoff. Having obtained and studied a copy of the memo, the *Miami Herald* wrote: "The scenario outlined in the Brinkerhoff memo resembled somewhat a paper Guiffrida had written in 1970 at the Army War College in Carlisle, Pa., in which he advocated martial law in case of a national uprising by black militants. The paper also advocated the roundup and transfer to 'assembly centers or relocation camps' of at least 21 million 'American Negroes.'"[85]

Two days after the article appeared, Lieutenant Colonel North began his sworn testimony before Congress in the Iran-Contra matter.

When Representative Jack Brook of Texas tried to ask North about Rex 84, he was silenced by co-chairman Senator Daniel Inouye because, in Senator Inouye's words, "that question touches upon a highly sensitive and classified area."[86] No more was heard about the matter.

The FBI's spying allegedly ended in July 1985. However, that date marks the beginning of a dramatic, nationwide escalation of break-ins into the offices of churches and citizen groups that opposed the administration's policies in Central America. During those break-ins, money or expensive office equipment was never taken, but files were invariably rifled and some were stolen. To list but a few incidents:

June 1985: In Los Angeles a list of fifteen hundred donors was stolen from the offices of Amnesty International.

16 July 1985: At University Baptist Church in Seattle, which offered sanctuary to Central American refugees, the offices of Rev. Donovan Cook were broken into, keys to the rooms of six Central American refugees were stolen, and files listing Sanctuary supporters were examined. Later the church's insurance company threatened it would dissolve the church's policy unless the refugees were removed.

25–26 October 1985: The offices of the Central America Refugee Project in Phoenix were broken into twice over the weekend. Telephone logs and clients' legal files were copied, but five hundred dollars in cash was left untouched.

4–5 December 1985: At the Old Cambridge Baptist Church, Cambridge, Massachusetts, the offices of the New Institute of Central America were burglarized for the fifth time. (The previous break-ins were on 27 November and 18–19 December 1984 and 20–21 April and 13–14 September 1985.) The Cambridge police report states, "The main targets in these breaks were desks and organizational files."

21–22 May 1986: The Manhattan offices of NACLA (North American Committee on Latin America) were burglarized just as the Committee was preparing a report on Oliver North's role in organizing of a support network for the contras. The offices were ransacked, and files were examined and scattered around the room.

29–30 October 1987: At Georgetown University, the offices of the Central American Historical Institute were burglarized, a file cabinet containing articles and stories on Central America was broken into. One hundred dollars in cash and a checkbook, which were in plain view, went undisturbed.[87]

The perpetrators of these crimes have never been found. The FBI denies having anything to do with the break-ins. Once the scandal about FBI surveillance broke in 1988, FBI director William S. Sessions admitted that the 1981–85 part of the operation, conducted under his predecessor, may have been "not properly directed," but nonetheless asserted that it was justified. President Reagan concurred in that judgment.[88]

From the war at home, we return to the war in El Salvador, and the murder of the Jesuits, in order to note the elaborate cover-up carried out by the United States and the government of El Salvador. Within days of the Jesuit murders, President Cristiani appointed Lt. Col. Manuel Antonio Rivas to head up the Special Investigative Unit (SIU) charged with solving the crime. Shortly thereafter, Col. Guillermo Benavides, head of El Salvador's Military Academy, confessed to Rivas that he had ordered the soldiers to carry out the killings. However, Rivas told Benavides to forget his confession and to start destroying evidence—both the guns that were used to murder the Jesuits and all records of the killers' movements that night. Benavides complied. From the beginning, Colonel Rivas and the SIU did their utmost to obstruct the investigation of the murders.[89]

Next, Lieutenant Colonel Rivas, with the assistance of the American embassy in El Salvador and the FBI, began intimidating the only witness to the events, Mrs. Lucía Cerna. On 16 November, from her lodgings on Calle Cantábrico only thirty meters from the scene of the crimes, Mrs. Cerna heard several shots on the campus shortly after 1:00 A.M. When she looked out her window, she saw five commandos in camouflage uniforms firing at the Jesuit residence, and she heard Father Martín-Baró, one of the victims, shout at them before he was shot.[90] From another window, her husband Jorge also saw a group of soldiers. The next morning at about 6:00 A.M. Mrs. Cerna, her husband, and four UCA watchmen discovered the bodies of the priests and reported the crime to the Jesuit provincial, José María Tojeira.

The Jesuits in El Salvador decided to send Mr. and Mrs. Cerna and their four-year-old daughter to the United States for their safety and protection. First, however, the Jesuits took her to the Spanish embassy, where she gave sworn testimony to a Salvadoran judge, the public prosecutor, and members of the SIU. France's state secretary of humanitarian affairs, who happened to be in San Salvador, agreed to accompany her on the flight to Miami and to deliver her to the French and Spanish consuls there, who in turn would hand her over to U.S. Jesuit officials.

The Jesuits intentionally did not inform the American embassy of their plans, but somehow Ambassador William G. Walker found out. He had Richard Chidester, legal officer of the embassy, telephone the Jesuits just hours before the Cernas' departure on 23 November. Chidester, over the Jesuits' objections, insisted that he be allowed to accompany Mrs. Cerna on the flight to the United States.[91]

Chidester brought with him on the flight FBI special agent Edward Sánchez. When the party arrived in Miami, Chidester, contrary to what he had agreed to do, did not deliver the Cerna family to the French and Spanish consuls. Instead he and Sánchez handed them over to the FBI, who held them in a guarded room at the Radisson Hotel in

Miami. When the U.S. Jesuits inquired after the Cernas, State Department officials told them the FBI needed time to do a "risk assessment" to determine how much protection the family might require.

However, each day from Monday, 27 November, through Thursday, 30 November, Chidester and Sánchez took the Cernas to an FBI office in Miami where Lucía and her husband were submitted, incommunicado, to an intensive and intimidating interrogation by Sánchez and another FBI agent, Fred Rivero. Moreover, Lieutenant Colonel Rivas, who was orchestrating the military cover-up in San Salvador, was invited by Chidester to come to Miami, where he participated in the interrogation of Mrs. Cerna.

After days of grueling questioning by Rivas and the FBI, which included insults, intimidation, and implied threats, Mrs. Cerna retracted her story and said she had seen nothing relevant to the murder of the Jesuits.[92]

In January 1990, less than two months after the Jesuits had been killed, U.S. major Eric Buckland, a senior military advisor in El Salvador, gave sworn testimony on three distinct occasions (1) that Salvadoran officers had planned and carried out the execution of the priests, and (2) that he, Buckland, had had prior knowledge—from three weeks before the killings right up to hours before they were carried out—that the military was going to take out the Jesuits. This was at a time when Colonel Rivas and the SIU were working overtime to conceal the perpetrators of the crime. Buckland gave his testimony as follows.

On 2 January 1990, six weeks after the murders, Buckland informed his immediate superior, Lt. Col. William C. Hunter Jr., senior U.S. advisor to the Salvadoran Joint Command, that Salvadoran colonel Guillermo Benavides had ordered the Atlacatl commandos to kill the Jesuits. Buckland had received this information on 20 December 1989 from his good friend, Salvadoran colonel Carlos Avilés, who in turn had it on excellent authority from Col. Nelson López y López, a member of El Salvador's Joint Command. On 3 January Buckland put the matter into writing for his superiors, and on 6 January he was flown to the United States.[93]

On 10 and 11 January 1990, in the presence of FBI agents, Buckland gave sworn testimony that went beyond his earlier statements: he revealed that he himself had had prior knowledge, going back some weeks before the event, that Benavides and other officers were planning to murder the Jesuits. As he put it, "Avilés told me they wanted to handle it the old way by killing some of the priests."[94]

Testifying on 12 January 1990, now on videotape in the presence of FBI special agent Paul Cully, Buckland further specified that on the afternoon of 15 November, just hours before the kill order was given, Avilés had told Buckland the army was planning to go onto the Jesuit campus and "clean out the UCA." Special Agent Cully asked Buckland, "What did this mean to you that they were going to go in and clear out the UCA?" Buckland replied, "To find out, you know, to get the dirty people in there." In addition Buckland told the FBI that he "understood" the military's "feeling of vengeance" against the Jesuits. That admission prompted the following exchange:

AGENT CULLY: So if those killings were to occur, you would have accepted that as a necessary thing, for the country?
BUCKLAND: I either accepted it as necessary and I really understood it, okay. You know, even though it might have been—superfluous isn't the word—you know, it might even have been stupid, and I understand, I understood the blood, the blood feeling, but it was their war and it was their country. . . .[95]

Buckland's testimony blew the case wide open. Up until then, the cover-up had been holding. The American embassy and President Cristiani were continuing to claim the FMLN had murdered the Jesuits. What, then, became of Buckland's explosive testimony?

Let us return for a moment to 2 January, the date of Buckland's original revelation to his superiors. Lt. Col. William Hunter immediately communicated Buckland's revelation to the head of the U.S. Military Group in El Salvador, U.S. colonel Milton Menjívar. That same day, Menjívar went directly to Col. René Ponce—the very officer who had ordered that the Jesuits be murdered—and revealed Buckland's information to him.

Ponce expressed surprise and anger, according to Menjívar, and then denied knowing anything about it. On the spot Ponce called Avilés, López y López, Buckland, and Hunter into his office and confronted them with Buckland's revelation. Caught between Ponce and Buckland, Avilés and López y López vigorously denied any knowledge of the matter, and Avilés denied having had the 20 December conversation with Buckland.

Whatever his intentions in the matter, Menjívar, by revealing everything to Ponce, (1) had alerted the chief perpetrator of the crime that the cover-up was coming unraveled, (2) had dangerously exposed two important witnesses who might have helped reveal the military's full role in the murders, and (3) gave Ponce and his colleagues the information and impetus they needed to begin a new cover-up.

The new cover-up began immediately. On 5 January, three days after the meeting, the Salvadoran Armed Forces, in private consultation with American officials, took the extraordinary step of setting up their own investigative body—the Armed Forces Honor Commission—to look into the Jesuit murders. The real purpose of this rump commission was to prevent the indictments from reaching any higher than Colonel Benavides: he was to be the fall guy, and higher ranking officers, especially the High Command, were to be insulated from indictment and trial.

The tactic worked. In less than a week the honor commission came up with a very limited list of low-ranking suspects—the eight commandos who had actually carried out the murders, plus Benavides, who had sent them. They and they alone would go to trial. No members of the High Command would ever be indicted for ordering the murder of the Jesuits.[96]

Why did the United States have an interest in limiting the investigation? Why would the U.S. embassy not want it known that the Salvadoran High Command, rather than just a single colonel, had ordered the killings of the Jesuits? "Because they would have to turn in their own client," replies Congressman George Miller, a member of the House task force investigating the murders. "Their client is the Salvadoran government and the Salvadoran military." For the Bush administration to turn in its client would mean that nine years of war and $6 billion in aid had been in vain. That was unacceptable.[97]

If the sworn testimony Buckland gave in El Salvador implicated the High Command in the Jesuits' murder, the information he gave the FBI in Washington DC raised serious questions about the role of the United States. Buckland's testimony indicated that at least one senior U.S. military advisor had had prior knowledge of the planned executions—ranging from weeks to hours before the crime—and had done nothing about it.

And if Buckland had prior knowledge of the crime, why not other U.S. military and diplomatic personnel? In the days before the murder of the Jesuits two other U.S. advisors—Colonel Porter and Major Lewis—had been working closely with C-2, the Salvadoran Army's intelligence section. Could they too have known the army was planning the murders? U.S. advisors often had close personal relations with their Salvadoran counterparts. Many shared offices with them. Buckland's office, and those of Lieutenant Colonel Hunter and other American advisors, were in the annex of the Joint Command Headquarters. Besides knowing that the executions were being planned, could other American advisors have also shared Buckland's "understanding" for the army's motives in carrying out the crime? Might they too, like Buckland, have "accepted it as necessary"?[98]

Buckland's prior-knowledge testimony could not be allowed to stand. The strategy for undoing it was twofold: bury the evidence and break the witness.

First, the FBI sent copies of Buckland's prior-knowledge testimony—both his affidavit of 10–11 January and the videotaped testimony of 12 January—to the U.S. embassy's legal affairs officer, Richard Chidester, the very one who, two months earlier, had helped hold Lucía Cerna incommunicado in Miami until she changed her testimony. The FBI briefed Chidester and his superiors on the seriousness of the matter.

Then, instead of passing Buckland's testimony on to the Salvadoran judge in charge of the case, Ambassador Walker, in an extraordinary move, invited President Cristiani to the ambassador's private residence for a secret viewing of the tape. Legal Officer Chidester and Deputy Chief of Mission Jeff Dietrich were also present at the viewing.

Shortly thereafter, U.S. diplomatic and military officials in Washington and El Salvador decided to bury Buckland's admission of prior knowledge. As Martha Doggett, the American lawyer who carried out the most thorough investigation of the case, puts it: "They decided not to disclose this information publicly, or to share it with the court. More than just concealing the evidence, State Department and Pentagon officials actually denied its existence when *The New York Times* printed rumors suggesting that a U.S. officer had prior knowledge of the murder plot."[99] But despite the denials the videotape still exists. The FBI keeps it logged under the case title "Shooting of Six Jesuit Priests" at the FBI's Polygraph Unit, section GRB, Suite 2, file number 00116093 PQI.[100]

The second part of the strategy entailed breaking Buckland. His admission of prior knowledge was too explosive; he had to take it back. And he did. On 14 January, the day after Chidester and Walker had received copies of his Washington testimony, Buckland announced at Fort Bragg that he wanted to change his story. In an article entitled "Cracking the Major," *Newsweek* cited sources in the Bush administration who knew what had been done with Buckland:

Newsweek has learned that an American Special Forces officer, who told U.S. authorities in January he knew of Salvador military plans to murder six Jesuit priests last November, was later pressured by FBI and State Department officials to recant. "He was grilled and grilled until he cracked."

U.S. officials told *Newsweek* that Buckland's original statement [in Washington DC] was "100 percent accurate." The administration "didn't want that story to come out," sources said, because it wasn't productive to the conduct of the war.[101]

When the administration advised *Newsweek* to retract the story, the magazine refused.

Representative Joseph Moakley of Massachusetts, who led the House task force investigating the murders, thinks he knows how

Buckland was pressured into retracting. By admitting prior knowledge of the crimes, the American major was possibly implicating himself in them: he not only knew the murders were being planned but even expressed understanding for the army's motives and for why the executions might be "necessary." In Moakley's words, "He couldn't have made up all those details [of the Washington revelations]. I think what happened was that after he testified, someone in a legal office somewhere must have pointed out to him that he had incriminated himself. That's when he decided to recant."[102]

On 18 January, in a written affidavit, Buckland retracted those parts of his previous testimony that indicated prior knowledge of the plot to kill the Jesuits. He swore: "I do not recall and am not aware of any specific information regarding any proposed threat to or attack on the University of Central America, including any of the Jesuit priests prior to the incident on November 16, 1989. I wish to specifically retract information or comments or suggestions made to FBI agents last week to that effect."[103] The legalistic language that characterizes Buckland's recantation is in marked contrast to the more discursive and even emotional tenor of his earlier testimony cited above. Moreover, as Long and Smyth report, after his retraction Buckland took an FBI lie detector test—and failed it. "In answer to the question, 'Did you have prior knowledge that the Jesuits would be killed?' Buckland said no, and the polygraph indicated 'deception,' according to official FBI documents."[104]

Nonetheless, the cover-up worked. Indictments in the case never reached the Salvadoran High Command, the true perpetrators of the crime, and the embassy was able to deny that any U.S. advisors in El Salvador had prior knowledge of the murders or agreed with the murderers' motives.

In the words of Father Charles Beirne, S.J., Ellacuría's successor at the UCA, "The Americans were helping to protect the High Command all along. They were afraid the whole house of cards would fall if the investigation went any further. They were involved with the cover-up from the very beginning."[105] The television network CBS got a taste of that some six months after the murders. When Ed Bradley of *Sixty Minutes* went to El Salvador to interview Ambassador Walker about the military's role in the crimes, the ambassador secretly taped their conversation and then sent the cassette across town to Colonel Ponce to help Ponce prepare for his own interview with Bradley.[106]

The trial for the murder of the six Jesuits, their housekeeper, and her daughter lasted only three days—26–29 September 1991. The defendants were limited to the eight men hand-picked by the military's Honor Commission: Colonel Benavides, plus seven soldiers who

ranked no higher than lieutenant. The jury found only Colonel Benavides and Lt. Yusshy Mendoza guilty of murder. The other six, including the confessed triggermen, were absolved of all crimes. On 1
April 1993, under a general amnesty law, Benavides and Mendoza were
released from prison.[107]

Colonel Ponce, the man who ordered the crimes in the first place,
was promoted from colonel to general, and from head of the Joint
Chiefs of Staff to minister of defense. He remained a client of the
United States and continued to serve his country until 30 June 1993,
when he retired with honors and full pension.

Was the U.S. war in El Salvador an exercise in fascism? Surely not, for
the United States is not a fascist country, and neither the Reagan nor
the Bush administration was a fascist regime. But one is left wonder-
ing what the war was really about and why the United States would ex-
pend an extravagant $6 billion on that tiny country.

In the early 1960s, as John F. Kennedy's anticommunist crusade was
about to unfold in Latin America, Arnold J. Toynbee wrote:

Today America is no longer the inspirer and leader of the World Revolution, and I
have an impression that she is embarrassed and annoyed when she is reminded that
this was her original mission. No one else laid this mission upon America. She
chose it for herself, and for one hundred and forty-two years, reckoning from the
year 1775, she pursued this revolutionary mission with an enthusiasm which has
proved deservedly infectious.

By contrast, America is today the leader of a world-wide anti-revolutionary
movement in defence of vested interests. She now stands for what Rome stood for.
Rome consistently supported the rich against the poor in all foreign Communities
that fell under her sway; and, since the poor, so far, have always and everywhere
been far more numerous than the rich, Rome's policy made for inequality, for injustice, and for the least happiness of the greatest number.

America's decision to adopt Rome's role has been deliberate, if I have gauged it
right. It has been deliberate, yet, in the spirit that animates this recent American
movement in reverse, I miss the enthusiasm and the confidence that made the old
revolutionary American irresistible.[108]

Mark Twain took a somewhat different tack. Whereas Toynbee would
put the turning point at the Bolshevik Revolution of 1917 (cf. "one
hundred and forty-two years, reckoning from the year 1775"), Twain
thought the American empire came into its own with the Spanish-
American War. And having followed the speeches of Republican Indiana Senator Albert Jeremiah Beveridge (1862–1927), Twain was hardly
convinced that Americans were "embarrassed" about becoming a new
Roman empire.

Twain had read Senator Beveridge's paean to America's God-given imperial mandate, delivered in the well of the Senate on 8 January 1900 during a debate on annexing the Philippine Islands. "We will not renounce our part in the mission of our race," Beveridge had thundered, "trustees under God, of the civilization of the world." He believed, as he told his colleagues, that God had been preparing "the English-speaking and Teutonic peoples" for this mission for a thousand years.[109]

Beveridge saw America's mandate as one of blood and business (Twain took to capitalizing the latter as "Business"), and nowhere did Beveridge better spell out that mission than in a speech he gave in Boston at the height of the Spanish-American War, in April 1898: "We are a conquering race. We must obey our blood and occupy new markets and if necessary new lands. . . . In the Almighty's infinite plan . . . debased civilizations and decaying races [are to disappear] before the higher civilization of the nobler and more virile types of man. . . . Fate has written our policy for us; the trade of the world must and shall be ours."[110]

Mark Twain's response to all of this came in February 1901, in an article titled "To the Person Sitting In Darkness." The United States had just acquired the Philippine Islands and was engaged in a bloody counterinsurgency war against the Filipinos, who, having just been freed from Spain, were not anxious to be colonized by America. It was America's first Vietnam: seventy-five thousand American troops on the ground, atrocities on both sides, the Americans frequently burning whole villages to the ground and killing each and every inhabitant.

A strong critic of this counterrevolutionary conflict, Twain addressed himself with bitter irony to the rebellious Filipinos, whom he called "the People Who Sit in Darkness" of Psalm 107:10. To them the imperial United States—or as Twain put it, the "Blessings-of-Civilization Trust"—promised the Light of Freedom, Progress, and Civilization—in a word, Business. But the question was how to get the message across to people who did not want the gift. "The Person Sitting in Darkness is almost sure to say: 'There is something curious about this—curious and unaccountable. There must be two Americas: one that sets the captive free, and one that takes a once-captive's new freedom away from him. . . .'" Twain paused and addressed to his readers a question that might resonate even today. "Shall we go on conferring our Civilization upon the peoples that sit in darkness, or shall we give those poor things a rest? Shall we bang right ahead in our old-time, loud, pious way, and commit the new century to the game; or shall we sober up and sit down and think it over first?" He then supplied the answer he thought the "Blessings-of-Civilization Trust" might give in response to his question:

Extending the Blessings of Civilization to our Brother who Sits in Darkness has been a good trade and has paid well, on the whole; and there is money in it yet, if carefully worked. But the People who Sit in Darkness have become suspicious of the Blessings of Civilization. More, they have begun to examine them. This is not well. We should say to him:

"There have been lies; yes, but they were told in a good cause. We have been treacherous; but that was only in order that real good might come out of apparent evil. True, we have crushed a deceived and confiding people; we have turned against the weak and the friendless who trusted us; we have debauched America's honor and blackened her face before the world; but each detail was for the best.

"Our Congress and our fifty State Legislatures are members not only of the Church, but also of the Blessings-of-Civilization Trust. This world-girdling accumulation of trained morals, high principles, and justice, cannot do an unright thing, an unfair thing, an ungenerous thing, an unclean thing."

That will convince the Person who Sits in Darkness. And it will give the Business a splendid new start.

Twain ended his essay by suggesting that, once the Philippine Islands were conquered and assimilated to the project of Business, America should adopt a new banner to fly over its far-flung colony:

As for a flag for the Philippine Province, it is easily managed. We can have just our usual flag, but with the white stripes painted black, and the stars replaced by the skull and cross-bones.

Progress and Civilization in that country can then have a boom, and will take in the Persons who are Sitting in Darkness. And we can resume Business as usual at the old stand.[111]

Notes

1. I have drawn on a number of sources: *From Madness to Hope: The 12-year War in El Salvador*, Report of the U.N. Commission on the Truth For El Salvador, ed. Belisario Betancur, chairman, with Reinaldo Figueredo Planchart and Thomas Buergenthal (New York: The United Nations, 15 March 1993), 62–66 (hereinafter referred to as U.N. Truth Commission Report). Martha Doggett, *Death Foretold: The Jesuit Murders in El Salvador* (Washington DC: Georgetown University Press, with Lawyers Committee for Human Rights, 1993), and her updated report, "The Assassination of the Jesuits: What the United States Knew," presented to the Latin American Studies Association Conference in Atlanta, Georgia, 10 March 1994 (typescript). Teresa Whitfield, *Paying the Price: Ignacio Ellacuría and the Murdered Jesuits of El Salvador* (Philadelphia: Temple University Press, 1994). Alejandro Artucio, *A Breach of Impunity: The Trial for the Murder of Jesuits in El Salvador*, Report of the Trial Observer of the International Commission of Jurists (New York: Fordham University Press, 1992). Instituto de Estudios Centroamericanos and El Rescate, *The Jesuit Assassinations: The Writings of Ellacuría, Martín-Baró and Segundo Montes, with a Chronology of the Investigation*, 11 November 1989–22 October 1990 (Kansas City: Sheed and Ward, 1990).

Documents referenced as "Lawyers Committee for Human Rights" are typed reports available from that group's offices at 330 Seventh Avenue, 10th Floor, New York NY 10001.

For an abundance of valuable information I am grateful to two veteran reporters in El Salvador: Eugene Palumbo (*Christian Science Monitor, Commonweal*, Canadian Broadcast Corporation) and Thomas Long (*Miami Herald, Village Voice*). Some of their published work is cited in these notes.

2. On death squad killings, see Douglas Farah, "Salvadoran Death Squads Threaten Resurgence," *Washington Post*, 28 August 1988, A1 and A26; Lindsey Gruson, "Salvadorans Consider Sweeping Amnesty for Military," *New York Times*, 18 March 1990, 3; and Benjamin C. Schwarz, *American Counterinsurgency Doctrine and El Salvador: The Frustrations of Reform and the Illusions of Nation Building*, prepared for the under secretary of defense for policy (Santa Monica CA: Rand Corporation, 1991), 35 and 42.

On death squad composition, see Amnesty International, *El Salvador: "Death Squads"—A Government Strategy*, report of October 1988, 9.

On private funding of death squads, see House Committee on Foreign Affairs, *The Situation in El Salvador. Hearing before the Subcommittee on Human Rights and International Organizations and on Western Hemisphere Affairs*, 26 January and 6 February 1984 (Washington DC: U.S. Government Printing Office, 1984), 41 and 46–49; Douglas Farah, "2 Salvadorans Detail Origin of A Death Squad," *Washington Post*, 29 August 1984, A1 and A20; Janet DiVicenzo, Scott Armstrong, Nicole Ball, and Thomas S. Blanton, eds., *El Salvador: The Making of U.S. Policy, 1977–1984* (Alexandria VA: The National Security Archive and Chadwyck-Healey Inc., 1989) (hereafter *El Salvador: The Making of U.S. Policy*), Document no. 04974 (1984/04/11), letter of W. Tapley Bennett Jr., assistant secretary of state for legislative and intergovernmental affairs, to Representative Thomas J. Tauke.

For annotated lists of death squads in El Salvador, see Ciarán ó Maoláin, *The Radical Right: A World Directory*, A Keesing's Reference Publication (Jarlow, Essex: Longman Group, 1987), 74–79; Peter Janke, *Guerrilla and Terrorist Organizations* (New York: Macmillan, 1983), 470–74.

3. The best analysis of the development of the FMLN as a fighting force is Francisco Emilio Mena Sandoval, *Del ejército nacional al ejército guerrillero* (San Salvador: Ediciones Arcoiris, n.d.). Much less well informed is the view from the government side presented by José Angel Moroni Bracamonte and David E. Spenser, *Strategy and Tactics of the Salvadoran FMLN Guerrillas: Last Battle of the Cold War, Blueprint for Future Conflicts* (Westport CT: Praeger, 1995). The figure of up to three thousand guerrillas attacking the capital city is from Artucio, *Breach of Impunity*, 17.

4. Thirteen U.S. Special Forces (Green Berets) were training the commandos up to forty-eight hours before the murders. Lawyers Committee for Human Rights, "Update on Investigation of the Murder of Six Jesuit Priests in El Salvador," 25 March 1991, 12; J. Donald Moran, "U.S. should not subsidize Salvadoran murderers," *Boston Globe*, 8 October 1991. See below.

5. Cited in Lawyers Committee for Human Rights, "Status of the Investigation of the Jesuit Murders in El Salvador: Memo to the U.S. Jesuit Conference," 12 April

1990, 7. Zepeda specifically blamed the Jesuits for planning an attack that had been carried out by FMLN urban commandos—Doggett, *Death Foretold*, 61. He made his charge in the newspaper *El Diario de Hoy*, which was owned by Enrique Viera Altamirano. In 1984 (see below) U.S. ambassador Robert White would name Viera Altamirano as one of the powers behind the death squads.

6. Ellacuría maintained correct but critical relations with both the Salvadoran army and the guerrillas, even though both groups often disagreed with his political analyses and positions. See José Ignacio López Vigil, *Rebel Radio: The Story of El Salvador's Radio Venceremos*, trans. Mark Fried (Willimantic CT: Curbstone Press, 1994), 143.

7. A bibliography of Ellacuría's writings appears in John Hassett and Hugh Lacey, eds., *Towards a Society that Serves its People: The Intellectual Contribution of El Salvador's Murdered Jesuits* (Washington DC: Georgetown University Press, 1991), 373–82. His political writings are published as Ignacio Ellacuría, *Veinte años de historia en El Salvador (1969–1989): Escritos políticos*, 3 vols. (San Salvador: UCA Editores, 1991). His chief work in philosophy is *Filosofía de la realidad histórica* (San Salvador: UCA Editores, 1990), which includes a bibliography of his philosophical works.

8. "They found no signs of any guerrilla presence, war matériel or propaganda" (U.N. Truth Commission Report, 50). On Cristiani's authorization of the search, see Lawyers Committee for Human Rights, "Update on Investigation of the Murder of Six Jesuit Priests in El Salvador," 25 March 1991, 11.

9. Thomas Long, "Jesuit Cover-up in Salvador: Videotape of U.S. Adviser Reveals Army Planned Priests' Murders," *Village Voice*, 16 July 1991, 26.

10. On Cristiani's being informed of the operation by High Command, see U.N. Truth Commission Report, 50. On the duration of Cristiani's stay at High Command headquarters, see Gen. Rafael Humberto Larios López, quoted in Doggett, *Death Foretold*, 57.

11. For Espinza and Guevara's testimony on the kill order, see Doggett, *Death Foretold*, 65.

12. On the night goggles, see Thomas Long, *Miami Herald* (International Edition), 2 July 1991, and *Village Voice*, 16 July 1991. See also Doggett, *Death Foretold*, 212. The training was conducted at Atlacatl Headquarters in Sitio de Niño, La Libertad, near the capital city. The American trainers were detached from the 7th Special Forces Group (Airborne) Deployment for Training, from Fort Bragg, North Carolina. This information on the Green Beret training sessions was supplied to Congressman Joseph Moakley by Carl W. Ford Jr., acting assistant secretary of defense for international security affairs.

13. For details on the shooting, see U.N. Truth Commission Report, 47. The description of the crime scene was given me by reporter Eugene Palumbo (22 February 1996), who arrived at the scene some five hours after the murders. The M-16 used to kill Fathers López and Moreno was produced by Colt Manufacturers in Hartford, Connecticut (ph. 203–236–6311), under contract with the U.S. government; and the 5.56mm cartridges employed to kill the priests were manufactured at the Lake City Army Ammunition Plant near Independence, Missouri (ph. 816–796–7101) under

contract with Olin Winchester. I am grateful to the offices of Mr. Gary Cox of the Lake City Plant, for supplying some of this information on 21 and 22 February 1996.

14. Doggett, *Death Foretold*, 68–69; Whitfield, *Paying the Price*, 13.

15. Lawyers Committee for Human Rights, "Status of the Investigation of the Jesuit Murders in El Salvador," 8.

16. See Philip Winters's letter to the *New York Times*, 29 November 1995, A18.

17. With a nod to John E. Peurifoy (1907–55), former ambassador to Guatemala. On 18 December 1954, following his first dinner with President Jacobo Arbenz of Guatemala, Peurifoy concluded his five-page telegram to Secretary of State John Foster Dulles (Dispatch No. 522) by saying that if Arbenz "is not a Communist, he will certainly do until one comes along." In Stephen Schlesinger and Stephen Kinzer, *Bitter Fruit* (Garden City NY: Anchor-Doubleday, 1982), 138 and 273 n.13.

18. Mary McGrory, "Salvador: Murder and Resurrection," *Washington Post*, 15 April 1990, D1.

19. See Thomas W. Lippman, "1989 Salvadoran Atrocity Posed Agonizing Choice for U.S.," *Washington Post*, 5 April 1994, A13.

20. For the cost of the Afghan adventure, see Anthony Lewis, "And We Walked Away," *New York Times*, 19 February 1996, A11; for the cost of the war in El Salvador, see Schwarz, *American Counterinsurgency Doctrine*, v and 2, with n.5. With the signing of the peace accords in January 1992, annual aid to El Salvador shrunk until by 1995 it was only $266 million.

21. Tim Weiner, "Documents Show U.S. Trained Salvadorans Linked to Death Squads," *New York Times*, 14 December 1993, A1 and A4; Clifford Krauss, "U.S., Aware of Killings, Worked With Salvador's Rightists, Papers Suggest," *New York Times*, 9 November 1993, A4, and his earlier "How U.S. Actions Helped Hide Salvador Human Rights Abuses," *New York Times*, 21 March 1993, 1 and 8; Dennis Volman, "Salvador Death Squads, A CIA Connection?" *Christian Science Monitor*, 8 May 1984, A1 and C1; Allan Nairn, "Behind the Death Squads," *The Progressive*, May 1984, 1, 20–29, and his "Confessions of a Death Squad Officer," *The Progressive*, March 1986, 26–30. Lawrence Ross, "Salvadoran's Arrest Raises Questions: Ex-Assassin Charged U.S. Was Involved with Death Squads," *San Francisco Chronicle*, 12 July 1990, A1 and A18, and his "Unwanted Testimony," *Pacific Sun*, 13 July 1990, 8–10.

22. Interview with Marc Cooper and Gregory Goldin, *Playboy*, November 1984, 73.

23. Cited in Allan Nairn, "Behind the Death Squads," *The Progressive*, May 1984, 21.

24. Nairn, "Behind the Death Squads," 29. On Kennedy in Costa Rica, see Richard N. Goodwin, *Remembering America: A Voice from the Sixties* (Boston: Little, Brown and Company, 1988), 221; and Alexander Cockburn, "Beat the Devil," *The Nation*, 15 May 1995, 659.

25. The text of the "Declaration of San José" (sometimes called the "Declaration of Central America") is printed in *The Department of State Bulletin* 47, no. 1241 (8 April 1963), 517; other relevant texts in "The Presidents' Meeting at San José," 511–40. The presidents attending were Orlich of Costa Rica, Rivera of El Salvador,

Ydígoras of Guatemala, Villeda of Honduras, Somoza of Nicaragua, Chiari of Panama, and Kennedy of the United States.

26. On the origins of ORDEN, see Michael McClintock, *The American Connection, vol. 1: State Terror and Popular Resistance in El Salvador* (London: Zed Books, 1985), 204–9.

27. Duarte, in Nairn, "Behind the Death Squads," 2.

28. Nairn, "Behind the Death Squads," 21.

29. Nairn, "Behind the Death Squads," 20.

30. From "The Nationalist Democratic Organization (ORDEN)," typescript prepared by Chase Brandon of the embassy's Political Section and sent from the U.S. embassy in El Salvador to the State Department, 2 April 1979; *El Salvador: The Making of U.S. Policy*, Document No. 00124 (1979/04/02), 5.

31. In *El Salvador: The Making of U.S. Policy*, Document No. 00124 (1979/04/02), 7. The report concludes by noting that Medrano, in an interview with the U.S. embassy, "admitted that the organization may be guilty of carrying out repressive actions against the church and other groups in rural areas," but the document goes on to mitigate the charges: "That is not to say, however, that ORDEN is at the heart of a systematic conspiratorial drive by the military government to defeat its enemies real or imagined." In *Making of U.S. Policy*, 6.

32. Nairn, "Behind the Death Squads," 23.

33. House Committee on International Relations, *The Recent Presidential Elections in El Salvador: Implications for U.S. Foreign Policy*. Hearings before the Subcommittees on International Organizations and on Inter-American Affairs, 9 and 17 March 1977 (Washington DC: U.S. Government Printing Office, 1977).

34. Nairn, "Behind the Death Squads," 23.

35. Barbara Crossette, "Honduras Sends Officer Linked to Abuse to U.N.," *New York Times*, 20 February 1996, A6. See the exposé of Battalion 3-16 by Gary Cohn and Ginger Thompson, *The Baltimore Sun*, 11–18 June 1995, reprinted as Special Report, "Unearthed: Fatal Secrets," *The Baltimore Sun*, 501 N. Calvert Street, Baltimore MD 21278.

36. On Salvadorans' yearly earnings, see *U.S. Foreign Policy: The Reagan Imprint* (Washington DC: Congressional Quarterly, Inc., 1986), 54; for more recent data, see Mike Edwards, "El Salvador Learns to Live With Peace," *National Geographic* 188, no. 3 (September 1995): 108–31, esp. 117, 121. On Salvadoran literacy rates, see Dr. Eduardo Molina, "Social Justice in the Aftermath of the El Salvador Civil War," lecture presented at Loyola University of Chicago, 25 March 1993.

37. Duarte's statement, made on 27 December 1980, appears in Raymond Bonner, *Weakness and Deceit: U.S. Policy and El Salvador* (New York: Times Books, 1984), 24.

38. Schwarz, *American Counterinsurgency Doctrine*, 24, 25. In 1984 former ambassador Robert White told Congress, "The fundamental error of the Reagan foreign policy team [in El Salvador] has been to hide the fact that death squads and butchery are intrinsic to the regime their policies have helped create." House Committee on Foreign Affairs, *The Situation in El Salvador*, 6 February 1984, 45.

39. Cited in *New York Times*, 26 September 1991, A14.

40. "El Salvador's Future—and How U.S. Can Influence It: Interview with Ambassador Robert White," *U.S. News and World Report*, 26 January 1981, 38.

41. House Committee on Foreign Affairs, *The Situation in El Salvador*, 6 February 1984, 45.

42. Interview with *La Prensa Latina*, 2 February 1980, on the occasion of his receiving an honorary doctorate in Louvain, Belgium. Quoted in Plácido Erdozaín, *Archbishop Romero: Martyr of Salvador*, trans. John McFadden and Ruth Warner (Maryknoll NY: Orbis Books, 1981), 76, x.

43. These quotations are taken from homilies dated 13 January, 24 February, 16 March, and 23 March 1980, published in James R. Brockman, S.J., *Romero: A Life* (Maryknoll NY: Orbis Books, 1989). See also Archbishop Oscar Romero, *A Shepherd's Diary*, trans. Irene B. Hodgson (Cincinnati OH: St. Anthony Messenger Press, 1993), 528; Erdozaín, *Archbishop Romero*, 76.

44. From President Reagan's fifth press conference, 10 November 1981, in *Reagan's First Year* (Washington DC: Congressional Quarterly, Inc., 1982), 154.

45. *Reagan's First Year*, p. 44.

46. "Transcript of the President's News Conference on Foreign and Domestic Matters," *New York Times*, 7 March 1981, 10.

47. Speech of April 27, 1983, cited in Eric Alterman, "Bosnia and the Credibility Trap," *New York Times*, 13 May 1993, A11.

48. Nixon's remarks are from his "Address to the Nation on the Situation in Southeast Asia" (televised speech from the Oval Office, 30 April 1970, announcing the U.S. invasion of Cambodia), in *Public Papers of the Presidents of the United States: Richard Nixon, 1970* no. 139 (Washington DC: Government Printing Office, 1971), 409a.

49. From one perspective—that of American casualties—the war in El Salvador was one of America's cheapest. Estimates of how many American military personnel died conflict-related deaths in El Salvador range from twenty to nine: William Blum, *Killing Hope: U.S. Military and CIA Interventions Since World War II* (Monroe ME: Common Courage Press, 1995), 358; Walter LaFeber, *Inevitable Revolutions: The United States in Central America*, 2d rev. ed. (New York: W. W. Norton and Co., 1993); Benjamin C. Schwarz, *American Counterinsurgency Doctrine*, 31. Michael Waller, *The Third Current of Revolution: Inside the "North American Front" of El Salvador's Guerrilla War* (Lanham MD: University Press of America, 1991). For allegations of wider combat roles played by American soldiers, see Bonner, *Weakness and Deceit*, 274–75; Blum, *Killing Hope*, 358, 438 nn.28–33; "The Pentagon Turned its Back on Them," *60 Minutes*, CBS News, 21 May 1995, transcript, 1–12. See also Ed Offley, "El Salvador Raid in 1985 Revealed: Fort Lewis Rangers Hit Guerrilla Camp, Killing 83," *Seattle Post-Intelligencer*, 15 June 1995, A1, A20; and Offley, "Former Ranger Tells of Raid to Destroy Terrorist Camp: Mission: 'There Are to Be No Survivors,'" *Seattle Post-Intelligencer*, 15 June 1995, A1, A21.

50. See, for example, Walter Isaacson, "A Lot of Show, But No Tell: The U.S. Bungles Its Evidence of Foreign Subversion in El Salvador," *Time*, 22 March 1982, 18–22. See also *Washington Post*, 21 February 1982; Bonner, *Weakness and Deceit*, 263; and Thomas Sheehan, "Recent Developments in El Salvador," *Three Penny Review* 16

(winter 1984), 10. Later on in the war, the Salvadoran rebels acknowledged they had received some military aid from Nicaragua, but American and Salvadoran intelligence had extraordinary difficulty in detecting it.

54. Hereafter cited as the *Santa Fe Report*, the formal title of the text is *A New Inter-American Policy for the Eighties*, and it is signed "by The Committee of Santa Fe." It was authored by L. Francis (Lynn) Bouchey, president of CIS; freelance writer Roger W. Fontaine; David C. Jordan; Lt. Gen. Gordon Sumner Jr.; and Lewis Tambs (who alone is listed as editor). It was published privately in summer 1980.

52. See Roger Reed, Director of Publications of CIS, "Editorial Note to the Second Printing"; also the curriculum vitae of Lewis A. Tambs in his "Mikhail Gorbachev: Still a Dedicated Marxist-Leninist," in Herbert London et al., *Communism: The Ideology Fades—The Threat Remains* (Buena Park CA: Americanism Educational League, 1990), 11. 53. Tambs, ed., *Santa Fe Report*, 2, 3.

54. Tambs, ed., *Santa Fe Report*, 17, 20.

55. Testifying at a Congressional hearing, former ambassador to El Salvador Robert White remarked: "For fifty years, El Salvador was ruled by a corrupt and brutal alliance of the rich and the military. The young officers' revolt of 1979 attempted to break that alliance. . . . When the Reagan Administration took office, it reidentified the United States with the military and economic elites—with disastrous results." House Committee on Foreign Affairs, *The Situation in El Salvador*, 46.

56. William F. Buckley, "Elliot Abrams Is on the Right Track," *Esquire*, December 1984, 498. Mr. Abrams's effort to explain and justify his actions in the 1980s is found in his *Undue Process: A Story of How Political Differences Are Turned Into Crimes* (New York: The Free Press, 1993).

57. U.S. Senate, Committee on the Judiciary, *Marxism and Christianity in Revolutionary Central America. Hearings before the Subcommittee on Security and Terrorism*, October 18–19, 1983 (Washington DC: U.S. Government Printing Office, 1984), 96, 109.

58. The other sister, Ita Ford, reported this incident to her family in a letter. Lawyers Committee for Human Rights, "A Decade of Failed Promises: The Investigation of Archbishop Romero's Murder," March 1990, 14, n.23.

59. U.S. Senate, Committee on the Judiciary, *Marxism and Christianity in Revolutionary Central America*, appendix, 289–305. Also U.N. Truth Commission Report, 62–66. See also Clifford Krauss, "How U.S. Actions Helped Hide Abuses in Salvador," *New York Times*, 21 March 1993, 8. In May 1984, Deputy Sergeant Luis Antonio Colindres Alemán and four members of the National Guard were convicted of the murder of the churchwomen, and sentenced to thirty years each. They were released from prison in April 1993.

60. Krauss, "How U.S. Actions Helped Hide Abuses," 8; and Anthony Lewis, "The Catharsis of Truth," *New York Times*, 22 March 1993, A17.

61. Mr. Haig's testimony was given before the House Foreign Affairs Committee on 18 March 1981. See Anthony Lewis, "Fear of the Truth," *New York Times*, 2 April 1993, A19.

62. Clifford Krauss, "How U.S. Actions Helped Hide Abuses," 8. Monterrosa died in a helicopter crash in Morazán on 23 October 1984. See López Vigil, *Rebel Radio*, 124–36; *Las mil y una historia*, 316–38.

63. See Mark Danner, *The Massacre at El Mozote* (New York: Random House/ Vintage, 1994), including a list of the names of the victims (280–304). Danner's text was first published as "The Truth of El Mozote," *The New Yorker*, 6 December 1993, 50–133. See also Larry Rohter, "Where Countless Died in '81, Horror Lives On in Salvador," *The New York Times*, 12 February 1996, A1 and A4.

64. The bill requiring the president's semiannual certification of improvement in human rights was signed into law on 29 December 1981, seventeen days after the massacre. Six weeks after the massacre President Reagan did certify to Congress that the government of El Salvador was "making a concerted and significant effort to comply with internationally recognized human rights [and was] achieving substantial control over all elements of its own armed forces, so as to bring to an end the indiscriminate torture and murder of Salvadorean citizens by these forces." Cited in Blum, *Killing Hope*, 359.

65. Greentree's words are cited from Alan Tomlinson's report, "Allegations Reagan Officials Lied to Congress Surface," National Public Radio, 3 May 1993, typed transcript supplied by NPR, 2. On Thomas Enders, see his obituary, *New York Times*, 18 March 1996, C12.

66. See Thomas Sheehan, "Ignoring the Facts," *Chicago Tribune*, 28 July 1982, sec. 1, 17; and "Should Congress Continue Military Aid to El Salvador?" *Los Angeles Times*, 15 August 1982, pt. 4, 3. For statistics on human rights abuses in El Salvador through June 1985, see Amnesty International, *Reports on Human Rights in El Salvador* (New York and Washington DC: Seventh Supplement, September, 1985).

67. House Committee on Foreign Affairs, *The Situation in El Salvador*, 51.

68. House Committee on Foreign Affairs, *The Situation in El Salvador*, 50. White continued: "The reliability of this military officer [who had reported on the meeting] as a trustworthy source has been established over the months and years. All of the above information was reported to Washington."

69. The letter was written by W. Tapley Bennett Jr., assistant secretary of state for legislative affairs, dated 11 April 1984. It has been declassified and is found in *El Salvador: The Making of U.S. Policy*, Document No. 04974 (1984/04/11).

70. The cable is given in two similar forms in *El Salvador: The Making of U.S. Policy*, Documents Nos. 02308 and 02309 (1981/12/21, 1817Z).

71. U.N. Truth Commission Report, 127 and 130. For an earlier review of the case, see Brockman, *Romero*, 249–55. Other sources implicate Edgar Pérez Linares, a detective in Salvador's National Police; see Douglas Farah, "2 Salvadorans Detail Origin of A Death Squad," *Washington Post*, 29 August 1984, A26.

72. Dan Quayle, *Standing Firm: A Vice-Presidential Memoir* (New York: HarperCollins/Zondervan, 1994), 121.

73. Farah, "Origin of a Death Squad," a26.

74. House Committee on Foreign Affairs, *The Situation in El Salvador*, 48; also 41, 49.

75. See "Minneapolis Law," *Bulletin of Municipal Foreign Policy* 4, no. 1 (winter 1989–1990), 50–51; also William Greidler, *Who Will Tell the People? The Betrayal of American Democracy* (New York: Simon and Schuster, 1992), 256–57.

76. Krauss, "How U.S. Actions Helped Hide Abuses," 8.

77. For a list of the organizations the FBI spied on, see "Groups Included in the

CISPES Files Obtained from FBI Headquarters," Center for Constitutional Rights, 666 Broadway. New York NY 10012, 27 January 1988, 11 pages, typescript.

78. See Ross Gelbspan, *Break-ins, Death Threats and the FBI: The Covert War Against the Central America Movement* (Boston: South End Press, 1991), 216; Bob Woodward, *Veil* (New York: Pocket Books), 110.

79. See Christopher Simpson, *National Security Directives of the Reagan and Bush Administrations: The Declassified History of U.S. Political and Military Policy, 1981–1991* (Boulder CO: Westview, 1995), 57, 94; also David Johnston with Michael Wines, "Spying Data on Sandinistas Involved U.S. Congressmen, Ex-Officials Say," *New York Times*, 15 September 1991.

80. A facsimile of the cable is reprinted in Ward Churchill and Jim Vander Wall, *The COINTELPRO Papers: Documents from the FBI's Secret Wars Against Domestic Dissent* (Boston: South End Press, 1990), 18–19.

81. See Gelbspan, *Break-ins, Death Threats and the FBI*; Churchill and Vander Wall, *COINTELPRO Papers*. Also House of Representatives, Committee on the Judiciary, *Break-Ins at Sanctuary Churches and Organizations Opposed to Administration Policy in Central America. Hearings before the Subcommittee on Civil and Constitutional Rights*, 19–20 February 1987 (Washington DC: U.S. Government Printing Office, 1987); Michael W. Hirschorn, "Newly Released Documents Provide Rare Look at How FBI Monitors Students and Professors," *Chronicle of Higher Education*, 10 February 1988, A1 and A13; Sandy Tolan and Carol Ann Bassett, "Informers in the Sanctuary Movement," *The Nation* 241 (20–27 July 1985): 40–43; Vince Bielski, Cindy Forster, and Dennis Bernstein, "The Death Squads Hit Home: Which Side is the FBI On?" *The Progressive* 51, no. 10 (18 October 1987): 15–19; Brian Glick, *War at Home: Covert Action Against U.S. Activists and What We Can Do About It* (Boston: South End Press, 1989).

82. U.S. House of Representatives, *Break-Ins at Sanctuary Churches*, respectively 464, 655, 458, and 457.

83. For more on the album, see Wayne King, "An F.B.I. Inquiry Fed by Informer Emerges in Analysis of Documents: Once-Discounted Tale of Invented Tips to Justify Spying on Policy Critics Is Bearing Out," *New York Times*, 13 February 1988, A33; and Gelbspan, *Break-ins, Death Threats and the FBI*, 97–102.

84. Gelbspan, *Break-ins, Death Threats and the FBI*, 184.

85. Alfonso Chardy, "Reagan Advisers Ran 'Secret Government,'" *The Miami Herald*, 5 July 1987, 1A, 14A, and 15A. The "U.S. military invasion abroad" was widely understood to refer to Nicaragua.

86. Gelbspan, *Break-ins, Death Threats and the FBI*, 185.

87. Details can be found in *Break-Ins at Sanctuary Churches*, 534, 537, 538, 555, etc. See also Gelbspan, *Break-ins, Death Threats and the FBI*, 194–207.

88. Philip Shenon, "F.B.I.'s Chief Says Surveillance Was Justified," *New York Times*, 3 February 1988, A1 and A13; and Philip Shenon, "Reagan Backs F.B.I Over Surveillance," *New York Times*, 4 February 1988, A21.

89. See Doggett, *Death Foretold*, 73–100.

90. Lucia Cerna heard Father Martín-Baró's last words—" ¡Esta es una injusticia! ¡Son una carroña!" (perhaps: "This is an injustice! You are utterly corrupt!"). Law-

yers Committee for Human Rights, "The Jesuit Murders: A Report on the Testimony of a Witness," 15 December 1980, 7.

91. On Walker's intervention, see Doggett, "Assassination of the Jesuits," 22 n.28, which here draws upon the embassy's "Mission Chronology," from volume 7 of the State Department's documents on the murder of the Jesuits. On Chidester, see Sam Dillon, *Comandos: The CIA and Nicaragua's Contra Rebels* (New York: Henry Holt, 1991), 221–22, 324; also Whitfield, *Paying the Price*, 76.

92. Lawyers Committee for Human Rights, "The Jesuit Murders: A Report on the Testimony of a Witness," 15 December 1989; also Doggett, *Death Foretold*, 220.

93. On the chain of information from Benavides to Buckland, see Doggett, *Death Foretold*, 222, 336–37.

94. Thomas Long and Frank Smyth, "Release the Jesuit Tapes: The FBI Has Videotaped Testimony That Accuses the Salvadoran Army of Killing Six Jesuits—and Proves the U.S. Knew in Advance," *Village Voice*, 13 November 1990, 22. See further also Thomas Long, "Jesuit Cover-up in Salvador: Videotape of U.S. Advisor Reveals Army Planned Priests' Murders," *Village Voice*, 18 July 1991, 25, 26. See also Doggett, *Death Foretold*, 225–26. Buckland's sworn statement (not handwritten, as formerly thought) is on file at the Lawyers Committee for Human Rights.

95. Cited from a transcript of the videotape in Long, "Jesuit Cover-up in El Salvador," 26.

96. Besides Benavides, the indicted were: Lts. José Ricardo Espinoza Guerra and Yusshy René Mendoza Vallecillos, and 2d Lt. Gonzalo Guevara Cerritos, the three who led the raid; Pvt. Oscar Mariano Amaya Grimaldi, nicknamed "Pilijay" ("Hangman"), who killed Frs. Ignacio Ellacuría, Ignacio Martín Baró, and Segundo Montes; Sub-Sgt. Ramiro Avalos Vargas, nicknamed "Toad" or "Satan," who killed Frs. Amando López and Juan Ramón Moreno; Cpl. Angel Pérez Vásquez, who finished off Fr. Joaquín López y López; and Sub-Sgt. Tomás Zarpate Castillo, nicknamed "Sampson" and (in absentia) Pvt. Jorge Sierra Ascencio, who, respectively, shot and finished off Elba Ramos and her daughter Celina. Benavides, Espinoza, Mendoza, Guevara, and Avalos were all graduates of the U.S. School of the Americas at Fort Benning, Georgia.

97. Representative Miller made his statement in response to questions from Ed Bradley, in "The Jesuit Murders," *Sixty Minutes*, 29 April 1990, CBS Television.

98. See Lawyers Committee for Human Rights, "Update on Investigation of the Murder of Six Jesuit Priests in El Salvador," 25 March 1991, 12.

99. Doggett, *Death Foretold*, 226–27.

100. This was first disclosed by Long and Smyth, "Release the Jesuit Tapes," 18.

101. "Cracking the Major," *Newsweek*, 19 November 1990, 6. See Doggett, *Death Foretold*, 228 n.457.

102. Cited in Long, "Jesuit Cover-up in Salvador," 26.

103. Cited in Doggett, *Death Foretold*, 226.

104. Long and Smyth, "Release the Jesuit Tapes," 22.

105. Long, "Jesuit Cover-up in Salvador," 26.

106. "The Jesuit Murders," *Sixty Minutes*, story by Ed Bradley.

107. AP Wire, "El Salvador Frees 2 In Murder of Priests," *New York Times*, 2 April

1993, A7. For a brief report on the trial, see Vincent T. O'Keefe, "The El Salvador Trial in the Jesuit Case," *America*, 19 October 1991, 260.

108. Arnold J. Toynbee, "The Shot Heard Round the World," in *America and the World Revolution, and Other Lectures* (New York and London: Oxford University Press, 1962), 92–93.

109. In Leon Wolff, *Little Brown Brother* (New York: Doubleday, 1961), 303; quoted here from Barbara Tuchman, "End of a Dream: The United States, 1890–1902," in *The Proud Tower* (New York: Bantam, 1962), 190. A more modest expression of the project might be simply: "promoting security and stability in our hemisphere," cited from a Bob Dole campaign working paper on foreign policy, in William Safire, "The Dole Doctrine," *New York Times*, 1 April 1996, A11.

110. In Tuchman, *Proud Tower*, 177.

111. Mark Twain, "To the Person Sitting In Darkness," *North American Review* 81 (February 1901): 161–76. See also Mark Twain, "Thirty Thousand Killed a Million," *Atlantic Monthly* 269, no. 4 (April 1992): 52–65, and the introduction, "Mark Twain on American Imperialism," 49–51 in the same issue.

Selected Bibliography

"1933–1934: Thoughts on National Socialism." Special feature, *Critical Inquiry* 17, no. 1 (1990).

Aly, Götz, Peter Chroust, and Christian Pross. *Cleansing the Fatherland: Nazi Medicine and Racial Hygiene.* Translated by Belinda Cooper. Baltimore: Johns Hopkins University Press, 1994.

Aubrac, Lucie. *Outwitting the Gestapo.* Lincoln: University of Nebraska Press, 1993.

Baldwin, Peter, ed. *Reworking the Past: Hitler, the Holocaust, and the Historians' Debate.* Boston: Beacon, 1990.

Bartov, Omer. "Intellectuals on Auschwitz: Memory, History, and Truth." *History & Memory* 5, no. 1 (1993): 87–110.

Ben-Ghiat, Ruth. "Fascism, Writing, and Memory: The Realist Aesthetic in Italy, 1930–1950." *The Journal of Modern History* 67 (1995): 627–65.

Berlin, Isiah. "Joseph de Maistre and the Origins of Fascism: I." *The New York Review of Books*, 27 September 1990, 57–64

———. "Joseph de Maistre and the Origins of Fascism: II." *The New York Review of Books*, 11 October 1990, 54–58.

———. "Joseph de Maistre and the Origins of Fascism: III." *The New York Review of Books*, 25 October 1990, 60–65.

Berman, Russell. "Modernism, Fascism, and the Institution of Literature." In *Modernism: Challenges and Perspectives*, edited by M. Chefdor, R. Quinones, and A. Nachtel, 94–110. Champaign: University of Illinois Press, 1986.

Bessel, Richard, ed. *Fascist Italy and Nazi Germany: Comparisons and Contrasts.* Cambridge: Cambridge University Press, 1996.

Blum, Cinzia Sartini. *The Other Modernism: F. T. Marinetti's Futurist Fiction of Power.* Berkeley: University of California Press, 1996.

Bracher, Nathan, ed. "A Time to Remember." Special issue, *Contemporary French Civilization* 19, no. 2 (1995).

Bunzl, Matti. "On the Politics and Semantics of Austrian Memory: Vienna's Monument against War and Fascism." *History & Memory* 7, no. 2 (1996): 7–40.

Caldwell, Lesley. "Madri d'Italia: A Cinematic Exemplification of Fascist Concern with Motherhood." *The Italianist: Journal of the Department of Italian Studies, University of Reading* 8 (1988): 79–95.

Capri, Daniel. *Between Mussolini and Hitler: The Jews and the Italian Authorities in France and Tunisia.* Tauber Institute for the Study of European Jewry Series, vol. 17. Hanover NH: University Press of New England, 1994.

Carroll, David. "Literary Fascism or the Aestheticizing of Politics: The Case of Robert Brasillach." *New Literary History* 23 (1992): 691–726.

————. *French Literary Fascism: Nationalism, Anti-Semitism, and the Ideology of Culture.* Princeton: Princeton University Press, 1995.

Castillo, Robert. *The Genealogy of Demons: Anti-Semitism, Fascism, and the Myths of Ezra Pound.* Evanston IL: Northwestern University Press, 1988.

Cheles, Luciano, Ronnie Ferguson, and Michalina Vaughan, eds. *The Far Right in Western and Eastern Europe.* 2d ed. London: Longman, 1995.

Childers, Thomas, and Jane Caplan, eds. *Reevaluating the Third Reich.* Europe Past and Present Series. New York: Holmes & Meier, 1993.

Cigar, Norman. *Genocide in Bosnia: The Policy of "Ethnic Cleansing."* Eastern European Studies, vol. 1. College Station: Texas A&M University Press, 1995.

Cobb, Richard. *French and Germans, Germans and French: A Personal Interpretation of France under Two Occupations, 1914–1918/ 1940–1944.* Hanover NH: University Press of New England, 1983.

Crew, David F., ed. *Nazism and German Society, 1933–1945.* New York: Routledge, 1994.

Dasenbrock, Reed Way. "Taking It Personally: Reading Derrida's Responses." *College English* 56, no. 3 (1994): 261–78.

De Grazia, Victoria. *How Fascism Ruled Women: Italy, 1922–1945.* Berkeley: University of California Press, 1992.

De Jong, Louis. *The Netherlands and Nazi Germany.* Cambridge: Harvard University Press, 1990.

"De Man and Heidegger Revisited." Special feature, *South Central Review* 11, no. 1 (1994): 1–55.

De Man, Paul. *Wartime Journalism 1939–43.* Edited by Werner Hamacher, Neil Hertz, and Thomas Keenan. Lincoln: University of Nebraska Press, 1988.

Eatwell, Roger. *Fascism: A History.* New York: Allen Lane/The Penguin Press, 1995.

Eco, Umberto. "Ur-Fascism." *The New York Review of Books*, 22 June 1995, 12–15.

Ezekiel, Raphael S. *The Racist Mind: Portraits of American Neo-Nazis and Klansmen*. New York: Viking Press, 1995.

"The Familiar Face of Fascism." Special issue, *Utne Reader*, no. 72 (November–December 1995).

Farías, Victor. *Heidegger and Nazism*. Edited by Joseph Mangolis and Tom Rockmore. Philadelphia: Temple University Press, 1989.

"Fascism and Culture." Special double issue, *Stanford Italian Review* 8, nos. 1–2 (1990).

"Fascism and Culture, Part Two." Special issue of *Modernism/Modernity* 3, no. 1 (1996).

"Fascist Aesthetics." Special issue, *South Central Review* 6, no. 2 (1989).

Ferry, Luc, and Alain Renault. *Heidegger and Modernity*. Chicago: University of Chicago Press, 1990.

Finkielkraut, Alain. *Remembering in Vain: The Klaus Barbie Trial and Crimes Against Humanity*. Translated by Roxanne Lapidus and Sima Godfrey. New York: Columbia University Press, 1992.

"The French New Right: New Right—New Left—New Paradigm?" Special double issue, *Telos: A Quarterly Journal of Critical Thought*, nos. 98–99 (1993–94).

Friedlander, Judith. *Vilna on the Seine: Jewish Intellectuals in France since 1968*. New Haven CT: Yale University Press, 1990.

Friedlander, Saul. *Reflections of Nazism: An Essay on Kitsch and Death*. Translated by Thomas Wyer. Bloomington: Indiana University Press, 1993.

Gaspard, Françoise. *A Small City in France*. Translated by Arthur Goldhammer. Cambridge: Harvard University Press, 1995.

Gättens, Marie-Louise. *Women Writers and Fascism: Reconstructing History*. Gainesville FL: University Press of Florida, 1995.

Gentile, Emilio. "Fascism in Italian Historiography: In Search of an Individual Historical Identity." *Journal of Contemporary History* 21, no. 2 (1986): 179–208.

———. *The Sacralization of Politics in Fascist Italy*. Translated by Keith Botsford. Cambridge: Harvard University Press, 1996.

Goldhagen, Daniel Jonah. *Hitler's Willing Executioners: Ordinary Germans and the Holocaust*. New York: Knopf, 1996.

Golsan, Richard J. "From the Heidegger Controversy to 'L'Affaire Derrida': Heidegger, Nazism, and the Anxiety of Influence." *Annals of Scholarship* 11, no. 3 (1997): 313–25.

Golsan, Richard J., ed. *Fascism, Aesthetics, and Culture*. Hanover NH: University Press of New England, 1992.

———. *Memory, the Holocaust, and French Justice: The Bousquet and Touvier Affairs.* Translated by Lucy Golsan and Richard J. Golsan. Contemporary French Culture and Society Series. Hanover NH: University Press of New England, 1996.

Gordon, Bertram. *Collaborationism in France during the Second World War.* Ithaca NY: Cornell University Press, 1980.

Green, Mary Jean. "Towards an Analysis of Fascist Fiction: The Contempestuous Narrator in the Works of Brasillach, Céline and Drieu la Rochelle." *Studies in Twentieth-Century Literature* 10, no. 1 (1985): 81–97.

Griffin, Roger. *The Nature of Fascism.* 2d ed. London: Routledge, 1993.

Griffin, Roger, ed. *Fascism.* New York: Oxford University Press, 1995.

Hamcher, Werner, Neil Hertz, and Thomas Keenan, eds. *Responses: On Paul de Man's Wartime Journalism.* Lincoln: University of Nebraska Press, 1989.

Harris, Geoffrey. *The Dark Side of Europe: The Extreme Right Today.* 2d ed. Edinburgh: Edinburgh University Press, 1994.

Hartman, Geoffrey H., ed. *Bitburg in Moral and Political Perspective.* Bloomington: Indiana University Press, 1986.

Hasselbach, Ingo, and Tom Reiss. *Führer-Ex: Memoirs of a Former Neo-Nazi.* New York: Random House, 1996.

Hawthorne, Melanie, and Richard J. Golsan, eds. *Gender and Fascism in Modern France.* Contemporary French Culture and Society. Hanover NH: University Press of New England, 1997.

"Heidegger and the Political." Special issues, *Graduate Faculty Philosophy Journal* 14, no. 2 (1985) and 15, no. 1 (1986).

Hellman, John. *The Knight-Monks of Vichy France: Uriage, 1940–1945.* Montreal: McGill-Queen's University Press, 1993.

Heschel, Susannah. "Anti-Semites Against Anti-Semitism." *Tikkun* 8, no. 6 (November–December 1993): 47–53.

Hewitt, Andrew. *Fascist Modernism: Aesthetics, Politics, and the Avant-Garde.* Stanford CA: Stanford University Press, 1993.

Higgins, Lynn A. *New Novel, New Wave, New Politics: Fiction and the Representation of History in Postwar France.* Stages, vol. 4. Lincoln: University of Nebraska Press, 1996.

Hirsch, David H. *The Deconstruction of Literature: Criticism after Auschwitz.* Hanover NH: University Press of New England, 1991.

Hockenos, Paul. *Free to Hate: The Rise of the Right in Post-Communist Eastern Europe.* New York: Routledge, 1993.

Hofer, Walther. "Fifty Years On: Historians and the Third Reich." *Journal of Contemporary History* 21, no. 2 (1986): 225–51.

"The Invasion and Occupation of France, 1940–1944: Intellectual and

Cultural Responses." Special issue, *Journal of European Studies* 23 (1993).

Jay, Martin. "Postmodern Fascism? Reflections on the Return of the Oppressed." *Tikkun* 8, no. 6 (1993): 37–46.

Jeansonne, Glen. *Women of the Far Right: The Mothers' Movement and World War II*. Chicago: University of Chicago Press, 1996.

Joffe, Josef. "Goldhagen in Germany." *The New York Review of Books,* 28 November 1996, 18–21.

Jones, Larry Eugene. *German Liberalism and the Dissolution of the Weimar Party System, 1918–1933*. Chapel Hill: University of North Carolina Press, 1988.

Joplin, Patricia Klindienst. "The Authority of Illusion: Feminism and Fascism in Virginia Woolf's *Between the Acts.*" *South Central Review* 6, no. 2 (1989): 88–104.

Kaes, Anton, Martin Jay, and Edward Dimendberg, eds. *The Weimar Republic Sourcebook*. Berkeley: University of California Press, 1994.

Kaplan, Alice Yeager. *Reproductions of Banality: Fascism, Literature and French Intellectual Life*. Theory and History of Literature, vol. 36. Minneapolis: University of Minnesota Press, 1986.

Kater, Michael H. *The Nazi Party: A Social Profile of Members and Leaders, 1919–1945*. Cambridge: Harvard University Press, 1983.

———. *Doctors under Hitler*. Chapel Hill: University of North Carolina Press, 1989.

Katz, Steven T. *The Holocaust in Historical Context*. Vol. 1, *The Holocaust and Mass Death before the Modern Age*. New York: Oxford University Press, 1994.

Kedward, Harry Roderick. *Vichy France: Collaboration and Resistance, 1940–1944*. New York: Blackwell, 1985.

Kedward, Harry Roderick, and Nancy Woods, eds. *The Liberation of France: Image and Event*. Oxford: Berg, 1995.

Kent, Peter C. *The Pope and the Duce: The International Impact of Lateran Agreements*. London: Macmillan, 1981.

Kershaw, Ian. *The "Hitler Myth": Image and Reality in the Third Reich*. Oxford: Oxford University Press, 1987.

———. *The Nazi Dictatorship: Problems and Perspectives of Interpretation*. 3d ed. London: Edward Arnold, 1993.

Knowlton, James, and Truett Cates, trans. *Forever in the Shadow of Hitler? Original Documents of the "Historikerstreit," the Controversy Concerning the Singularity of the Holocaust*. Atlantic Highlands NJ: Humanities Press, 1993.

Knox, MacGregor. *Mussolini Unleashed, 1939–1941: Politics and*

Strategy in Fascist Italy's Last War. Cambridge: Cambridge University Press, 1982.

Koch, Hannsjoachim Wolfgang. *In the Name of the Volk: Political Justice in Hitler's Germany.* New York: St. Martin's Press, 1989.

Kofas, Jon V. *Authoritarianism in Greece: The Metaxas Regime.* Boulder CO: East European Monographs, 1983.

Kuhl, Stefan. *The Nazi Connection: Eugenics, American Racism, and German National Socialism.* New York: Oxford University Press, 1993.

Landy, Marcia. *Fascism in Film: The Italian Commercial Cinema, 1931–1943.* Princeton: Princeton University Press, 1986.

Laqueur, Walter. *Black Hundred: The Rise of the Extreme Right in Russia.* New York: HarperPerennial, 1993.

———. *Fascism: Past, Present, Future.* New York: Oxford University Press, 1996.

Lewis, David Stephen. *Illusions of Grandeur: Mosely, Fascism and British Society, 1931–81.* Manchester: Manchester University Press, 1987.

Lewis, Wyndham. *The Art of Being Ruled.* 1926. Edited by Reed Way Dasenbrock. Reprint, Santa Rosa CA: Black Sparrow Press, 1989.

Lottman, Herbert R. *The Purge.* New York: Morrow, 1986.

Löwith, Karl. *Martin Heidegger and European Nihilism.* Translated by Gary Steiner. European Perspectives. New York: Columbia University Press, 1995.

Lyotard, Jean-François. *Heidegger and "the jews".* Minneapolis: University of Minnesota Press, 1990.

Maier, Charles S., et al. *The Rise of the Nazi Regime: Historical Reassessments.* Boulder CO: Westview Press, 1986.

Mancini, Elaine. *The Struggle of the Italian Film Industry during Fascism, 1930–1935.* Ann Arbor MI: UMI Research Press, 1985.

Marcus, Jonathan. *The National Front and French Politics: The Resistible Rise of Jean-Marie Le Pen.* New York: New York University Press, 1995.

"Marinetti and the Italian Futurists." Special issue, *Modernism/Modernity* 1, no. 3 (1994).

Marrus, Michael Robert. *The Holocaust in History.* Tauber Institute for the Study of European Jewry Series, vol. 7. Hanover NH: University Press of New England, 1987.

Marrus, Michael Robert, and Robert O. Paxton. *Vichy France and the Jews.* New York: Basic Books, 1981.

Martin, Elaine, ed. *Gender, Patriarchy, and Fascism in the Third Reich: The Response of Women Writers.* Detroit: Wayne State University Press, 1993.

Mason, Timothy W. *Social Policy in the Third Reich: The Working Class and the National Community.* Providence: Berg, 1993.

———. *Nazism, Fascism and the Working Class.* Cambridge: Cambridge University Press, 1995.

McCarthy, Patrick. *The Crisis of the Italian State: From the Origins of the Cold War to the Fall of Berlusconi.* New York: St. Martin's Press, 1995.

Mehlman, Jeffrey. *Legacies of Anti-Semitism in France.* Minneapolis: University of Minnesota Press, 1983.

Michaud, Eric. "National Socialist Architecture as an Acceleration of Time." Translated by Christopher Fox. *Critical Inquiry* 19 (1993): 220–33.

Miller, Judith. *One, by One, by One: Facing the Holocaust.* New York: Simon & Schuster, 1990.

Mizejewski, Linda. *Divine Decadence: Fascism, Female Spectacle, and the Makings of Sally Bowles.* Princeton: Princeton University Press, 1992.

Morrison, Paul. *The Poetics of Fascism: Ezra Pound, T. S. Eliot, Paul de Man.* New York: Oxford University Press, 1996.

Mühlberger, Detlef, ed. *The Social Basis of European Fascist Movements.* New York: Croom Helm, 1987.

Neaman, Elliot. "Fascism and Postmodernism: A Reply to Martin Jay." *Tikkun* 8, no. 6 (1993): 42–46.

Nicholls, Anthony James. *Weimar and the Rise of Hitler.* 3d ed. The Making of the 20th Century. London: Macmillan, 1991.

"The Occupation in French Literature and Film, 1940–1992." Special issue, *Ésprit Créateur* 33, no. 1 (1993).

O'Sullivan, Noël. *Fascism.* Modern Ideologies. London: J. M. Dent and Sons, 1983.

Pauley, Bruce F. *Hitler and the Forgotten Nazis: A History of Austrian National Socialism.* Chapel Hill: University of North Carolina Press, 1981.

———. *From Prejudice to Persecution: A History of Austrian Anti-Semitism.* Chapel Hill: University of North Carolina Press, 1992.

Paxton, Robert O. *Vichy France: Old Guard and New Order, 1940–1944.* New York: Columbia University Press, 1982.

———. "The Uses of Fascism." *The New York Review of Books*, 28 November 1996, 48–52.

Payne, Stanley G. "Fascism and Right Authoritarianism in the Iberian World—The Last Twenty Years." *Journal of Contemporary History* 21, no. 2 (1986): 163–77.

———. *The Franco Regime, 1936–1975.* Madison: University of Wisconsin Press, 1987.

————. *A History of Fascism, 1914–1945*. Madison: University of Wisconsin Press, 1995.

Perloff, Marjorie. *The Futurist Movement: Avant-garde, Avant guerre, and the Language of Rupture*. Chicago: University of Chicago Press, 1986.

Peukert, Detlev. *Inside Nazi Germany: Conformity, Opposition, and Racism in Everyday Life*. New Haven CT: Yale University Press, 1987.

————. *The Weimar Republic: The Crisis of Classical Modernity*. London: Penguin Books, 1993.

Pickering-Iazzi, Robin. *Mothers of Invention: Women, Italian Fascism, and Culture*. Minneapolis: University of Minnesota Press, 1995.

Pinkus, Karen. *Bodily Regimes: Italian Advertising under Fascism*. Minneapolis: University of Minnesota Press, 1995.

Preston, Paul. *The Politics of Revenge: Fascism and the Military in Twentieth-Century Spain*. London: Routledge, 1990.

Pulzer, Peter G. J. *The Rise of Political Anti-Semitism in Germany and Austria*. Rev. ed. Cambridge: Harvard University Press, 1988.

Redman, Tim. *Ezra Pound and Italian Fascism*. Cambridge Studies in American Literature and Culture. Cambridge: Cambridge University Press, 1991.

Roth, Jack Joseph. *The Cult of Violence: Sorel and the Sorelians*. Berkeley: University of California Press, 1980.

Rousso, Henry. *The Vichy Syndrome: History and Memory in France since 1944*. Translated by Arthur Goldhammer. Cambridge: Harvard University Press, 1991.

Schmidt, Michael. *The New Reich: Violent Extremism in Unified Germany and Beyond*. Translated by Daniel Horch. New York: Pantheon Books, 1993.

Schnapp, Jeffrey T. *Staging Fascism: 18 BL and the Theater of Masses for Masses*. Stanford CA: Stanford University Press, 1996.

Sheehan, Thomas. "Heidegger and Nazism: An Exchange." *The New York Review of Books*, 8 April 1993, 49–50.

Shrivastava, Anjana. "German Neo-fascism and the Politics of Meaning." *Tikkun* 9, no. 4 (1994): 9–12.

Smith, Bradley F. *The Road to Nuremberg*. New York: Basic Books, 1981.

Smith, Woodruff D. *The Intellectual Origins of Nazi Imperialism*. New York: Oxford University Press, 1986.

Soucy, Robert. *French Fascism: The First Wave, 1924–1933*. New Haven CT: Yale University Press, 1986.

———. *French Fascism: The Second Wave, 1933–1939.* New Haven CT: Yale University Press, 1995.

"Special Issue on Ernst Jünger." *New German Critique,* no. 59 (1993).

Steinberg, Jonathan. *All or Nothing: The Axis and the Holocaust 1941–43.* London: Routledge, 1990.

Steiner, George. "Heidegger, Again." *Salmagundi,* nos. 82–83 (1989): 31–55.

Steinweis, Alan E. *Art, Ideology, and Economics in Nazi Germany.* Chapel Hill: University of North Carolina Press, 1993.

Sternhell, Zeev. *Neither Right nor Left: Fascist Ideology in France.* Translated by David Maisel. Berkeley: University of California Press, 1986.

Sternhell, Zeev, Mario Sznajder, and Maia Asheri. *The Birth of Fascist Ideology: From Cultural Rebellion to Political Revolution.* Translated by David Maisel. Princeton: Princeton University Press, 1994.

Sweets, John F. *Choices in Vichy France: The French under Nazi Occupation.* New York: Oxford University Press, 1986.

"Symposium on Heidegger and Nazism." Special feature, *Critical Inquiry* 15, no. 2 (1989).

Tarrow, Sidney. *Democracy and Disorder: Protest and Politics in Italy, 1965–1975.* Oxford: Clarendon Press, 1989.

Tartar, Maria. *Lustmord: Sexual Murder in Weimar Germany.* Princeton: Princeton University Press, 1995.

Taylor, Telford. *The Anatomy of the Nuremberg Trials: A Personal Memoir.* New York: Knopf, 1992.

Thelweleit, Klaus. *Male Fantasies: Vol. 1, Women, Floods, Bodies, History.* Minneapolis: University of Minnesota Press, 1987.

———. *Male Fantasies: Vol. 2, Male Bodies: Psychoanalyzing the White Terror.* Minneapolis: University of Minnesota Press, 1989.

Todorov, Tzvetan. "The Heidegger/De Man Debates." *Times Literary Supplement,* 17–23 June 1988, 676ff.

Tratner, Michael. *Modernism and Mass Politics: Joyce, Woolf, Eliot, Yeats.* Stanford CA: Stanford University Press, 1995.

Ungar, Steven. *Scandal and Aftereffect: Blanchot and France since 1970.* Minneapolis: University of Minnesota Press, 1995.

Veen, Hans-Joachim, Norbert Lepszy, and Peter Mnich. *The Republikaner Party in Germany: Right-Wing Menace or Protest Catchall?* The Washington Papers, vol. 162. Westport CT: Praeger, 1993.

Weinberg, Gerhard L. *A World at Arms: A Global History of World War II.* Cambridge: Cambridge University Press, 1994.

———. *Germany, Hitler, and World War II: Essays in Modern German and World History.* Cambridge: Cambridge University Press, 1995.

Welch, David. *Propaganda and the German Cinema, 1933–1945*. 2d ed. Oxford: Clarendon Press, 1987.

———. *The Third Reich: Politics and Propaganda*. London: Routledge, 1993.

Willson, Perry R. *The Clockwork Factory: Women and Work in Fascist Italy*. Oxford: Clarendon Press, 1993.

Wolin, Richard. *The Politics of Being: The Political Thought of Martin Heidegger*. New York: Columbia University Press, 1990.

———. *The Terms of Cultural Criticism: The Frankfurt School, Existentialism, Poststructuralism*. New York: Columbia University Press, 1992.

———. "Mussolini's Ghost: Europe and the Specter of Fascism." *Tikkun* 9, no. 4 (1994): 13–16ff.

Wolin, Richard, ed. *The Heidegger Controversy: A Critical Reader*. New York: Columbia University Press, 1991.

Ziegler, Herbert F. *Nazi Germany's New Aristocracy: The ss Leadership, 1925–1939*. Princeton: Princeton University Press, 1989.

Zuccotti, Susan. *The Italians and the Holocaust: Persecution, Rescue, and Survival*. Lincoln: University of Nebraska Press, 1987.

———. *The Holocaust, the French, and the Jews*. New York: Basic Books, 1993.

Contributors

Reed Way Dasenbrock is Associate Dean and Director of the Research Center in the College of Liberal Arts at New Mexico State University, where he has taught in the English Department since 1981. He has authored or edited seven books, including, most recently, *Literary Theory after Davidson* (Pennsylvania State University Press, 1993). He has just completed a book-length manuscript entitled *Truth and Consequences: From Conventionalism to Intentionalism in Literary Studies.*

Christopher Flood is Head of European Studies at the University of Surrey, England. He is author of *Pensée politique et imagination historique dans l'oeuvre de Paul Claudel* (Université de Besançon; Diffusion, 1991), *Political Myth: A Theoretical Introduction* (Garland, 1996), and numerous articles or chapters on aspects of French politics and culture. He is coeditor of *Political Ideologies in Contemporary France* (Pinter, 1997) and is currently coediting a collection of essays dealing with French debates over decolonization, immigration, and postcolonialism.

Richard J. Golson is Professor of French at Texas A&M University and Editor of *South Central Review.* He has written books on Henry de Montherlant and René Girard and has recently edited *Memory, the Holocaust, and French Justice* (Dartmouth/University Press of New England, 1996) and *Fascism, Aesthetics, and Culture* (University Press of New England, 1992). His articles have appeared in *SubStance, The French Review, Mots Romance Quarterly, L'Esprit Créateur,* the *Journal of European Studies,* and elsewhere. He is currently researching a book on the trial of Maurice Papon.

Bertram M. Gordon, Frederick A. Rice Professor of History at Mills College, is the author of *Collaborationism in France during the Second World War* (Cornell University Press, 1980) and the Editor of the *Historical Dictionary of World War II France: The Occupation, Vichy, and the Resistance, 1938–1946,* to be published by Greenwood Press in 1998. A frequent contributor of articles on World War II France, the French Right, and the Collaboration, he has also written on the history of gastronomy and the history of tourism. He serves on the editorial board of *French Historical Studies*, the international editorial advisory board of *Modern and Contemporary France*, and as coeditor of the H-France electronic history network.

Lynn A. Higgins is Professor of French and Comparative Literature and Chair of the Department of French and Italian at Dartmouth College. She is the author of *Parables of Theory: Jean Ricardou's Metafiction* (Summa, 1984) and coeditor of *Rape and Representation* (Columbia University Press, 1991). Her most recent book is *New Novel, New Wave, New Politics: Fiction and the Representation of History in Postwar France* (University of Nebraska Press, 1996).

Wulf Kansteiner, Assistant Professor of History at the University of Tennessee at Chattanooga, studied at the Ruhr-Universität Bochum and UCLA. He has published on the interpretation of Nazism and the "Final Solution" in historiography, philosophy, and criticism. He currently studies the representation of Nazism and the Holocaust in German television.

Elliot Neaman teaches European History at the University of San Francisco. He is the author of the forthcoming book *A Dubious Past: Ernst Jünger and the Politics of Literature after Nazism* (University of California Press).

Jeffrey T. Schnapp is Professor of Italian and Comparative Literature at Stanford University. He is the author of *The Transfiguration of History at the Center of Dante's Paradise* (Princeton, 1986) and of *Staging Fascism: 18 BL and the Theater of Masses for Masses* (Stanford; Garzanti, 1996), as well as of a body of essays concerning Hildegard of Bingen, Boccaccio, Machiavelli, D'Annunzio, and Marinetti. An Ailsa Bruce Mellon Senior Fellow at the National Gallery of Art during 1996–97, he is currently completing *Crash*, a cultural history of speed and accident.

Thomas Sheehan is Professor of Philosophy at Loyola University Chicago and a specialist in the philosophy of Martin Heidegger. He has frequently visited and written about Central America over the past fifteen years. His 1982 article in the *New York Times* was the first to expose the fraud of the U.S.-sponsored elections in El Salvador that year.

Robert Soucy, Professor of History at Oberlin College, is the author of four books: *Fascism in France: The Case of Maurice Barres; Fascist Intellectual Drieu La Rochelle; French Fascism: The First Wave, 1924–1933,* and *French Fascism: The Second Wave, 1933–1939.*

Richard Wolin teaches European intellectual history at Rice University. Among his books are *The Politics of Being: The Political Thought of Martin Heidegger* (Columbia University Press, 1990) and *Labyrinths: Explorations in the Critical History of Ideas* (University of Massachusetts Press, 1995).

Index

Fay, Sidney B., 229
FBI human rights investigation, 279–81. *See also* El Salvador
FBI Jesuit murder investigation, 286
FBI "Terrorist Photo Album," 279–80
Federal Emergency Management Agency (FEMA), 280
Federal Republic of Germany. *See* Germany
Fédération Nationale Entreprise Moderne et Libertés, 37
fichier juif (French Jewish census), 157, 158, 160
Le Figaro (newspaper), 54, 141
Figaro-Magazine, 155
"Final Solution": Historians' Debate on, 91; recent research about, 90; structuralists' interpretation of origins of, 106. *See also* Holocaust
Fini, Gianfranco, 3, 13, 50, 63, 74, 78–80, 169
Finkielkraut, Alain, 2, 183, 203, 205–6
Fischer, Fritz, 104
Fischer Debate (1960–65), 103–5, 107
Fishman, Sarah, 161
Flemish Block Party (Vlaams Blok), 49
Flood, Christopher, 5, 13, 19
Fontaine, Roger, 272
forest walk (*Der Waldgang*), 230–31
former Soviet Union, 152. *See also* Soviet Union
Forza Italia, 3
Foucault, Michel, 227, 251, 252, 254
Foucault's theory of power, 97
the Foulard (Islamic headdress) petition (France), 57
Français d'abord, la lettre de Jean-Marie Le Pen (FN magazine), 27
France: amnesty laws of, 204; attempts to maintain enormity of Nazi crimes, 181 n.113; cancer metaphor on Algeria and, 211–12; Chirac's apology for complicity during Occupation, 152, 166, 172, 195; crimes against humanity laws in, 188–89, 205; "duty to memory" by, 185; elections of 1988/1995, 24, 25; emer-

gence of political moderation in, 23–24; German occupation (1940–44) of, 21; historians' debate (1980s and 1990s) in, 153–63; immigration as political issue in, 21–22, 29–30, 57, 213; "mode rétro" experience of, 154, 156–57, 158, 164, 166, 174, 176 n.25; "obsession" with Vichy past by, 160, 182–86; political embrace of national identity in, 55–56; polls on Vichy syndrome interest within, 171; proposed parliamentary ethnic cleansing in, 55; Right and Left war in, 146; rise of far Right in, 3, 51–58; roots of the extreme Right in, 20–21; social/political tension in, 22–23; undefined northeastern border of, 174; Vichy anti-Jewish statutes (1940–41), 10; Vichy syndrome of, 9–10, 14, 146, 154, 170–74, 175 n.7, 182–83. *See also* French fascism; French Occupation; French wartime collaboration
La France à l'heure allemande (Burrin), 160
France-Observateur, 206
Franciste party (France), 131
"Franco-French civil war," 146
Frankfurter Allgemeine Zeitung (newspaper), 89
Frankfurt School neo-Marxism, 96
Frankreich in Hitlers Europa (Jäckel), 155
Freedom of Information Act, 278–79
Freedom Party (Austria), 3, 4, 5, 6, 152
Freiheitliche Partei Österreichs, 20
"French Children of the Holocaust: A Memorial Exhibition" (photography show), 181 n.113
French Communists, 135, 153, 161, 162, 167–68
French Fascism (Soucy), 8
French fascism: consensus school of, 133–34; debate over anti-Semitism and, 136–37; debate over Croix de Feu as, 134–35; debate over extent of 1930s, 139–41; debate over Ger-

genealogical study, 163
"Le Génocide en Algérie" (Vergès), 208
Gentile, Giovanni, 65, 70
The German Catastrophe of 1946
 (Meinecke), 233
German People's Union (Deutsche
 Volksunion), 50
Germany: *Alltagsgeschichte* movement of, 96–99, 101, 103, 106, 113,
 115; attacks on "Americanization"
 of, 226–27, 231, 237; Bitburg affair
 (1985), 12, 91, 94, 95; efforts to deal
 with Nazi past by, 11–12; Fischer debate on World War I and, 104–5; historical museum projects proposed
 in, 92; history and memories of,
 228–29; Hitler-Youth Generation
 of, 88, 108–12, 127 n.72; immigration restrictions of, 51, 240 n.30;
 Jenninger's speech affair, 86–88, 94,
 115, 116; Jünger as radical of Weimar
 Republic, 220–24; malaise of
 Weimar Republic, 2; re-creation of
 historical identity of, 91–92, 100–
 102; state of culture in, 226–27. *See
 also* Historians' Debate; New Right,
 German
Gherardi, Sophie, 169
Ginzburg, Carlo, 97
Girardet, Raoul, 155
Giudizio sul bolscevismo (Ciocca), 72
Glucksmann, André, 57–58, 194
"Gnade der späten Geburt" (mercy of
 late birth), 108–9, 127 n.71
Goebbels, Joseph, 147, 221
Golsan, Richard J., 14, 182
Goodfellow, Sam, 135, 138, 144, 145
Gordon, Bertram M., 7, 13, 152
"government of professors" (Italy), 67
Graficus, 73
Gramsci, Antonio, 71, 248
Graw, Ansgar, 228
GRECE (French New Right think tank),
 27, 51–53. *See also* New Right,
 French
Greenberg, Clement, 245
"green notebooks" (Touvier), 192

Greentree, Todd, 275
Grosser, Alfred, 159, 161
La Guerre sans nom (film), 208–10
Guevara, Gonzalo, 262
Guiffrida, Louis O., 280

Habermas, Jürgen, 90, 91, 94, 95, 96, 99,
 100–101, 247
Hahn, Karl-Eckhard, 228
Haider, Jörg, 3–4, 6–7, 11, 20, 49
Haig, Alexander, 274, 276
Halbwachs, Maurice, 114
Halter, Marek, 156
Hardy, René, 202, 203
Hasselbach, Ingo, 4, 224
Haushofer, Karl, 223
Hegel, Georg Wilhelm Friedrich, 218
Heidegger, Martin, 12–13, 14, 17 n.42,
 219, 230, 231, 237, 238, 245, 248,
 251, 252–54, 256
Heidegger and the Jews (Lyotard), 253
Heidegger, Art and Politics (Lacoue-
 Labarthe), 253
Heidegger et le nazisme (Farias), 12
Heimat (German soap opera), 96, 98,
 102, 123 n.47
Hellman, John, 146, 161
Helms, Jesse, 278
Henriot, Philippe, 158, 187, 192. *See
 also* Touvier affair
Higgins, Lynn A., 14, 200
Hillgruber, Andreas, 91, 109, 110, 228
Hinton, Dean, 275, 276
Hiroshima mon amour (film), 206
L'Histoire (magazine), 165
Histoire de Vichy (Dreyfus), 157, 185
Historians' Debate (1986–88): by histo-
 rians of Hitler-Youth Generation,
 88, 108–12, 122 n.43; comparison
 between Fischer Debate and, 104–5,
 107; generational dimension of,
 108–12; historiographical dimension of, 103–8; major issues/accusa-
 tions of, 91–92; neo-Revisionists'
 side during, 228–29; Nolte on attempts to blame Asian influences,
 184; overview of, 89–91; political

In the Stages series